T0301587

# Global Threats, Global Futures

Critical Issues, Global Concerns

# Global Threats, Global Futures

## Living with Declining Living Standards

Thayer Scudder

*Professor Emeritus of Anthropology, California Institute of Technology, USA*

**Edward Elgar**

Cheltenham, UK • Northampton, MA, USA

Published by
Edward Elgar Publishing Limited
The Lypiatts
15 Lansdown Road
Cheltenham
Glos GL50 2JA
UK

Edward Elgar Publishing, Inc.
William Pratt House
9 Dewey Court
Northampton
Massachusetts 01060
USA

A catalogue record for this book
is available from the British Library

Library of Congress Control Number: 2009940658

Mixed Sources
Product group from well-managed
forests and other controlled sources
www.fsc.org Cert no. SA-COC-1565
© 1996 Forest Stewardship Council
FSC

ISBN 978 1 84844 847 6 (cased)
ISBN 978 1 84844 849 0 (paperback)

Printed and bound by MPG Books Group, UK

# Contents

# Figures

# Acknowledgments

Conceptualizing, writing, editing and revising this book involved over four years of work. During that time the assistance, critiquing and encouragement of colleagues and family members have been essential. David Brokensha, Elizabeth Colson, John Gay and David McDowell have not only critiqued the content of every chapter but also provided editorial comments and advice on writing style. Joseph Jorgensen would have done the same if not for his untimely death on 5 March 2008. Robert Bates, Harald Frederiksen, Robert Goodland and Burt Singer provided encouragement when I most needed it and critiqued key sections. Michael Clemens, Jean Ensminger, Philip T. Hoffman, Charles W. Howe, Lee Talbot and Susan Wood provided advice during the early days of conceptualization. Elizabeth Colson, Lisa Cliggett and Jairos Mazambani updated me from the field on Zambia and the Gwembe Tonga. Eliza, my wife of 60 years, provided necessary encouragement when the task grew too onerous, while daughters Eliza Scudder and Alice Thayer Scudder maintained interest and provided encouragement as the years went by. Son-in-law John Williamson spent hours listening to me and passed on relevant information.

I am especially indebted to Alex Pettifer, who was willing to take the risk and responsibility for publishing this work. My thanks go also to Jenny Wilcox and Elizabeth Clack. Sara Lippincott provided early editorial advice, as more recently did Roby Harrison, Donald S. Lamm and Rob West. The Government of Laos with the Nam Theun Power Company, Carine Petit and Erik Lambin provided the remote sensing images. At Caltech, Victoria Mason helped edit and protected the manuscript as it grew, even taking it home with her for safe keeping.

# Introduction

## INTRODUCTION

My research and consulting in 30 countries on three continents over a 55-year period have convinced me that future generations throughout the world can expect a continuing decline in living standards due to existing global threats. I am a social and cultural anthropologist, unlike the large majority of other authors and scholars who have written on global topics. They tend to be biologists, development practitioners, journalists and other social scientists who have seldom done detailed micro-studies of human populations, including on how they impact upon their environment, on how national and international development policies and globalization impact upon them and on how affected individuals, households and communities respond to those impacts.

My research and consulting have concentrated on micro-studies, the results of which, I believe, have major policy implications for all high-, middle- and low-income countries. More specifically, my conclusions, experience and observations draw on systematic, longitudinal socio-economic research, during which I have worked for years in some of the world's most impoverished communities.

The origins of this book date back to the second half of the 1990s, when I was preparing for the Society of Applied Anthropology's 1999 Malinowski Award Lecture. My title was 'The Emerging Global Crisis and Development Anthropology: Can We Have An Impact?' The previous year I sent a questionnaire to 89 development anthropologists who had experience with the economic and social impacts of development on poor people and communities around the world. I asked my colleagues to list in order of importance three social and three environmental issues that posed 'the most serious constraints to a sustainable future' in the 21st century.[1]

The 53 answers that I received from colleagues in 25 countries in the major regions of the world are reflected in my categories of threats. Among social issues, poverty was listed as the most serious (57 per cent of responses), followed by globalization (49 per cent), community unraveling (36 per cent), population pressure (23 per cent), increasing marginalization

(21 per cent) and fundamentalism (19 per cent). Among environmental issues, misuse of natural resources was named as the most critical (74 per cent) and water scarcity and water pollution received the most emphasis. In this book I will be discussing all of these issues and the global threats they involve.

I am fascinated by how few experts anticipated the current global financial and economic crisis and by the inability of policy makers at national and international levels to cooperate in addressing that threat and other current threats such as global warming. Even a small number of such threats, including those I discuss, can cause living standards to decline not just in poor societies but in all societies and nations. I also discuss the type of transformations which might slow the rate and magnitude of decline. Whether or not quality of life can be maintained or even improved remains to be seen.

The difference between living standards and quality of life is analogous to the difference between growth and development. Definitions of living standards emphasize material comfort as measured by per capita income and Gross Domestic Product (GDP), which also are the usual indices for measuring growth. They largely ignore the fact that the world in which we live does not have unlimited natural resources, the overuse of which already is a global threat to humanity. Overemphasis on per capita income plays down two other major threats: poverty and the rising gap between rich and poor within and between countries. That said, readers should not conclude that growth is unimportant, for it is a key component of development and especially for the alleviation of global poverty.

Development, like quality of life, is a much broader concept, and includes a person's access to a wider range of non-material attributes such as those available to people in every viable society and culture. Moreover, there is increasing evidence that such attributes as happiness and wellbeing are not dependent upon an ever-increasing living standard.[2] As for a further distinction between growth and development, there is little evidence that sustainable high growth rates for all nations are possible. On the other hand, development, if it does not exceed the earth's biophysical carrying capacity, can continue and can enrich human life.

I believe I provide a more realistic analysis of the implications of current trends than those presented in other books about our future. Some such books are written by what I call Global Boomers, such as global futurist Herman Kahn in the 1970s and economist Jeffrey Sachs more recently. Global Boomers foresee a better future with higher living standards lasting centuries. Other authors, including biologists Paul and Anne Ehrlich and geographer Jared Diamond, make a Wake-Up Call.

The Ehrlichs and Diamond expect a decline in living standards if present trends continue, but still anticipate, unlike myself, a change for the better if their proposals are implemented.

I combine a number of global threats to living standards in three unprioritized but interrelated categories. They are:

1.   poverty and an increasing gap between rich and poor
2.   cultural, economic, political and religious fundamentalism
3.   global environmental degradation.

These global threats are analyzed in the first three chapters. The next three chapters focus on case studies of the United States, China and Zambia, to illustrate current situations in high-, middle- and low-income countries. The last chapter introduces the type of transformational changes that might reduce the rate and magnitude of decline in living standards while possibly improving quality of life.

My list of threats, of course, is far from comprehensive, but it is drawn from those associated with situations that I have researched. I also incorporate into the text threats associated with consumerism, population increase and urbanization. Already unsustainable levels of consumption pose a major global threat. Population increase is threatening because 90 per cent occurs in low-income countries, and 90 per cent of that growth 'will be concentrated in the poorest of these countries.'[3] By 2007, 50 per cent of the world's population had become urban dwellers, one-third of whom lived in slums, which are expected to increase in the years ahead since 'more than 95 per cent of the population growth in the world's poorest regions will occur in urban areas, with the result that cities will become the predominant sites of poverty in coming years.'[4]

I intentionally do not include the threat of terrorism but rather emphasize two threats which are major contributory factors to terrorist movements. One is relative poverty, dealt with in Chapter 1. The other is fundamentalism, dealt with in Chapter 2. The serious threats of global climate change and nuclear war, briefly dealt with in Chapter 7, are better detailed by more knowledgeable experts.

As for transformational changes, one will emphasize the need for far more concentration on food production, manufacturing, enterprise development and entrepreneurial activities in rural areas and on improving the connections between those areas and cities and ports. A development strategy emphasizing rural areas has several advantages over the current emphasis in China, for example, on state industrial and urban growth. Not only is such a strategy more equitable in addressing rising gaps between rich and poor, but it is closer to the natural environment, and facilitates social networking and community and cultural development. And, for those who look, the evidence is overwhelming that the world's low-income majority wants such broadly defined development and will respond to opportunities and supportive government policies.

Another advantage of a global strategy that revisits rural development is that facilitating the emergence in rural areas of agricultural, manufacturing and other non-farm enterprise can match in late-developing countries increases in GDP and individual income associated with capital-intensive urban and industrial development. Such activities, moreover, are essential for economic and political survival in countries which have rural majorities. China's annual growth rate of approximately 10 per cent over the last thirty years is based on two very different development policies, as analyzed in Chapter 5.

During the 1980s the Chinese government's emphasis was primarily on realizing the potential of the rural majority through the household responsibility system and related economic reforms. After 1989, new leadership switched emphasis to state-controlled industrial and urban development. Both strategies have achieved similar growth rates. But personal income grew faster than GDP in the 1980s and slower than GDP in the 1990s, indicating the importance of a rural emphasis.[5] There was also greater improvement in the majority's social and cultural wellbeing in the 1980s as well as less environmental degradation, which can be generalized as a further advantage of increasing emphasis on a rural development strategy.

In this book I also stress several other transformational themes that I believe are necessary for trying to cope with global threats. Most involve changes in the values of individuals, societies and belief systems. Empowerment of women is one. Capacity building that starts with preschool education and ends with national service is another.

I wish to emphasize from the start that I am not a prophet of doom. The late economist Robert L. Heilbroner foresaw a link between economic decline and an authoritarian system of governance. I do not go that far; rather, I am an 'optimistic pessimist.' While I am convinced that downturn will occur, I agree with Donella Meadows and her colleagues of the Systems Dynamics Group at the Massachusetts Institute of Technology (MIT) that a future society that is 'sustainable, functional and equitable'[6] is possible – though at a lower standard of living worldwide.

Forecasting a global future is, of course, fraught with difficulty. Complexity is one problem. Another derives from our genetic heritage. Like our primate relative the chimpanzee, with whom we share 98 per cent of our genes, our concerns deal primarily with the present. This is true for both small-scale societies of foragers and high-income, developed industrial societies. In the United States, voters and politicians alike focus on current events and the next election, while the business community is especially concerned with quarterly and annual returns. Cost-benefit analysis as used by development economists to evaluate different courses of action is more concerned with such current and important issues as poverty, infant mortality and malnutrition and disease, as opposed to more long-term but possibly more serious issues, such as global climate change.

## WAKE-UP CALL AUTHORS AND GLOBAL BOOMERS

Skepticism as to the inevitability of decline is understandable because the writings of such influential doomsters as Malthus and the Ehrlichs have proved wrong. The problem is not so much that they cried 'wolf' but that they underestimated the complexities of the processes involved. Take food production: present concerns relate more to the ability of the low-income majority to buy food, and to inadequate infrastructure and institutional capacity to distribute food in times of need, than to food's global availability. In the future, genetic engineering is likely to produce salt- and drought-tolerant food staples; nonetheless, food availability cannot be assumed indefinitely. Expected events such as increased consumption of grains and grain-fed meat in China's growing middle class and the use of food staples for fuel alternatives, as in Brazil, will affect supplies and thus increase prices, reducing availability to the poor.

   Also causing confusion about future trends are the opposing views of Wake-Up Call authors and Global Boomers. Both types make good sense but they talk past each other. Recent books by Wake-Up Call authors include Yale University environmentalist James Speth's 2008 *The Bridge at the Edge of the World: Capitalism, the Environment, and Crossing from Crisis to Sustainability*. Worldwatch president Christopher Flavin writes in the preface to the Worldwatch Institute's *State of the World* (2006) that 'it is clear that the current western development model is not sustainable. We therefore face a choice: rethink almost everything, or risk a downward spiral of political competition and economic collapse.'[7]

   There are also numerous Wake-Up Call statements signed by scientists and distinguished citizens. Two examples are worth quoting. In the 1993 'World Scientists' Warning to Humanity,' 1680 scientists from 49 countries wrote that '[h]uman beings and the natural world are on a collision course.'[8] In a 2001 statement on 'The Next Hundred Years,' 120 Nobel Laureates in literature, medicine, natural science, politics, religion and social science emphasized that 'the only hope for the future lies in cooperative international action, legitimized by democracy.'[9]

To date, such alarms have had little impact on national and international policies. One reason is the optimism of the Global Boomers, who believe that a combination of science, technology, democracy, free-market capitalism without regulation and globalization can significantly improve human livelihoods in the decades and centuries to come. Their initial stimulus was to refute the pessimism of such publications as Rachel Carson's *Silent Spring* (1962) and the 1972 *Limits to Growth* by the Social Dynamics Group of MIT's Sloan School of Management.

The main challenger to the MIT Group's pessimistic assessment was Herman Kahn (1922–1983), whose interests shifted in the 1970s from nuclear strategies to global scenarios. He authored or co-authored a series of books arguing that a combination of technology and capitalism could lead not just to sustainable futures for hundreds of years but also to the colonization of space. Julian Simon (1932–1998), for many years a senior fellow at the Cato Institute, was another prominent Global Boomer. His 1981 book *The Ultimate Resource* held that an increasing population could use science and technology to develop substitutes for whatever natural resources might run out. In 1984, Simon joined forces with Kahn to edit *The Resourceful Earth: A Response to Global 2000*.

Other books by Global Boomers include Jeffrey Sachs's 2005 *The End of Poverty: Economic Possibilities for Our Time*. Sachs, a macroeconomist who is director of Columbia University's Earth Institute, is what I call an 'optimistic optimist.' He believes that it is not only possible to end poverty in our time but that 'all parts of the world have the chance to join an age of unprecedented prosperity building on global science, technology, and markets.'[10] The 2008 World Bank-initiated Commission on Growth chaired by Michael Spence, Nobel Prize Laureate in Economics, presents a similar world view.[11] Various business-oriented sources have presented similar arguments. They include the 31 August 1998 special double issue of *Business Week* on the 21st Century economy and Knight Kiplinger's 1998 *World Boom Ahead: Why Business and Consumers Will Prosper* ('On the eve of the 21st century, the world stands on the threshold of a long, strong surge in economic growth and living standards, unprecedented in world history').[12]

It would be a mistake to ridicule the future scenarios of Global Boomers any more than those of Wake-Up Call authors. More importantly, because of the disjuncture between the two types of scenario, we should attempt to learn from them. Neither side adequately addresses the other's arguments. Global Boomers have not shown how science and technology can offset the increasing consumption of natural resources, can resist cultural, economic, political and religious fundamentalism, and can stem the degradation of the global environment. Yet many of their suggestions can indeed help reduce the living standard drop that I envision and that Wake-Up Call authors fear. Global Boomers, for example, emphasize the importance of the problem-solving potential of people – a theme which I stress throughout this book. Simon states it nicely in the conclusion of *The Ultimate Resource*: 'The ultimate resource is people – skilled, spirited and hopeful people who will exert their wills and imaginations for their own benefit and inevitably they will benefit not only themselves but the rest of us as well.'[13]

My research emphasizes that people are the greatest single resource that planners must utilize. This is not a common view among politicians, development planners or even social scientists. Within the World Bank, for example, the myth of the conservative peasant still exists. On the contrary, a large majority of families that I have studied want better health care, education for their children and improved wellbeing. That conclusion applies especially to low-income households living in communities under extreme stress due to such crises as conflicts and civil wars, natural disasters and development-induced involuntary resettlement.

During our long-term study of 57 000 Africans forced to move in the 1950s during the construction of a large dam on the Zambezi River, social anthropologist Elizabeth Colson and I observed that each time we returned to the resettled villages, only a small minority of village households were experimenting with new income earning or other innovations, such as shifting from cultivation with hoes to plowing larger holdings with oxen. Subsequently we learned that different households were innovating at the time of each revisit and that most households had either initiated risky experiments or had adopted the successful ones of their neighbors. This propensity to take risks occurred in spite of a high failure rate due to environmental constraints (drought and floods especially) and inadequate government policies and institutions over which villagers had no control, such as inept pricing policies and inefficient marketing institutions.

The Gwembe Tonga experience (see Chapter 6) can be generalized to the millions of poor people involuntarily resettled in connection with dams. Such resettlement is stressful and is initially associated with risk-adverse behavior by the majority. Yet in a statistical analysis of 50 dam projects around the world, mathematician and anthropologist John Gay and I found that most of those resettled would nonetheless respond to appropriate development opportunities and that the availability of such opportunities, and the active participation of resettlers in their planning and implementation, were statistically related to a successful resettlement outcome.[14]

It is also important to keep in mind that advances in science and technology can have adverse impacts. They can increase unemployment and
underemployment, an outcome often ignored by development economists,
as discussed in the next chapter. They can adversely affect living standards
and quality of life in other ways. In *The World is Flat: A Brief History of
the Twenty-First Century* (2005), journalist Thomas Friedman analyzes
ten globalizing forces (or flatteners) which have begun to work in a 'complementary, mutually enhancing fashion'[15] to create a more level playing
field. One result will be a world made 'more equal and more intense', in
which '[w]e Americans will have to work harder, run faster, and become
smarter to make sure we get our share.'[16] Hardly an appealing future for
citizens of what is currently the world's greatest power and who already
spend more hours at work than people in other industrial societies!

I disagree with most Wake-Up Call authors in their faith that global
living standards can improve, or at least not deteriorate, if their solutions to current problems are implemented. I do not mean to denigrate
their proposals, which offer critically important ways to reduce declines
in living standards and quality of life. But I question their optimism
that an overall living standard decline can be avoided. Jared Diamond
believes that having caused the world's environmental problems, 'we are
the ones in control of them.'[17] All we need do to deal with those problems is to 'reconsider core values' and have the 'political will' to implement 'solutions already available' via a process of long-term planning.[18]
James Speth is more specific in discussing ways to avert environmental
disaster, but he too believes that the natural beauty he has known 'will
be there for our children and their children and so on forever if we have
the wisdom to protect it.'[19] Stern, the leading economist writing on the
threat of global warming, nonetheless titles his most recent book *The
Global Deal: Climate Change and the Creation of a New Era of Progress
and Prosperity.*[20]

## MY BACKGROUND AND QUALIFICATIONS

I am currently emeritus professor of anthropology at the California
Institute of Technology. Prior to attending college, my main interests
were nature, mountains and people. I began a bird diary when I was ten,
in which I recorded the birds seen each day. I expanded my diary's contents during the next twelve years to include people met, rock climbing in
Eastern North America and mountaineering in Western North America,
including Alaska and British Columbia. At Harvard College, while president of the Harvard Mountaineering Club, I almost began a career as a

professional mountaineer. I also hitchhiked during those years over 20 000 miles throughout the United States. Hitchhiking then was a wonderful experience for a young person and I am convinced had a major impact on my later shift from the natural sciences to the social sciences.

My formal education has been wide-ranging and eclectic. At Harvard College and Graduate School it included biology, archeology, history and ecology as well as social and cultural anthropology. I wrote my PhD dissertation on the human ecology of a Central African ethnic group. I also spent a year studying world religions at the Yale Divinity School and a year doing postdoctoral research in African anthropology and ecology at the London School of Economics. So from its very beginning my academic education and research has required me to cross disciplinary boundaries.

My overseas social science research began in 1956 when Elizabeth Colson, now professor emerita at the University of California, Berkeley, and I initiated our long-term study in Central Africa of 57 000 Gwembe Tonga villagers soon to be involuntarily resettled due to the construction of Kariba – the first mainstream dam on the Zambezi River. Now in its fifty-fifth year, our research has become the most systematic long-term study of how people are impacted by, and respond to a large-scale development project. My 18 research visits and over four years' residence in what is now Zambia also have had a major impact on me and especially on my thinking about such global issues as poverty, development and environmental degradation.

Wanting to expand my knowledge of how large-scale development projects affect different ethnic communities, in 1962 I joined a research team conducting a study of 50 000 Egyptian Nubians soon to be displaced by the Aswan High Dam.[21] In September 1964, before joining the faculty of Caltech later that year, I was recruited by the World Bank to work with three economists and an agronomist on the first major comparative analysis of small-scale African agriculture.[22] That assignment began a close advisory and consultancy relationship with the World Bank that continues to this day. It has been advisory when I served on World Bank-required independent panels of environmental and social experts for large-scale dams in China, Laos and Lesotho and, at the request of the Bank, as resettlement adviser on a Canadian feasibility study of China's Three Gorges Project.[23] It has been as a consultant in India and in four African countries. My relationship with the World Bank requires some explanation since the Bank, as the premier development agency in the world, figures prominently in this book.

A global development bank is needed today and the World Bank, initially called the International Bank for Reconstruction and Development, was established in 1946 to play that role. The World Bank's record in achieving development in low-income countries, however, has been defective. For that reason, I have been very critical over the years of the Bank as, to use a British parliamentary phrase, a member of the loyal opposition. It is also important to emphasize that the World Bank is not a monolithic agency. Its staff has included a good number of constructive critics who have achieved important policy and institutional changes within the Bank.

I have continued throughout my career global research on low-income societies, poverty and dry land and irrigated agriculture (which employ more people worldwide than any other occupation). I completed during the 1970s and 1980s global reviews of large-scale government and private sector agricultural settlement projects for the United States Agency for International Development (USAID) as well as for the World Bank. Shorter consultancies for international organizations included the Food and Agriculture Organization (FAO) of the UN (small-scale fisheries worldwide and large-scale dam impacts in Nigeria), the World Health Organization (WHO) on schistosomiasis (liver fluke) in Ghana, and the United Nations Development Programme (UNDP) on the human impact of the Jonglei Canal in the Sudan, dam resettlement planning in the Ivory Coast and onchocerciasis (river blindness) in several West African countries. I have also consulted for Environmental Defense and The Nature Conservancy as well as for the Ford Foundation and the Navajo Nation. Most of these consultancies were sponsored by the not-for-profit Institute for Development Anthropology, which I co-founded with two colleagues in the mid-1970s in order to incorporate environmentally, economically and socially sound research into development planning and implementation.[24]

My interest in people affected by large-scale development projects continues today. Large dams, for example, tend to be the biggest single investment in a country's development portfolio at the time of their construction. This is true, for example, of the Aswan High Dam, China's Three Gorges Dam, India's Sardar Sarovar Project, Sri Lanka's Mahaweli Project, Ghana's Volta Project at Akosombo, Nigeria's Kainji Dam and Lesotho's Highland Water Project. My involvement in those projects also allowed me to work with (and study) officials in governments, engineering firms and international, national and private-sector financing institutions. In Sri Lanka, for example, I was unofficial adviser to the Minister for Mahaweli Development, who arranged meetings with President Jayawardene and the chairman of the party in power. Currently I am one of three members on an international panel of environment and social experts for Laos's Nam Theun 2 Dam Project; we report to the Minister of Energy and Mines and to the Office of the Prime Minister.

Dam construction provides a quasi-laboratory situation in which impacts on affected people, and their responses, can be compared with development-induced resettlement elsewhere. Similar responses, regardless of environmental, cultural or national differences, have allowed me to develop a theoretical and policy-relevant frame of reference that predicts how a majority of those involved can be expected to behave over two generations during the different stages of the resettlement process.[25]

I have also had the opportunity to observe cultural, economic, political and religious fundamentalism in different settings in many countries (including those in which Buddhism, Christianity, Hinduism and Islam are the dominant religions). In these countries I have also studied how different populations respond to poverty and development constraints and opportunities.

My background is similar in some ways to that of other authors, such as Jared Diamond, Paul Ehrlich and E.O. Wilson, who have also dealt with global threats. We have all been professors at major research universities with lengthy research careers that have brought us in contact with life-threatening global issues. Where my career differs from theirs is that, as a social anthropologist, I have researched a wider range of global issues from the bottom up, including the threats that are the focus of this book. As for my colleagues in anthropology, none have combined to the same extent systematic long-term research in a single area (in my case, the Middle Zambezi Valley in Zambia) with comparatively briefer studies throughout Africa, Asia and the Middle East, as well as in Canada and the United States – research that has brought me more public policy awards and recognition dealing with global development issues than any other anthropologist.

## NOTES

1. See Thayer Scudder (1999). 'The Emerging Global Crisis and Development Anthropology: Can we have an impact?' 1999 Malinowski Award Lecture. *Human Organization.* **58** (4). Pages 351–364.
2. See, for example, Richard A. Easterlin (1995). 'Will Raising the Incomes of all Increase the Happiness of All?' *Journal of Economic Behavior and Organization.* **27**. Pages 35–47.
3. 'Return of the Population Growth Factor.' Page 4. This 31 January 2007 report, prepared by the United Kingdom's All Party Parliamentary Group on Population, Development and Reproductive Health, explains why the UN's eight Millennium Development Goals 'are difficult or impossible to achieve with the current levels of population growth in the least developed countries and regions.'
4. United Nations Human Settlement Programme Report (2007). *State of the World's Cities 2006/7: The Millennium Development Goals and urban sustainability: 30 years of shaping the habitat agenda.*

5.  Yasheng Huang (2008). *Capitalism with Chinese Characteristics*, Cambridge: Cambridge University Press. Page 253.
6.  Donella Meadows, Jorgen Randers and Dennis Meadows (2004). *Limits of Growth: The 30-year update*. White River Junction, VT: Chelsea Green Publishing Company.
7.  *State of the World: 2006*. Page xxii. New York: W.W. Norton and Company, Inc.
8.  *World Scientists' Warning to Humanity* (1993). Cambridge, MA: Union of Concerned Scientists. Page 1.
9.  http://www.sciencemag.org/feature/data/nobel.dtl.
10. Jeffrey D. Sachs (2005). *The End of Poverty: Economic possibilities for our time*. New York: Penguin Press. Page 2.
11. Commission on Growth and Development (2008). *The Growth Report: Strategies for sustained growth and inclusive development*. Washington DC: The World Bank.
12. Knight Kiplinger (1998). *World Boom Ahead: Why business and consumers will prosper*. Washington DC: Kiplinger Books. Page 1.
13. Available at http://www.juliansimon.com/writings/Ultimate_Resource/TCONCLUS. txt. Page 10.
14. Thayer Scudder (2005). *The Future of Large Dams: Dealing with social, environmental, institutional and political costs*. Oxford: Earthscan.
15. Thomas L. Friedman (2005). *The World Is Flat: A brief history of the twenty-first century*. New York: Farrar, Straus and Giroux. Page 176.
16. *Ibid.* Page 469.
17. Diamond, J. (2005). *Collapse: How societies choose to fail or succeed*. New York: Viking. Page 521.
18. *Ibid.* Page 522.
19. Speth (2004). *Red Sky At Morning: America and the crisis of the global environment*. New Haven, CT: Yale University Press. Page xiv.
20. Nicholas Stern (2009). *The Global Deal: Climate change and the creation of a new era of progress and prosperity*. New York: Public Affairs.
21. See Thayer Scudder and Maher Habbob (forthcoming). 'Aswan High Dam Resettlement.' In A.K. Biswas and C. Tortajada (eds). *Conference Proceedings of the February 2007 Cairo Workshop on the Aswan High Dam*. Berlin: Springer.
22. John C. de Wilde, assisted by Peter F.M. McLoughlin, André Guinard, Thayer Scudder and Robert Mabouché (1967). *Experiences with Agricultural Development in Tropical Africa*. Vols. I and II. Baltimore. MD: Johns Hopkins University Press for the International Bank on Reconstruction and Development (the World Bank).
23. That assignment was in the mid-1980s. I did not sign off on the feasibility study because I considered the Three Gorges Project to be a bad one for several reasons.
24. After 20 years involvement as a founding director I resigned in the mid-1990s when it was clear that the type of research that we had pioneered in the 1970s was now well established in university international programs and private consultancy firms within the United States as well as increasingly within universities and research programs within low- and middle-income countries.
25. Thayer Scudder. 2005. Op. cit.

# 1.   The threat of global poverty

## INTRODUCTION

My research and consulting have dealt primarily with poor communities over the past 55 years. This includes Elizabeth Colson's and my long-term study of the Gwembe Tonga – one of the poorest ethnic groups in Zambia, which is one of the poorest countries in the world. The Gwembe study is one of 21 cases of government-induced community relocation that I have studied in 19 countries in Africa, Asia, the Middle East and North America. All involve poor communities including indigenous people and ethnic minorities.

I have also made a special effort to visit communities of the poor studied over the long term by colleagues, to discuss results with them, to contribute to books on long-term community studies[1] and to visit poverty-stricken communities in major cities in low- and middle-income countries. My early morning walks through Mexico City, Cairo, Khartoum, Lagos, Lusaka, Mumbai (Bombay), Delhi, Colombo, Bangkok and Beijing are well known among my colleagues.

Only once was I afraid when walking in some of the largest slum communities in the world. That was in perhaps the most impoverished slum community in Delhi, which was built on the exposed flood plain of the Yamuna River. Suddenly I was surrounded by a pack of snarling pariah dogs. Expecting to scare them off – the technique had worked elsewhere – I opened my rolled umbrella and whirled around thrusting it at my attackers. The result only further infuriated them, leaving me helpless as they closed in on my ankles and legs. But just as quickly as they had surrounded me, they turned and fled when a man, emerging from a nearby hovel, routed them with a fuselage of rocks. We looked at each other for several moments; then he invited me in for a cup of tea. That was the kind of personal contact and interesting interaction that I continue to associate with my slum community walks.

Without question, poverty reduction is seen, nationally and internationally, as a major development goal and human-rights requirement. The first of the UN Millennium Development Goals is to '[e]radicate extreme poverty and hunger,' while the next five of the eight goals are related to poverty reduction. The first slogan seen by staff entering the World Bank's Washington DC headquarters is that the Bank's goal is 'achieving a world without poverty.'

Gatherings of the international elite, such as the annual meetings at Davos, Switzerland, of the World Economic Forum as well as of the 30 Organisation of Economic Co-operation and Development (OECD) countries, continually stress the importance of poverty alleviation. At the February 2007 San Francisco meeting, the President of the American Association for the Advancement of Science mentioned global poverty as the first of four key challenges to which scientists should volunteer 10 per cent of their time.[2]

In this chapter, I pay special attention to threats associated with relative poverty, new poverty and increased consumption associated with successful poverty alleviation. Additional sections deal with the impoverishing role of current international and national policies and methodologies.

## DEFINING, MEASURING AND STUDYING POVERTY

### Introduction

Poverty is complex. It is not surprising that experts differ on how to define, measure and study it. Current definitions, used by the World Bank and most development economists, distinguish three types: absolute, moderate and relative. In my analysis I add new poverty as a fourth category which arises from both the poor and the non-poor.[3]

Households living in absolute poverty are unable to meet basic needs: food, potable water, shelter and access to educational and health services. Those living in moderate poverty are barely able to meet basic needs. The World Bank, other development agencies and the UN's Millennium Development Goals use global estimates of those living on less than $1 a day and less than $2 a day as simplifying standards for estimating the global scale and distribution of absolute and moderate poverty.

Narrow definitions of relative poverty are also based on income.[4] They emphasize households that live below a country's poverty line. Though poverty lines vary between upper-, middle- and low-income countries, usually daily income levels exceed per capita income of two dollars. A broader definition of relative poverty, which I use, follows from the wording of the United Nations' 1986 Declaration on the Right to Development. This defines relative poverty as exclusion from active participation in the societies to which the relatively poor belong. New poverty results from the implementation by governments and private sector agencies of what are advertised as development projects. Included are urban redevelopment, extractive industries, dams and special economic zones.

To date development agencies and practitioners have concentrated on absolute and moderate poverty. The result has been a flawed and dangerous analysis that has downplayed the threat of relative poverty to individual nations and global society – especially where the relatively poor are dynamic individuals who are unwilling to accept their exclusion from the political economies of the nations to which they belong or from global society.

Without support from strong leaders, the large majority of the poor are sufficiently apolitical (as defined by not voting or otherwise participating in the political process) that governing elites can ignore and/or exploit them. Ignoring them certainly has been the approach of both political parties in the United States (see Chapter 4). Even under extreme provocation, violent resistance by the very poor has been rare. Involuntary community resettlement from a beloved homeland is an excellent example of extreme provocation. Yet I continue to be amazed by the non-violent reactions of the tens of millions of poor people who have been victimized by such removal.

Where relative poverty is involved, however, influential revolutionary leaders are more likely to emerge. I will be analyzing a number of cases later in this chapter as well as in Chapter 2. The seriousness of the situation can become especially volatile where governments go out of their way to exclude ethnic or religious minorities from national participation, as has been the case in Sri Lanka in regard to Tamil-speaking Hindus.

**Defining Poverty**

Definitions of poverty based on income alone are too restrictive because they de-emphasize a range of material and non-material assets that the poor themselves consider necessary solutions to their current poverty. For that reason, definitions must pay attention to a much wider range of assets including the extent to which the poor participate politically in the communities and nations in which they live. The Asian Development Bank, for example, defines poverty in a single sentence as 'a deprivation of basic assets and opportunities which every human being is entitled to have.'[5] According to the World Bank's *Voices of the Poor: Can Anyone Hear Us?* 'the poor rarely speak about income, but they do speak extensively about assets that are important to them.'[6]

*Voices of the Poor* divides assets into four categories.[7] One includes environmental assets arising from biodiversity such as food, and materials for building crafts, medicines and other uses. A second category of assets relates to the ability of household members to work: good health, education, initiative and, especially important, expertise that creates wealth and provides security. All sorts of property, especially legal or customary access to land and water for cultivation, livestock management and other uses, constitute a third category. The fourth category is recognized membership in one or more communities and social networks that provide one's livelihood with social and cultural meaning. Security,[8] freedom to travel and possibility of social and political upward mobility would be other important asset categories. It is the combination of these asset categories that allows household members to create diversified production systems on which they can subsist and then move beyond subsistence.

Taken together, the four categories of assets provide much more than material wellbeing. They also provide a sense of security, self-respect and hope, the absence of which are major defining characteristics of poverty. Researchers, and the poor themselves, stress the impoverishing effect of feeling powerless to deal with relevant issues. A sense of powerlessness has increased significantly since the 1940s because of rising gaps between rich and poor, increasing globalization and a wide range of development policies and plans that have left millions of households and innumerable communities behind.

The current trend to restricting definitions of poverty to income alone is problematic not just because it is too restrictive but also because in some situations it is too inclusive. Millions of people living in indigenous and ethnic communities earn less than $2 a day but still have relatively satisfying lives based on dense networks of social relations and viable and resilient cultures that are only loosely attached to the market economy. Money may be less important than household self-sufficiency, while barter may serve as an alternate currency. Such households, communities and societies could become more important as models for the future, if scenarios emphasizing the importance of community and localization advocated by Wake-Up Call authors such as Herman Daly and John Cobb are institutionalized.

Even if living standards are significantly lower in relatively self-sufficient communities, their quality of life may be higher, as measured by degree of self-sufficiency (including access to arable land and other natural resources), belief systems held and the intense group interaction that, for example, characterized the Gwembe Tonga when I first lived among them in the 1950s. Analysis of the extent of poverty in such societies is difficult because adequate indices and procedures have yet to be developed for defining cultural poverty. Poverty of this type can arise with the breakdown of social and/or political organization and values among individuals and in households, communities and states that have only recently joined the ranks of the poor.

## THE EXTENT OF POVERTY

The distribution of the poor is global. Numbers are constantly chang-ing due to natural catastrophes (recent tidal waves in Asia, for example), strife, including civil wars, and economic events such as rising food prices and the current (2007–09) financial and economic crisis. Notwithstanding China's and India's recent success in reducing the proportion of their citizens living in absolute and moderate poverty, impoverished people most likely continue to constitute a majority of the world's population. In 2000, the World Bank estimated that those living on less than $2 a day were 'almost half' of the world's six billion people.[9] In 2001, World Bank authors Shaohua Chen and Martin Ravallion[10] estimated that 21.1 per cent of the global population in low- and middle-income countries still lived on less than $1.08 per day, while 52.9 per cent lived on less than $2.15. Those totals would not have included an unknown number living in relative poverty.

The proportion of the world's population living in poverty, however, is not the only way to assess the extent and distribution of poverty.[11] Another is to count changes in the total number of the poor. Indian econo-mist Ravi Kanbur, now T.L. Lee Professor of World Affairs at Cornell University, refers to World Bank calculations that suggest that between 1990 and 1999 those living on less than $2 per day increased from 2.7 to 2.8 billion.[12] During that same period, the percentage of the global population with that income level fell to 55.6 per cent from 61.2 per cent. So, Kanbur asks, during the decade of the 1990s has global poverty gone up or down? He also is concerned that more emphasis is paid to celebrating those who escape from poverty as opposed to those who, at the same time, fall into poverty,[13] as has been the case with new poverty.

## RELATIVE POVERTY: AN INCREASING GLOBAL THREAT

Relative poverty is especially sensitive to the increasing gap within nations between rich and poor due primarily to income gains among the rich. In the United States, the 2006 survey of the world economy by *The Economist* notes that 'America's top 1 per cent of earners now receive 16 per cent of all income, up from 8 per cent in 1980.'[14] Initial economic growth among the Asian tigers was associated 'with relatively low and sometimes even falling income inequality.' In recent years, 'the rich are now growing richer much faster than the poor'[15] in 15 of 21 countries assessed by the Asian Development Bank.[16] That is especially true in China, which has a higher

Gini coefficient than the United States and one close to those of Brazil, Argentina, Chile and Mexico.

In China, rural–urban inequality and inequality within cities are increasing to an extent that should be of major concern to China's central government since employment is not keeping up with population increase. That conclusion applies not just to peasants, non-farm rural workers and urban migrants but also to students with higher education. Peasants are at a disadvantage because they do not own their land, which under-budgeted and corrupt local officials are tempted to take, with inadequate compensation, for more lucrative industrial enterprises. As a result, 'among more than 700m left-behind peasants, frustrations are building.'[17]

In terms of risks associated with relative poverty, jobs are increasingly unavailable in China even for the millions of college and university graduates. *Los Angeles Times* staff writer Mitchell Landsberg describes a situation in which graduates were expected to increase by 820 000 between 2006 and 2007. Yet already in 2006, graduates were competing for too few jobs: 'a graduate's nightmare that mirrored a national problem: too many people, too few jobs.'[18]

In China, as in other middle- and upper-income countries:

> [W]orkers are not getting their full share of the fruits of globalization. This is true not just for the lowest-skilled ones but increasingly also for more highly qualified ones . . . Thus the usual argument in favour of globalization—that it will make most workers better off, with only a few low-skilled ones losing out – has not so far been borne out by the facts. Most workers are being squeezed.'[19]

That relative poverty is an important cause of civil strife, civil war and terrorism in some countries has yet to receive the attention that it deserves. Recent examples leading to civil wars between standing governments and excluded minorities include Sri Lanka (see Chapter 2) and Sierra Leone. In both cases, the rebels have been classified as terrorists who inflicted serious crimes against humanity. In both cases the media, governments and policy analysts have paid far too little attention to why youths started civil wars that led to criminal activities.

The Sierra Leone case involves the rebellion of the Revolutionary United Front (RUF) against the government and, later on, international forces between 1991 and 2002. My analysis will emphasize the causes leading up to the rebellion and the backgrounds of the rebel leaders and the militia that they led. My main source is the research and publications between the mid-1980s and 2005 of Wageningen University's Paul Richards.[20] Though the leading analyst of the RUF, the inadequate attention paid to Richards' work illustrates the emphasis on RUF atrocities at the expense of the causes of the civil war.

According to former De Beers diamond specialist Caspar Fithen and Paul Richards, 'the civil war in Sierra Leone (1991–2002) mobilized young people marginalized by poverty, educational disadvantage, and injustice.'[21] Those youth lived in a corrupt and failing state that favored the urban sector of the economy and no longer had the resources to maintain its characteristic patron–client relationships, including such vital services as education. Rural teachers had no way of knowing when their next pay check would arrive, if ever. Rural students had 'few prospects of continuing education and progressive employment through established channels.'[22] The impoverishing situation in which they found themselves was worsened by the structural adjustment policies of the World Bank and other international financial institutes (IFIs), to which the government responded by cutting back on education, health and agricultural services.

Rural youth were not unaware, however, of intellectual trends in other countries, including the pan-African thinking associated with Ghana's President Nkrumah, the utopian ideas in *The Green Book* of Libya's President Gaddafi and *The Third Wave* futurology of American author Alvin Toffler. The rebellion began when a small group of RUF's founding leaders returned from exile in Libya with some financing and military training. Within Sierra Leone, the leadership was augmented by others, including former rural teachers. Young recruits were captured by raiding rural primary schools and were indoctrinated in forest camps where leaders tried 'to construct a model egalitarian society of their own.'[23] They obviously succeeded to an extent since some of the boys and girls captured in time became trusted fighters and leaders.

This brief background analysis should not be interpreted as an attempt to belittle RUF's kidnapping and terrorizing of primary school students, murdering those who tried to escape, atrocities committed on thousands of villagers and poverty imposed on hundreds of thousands of refugees. In several publications, Richards endorses British anthropologist Mary Douglas's analysis of (in Richards' words) 'the irresponsible world of the excluded intellectual.'[24] Rather the point that I wish to emphasize is the risks to society, nations and the world of relative poverty associated with exclusionary policies.

The Sierra Leone case is not unique. Richards compares it to the rise of Shining Path in Peru. The rise of various Muslim Brotherhoods in the Middle East is another example and in the next chapter I analyze the background to the Hindu rebellion in Sri Lanka. Elsewhere in Africa relative, moderate and absolute poverty are certainly a factor in recent civil strife in the Ivory Coast, where successive governments dominated by politicians from the central and southern regions withheld citizenship from many living in the rebelling northern region.[25] Nor should the policies and impacts of other nations and international agencies be ignored in the analysis of other cases where poverty is one of a number of causes of civil strife and civil war.

As one grim example which requires more background analysis, the report of a Finnish Inquiry Commission on genocide in Cambodia discusses how America's illegal carpet bombing in the first half of the 1970s was responsible for the influx of over a million refugees into the capital, which presumably had a bearing on their forced evacuation after the Khmer Rouge entered in 1975.[26] Each such case requires, as Richards emphasizes, social and cultural analysis to illustrate its distinguishing features, since coping with strife and reconstruction 'depends on cultural and institutional resourcefulness in civil society.'[27]

## NEW POVERTY

New poverty results from international and national policies, programs, plans and legislation that are supposed to foster development but in the process create massive poverty. Examples include unintended impacts of the structural adjustment programs of the World Bank (see Chapter 6), attempts by the United States Agency for International Development (USAID) and other national donor agencies to push privatization policies too rapidly or indiscriminately on aid recipients, and policies and legislation of national governments for the benefit of the upper classes at the expense of the poor.

I have direct experience with two cases where national governments and supportive elites passed legislation that impoverished local communities. Both involved legislation to privatize the common-property resources of poor rural communities so that their ownership could be transferred to politicians, civil servants, military officers and other elites. In both cases legislation was associated with planned dam constriction that would significantly increase downstream land values.

Construction of Mali's Manantali Dam almost caused war to break out between Senegal and Mauritania, while plans for building a large dam on Somalia's Juba River was a factor in the outbreak of civil war in a country that continues to remain ungovernable. In both the Mauritanian and Somali cases, national legislatures passed land-registration acts that enabled the elite to privatize, at the expense of local downstream communities, common-property resources whose value would increase significantly as a result of dam-supplied irrigation. In the Senegal River case, after the Mauritanian government passed a land-privatization act, the national elite evicted tens of thousands of local people from their villages and riparian lands, killing some and driving 50000 across the river into Senegal. In the Somali case, following passage of the land-registration act, elite from the capital city of Mogadishu began to privatize land below a planned dam[28] on the Juba River that belonged to local people under customary tenure. Conflict followed. Elsewhere, a more common result following government-instigated large dam construction is for wealthy and influential outsiders to privatize or seize valuable reservoir frontage for private residences or tourist facilities at the expense of communities that already have lost their most valuable agricultural resources to reservoir formation.[29]

Other forms of national legislation can cause new poverty in other countries. Examples include farm subsidies, tariffs and export credit agency policies. Then there is legislation prohibiting cultivation of certain high-value cash crops (like coca in Latin America, opium in Afghanistan and Asia and marijuana in Africa) which are the major sources of livelihood for millions living in poor rural communities throughout the world. I have studied the adverse impacts of such legislation in Lesotho, where dam-induced resettlers were further impoverished when refused compensation for marijuana, their highest value crop. Once relocated, they also found marijuana more difficult to grow because of tighter government control.

Another form of new poverty occurs when governments, with and without the assistance of international financial institutions, use eminent domain policies to evict millions of households, as well as entire communities, to make way for economic and conservation projects. Global research, including my own, documents how such involuntary resettlement causes increased impoverishment in the large majority of cases.[30]

While there are no accurate figures on the number of people involuntarily resettled or otherwise impoverished by development activities, the total certainly exceeds several hundred million and is one reason why the World Bank considers development-induced involuntary resettlement to be 'A Worldwide Challenge.'[31] Over a ten-year period from the mid-1970s, the World Bank estimates that 'about 80 to 90 million people' have been resettled in connection with 'dam construction, and urban and transportation development.'[32] That number is probably a major underestimate since planners of the large majority of such projects underestimate the number of people who must be moved. That is true even for World Bank-funded projects, where at least an attempt is made to estimate the numbers in order to provide adequate funding for the resettlement process. During the Bank's 1994 review of 192 assisted projects involving resettlement between 1986 and 1993, 'the total number of people to be resettled is 47 per cent higher than the estimate made at the time of appraisal.'[33] In my own analysis of resettlement in connection with large dams, I found a similar deficiency, with the number finally resettled being 50 per cent higher than appraised.[34]

Examples of development projects causing involuntary resettlement are worldwide. They include urban renewal, infrastructure projects, extractive industries, conservation areas and national parks and the creation of industrial parks and special economic zones. Urban renewal as in China (Beijing) and India (Mumbai) currently causes the most involuntary resettlement of poor people. It also has the most negative impact on small businesses. Their relocation can be expected to reduce employment opportunities, for often businesses are unable to re-establish themselves elsewhere.

Until overtaken by urban development in the mid-1990s, dam construction was the main cause of involuntary resettlement. The shocking deficiency in knowing the numbers of people involuntarily resettled is illustrated by a two-year study by the World Commission on Dams, on which I was one of 12 commissioners; the best estimate that it could make was somewhere between 40 and 80 million resettlers. Though research is lacking, the living standards of a still larger number of people living below dams have been adversely affected due to the regularization of rivers' natural flow regimes for hydropower generation and irrigation.[35]

Figures for other types of development-induced change are even harder to come by. Though such extractive industries as mines cause less involuntary resettlement than do dams and urban development, individual projects can require the removal of tens of thousands of people. Such is the case with coal-powered thermal power projects. In India, the World Bank estimates that between them the coal-fired Farakka II and Singrauli II thermal power plants caused the involuntary removal of approximately 100000 people. Though data on evictions are even less available for national parks and other protected areas, social scientists Kai Schmidt-Soltau and Dan Brockington conclude after a survey of the literature that 'forced displacements have been used widely and systematically as the approach to "cleanse" protected areas of people, rather than being confined to a few instances.'[36] Noting that protected areas cover approximately 10 per cent of the world's surface area and that, at a conservative estimate, 50 per cent of those in poor countries are occupied, they are especially concerned about the forced relocation that may follow from increased enforcement of conservation regulations. They refer, for example, to recent reports from India and Africa that 'suggest that nearly four million people face eviction following amendments to protected area policy,' while 'up to 16 million people in Africa could become environmental refugees from protected areas.'[37] As for the expansion and creation of industrial parks and special economic zones, in China, and more recently in India, uncounted households of rural farmers as well as entire communities are being displaced with inadequate compensation and little to no livelihood development opportunities (see Chapter 5).

## OTHER WAYS FOR CATEGORIZING POVERTY

Categories of poverty change through time. Relatively recent examples include the rapid growth of urban poverty, poverty associated with failed states and poverty induced by environmental degradation. Then there is what I have labeled, for lack of a better phrase, 'poverty caused by the poor or former members of poor communities exploiting other poor.' There is also poverty that results from protectionist and self-serving policies of the more powerful industrial societies.

When I first taught courses in anthropology to Caltech students in the 1960s, rural poverty was considered the most prevalent and the most deserving of attention. It included small-scale farmers cultivating marginal land or land subdivided over the years among an increasing number of heirs, as well as those with neither land nor employment. Migration to cities and towns was a logical response to such poverty – not just because of more job opportunities but also because of better access to educational and medical facilities.

The capacity of the rapidly growing mega-cities, especially in developing countries, to absorb migrants shrank as millions of rural poor packed into unauthorized settlements in and around urban centers. The situation has deteriorated to such an extent that UN-Habitat's 2006 report[38] states that urban poverty may well be worse than rural poverty, since cities in which too many people are crowded can no longer raise the living standards of their own urban poor, let alone absorb more immigrants.

In an increasing number of failed states (as of 2006 the World Bank lists 26), civil strife, corruption and dysfunctional governments and/or policies have increased the number of people in poverty. Civil wars are especially impoverishing. World Bank-funded research in Sri Lanka estimates that civil war has reduced economic growth annually by two to three per cent,[39] while the Oxford University economist Paul Collier estimates a 2.2 per cent annual decline in per capita Gross Domestic Product as economic consequences of civil war.[40] More directly affected are internally displaced people (IDP) and refugees. During the first half of 2009, for example, UN OCHA (Office for the Coordination of Humanitarian Affairs) reported that the number of IDPs and refugees in 16 East and Central African countries increased from 10.9 million to over 11 million due to national disasters and armed conflict.[41] Then there are environmental IDPs and refugees whose number is already beginning to increase because of global warming. They include people who have left their homes because of desertification in the African Sahel, Iran and China[42] and flooding in Bangladesh.

Exploitation of the poor by community members or former members is seldom analyzed in the development literature, perhaps because it is more the domain of anthropologists and sociologists who have studied communities of the poor in the field. Both disciplines continue to be under-represented in international and national development institutions, as does research on communities of the poor. But then very few staff members in development agencies have studied poverty by living within poor communities or communities in which the poor are an important component.

In such communities a major problem is the extent to which the poor or former poor 'feed upon the poor.' Two types of situation need be dealt with in poverty reduction programs. One is kin-based. In Gwembe Tonga villages, current poverty is so extreme that family members or members of extended kin groups increasingly steal from each other. Children, for example, steal livestock from their parents. Such poverty accompanies a breakdown in social organization and values; in the Gwembe Tonga case worsened by fear of witchcraft among family members.

The second situation is more complicated. It can involve community members stealing from one another, as also among the Gwembe Tonga today, where intra-community theft of standing and stored crops is more common than in the past. But it can also involve formerly poor 'specialists' from within rural and urban communities alike, or from the wider society, who steal, as individuals and members of gangs, from poor households or sell drugs within the community. In low-income urban communities, for example, family members can return home to find that all their furnishings have been stolen, a situation I have come across in Old Kanyama, an unauthorized settlement in Lusaka, Zambia. Intra-community drug dealing by members of poor communities has been reported throughout the world, including among the urban poor in U.S. inner cities and among such indigenous people as Native Americans. Not infrequently the thieves and drug dealers suffer from relative poverty, in that they find themselves excluded from the wider society.

Exploiters of the poor in this second situation also include those who were born poor in the community but managed to escape it through such means as education to join the middle or upper classes. As communities of the poor become increasingly diversified (another situation that makes poverty reduction harder, because heterogeneity makes community participation in the development process more difficult), such members use their knowledge and influence to privatize common-property resources in their natal community to the communities' harm. As one example, I came across a case in Botswana where a retired civil servant used his influence to privatize communal grazing land and water resources in his village of origin. In Zambia I documented a case in which a high official used his knowledge and influence to privatize in his home community an extensive area of the most valuable common-property resource for agriculture and grazing.

Additional categories of the poor include people who have been either marginalized within particular societies or by the expansion of more dominant societies and nations. Those marginalized within specific societies would include the various ethnic groups labeled Roma or Gypsies in Europe, the Middle East and Asia, hundreds of thousands of members of scheduled castes and scheduled tribes in India, the large majority of those living in urban ghettoes such as African Americans in South Los Angeles and North African and Asian immigrants in Europe, and immigrants from other African countries in the Ivory Coast and South Africa.

Those marginalized due to the expansion of dominant outsiders would include most Native Americans in Canada and the United States and Australian aborigines, most of whom have been pushed into ethnic reserves. Still other categories include the millions with HIV/AIDS who have inadequate access to medication and most members of urban gangs, of which there are an estimated 100 000 in Cape Town (population 3.4 million) and 34 000 in Los Angeles (population 4 million). Then, as also in the United States, there are the homeless and those institutionalized because of mental illness or crimes committed.

# POVERTY ALLEVIATION AND DEVELOPMENT

## Introduction

It is assumed by national governments and international agencies that poverty alleviation requires the successful implementation of development policies, programs, plans and projects. For that reason it is necessary to explore how the term 'development' is defined and implemented, and then to ask whether or not the majority of the poor actually want development. My starting point is to examine first the United Nations' Declaration on the Right to Development, which the General Assembly adopted, with some opposition, on 4 December 1986. Subsequently at the 1993 World Conference on Human Rights, the Vienna Declaration and Programme of Action, which included the Right to Development, was 'unanimously adopted' by 171 member nations.[43]

The first of 10 articles in the 1986 Declaration states that 'the right to development is an inalienable human right' which entitles all people 'to participate in, contribute to, and enjoy economic, social, cultural and political development.' It also implies the right to self-determination. Since development is centered on people, nation states have the 'duty to formulate appropriate national development policies that aim at the constant improvement of the well-being of the entire population' through their participation in the development process and in the distribution of its benefits (Article 2).

Like all such declarations, the meaning of the different articles is 'fuzzy' so that interpretations can and do vary between different interest groups. Indigenous people with customary rights over the lands in which they live can be expected to have different interpretations as to the meaning of the right to self-determination. Interpretations also differ as to the extent to which active participation in political development implies or requires a democratic form of government. Distinguished economist and Nobel Laureate Amartya Sen stated in a 1999 talk that the rise of democracy was the most important event during the previous hundred years, being a 'constituent of development – indeed as an integral part of a good society in the contemporary world.'[44] In other writing, Sen supports his conclusion by noting that 'no substantial famine has ever occurred in any independent country with a democratic form of government and a relatively free media.'[45]

Also important is the extent to which the stronger industrial countries, the United States in particular but also the OECD countries, define the development process (as implemented through their export credit agencies as well as through their influence on the international financial institutions) in ways that disproportionately benefit their own economies and values. More recently China has been tying its financial aid in Africa to use of Chinese construction companies, equipment and access to natural resources and other economic opportunities (Chapter 5). Hence the need to avoid confusion between national definitions of development that vary in significant ways from that defined in the Declaration on the Right to Development.

A major weakness in that Declaration, and in the way it is implemented, is that it is centered on people, their cultures and their nation states as if they existed in a vacuum rather than being a part of, and dependent upon, a global ecosystem. It is interesting, for example, that there is no reference in the Declaration's ten articles to human dependence on the world's natural resource base. A similar inadequacy characterizes such national measures of annual development as Gross Domestic Product which include, for example, market value arising from the non-sustainable use of natural resources. Such non-sustainable income generation I would label as a form of 'growth without development.' I first came across that designation in a 1966 book dealing with the economy of Liberia, where the authors expanded its meaning to a situation where 'enormous growth in primary commodities produced by foreign concessions for export has been unaccompanied either by structural changes to induce complementary growth or by institutional changes to diffuse gains in real income to all sectors of the population.'[46] Subsequently such growth without development was fueled by unsustainable timber removal that also was an important source of finance for Liberia's two civil wars and especially for the government of Charles Taylor,[47] who is now being tried before the International Court of Justice for crimes against humanity.

## Do the Poor want Development?

### Introduction

During my research among poor populations in North America, Africa, the Middle East and Asia, I have never worked in communities, including indigenous ones, in which the majority did not want some form of development as defined by the Declaration on the Right to Development. Nor have I come across contemporary cases in the social science and development literature where other communities have stated a lack of interest in participating in development opportunities. Perhaps that was not the case before the Second World War. But thereafter, attitudes favoring development have been influenced by radio and television, temporary and permanent labor migration within countries and from low-income and unstable nations to middle- and upper-income ones, and the more recent spread of information technology and globalization. All such influences and activities have, for better or worse, significantly increased contact between cultures, nations and societies and rates of social change.

On the other hand, it is of critical importance to emphasize that what constitutes development varies between nations and ethnic groups. Due especially to increasing heterogeneity, definitions vary as well within ethnic groups and within communities. Such is also the case within families, not just between young and old, and men and women, but also within the same age and gender categories.

The two case histories given below involve ethnic groups that I have visited in the field. I selected them to represent the type of society that one might assume would be least interested in development. Both have maintained distinctive cultures, including their own language. But they have also remained relatively open to change influenced through contacts with the outside world. As for development, their members want it. Though their definitions of what constitutes development vary, greater availability of health and educational services and access to a wider range of opportunities for improving livelihood are common features. In other words, like ethnic groups everywhere they have histories which involve both cultural continuity and culture change.

### The James Bay Cree Nation (Quebec Province, Canada)

The James Bay Cree[48] are indigenous First Nation Canadians numbering over 13 000. Though in contact with, and influenced by, other Native American groups in pre-colonial days, their livelihood was based on hunting, fishing and gathering. Following contact with colonial trappers in the 17th century, they began selling furs as a cash crop through the Hudson Bay Company. Contact and influence by missionaries increased during the 19th century and with Canadian government agencies during the 20th century, at which time some wage labor further diversified their livelihood. But hunting has continued to remain a key component of the economy of the Cree's nine isolated communities, with its influence permeating throughout Cree culture.

In 1971 Quebec's Premier announced that one of the world's largest programs for the generation of hydroelectric power was to be implemented by Hydro-Quebec, a provincial organization, by damming and diverting major rivers within Cree customary territory. No Cree had been involved in the program's planning nor were they even aware of its existence until a few local leaders heard the news on the radio.

Initially the leaders of the nine communities were at a loss about how to respond to what they saw as a major threat to their livelihood. Within three years, however, they had formed a Grand Council of the Crees that mobilized the people into an effective institution for negotiating their future. Help from outsiders was welcomed and was provided especially by non-governmental organizations (NGOs) and university researchers.

In November 1975 a year of negotiations produced The James Bay and Northern Quebec Agreement, which probably was the best that the Cree could expect at the time, since an earlier court case opposing the first dam had been lost. Ten years later, however, when planning began for another dam, the Crees' negotiating ability was much stronger. Arguing that the new dam was not covered by the 1975 agreement and that agreement-stipulated benefits had not been fully implemented, the Cree launched effective international opposition. Not only did they work closely with anti-dam NGOs in both Canada and the United States, but they also received support from state governments in the northeastern portion of the United States which refused to purchase power produced by the disputed dam. Support was also received from the United Nations and from the Pope. Opposition paid off when Quebec's Premier announced in 1994 that the disputed dam had been 'put on ice.'

Thereafter the federal government stepped in and began to explore with the Cree better ways for implementing the 1975 James Bay Agreement. Meanwhile, under pressure, Hydro-Quebec had improved its policies for dealing with project-affected people and the environment, and, joined by Quebec provincial leaders, had begun negotiations with the Cree on a new agreement in which Hydro-Quebec and the Cree would be partners in hydropower development. In a January 2001 referendum, 70 per cent of a large turnout of Cree voters approved the new agreement.

Why did the Cree agree? Not only did they realize that hydropower development was inevitable in their customary lands, but they knew that development was necessary for a Cree population that had more than doubled since 1974. Foraging, fishing and especially hunting remained very important, with at least a third of Cree families benefiting during the 1990s from the Income Security Programme for Hunters and Trappers that had been negotiated as part of the James Bay Agreement. But hunting and trapping alone could not provide employment for the approximately 500 youths who entered the job market each year. In supporting the 2002 agreement a month before its approval by Cree voters, the then Grand Chief of the Grand Council said in a speech '**The Cree Nation is no longer seen as being in the way of development. Instead the Crees are recognized as essential to development – the logical centre for development in the territory**' (bold print as in the Grand Chief's statement).

### The Dinka (Southern Sudan)

The Dinka are the largest ethnic group in Southern Sudan. Their number today is well over a million. Prior to formation of Sudan's Government of National Unity in 2005, the Dinka contributed by far the largest number of fighters in the civil war in which the Southern Region sought independence from the national government. They also suffered the largest number of casualties and in-country and international refugees. Today, they are Southern Sudan's dominant ethnic force within the Government of National Unity.

In March 1978 British livestock expert Bill Payne and I were traveling in the Central Sudan during an extended break in the civil war. Conditions were grim for local people and consultants alike. On our arrival at Malakal, we camped in a bombed-out bank where, with our Sudanese colleagues, we groped for beans at the bottom of a common pot to avoid the surface of dead and dying flies which were hatching from maggots swarming in the adjacent unflushable toilets.

Several days later our destination was a Dinka cattle camp that young men and women had recently established to take advantage of new grazing on floodplains from which the Nile's annual flood was receding. En route we passed by other camps with hundreds of cattle partially obscured by smudge fires of dung that had been kept going all night to discourage the swarms of mosquitoes which we too had encountered when they found holes in our mosquito nets.

We reached our destination shortly after dawn. Young men, thin of body and over six feet tall, were reciting poetry to, and simulating the trained horns of their favorite oxen as they ran 50 yard dashes off an elevated mound that served as a sleeping platform at night. Immediately I noticed cultural continuity with anthropologist Evans-Pritchard's similar description from the 1930s among the neighboring Nuer. The thought occurred to me that perhaps these Dinka had not changed much during the past forty years.

Once introductions were made (Payne and I were UNDP consultants at the time), we asked the young men grouped around us what were their activities, besides herding cattle and making love, as well as their needs and problems. They wanted development all right, but – and there is a major lesson here for all planners – only as they defined it. That definition included as the number one priority reconstituting herds devastated during the war years and improved veterinary care for their remaining livestock. Improved medical facilities for people were also stressed along with access to education for children.

The men then launched into a long discussion of past and ongoing problems they had in marketing their cattle. At first they had driven old stock to the market but low prices and a high death rate en route quickly taught them to market prime steers. But then there was the problem of purchasing supplies in war-affected towns, and of acquiring the trucks to carry them back to their villages. Finally, when everyone was more relaxed, a few young men brought out their Uzi submachine guns and told us about the difficulties they had in maintaining them and acquiring the necessary parts.

## THE CONSUMPTION THREAT ASSOCIATED WITH SUCCESSFUL POVERTY ALLEVIATION

If global poverty was eliminated, try to imagine what might be the impact of the increased consumption of billions more people on the world's natural resources, pollution, and land and other forms of environmental degradation. In the process keep in mind that approximately 70 per cent of American GDP came from private consumption before the current (2009) financial and economic crisis. In India the figure was about 60 per cent.

Various estimates expect the world's current six billion people to increase to nine billion between 2040 and 2050. The majority of that three billion increase will be poor people, most of whom will be born in the poorest countries. Since global leaders are committed to poverty alleviation, with the first Millennium Development Goal being to eradicate extreme poverty and hunger and economist Jeffrey Sachs discussing the end of poverty as an economic possibility for our time, successful poverty alleviation could easily double and even triple the number of non-poor consumers over the next thirty to forty years.

The seriousness of the above threat is based on my assumption that as the poor emerge from poverty they will increase their consumption like the rest of us, hence increasing the risk of disastrous environmental impacts. I believe the evidence justifying that assumption is overwhelming – certainly I have come across no major exceptions in my own work. Others, however, are not convinced. The authors, for example, of the 2006 *An Introduction to Sustainable Development* state that 'poverty reduction is not likely to create overconsumption, which could, in turn, enhance environmental degradation.'[49]

My opposite conclusion is based on my own comparative research and long-term studies dealing with consumption changes in communities and households escaping poverty in the major regions of the world, as well as on the experience of others.[50] Let me make it clear, not only do I applaud poverty reduction but consider it absolutely essential if countries, like Zambia, with impoverished rural majorities are to improve the quality of life of their citizens. But, at the same time, the consumption threat posed by success needs to be anticipated and addressed.

My own comparative research on government-sponsored land settlement schemes for both poor volunteers and involuntary development-induced resettlers illustrates increasing consumption trends as the incomes and livelihoods of formerly poor people improve.[51] Once subsistence needs are met, the large majority of households shift their labor to farm and non-farm activities to increase income. Around the world that income is spent in identical ways. Improved housing has a high priority, with houses furnished in almost identical ways. Furniture includes a stuffed couch and chair suite for the family room along with a cabinet to show, through the glass or clear plastic front paneling, children's toys, a tea or coffee set and valued family possessions. A wall clock can be expected along with a radio, cassette and video player, a color television and framed pictures of school graduates, soldiers and elaborate weddings. The kitchen is furnished usually with a wooden table and chairs along with upgraded cooking facilities.

As income increases, consumption increasingly shifts from locally

manufactured goods (which provide a critical source of national employment) to imported goods and services. Both make demands on the home
environment (on forests, for example, for wood for housing, tables and
other furniture and for charcoal) and on the natural resources of other
countries where manufactured goods are made.

Results from individual countries provide similar details. Take for
example the current situation in the Chinese village of Kaihsiengkung,
which I visited during the 1980s. When Chinese anthropologist Fei
Hsiaotung began his research there in 1936, the large majority of residents
lived in poverty. Today the majority would be considered middle class.
Their possessions in 2004 included 730 new houses for a population of
about 3000, 850 air conditioners, 1230 mobile phones, 650 motorcycles
and 21 cars. Two years later there were 850 motorcycles and 28 cars.

A similar consumption pattern, taking only five years to occur, is underway in Laos among 1200 households resettled in connection with the Nam
Theun 2 dam project. When I first visited their pre-resettlement villages
around the turn of the century, the occupants were among the poorest in
Laos. By the end of 2007 they had used their increased income to buy televisions for practically every house, 728 motorcycles, 196 satellite receivers
and 167 hand tractors. The transformation in the number and stocking of
shops in the district center by 2008 was astonishing, with two shops selling
and repairing motorcycles and several others fully stocked with TVs,
boom boxes, refrigerators, electric fans, submersible pumps and quantities
of cell phones. Another shop specialized in making Buddhist shrines for
the household market.

Though Gwembe Tonga villages in the Middle Zambezi Valley have
fallen back into poverty since the mid-1970s, during the good years in the
1980s, income from reservoir fishing and sale of cash crops was used to
purchase spring beds and mattresses, wooden tables and chairs, bicycles
and radios. The few with tertiary education aspired to middle-class status,
including elaborate Christian weddings.

# THE IMPOVERISHING ROLE OF NATIONAL AND INTERNATIONAL ECONOMIC POLICIES AND METHODOLOGIES

## Structural Adjustment Programs and the Washington Consensus

Structural adjustment programs and the Washington Consensus refer
to the development policies of the main international financial institutions, the United States Treasury and the financial institutes of other G7

**The threat of global poverty**      33

countries[52] and the financial press. They are intended to produce growth (defined as real increases in per capita income and Gross Domestic Product). Critics state that too much emphasis has been placed on growth alone, that policy implementation results have been unsatisfactory in regard to poverty alleviation as well as the global environment, and that the policies continue to be too favorable to the United States, Western European countries and Japan.[53]

As implemented by the World Bank and the regional banks as conditions tied to borrower loans, structural adjustment programs emphasize conservative fiscal policies, including fiscal discipline and major reductions in government funding, as well as export-led growth, privatization of public industries, and trade liberalization with an emphasis on tariff reduction. The phrase, Washington Consensus, originated from a 1990 paper by economist John Williamson, called 'What Washington means by Policy Reform.' By Washington he meant the international financial institutions (IFIs) including the World Bank and the International Monetary Fund, the United States government and various think tanks. Though he admits now that such a policy consensus no longer exists,[54] if it ever did, he identified '10 policy instruments about whose proper deployment Washington can muster a reasonable degree of consensus.'[55] Like the structural adjustment policies, they emphasized, in Williamson's words, 'macro-economic discipline, a market economy, and openness to the world'.[56] Williamson's ten points also emphasized tax reform, liberalizing interest rates, and property rights.

Many books and reports have been written by influential supporters and critics of differing viewpoints on the effectiveness of poverty reduction policies and confrontation over them. My more restricted approach is to concentrate on different viewpoints involving the World Bank. I focus on controversy over the approach taken to growth and globalization on two occasions. The first approach was taken during and following the preparation of the 2000 World Bank's *World Development Report 2000/2001: Attacking Poverty*, and on the analysis of its team director, Ravi Kanbur, who resigned in protest over efforts within the World Bank and the U.S. Treasury to rewrite the report.[57] The second is the current controversy over the World Bank-initiated 2008 *Growth Report* by the Commission on Growth and Development.

Kanbur's view is relatively close to my own research-based views on human nature, on socio-cultural systems and on creation and alleviation of poverty.[58] Unlike most development economists, I share the evolving views of behavioral economists and other social scientists who disagree with the overemphasis on the rationality of human decision making in regard to economic and other matters. Human nature is far more complicated than that, with decision making also heavily influenced by genetics and by cultural learning and belief systems, not to mention behavioral inconsistencies. As for socio-cultural systems, I assess them as complex, many stranded, open-ended coping systems, unlike most academic economists, who see them as equilibrium systems. Of course, under certain circumstances, socio-cultural systems and societies can behave temporarily as if they were equilibrium systems, an example being when a majority of members respond to the multidimensional stress that is associated with involuntary community resettlement.

In 1998 The World Bank appointed Ravi Kanbur as team director to prepare a World Development Report focusing exclusively on poverty. A former Principal Adviser to the Bank's Chief Economist, Kanbur at that time was Professor of Economics at Cornell University. Published annually, World Development Reports are the responsibility of the Chief Economist. They are prepared by Bank staff with help from advisers and consultants writing issues papers. Those published at the beginning of each decade are especially prominent.

During his tenure, Kanbur broadened reliance on information from sources outside the Bank, including NGOs and individual experts. An electronic conference was held in January 2000 to discuss the report's first draft. There were 1523 participants from 80 countries. The general impression was favorable, though some wanted still bolder conclusions. On the other hand, the Bank's Chief Economist and other senior personnel in the Bank felt that the draft was too critical of past Bank policy and actions, and of Bank emphasis on growth and globalization. Substantial rewriting was required, with the result that Kanbur resigned in May 2000. A report that was supposed to be published in September 2000 was not released until 2001, with the title *World Development Report 2000/2001: Attacking Poverty.*

Kanbur emphasized that IFI policies paid insufficient attention to the impacts of growth and globalization on income distribution and inequality. Furthermore the IFIs also pushed too rapidly a uniform development approach on all countries. Instead governments should have more influence in formulating policies and the speed at which those policies should be implemented. Tariff reduction, for example, requires a careful approach, the timing and extent of which should vary from country to country. That is an approach that my experience in Zambia supports (see Chapter 6).

Kanbur also emphasized the need for more emphasis on single-country studies which would document what policies have worked through time and would show the extent to which development experiences vary from one country to another. In addition to diversity between Asian countries, he noted in a number of papers the recent increasing inequality in China and India between rich and poor as well as people falling into poverty as a result of government policies.[59] Those examples are important, for they illustrate the weakness in the position of those who used the Chinese and Indian cases to 'prove' how an emphasis on growth alone would also reduce poverty.

I would add microanalysis based on long-term studies of community change and continuity through several generations to the need for more in-country analysis. Stated differently, development economists have relied too much on time-series data gathered by other institutions and researchers, often for rather different purposes, and on use of those data for cross-country regression analyses based on a restricted number of variables to reach their conclusions about development outcomes. These conclusions can differ greatly from those of anthropologists like myself and local and international NGOs. There are also situations where privatization should not occur and, where it does occur, can cause poverty, conflict and environmental degradation. Such is especially the case in regard to limited access common-property rights where a community or an ethnic group has restricted customary rights to land and water resources, as in the previously mentioned Mauritanian and Somali cases.

The 2008 *Growth Report* is important reading for two major reasons. Positive is reinforcement of the areas of agreement among development practitioners. These include the authors' realization the 'the global economy has outrun our capacity to manage it' and insistence that 'no generic formula exists. Each country has specific characteristics and historical experiences that must be reflected in its growth strategies.'[60] Moreover, '[o]ur model of developing economies is too primitive at this stage to make it wise to pre-define what governments should do.'[61] The authors also emphasize, as I do in Chapter 7, the importance of equal educational opportunities for both sexes from the preschool level through tertiary education. Not only must committed governments and strong political leaders be actively involved but there is a need for a new international organization for carrying out two tasks. Monitoring would be one. Anticipating and responding to instabilities in the global financial systems would be the other.

On the negative side, the authors not only underestimate environmental threats but 'do not know if limits to growth exist . . . The answer will depend on our ingenuity and technology, on finding new ways to create goods and services that people value on a finite foundation of natural resources.' (2008 *Growth Report*, p. 12). Meanwhile, as with other Global Boomers, it is full-speed ahead with high-growth policies. Yet, as former World Bank environmental economist Herman E. Daly asks, 'what makes this blue ribbon Commission believe that the extra ecological and social costs of growth are not already larger than the extra production benefits?'[62]

I am perplexed as to why the authors' consideration of environmental issues is largely limited to pollution and to global warming and climate change. Robert Goodland, the World Bank Group's now retired chief environment adviser, wants to know why the report ignores the fact that the atmosphere and the oceans, the two biggest sinks for the wastes of growth, 'are full or over-full.'[63]And why, Daly asks, do the authors ignore 'alternate indexes bearing on human well-being' such as the Human Development Index, the Ecological Footprint, and Daly and Cobb's own Index of Sustainable Economic Welfare?[64]

**Inadequate Policy Emphasis on the Need for Employment**

Policies for reducing poverty advocated by influential development economists place far too little emphasis on the necessity for increasing employment. Take Jeffrey Sachs, author of the 2005 *The End of Poverty* and Special Adviser to former UN Secretary-General Kofi Annan on the Millennium Development Goals. The words 'employment', 'unemployment' and 'jobs' or 'job creation' do not even occur in the index to *The End of Poverty*. Nor is the employment issue prominent within the text. It is not mentioned, for example, when Sachs lists India's four major economic challenges, in spite of the fact that several hundred million Indian citizens are unemployed or seriously underemployed in a country which continues to ignore its rural and urban poor. Moreover, individual Indian states push large dams, urban redevelopment, and more recently, as in China, special development zones that impoverish residents when they are forced from their homes and/or land without employment or other development opportunities to even restore their previous level of poverty.

Even in the eight UN Millennium Development Goals, job creation is not highlighted except as one of seven bullet points in the eighth goal – Develop a Global Partnership for Development. Yet without being linked with job creation, realization of some of those important goals can contribute to further poverty. Take, for example, the goal to achieve universal primary education. As a stand-alone goal, universal primary education would appear to be 'a no brainer.' Surely teaching rural children to read instructions for applying fertilizer and to keep simple accounts of income and expenditures makes sense. Agreed. But as John Gay emphasizes in his critique of Sachs' *The End of Poverty*, 'Without employment, primary education is a trap and a dead end.'[65] Completing primary school in low-income countries also raises expectations of a better standard of living which, if not met, can lead to relative poverty, which in turn can encourage revolutionary behavior, especially where non-exclusionary alternatives are unavailable, as was the case in the recent civil war in Sierra Leone. The unemployment problem is global and is increasing. In commenting on his organization's January 2006 annual jobs report, the Director-General of the International Labour Organization stated that 'this year's report shows once again that economic growth alone isn't adequately addressing global employment needs . . . We are facing a global jobs crisis of mammoth proportions, and a deficit in decent work that isn't going to go away by itself. We need new policies and practices to address these issues.'[66] Most recently Martti Ahtisaari, a day after receiving the 2008 Nobel Peace Prize, emphasized that only 300 million of 1.2 billion people aged 15 to 30 entering the job market in Asia and the Middle East will find jobs 'with the means now at our disposal . . . what will we offer these young . . . or will we leave them to be recruited by criminal leagues and terrorists?'[67]

**Tariffs and Subsidies**

Expectations had been high prior to the July 2008 failure of the World Trade Organization's Doha Round of negotiations that two types of compromise would be approved. One, demanded by low- and middle-income countries with large numbers of small-scale farm families, would involve substantial reduction of high-income country tariffs on agricultural imports and on their subsidies to in-country farmers. The other type of compromise, primarily for the benefit of the high-income countries, would involve global reduction of tariffs restricting non-agricultural market access.

Low- and middle-income countries, with strong support from Brazil, China and India, wanted the United States, the European Union and Japan to reduce their agricultural tariffs and subsidies. In Japan, the main crop protected is rice, in the United States feed grains, cotton, wheat, rice and soya, and in the European Union a wide variety of produce, including dairy products. The main beneficiaries in those countries are not just farmers but all businesses that benefit from backward and forward linkages to agriculture. Losers include the urban and rural poor (some of whom are small-scale farmers growing other crops which are not subsidized) who have to pay higher than world market prices for food.

Capital transfers subsidizing farmers in high-income countries are substantial. It is easier to understand the position of Japan and various European countries, which have many small farms and a culturally important appreciation of rural landscapes and life styles, than that of the United States. Farm subsidies are America's 'largest corporate welfare

program.' The main beneficiaries are large-scale farms and vertically integrated agribusinesses whose profits enable them to reduce the proportion
of smaller farms by buying them up.

In 2002 approximately $40 billion were transferred to American
farmers.[68] In the European Union, 2002 transfers of $100 billion consti-
tuted 36 per cent of total farm receipts versus 18 per cent in the United
States. In 2003, 25 per cent of American farms received 90 per cent of agricultural support.[69] The 2008 farm bill, which the European Union's trade
commissioner called 'one of the most reactionary farm bills in the history
of the US,' initially would continue crop subsidies to farms with incomes
of $2.5 million; this would drop to $750000 over a five-year period.

Globally the main losers to such high subsidies are the economies and
farming households in those low-income countries where agriculture continues to play a dominant or major role in efforts to industrialize. That is
because it is the rising income and purchasing power of millions of farm
households for a wide range of locally produced goods and services (as
opposed to luxury goods imported by small elites) that drives the economy
forward during the early stages of national development.[70] During Doha
Round negotiations, African countries emphasized how U.S. cotton subsidies damaged their economies and drove millions of farmers further into
poverty. As Oxfam pointed out, 'the statistics are compelling.'[71] In 2005, in
spite of their illegality following a 2004 World Trade Organization ruling,
over $4.2 billion in subsidies were paid to 25000 American cotton farmers
who sold 3.3 million tons of cotton on the world market. Citing a World
Bank source, Oxfam stated that 'removing US cotton subsidies alone
would raise the price of cotton on the international markets by an average
of 12.9 per cent.'[72]

The breakdown in the 2008 Doha Round negotiations was largely due
to disagreements as to when the Agriculture Special Safeguard Mechanism
would restrict cheap imports and import surges of agricultural produce
from the United States and other major agricultural exporters. Led by
China and India, countries with large populations of small-scale farmers
wanted higher thresholds, which the United States rejected, for restricting
imports.

**Over-reliance on Cost-Benefit Analysis**

Since the end of the Second World War, cost-benefit analysis has been
the main economic methodology for rating and ranking development
programs and projects according to the relationship of benefits to costs.
More recently even U.S. politicians have discovered cost-benefit analysis as a procedure for evaluating government programs. Where poverty

is involved, however, cost-benefit analysis has three major liabilities. It ignores how costs and benefits are distributed, with the frequent result that the rights of, and risks to, the poor are underestimated except in that minority of programs and projects that directly target the poor. Even where the poor are involved, cost-benefit analysis underestimates costs that are hard to quantify, receive low priority or are ignored altogether, and where costs exist in the more distant future, it employs discount rates that are too high.

My experience with the inadequacies of cost-benefit analysis relates to the underestimated costs and overestimated benefits associated with the construction of large dams. Social and environmental costs are systematically undervalued during project appraisal and discount rates are too high because they ignore future environmental and decommissioning costs. Moreover, 'sensitivity and risk analysis is inadequate.'[73] Ironically, cost-benefit analysis of dams as used by the World Bank during project appraisal also underestimates the beneficial multiplier effects that could be expected from the improved implementation of such large-scale water development projects.[74]

Involuntary resettlement illustrates the weaknesses of cost-benefit analysis where poverty is involved. Adverse impacts invariably have been underestimated and potential benefits ignored. While use of cost-benefit analysis is not the only deficiency, economic, social and cultural costs to communities, and the societies of which they are part, are under-assessed, as are adverse health and psychological impacts to individual resettlers. But more fundamentally, as the World Bank's now retired senior sociological adviser Michael Cernea emphasizes, '*even at its best, without distortions* [author's italics], the standard cost-benefit method is incapable of answering the economic and ethical questions involved in forced displacement.'[75] For that a wider range of economic methodologies, including distribution and risk analysis, should be included within a wider decision support system that incorporates a multi-criteria approach.[76]

## SUMMARY

Not only does approximately half of the world's population live in absolute, moderate, relative or new poverty, but the threat posed by poverty to the rest of humankind and to the environment is increasing. Reasons include the accelerating movement of the poor to cities, which are increasingly unable to meet their basic needs for employment, social services and meaningful participation in social and political activities. While the rural poor are spread out over the landscape, the consolidation of the poor in urban areas also puts them at greater risk from crime and other forms of exploitation including that by populist political leaders.

In dealing with conflict situations in which poverty is a factor, it is important to assess the relevance of all four types. Especially threatening is relative poverty involving educated individuals who are excluded from participating in the societies and nations to which they belong. Relative poverty has produced recent leaders of civil wars and other conflicts, while those suffering from absolute, moderate and new poverty, youths in particular, become their foot solders. New poverty has increased since the end of the Second World War. It includes development-induced involuntary removal from homes and land due to urban redevelopment, extractive industries, infrastructure such as large dams, special economic zones, new national conservation areas and parks and implementation of other government and private sector activities and policies.

While poverty alone is neither a necessary nor sufficient cause for conflict, it is one of a number of underlying factors that come up again and again in case studies.[77] Other situations in which poverty is a dominant factor include food riots in urban areas following a government-imposed rise in the price of food staples, as reported from many developing countries, or natural catastrophes that destroy crops and cut off populations from receiving outside aid. Conflict over scarce arable land and other natural resources by increasing populations of the rural poor was a major concern of some of the anthropologists replying to my 1998 questionnaire on constraining environmental and social issues. Cyprian Fisiy, a World Bank staff member from Cameroon, wrote in his questionnaire that '[i]n my work in Sub-Saharan Africa the evidence suggests that as natural resources are diminishing, there has been a strong re-emergence of confrontational ethnicity.' Gordon Appleby, a World Bank consultant from the United States, wrote that 'as economic conditions deteriorate, more and more people resort to common property resources to survive, destroying those resources and causing conflict among themselves.'

Underlying the United Nation's human rights emphasis is a series of covenants that include the 1986 Declaration on the Right to Development. Failure to realize broader development rights presents a major threat to the living standards of future generations. National and international economic policies and methodologies have slowed poverty alleviation by confusing growth with development and have inadvertently caused poverty and increased impoverishment. Policies have, for example, paid insufficient attention to employment generation, income distribution and the rising gap between rich and poor. The unwillingness of the highly industrialized nations, the United States and the European Union in particular, to lower their agricultural tariffs, reduce agricultural subsidies and agree to reasonable agricultural safeguard mechanisms jeopardize efforts by late-developing countries to reduce poverty and to develop. The economic fundamentalism of the international financial institutions and other donors, in pushing a 'one fits all' set of policies, has underestimated the complexity of the development process in different countries and in the same country at different times. The importance of agricultural development in the earlier stages of industrialization has been seriously underestimated. Conversely the speed with which new policies can be implemented, such as unrestricted capital flows, tariff reduction and privatization of government assets, has been overestimated.

Over-reliance on cost-benefit analysis and high discount rates have resulted in an underestimate of the length of time it takes for late-developing countries to shift from agricultural to industrial and post-industrial economies. Where poverty exists, cost-benefit analysis of such major projects as dams ignores how costs and benefits are distributed. Even where the poor are involved, cost-benefit analysis underestimates costs that are hard to quantify, receive low priority, or are ignored altogether, and where costs exist in the more distant future, it employs discount rates that are too high.

Poverty alleviation must not be seen as an end in itself but rather part of a dynamic development process to produce a more sustainable livelihood for the world's citizens. A major threat associated with success will be a significant increase in private consumption which, if not reduced, will accelerate exhaustion of the earth's natural resources, environmental degradation, global warming and the rate and magnitude of declining living standards.

# NOTES

1.  See George Foster, Thayer Scudder, Elizabeth Colson and Robert Van Kemper (eds) (1979). *Long Term Field Research in Social Anthropology.* London: Academic Press, and Thayer Scudder and Elizabeth Colson (2002). 'Long Term Research in Gwembe Valley, Zambia.' In Robert V. Kemper and Anya Peterson Royce (eds). *Chronicling Cultures: Long term field research in anthropology.* Walnut Creek, CA: Altamira Press.
2.  Mentioned in *Science* (23 February 2007). **315**. Page 1068.
3.  Michael M. Cernea, senior sociological adviser at the World Bank prior to retirement, has used the phrase 'new poverty' for various forms of development-induced poverty which have increased significantly since the end of the Second World War.
4.  Researchers concerned with relative poverty use several procedures for measuring the inequality that exists in all societies and nations. One is the Gini coefficient, which measures income inequality on a scale of 0 to 1 with 0 indicating complete equality. Another is the Decile Dispersion Ratio, which the World Bank Institute defines as 'the ratio of the average consumption of income of the richest 10 per cent of the population

divided by the average income of the bottom 10 per cent' (see World Bank (2000). *World Development Report 2000/2001: Attacking poverty: Opportunity, empowerment, and security.* Page 3). Neither definition is adequate because both are based on income alone.

5. Asian Development Bank (1999). 'Fighting Poverty in Asia and the Pacific: The poverty reduction strategy.' Manila: ADB.
6. Deepa Narayan (ed.) (2000). *Voices of the Poor: Can anyone hear us?* Page 49. New York: Oxford University Press for World Bank. The Bank analysis is based on recorded statements of over 40 000 poor men and women living in 50 countries during the 1990s.
7. Three the World Bank labels as physical, human and social capital, the fourth being environmental assets. I prefer not to extend the conventional dictionary definition of capital to such important attributes of individuals and of social and cultural variables.
8. Worldwide, poor women are especially concerned about their security because they are more subject than wealthier women to crime, sexual assault and exploitation at work and in the home.
9. The World Bank (2000).Op. cit.
10. Shaohua Chen and Martin Ravallion (2004). 'How Have the World's Poorest Fared Since the Early 1980s?' Washington DC: World Bank, Development Research Group.
11. See R. Kanbur (January 2004). 'Growth, Equity and Poverty: Some Hard Questions.' Commentary Prepared for *State of World Conference*, Princeton University, February 13–14.
12. *Ibid.*
13. *Ibid.* Page 8.
14. *The Economist* (16 September 2006). 'The New Titans. A Survey of the World Economy.'
15. *The Economist* (11 August 2007). 'Income Inequality in Emerging Asia is Heading Toward Latin American Levels.' Page 36.
16. Asian Development Bank (2007). 'Inequality in Asia: Key Indicators 2007. Special Chapter: Highlights.'
17. *The Economist* (13 October 2007). 'China Beware.' Leaders. Page 15.
18. Mitchell Landsberg (28 December 2006). 'Jobs Scarce for China's Graduates.' *Los Angeles Times.*
19. *The Economist* (16 September 2006). Op. cit.
20. See especially Paul Richards (1996). *Fighting for the Rain Forest: War, youth and resources in Sierra Leone.* Oxford and Portsmouth, NH: The International African Institute in association with James Currey and Heinemann; Paul Richards (2005a). 'New War.' In Paul Richards (ed.). *No Peace, No War: An anthropology of contemporary armed conflicts.* Athens, OH and Oxford: Ohio University Press and James Currey; and Paul Richards (2005b). 'Green Book Millenarians? The Sierra Leone War within the perspective of an anthropology of religion.' In Niels Kastfelt (ed.). *Religion and African Civil Wars.* New York: Palgrave Macmillan.
21. Caspar Fithen and Paul Richards (2005). 'Making War, Crafting Peace: Militia solidarities and demobilization in Sierra Leone.' In Paul Richards (ed.). *No Peace, No War: An anthropology of contemporary armed conflicts.* Athens, OH and Oxford: Ohio University Press and James Currey. Page 117.
22. Paul Richards (1996). Op. cit. Page 28.
23. *Ibid.* Page 162.
24. *Ibid.* Page 84. See Mary Douglas (1986). 'The Social Preconditions of Radical Skepticism.' In J. Law (ed.). *Power, Action and Belief: A new sociology of knowledge.* London: Routledge and Kegan Paul.
25. In his 1999 essay 'Poverty, Conflict and Development Interventions in Sub Saharan Africa,' Dutch geographer Pyt Douma states that 'patterns of relative poverty provide a strong incentive for groups to engage in violent conflict, as so-called power brokers can manipulate feelings of marginalization.'
26. Kimmo Kiljunen (ed.) (1984). *Kampuchea: Decade of the genocide: Report of a Finnish*

*Inquiry Commission.* London: Zed Books Ltd. Composed of 23 members from different sectors of Finnish society including four universities, this report attempts to present an unbiased assessment of events during the 1970s.

27. Richards (1996). Op. cit. Page 163.
28. This was the yet to be built Baardheere Dam.
29. Examples include Lake Kariba in Zambia, while on the Zimbabwe side of the reservoir communal lands were seized by the government for game reserves and parks.
30. For development-induced resettlement see Michael M. Cernea (ed.) (1999b). *The Economics of Involuntary Resettlement: Questions and challenges.* Washington DC: The World Bank. See also Thayer Scudder (2005). *The Future of Large Dams: Dealing with social, environmental, institutional and political costs.* London: Earthscan.
31. *Resettlement and Development: The Bankwide review of projects involving involuntary resettlement 1986–1993.* Washington DC: The World Bank, Environment Division. 8 April 1996.
32. *Ibid.* Page 1.
33. *Ibid.*
34. Thayer Scudder (2005). Op. cit.
35. See Brian D. Richter, Sandra Postel and Carmen Revenga *et al.* (forthcoming). 'Lost in Development's Shadow: The downstream human consequences of dams.' Manuscript. Nigeria's Kainji Dam, for example, has adversely affected hundreds of thousands of downstream residents.
36. Kai Schmidt-Soltau and Dan Brockington (2006). 'Do Conservation and Development Programs Differ When they Displace People.' Manuscript. Page 15.
37. *Ibid.* Page 18.
38. United Nations Human Resettlement Programme. *State of the World's Cities Report 2006/7.* London: Earthscan.
39. 'Toward a Conflict Sensitive Poverty Reduction Strategy: Lessons from a retrospective analysis.' (30 June 2005). Washington DC: The World Bank. Page 263.
40. See Paul Collier (1999). 'On the Economic Consequence of Civil War.' *Oxford Economic Papers.* **51**. Page 175.
41. UN News Service (18 May 2009). 'Over 11 Million People Displaced in Central and East Africa.' UN Reports. Available at http://www.un.org/apps/news/story. asp?NewsID=30826. According to UNHCR, UNRWA and Internal Displacement Monitoring Center estimates the number of currently displaced people in the world exceeds 35 million.
42. Lester Brown (28 January 2004). Earth Policy Institute Update 33. Page 2.
43. Felix Kirchmeier (July 2006). 'The Right to Development: Where do we stand?' State of the Debate on the Right to Development. Dialogue on Globalization. Occasional Papers, No. 23. Geneva: Friedrich Ebert.
44. Amartya Sen (1999a). 'Democracy and Social Justice.' Talk given at the *International Conference on Democracy, the Market Economy and Development.* Seoul, Korea. 26–27 February.
45. Amartya Sen (1999b). *Development as Freedom.* New York: Anchor Books.
46. R.W.Clower, G. Dalton, M. Harwitz and A.A. Walters (1966). *Growth without Development: An economic survey of Liberia.* Evanston, IL: Northwestern University Press.
47. See Global Witness (January 2001). 'The Role of Liberia's Logging Industry: Briefing to the UN Security Council on National and Regional Insecurity.'
48. I gained personal familiarity with the Cree case in 1994 while being a member of Hydro-Quebec's International Panel of Experts that evaluated, and rejected, Hydro-Quebec's Grande-Baleine Environmental Impact Study. See Scudder (2005). *The Future of Large Dams* for a more detailed analysis of the Cree case that includes references. See also I.W. Dickson *et al.* (1994). 'Hydro-Quebec's Grande Baleine Environmental Impact Study: An assessment report prepared for Hydro-Quebec'; H.A. Feit (1995). 'Hunting and the Quest for Power: The James Bay Cree and white men in the 20th Century.'

In R.B. Morrison and C.R. Wilson (eds). *Native Peoples: The Canadian experience.* Toronto: McClelland and Stewart; and R.F.Salisbury (1986). *A Homeland for the Cree: Regional development in James Bay 1971–1981.*Quebec: McGill-Queens University Press.

49. Peter P. Rogers, Kazi Jalal and John Boyd (2006). *An Introduction to Sustainable Development.* Pages 51–52.
50. See, for example, Gary Gardner, Erik Assadourian and Radhika Sarin (2004). 'The State of Consumption Today.' In *State of the World 2004.* New York: W.W. Norton and Company for the Worldwatch Institute.
51. See Scudder (1981). *The Development Potential of New Lands Settlement in the Tropics and Subtropics: A global state-of-the-art evaluation with specific emphasis on policy implications.* Binghamton, NY: Institute for Development Anthropology for U.S. Agency for International Development; and, with the assistance of Gottfried Ablasser (1984). *The Experience of the World Bank with Government-Sponsored Land Settlement.* Report No. 5625. Washington DC: World Bank, Operations Evaluation Department.
52. Canada, France, Germany, Italy, Japan, the United Kingdom and the United States.
53. See Ravi Kanbur (July 2005). 'The Development of Development Thinking.' Text of a public lecture given at the Institute for Social and Economic Change, Bangalore, India, 10 June, 2004.
54. See John Williamson (2002). 'Did the Washington Consensus Fail?' Outline of Speech at the Center for Strategic and International Studies. Washington DC. 6 November.
55. John Williamson (1990). 'What Washington Means by Policy Reform.' In John Williamson (ed.) *Latin American Adjustment: How much has happened?* Washington DC: Institute for International Economics.
56. *Ibid.*
57. All sides agree about differences in opinion within the Bank. Less clear is the role played by the U.S. Treasury and especially by Secretary of the Treasury, Larry Summers, who had been the World Bank's Chief Economist during 1991–1993.
58. Kanbur was born in India and educated at Cambridge (bachelor's degree) and Oxford (PhD degree). According to his home page résumé he served on the staff of the World Bank as Economic Adviser, Senior Economic Adviser, Resident Representative in Ghana, Chief Economist of the African Region and Principal Adviser to the Chief Economist. Currently he has joint appointments as professor in the Department of Applied Economics and Management in Cornell University's College of Agriculture and Life Sciences and in Cornell's Department of Economics in the College of Arts and Sciences. As his résumé suggests, he is a strong believer in the need for a multi-disciplinary approach to development and to poverty alleviation.
59. See Ravi Kanbur (March 2006). 'Three Observations on the Challenges of Growth and Poverty Reduction in Asia.' Available at http://www.arts.cornell.edu/poverty/kanbur/AsiaGrowthThreeObservations.pdf.
60. Commission on Growth and Development (2008). *The Growth Report: Strategies for sustained growth and inclusive development.* Washington DC: The World Bank. Pages 103 and 2.
61. *Ibid.* Page 30.
62. Herman E. Daly (September 2008). 'Growth and Development: Critique of a credo.' Notes and Commentary. *Population and Development Review.* **34** (3). Page 512.
63. Robert Goodland (5 August 2008). Email to Friends.
64. Daly (September 2008). Op. cit. Page 514. See also United Nations Development Programme (1990). *Human Development Report 1990.* New York: Oxford University Press; William E. Rees and Mathis Wackernagel (1994). 'Ecological Footprints and Appropriate Carrying Capacity: Measuring the natural capital requirements of the human economy.' In Ann Mari Jansson *et al.* (eds.) *Investing in Natural Capital: The ecological economics approach to sustainability.* Washington DC: Island Press; and Herman E. Daly and John B. Cobb, Jr. (1994). *For the Common Good: Redirecting the economy toward community, the environment and a sustainable future.* Boston, MA: Beacon Press.

65. John Gay (2005). 'An Analysis of *"The End of Poverty"* and the Millennium Development Goals, by Jeffrey D. Sachs.' *Higher Education in Europe.* **XXX** (3–4). Pages 249–265.
66. International Labour Organization (24 January 2006). 'ILO Annual Jobs Report Says Global Unemployment Continues to Grow, Youth Now Make Up Half Those Out of Work'. Press Release. Available at http://www.ilo.org.global/About_the_ILO/ Media_and_public_information/Press_Releases/lang--en/WCMS_065176/index.htm.
67. *International Herald Tribune* (11 October 2008). 'Nobel Peace Prize Winner Wants Jobs for the Young.'
68. *OECD in Washington* (August/September 2003). 'Subsidies to Agriculture: Why?' No. 46.
69. *OECD in Washington.* Op. cit.
70. See B.F. Johnston and P. Kilby (1975). *Agriculture and Structural Transformation: Economic strategies in late developing countries.* New York: Oxford University Press.
71. Oxfam (2006). 'A Recipe for Disaster: Will the Doha Round fail to deliver for development?' Oxfam Briefing Paper 87. Page 7.
72. *Ibid.*
73. *Ibid.* Pages 180-182.
74. See Ramesh Bhatia, Rita Cestti, Monica Scatasta and R.P.S. Malik (eds) (2008). *Indirect Economic Impacts of Dams: Case studies from India, Egypt and Brazil.* New Delhi: Academic Foundation for the World Bank.
75. Michael M. Cernea (1999a). 'Why Economic Analysis is Essential.' In Michael M. Cernea (ed.). *The Economics of Involuntary Resettlement: Questions and challenges.* Washington DC: The World Bank. Page 21.
76. World Commission on Dams (2000). Dams and Development: A new framework for decision-making. London: Earthscan. Page 182.
77. See World Bank (2005). *Toward a Conflict-Sensitive Poverty Reduction Strategy: Lessons from a retrospective analysis.* Washington DC: World Bank. Factors mentioned include competition at all levels of society over scarce natural resources and governments with weak institutions, such as corrupted or weak legal systems, which are unable to deal with conflict when it arises. A small middle class, as in many developing countries, and lack of democracy or inadequate opportunities for selection of policy makers, are also factors. Even more important are perceived inequities including lack of access to government benefits such as education, jobs within the civil service and the military, unfair taxes on households and produce (through government marketing boards and other institutions that favor one sector over another), and incapacity to influence decisions at all levels of society.

# 2. The threat of fundamentalism

## INTRODUCTION

I define fundamentalists as those who are committed to following an exclusive ideology which they believe every one should share. At best they are unaware or unconcerned about other belief systems. At worst they are committed to using destructive means to convert others to their own beliefs. Today fundamentalism has a global impact as a threat. The threat posed by religious fundamentalism has a history dating back over thousands of years. The nature of the threat intensified when national governments exported a broader range of cultural, economic and political fundamentalist policies during the era of Western colonialism.

In recent years there have been the fundamentalist efforts of the second Bush administration in the United States to export American democracy to the Middle East and to superimpose the Christian fundamentalism of a minority of U.S. citizens on the nation's majority, and, through restrictions on foreign aid, on the international community. In Sri Lanka, Buddhist-dominated governments have implemented fundamentalist cultural, political and religious policies that marginalized, and led to civil war with the country's Tamil-speaking Hindu minority. In the Middle East, Israeli religious and political fundamentalism has marginalized millions of Palestinians. The potentially destructive structural adjustment and Washington Consensus policies of the World Bank, as explained in Chapter 1, have been a form of economic fundamentalism in that they involved an untested 'one fits all' set of economic policies that borrower nations were expected to immediately adopt.

Different kinds of fundamentalism are major threats to global living standards today and in the future because they share belief systems that are fixed, or at least relatively impervious to change, and a system of action that believers require others to follow. They constitute dangerous ideologies that share a number of faith-based distinguishing features that include oversimplification of complex situations, rejection of other explanations, conviction of rectitude and willingness to gain and use power to convert or force others to comply with the views held.

Coping with the uncertainty accompanying such future threats as global warming and the occurrence of other unexpected events will require flexibility in making, monitoring and altering policies and making and implementing novel decisions at all levels of society from the family to the global level. Fundamentalism not only does not involve the necessary flexibility but frequently is opposed to it. There are other belief systems, such as witchcraft as practiced in Africa, that share features with fundamentalism and are incompatible with the type of transformational change necessary to slow and reduce future declines in living standards.

It is important to emphasize that there are major differences between and within religious, political, economic and cultural fundamentalist movements. During the 1990s the American Academy of Arts and Sciences contracted scholars to work together during a five-year study of religious fundamentalism.[1] Differences between the religions studied and the interpretations and beliefs of the scholars made definitions difficult. Nonetheless the authors were able to agree on nine 'family resemblances.' Five are at least partially applicable to other forms of fundamentalism. They are: idealism as a basis for personal and communal identity; envisioning one's movement as part of a much wider struggle (cosmic for religious fundamentalism, global for political, economic and cultural fundamentalism); demonizing any opposition and being reactionary; selective in what parts of tradition and heritage are stressed; and being led by males (a less reported characteristic is the subjugation of women within fundamentalist movements). Not applicable to political, economic and cultural fundamentalism is an emphasis on truth as revealed, while only the second part of the ninth characteristic ('efforts to overturn the distribution of power') is applicable.

I have placed religious fundamentalism first because readers will be most familiar with it, because it is best studied and because of its long history of bloodshed, conflict and exploitation of humanity and especially of women and children.[2] A major question is whether or not the religions in which fundamentalism is imbedded can control fundamentalism among their members. There is little historical evidence that they can. Today politically influential Buddhist monks in Sri Lanka are in the forefront of those discriminating against the Hindu minority, while Buddhist monks have marched recently in Thailand's capital demanding that the country be declared a Buddhist nation.

In Israel, it is rabbis and their followers in the more conservative Jewish sects who have disproportionate influence on government policies toward returning illegally acquired land to Palestine and Palestinians. Within Islam, it is fundamentalist mullahs who have the greatest influence on militant youth. In Christianity, fundamentalists consider neither liberal Christians nor Catholics as 'saved.' Moreover, the number of liberal

Christians in the mainline churches is declining. As for Catholics, it is the Pope himself, and those in the Catholic hierarchy that have attacked liberation theology in Latin America, efforts in Brazil, Mexico and Spain to legalize abortion and/or civil unions among gays, and use of condoms as protection against HIV/AIDS.

Religious fundamentalism feeds upon poverty and especially upon relative poverty. Throughout history, men – excluded from participating in the societies in which they live – have participated in, led or initiated religious movements including fundamentalist ones. A key example of a world religion is the birth of Christianity in opposition to the Roman Empire and the local Jewish leadership. A more recent example is the rise of the Mormon religion. Both are examples of revitalization movements arising in situations where believers were a discriminated-against minority.

The history of colonialism is full of small-scale revitalization movements in which the large majority consisted of uneducated 'natives' in the vocabulary of the time. Examples included the cargo cults in Melanesia, the Ghost Dance among Native Americans in the United States and the hundreds of revitalization movements in South Africa during the Apartheid era. Many were fundamentalist movements including some in which believers, who thought themselves impervious to injury from bullets or other causes, turned to violent resistance. The Maji Maji Movement in German East Africa is an example from the early part of the 20th century while the Lord's Resistance Army is a current example from Northern Uganda.

Recent larger-scale contemporary movements involving violence and death include Catholic and Protestant fundamentalism in Northern Ireland, Jewish fundamentalism in Israel and Palestine, Muslim fundamentalism in the Middle East, Hindu fundamentalism in India and Buddhist fundamentalism in Sri Lanka. In addition to violence, many such movements also create large numbers of refugees. Especially horrendous examples include the millions of Hindu and Muslim refugees created by the partition of India and hundreds of thousands of Palestinian refugees who, failing repatriation or other resettlement into the third generation, now number in the millions.

Rather than trying to further define fundamentalism in the abstract, my approach is to analyze and illustrate the threatening impacts of a series of contemporary fundamentalist movements. The first deals with Sri Lanka. It is selected for two major reasons. One is that the movement there involves strong religious, political and cultural components which are so closely fused that it is often not possible to separate out their specific effects. The other is that the religion involved is Buddhism, which, according to conventional wisdom, is supposed to be non-violent. The second case deals with religious and political fundamentalism in Israel and the third with cultural, political and religious fundamentalism in the United States. Cases involving Buddhism and Judaism are emphasized because as threats, fundamentalism in these two religions has been less analyzed than in Christianity and Islam.

Before proceeding I wish to add a few words about my own relationship with individual and institutionalized religion. Both have influenced and fascinated me since early childhood. In primary school I sang in the choir of the Episcopal Church and, while in secondary school, in the choir of an interdenominational church. Since that time I have enjoyed Christian religious music and during my travels have gone out of my way to visit churches, mosques and temples.

At Harvard College I took a course on primitive religion. Following graduation I spent a year as a special student at the Yale Divinity School, where I could also take courses in the Graduate School of Arts and Sciences. That year at Yale was perhaps the most interesting year of my education. In the Divinity School I took courses in Church History, Systematic Theology, and Old Testament and Non-Western Religions. And I discussed religion with other divinity students.

My fascination and interest in religion as a cultural universal has con-tinued to the present, while as a social anthropologist I have continued studying a wide variety of belief systems. As for my own beliefs, my wife, Eliza, and I accept no institutionalized belief system. Because my courses at Caltech included the study of religion, my students invariably would ask about my own views. I replied that I was a non-believer and had my own hypotheses as to why religious systems existed. They were all based on natural explanations. As many scholars have emphasized in great detail, reasons included a consoling way to deal with uncertainty, especially death (I showed students slides of Neanderthal man burying the dead with red ochre to demonstrate that religious concerns have existed for tens of thousands of years). I asked them to think about why most religious belief systems, and especially the great world religions, were dominated by older, indeed, elderly men. Might it be that they had invented such systems in part to continue their domination over younger men, women and children when their physical strength ebbed? And why the change from thousands of relatively isolated ethnic-specific religious systems to the great world religions that incorporated believers and non-believers alike within a single system? Could that be associated with the rise of cities and the need for an encompassing belief system to deal with strangers from many differ-ent cultural backgrounds that were being brought together in the market place of increasingly complex civilizations?

I find such cultural hypotheses satisfying and sufficient. But are they sufficient to address future threats without the commitment and action that arises from faith-based beliefs? That is a question that scholars like Dawkins (in *The God Delusion*) and Sam Harris (in *The End of Faith*), in oversimplifying the issues involved, do not address. Two issues need much more consideration. One concerns the issue as to whether or not our DNA includes a predisposition for religion that has evolved over the millennia. Some evolutionary biologists as well as behavioral and information scientists increasingly believe that to be the case; that the need for religion is a 'built-in' characteristic of humankind and hence immutable in the short run. If so, then we need think more about the future implications of that genetic inheritance as both a source of strength and of weakness.

The second issue, of more interest to me in this book, is the unique ability that religion has to enable believers to work in dangerous but important situations that I would not dare enter nor would, I suspect, most non-believers. I am referring to the willingness of religious men and women to put their lives in danger throughout their careers by serving the poor and the sick in areas, like Darfur in the Sudan, where their lives are continually at risk. Of course not all humanitarian workers are religious, but I suspect that a disproportionate number are. In the years ahead we are going to need just that sort of commitment to deal with expected threats and uncertainties. Without religion, will enough people be available to work continually with those life-threatening situations which must be dealt with? Then there is the question as to whether religious fundamentalists not only are more willing to take such risks but also are able to expand their concerns to give priority to poverty elimination and sustainable development. Within the United States there is an observable trend in Protestant fundamentalism in which some leaders and the younger generation are placing more emphasis on poverty alleviation and on the need to protect 'the Creation.'[3]

## RELIGIOUS, POLITICAL AND CULTURAL FUNDAMENTALISM IN SRI LANKA

### Introduction

I intentionally focus on successive governments of Sri Lanka's Sinhala-speaking Buddhist majority. Their fundamentalist policies since independence in 1948 have caused relative poverty among, and radicalized, the Tamil-speaking Hindu minority and have played a major role in causing the recently ended civil war between the government and the Liberation Tigers of Tamil Ealam (LTTE), who developed suicide bombing as a major instrument of twentieth century conflict. Tamil Tigers that I have met were well-dressed, educated youth who, with considerable justification, saw themselves excluded from contributing to the political economy of Sri Lanka. Do not misunderstand me. I am not an apologist for the Tigers but just an analyst of how fundamentalism on the part of a government can lead to conflict and unacceptable behavior on the part of the conflicting parties. During much of my work in Sri Lanka I was an unofficial adviser to Gamini Dissanayake, the Minister of Mahaweli Development. I considered him a friend. He was killed by a suicide bomber in 1994 while campaigning for the presidency which he might well have won.

It would be hard to find a better example than contemporary Sri Lanka of a democratically elected government's emphasis on several aspects of fundamentalism as well as an authoritarian approach to opposition.[4] I made ten visits to Sri Lanka between 1979 and 1999. Most were in the 1980s after the civil war had commenced. During that time my colleague Kapila P. Wimaladharma (now deceased) and I were periodically working in areas in which both government security forces and Tamil Tigers were operating.

My first visit was at the invitation of Sarah Jane Littlefield, the Sri Lankan Director of the United States Agency for International Development (USAID). She and her staff wanted me to assess Sri Lanka's experience with government-sponsored land settlement projects and to complete a series of evaluations of the government's Accelerated Mahaweli Project that the United States was assisting. I examine Mahaweli to illustrate the government's fundamentalist approach to development and to the country's Tamil-speaking Hindu minority. But first it is necessary to place the Mahaweli Project within a wider Sri Lankan context.

**Sri Lankan Civilization before Independence in 1948**

Sri Lankan history incorporates some of the world's greatest hydrologic civilizations, with major works dating back at least 2500 years. Construction in the 1970s and 1980s of Mahaweli Project infrastructure exposed the remains of well-engineered ancient works. Builders of these ancient structures were both Sinhala-speaking Buddhists and Tamil-speaking Hindus who brought civilization to Sri Lanka in a succession of migrations from India. Both established kingdoms that alternately fought and lived at peace with each other.

During the Colonial Era the remaining Tamil kingdom was conquered first by the Portuguese and then by the Dutch in the 16th century, while the remaining Sinhalese kingdom held out against the British until 1815. Both, according to the Sinhalese anthropologist Gananath Obeysekera, 'claimed sovereignty over the whole island. No king was content to see himself as a ruler of a part since the island was always considered a totality. The call for a separate state of Tamil-speaking peoples is thus a contemporary historical phenomenon.[5] The point is an important one for combatants on both sides exaggerated, as a form of cultural, political and religious fundamentalism, their claims to land and to national legitimacy.

The British favored the Sri Lankan Tamil minority.[6] The Tamils also benefited from English language education in higher quality Christian mission and other private schools established in the north. Better education, combined with British favoritism, allowed them to fill a disproportionate number of positions in the colonial bureaucracy as well as within the business community – a situation that was a factor in the government's exclusionary policies and in worsening Sinhalese–Tamil public relations following independence.

### The Independence Years: 1948 to the Present

Civil war broke out between the two populations in the late 1970s and escalated during the early 1980s. At that time the national population was about 14 million people. Approximately 75 per cent were Sinhalese and 18 per cent Tamils. Slightly over two-thirds of the Tamils were ancient citizens of Sri Lanka. The remainder, the so-called Indian Tamils (though they had lived in Sri Lanka for generations) were mainly arrivals from India brought in by the British to work on tea estates in the country's upland areas. Muslims, at about 7 per cent, made up the next largest segment of the population.[7]

Though divided among different political parties, the Sinhalese majority selected successive Sinhalese governments from the start. Over the years, the government tendency, with occasional interruptions, was to apply increasingly exclusionary policies toward the Tamil minority, while the largely Buddhist Sinhalese public periodically killed Tamil men, women and children and destroyed Tamil businesses in riots which were unknown before independence.[8] Successive governments have also become more authoritarian through efforts to control any form of Sinhalese or Tamil political opposition.[9]

Discrimination against Sri Lankan Tamils has occurred in many forms. In the late 1940s legislation took away the vote from, and made stateless, the approximately 900 000 upcountry Indian Tamils – an act which Tamil leaders perceived as discriminatory against all Tamils.[10] In 1956 the government passed an Official Language Act which prescribed '[t]he Sinhala language as the one official language.' Subsequently the 1972 Constitution not only referred to Sinhala as the official language but also stated that Buddhism had the 'foremost place' in the country.

Since Tamil continued to be the language of instruction in primary and secondary schools in Tamil communities, this legislation had far-reaching implications for Tamil employment. Non-violent objections to the Act by a group of Tamils precipitated the 1956 riots by the Sinhalese public. Tamils involved in a sit-in in the capital were beaten while the police looked on. Over 100 Tamils were killed when the riots spread to other cities and towns. Subsequent Sinhalese-instigated riots against Tamils occurred in 1958, 1977, 1981, 1983 and 2006. The 1983 riots are reported to have killed over 3000 people and made thousands more refugees.

Also in 1956, admittance to the country's leading teacher training college was restricted to Sinhalese applicants. The government's affirmative action policies also favored Sinhalese youth seeking university access over minority Tamil students who had, for example, to do better on science entrance examinations to qualify for admission.[11] Harvard anthropologist S.L Tambiah notes that in the first half of the 1980s there had been 'virtually no recruitment of Tamils into the armed forces, and very little into the police force, for nearly thirty years.'[12] As the World Bank reports, such discriminatory policies along with high unemployment rates during the 1970s 'provided fertile grounds for the birth of youthful militant Tamil separatist groups, including the Liberation Tigers of Tamil Eelam (LTTE).'[13]

**Government Religious, Political and Cultural Fundamentalism in the Mahaweli Project**

At the time of its construction in the late 1970s, and throughout the 1980s, the Accelerated Mahaweli Project (AMP) was one of the world's largest and most expensive development projects. It involved the construction of five large hydropower dams on the Mahaweli, the country's major river. Canals then funneled water into the sparsely settled and well-forested dry zone to irrigate approximately 75000 hectares of new land. Water was also provided for perennial irrigation of 100000 hectares in several older irrigated settlement schemes. Planners intended the newly irrigated lands to be farmed by 75000 households, each of which would be allotted a one hectare farm lot and a smaller home lot.

The AMP was by far Sri Lanka's largest project over the last 2500 years. Its multipurpose goals were developmental, cultural, political and religious. As a development project, a disproportionate amount of the national budget and foreign assistance was supposed to extend the project's economic benefits over the entire nation. Fundamentalism came in where the government was willing to ignore several of its major AMP goals which had been widely advertised to secure billions of dollars of foreign aid. One such goal was to hasten national unification by involving all ethnic and religious groups according to their numerical importance. That goal was subverted to realize more fundamentalist cultural and religious goals.

All major Mahaweli areas had been the sites of previous Sinhala-speaking, Buddhist civilizations which had collapsed by the 12 century AD. Though drought and malaria were likely involved, many Sinhalese blamed invading Tamils, with the AMP seen as a way to recolonize former heartlands currently settled by a mixed population of Sinhalese and Tamil villagers. Minister Gamini Dissanayake emphasized recolonization in a 1981 conference, when he stated 'It was thus possible to return to the great hydraulic civilization of the past' and it is not an accident that Mahaweli waters 'will be taken along canals built 1,500 years ago.'[14] Wimaladharma emphasized at the same conference that 'to us in Sri Lanka, colonization meant symbolically and materially, a return to the past and to the habitat of the ancestors.'

After his election in 1977, President Jayawardene emphasized that households settled in the AMP's three major irrigated zones would reflect the country's ethnic, linguistic and religious make-up. Yet after more than 75000 households had been settled, only 1.9 per cent were Hindu. The imbalance could have been even worse. In early 1983 a cabal of senior officials in the Ministry of Mahaweli Development began planning a large-scale illegal settlement of thousands of poor land-hungry Sinhalese into Tamil-speaking Mahaweli project areas. The land invasion was initiated in September 1983 with the active involvement of Dimbulagala, the nationally prominent senior Buddhist religious leader in the area. He advertised through the media the availability of free land for the taking, blessed the land invasion as a sacred duty and personally led an initial procession of trucks and tractors full of local men prepared to clear and occupy Mahaweli Project land.[15]

The motivation of those in the cabal and of Dimbulagala were both religious and political – to restore in a sparsely populated, largely Tamil area a former Sinhala-speaking and Buddhist society and to subvert any intentions of Tamil separatists to establish an independent Tamil nation.[16] Soon out of control, the entire operation was badly planned, timed and implemented. Criticism was almost immediate from the Indian government and from the head of Canada's international development agency, which provided the main source of funds for the dam serving the contested area. All encroachers were removed at President Jayawardene's insistence. Dimbulagala was killed by Tamil Tigers in 1995.

1983 also saw an increase in fighting between government security forces and Tamil separatists – the Tamil Tigers in particular. That year

Wimaladharma and I began our interviewing in project-affected Tamil villages. During daylight hours the Sri Lankan army controlled the area, while the Tamil Tigers moved freely during the hours of darkness; indeed also during the day, as when they listened in on our household interviews. These interviews, as well as interviews with local leaders, convinced us that too many still-resident Tamil households were being intentionally denied one hectare irrigated farm lots even though the official policy was to give first priority to pre-existing villages in future project areas.

Communal strife increased, exacerbated by ongoing official settlement of a disproportionate number of poor Sinhalese households in Tamil-speaking areas. That policy we knew would place those settlers at risk of attack by Tamil separatists. I was so convinced that government policy would also put at risk Tamil-speaking households when government security forces retaliated that I wrote a lengthy memo to USAID and the World Bank in the unrealized hope that they, as Mahaweli donors, might be able to influence the government to change its policies.[17]

In that same memo I described how government security forces were harassing Tamil villagers. The Army, for example, had taken away over half of the younger men from one of our study villages. None had returned when we visited that village several weeks later, 'nor had their parents, relatives and friends received any news as to where they were, what had happened to them, or when they might be coming back.'[18] One mother was so distraught that she fell to the ground, clasped my feet and implored us to help her children to return. On a return visit four years later, we inter-viewed one man who had been tortured and permanently disabled before being released.[19]

## RELIGIOUS AND POLITICAL FUNDAMENTALISM IN ISRAEL

### Introduction

The religious fundamentalism of a minority of Jews has enabled religious and secular politicians in Israel to strengthen the political fundamental-ism of the government at the expense of the Palestinian people. In 1979, while on a consultancy in Jordan, I had the opportunity to discuss with Palestinian colleagues the impacts of the 1948 and 1967 Arab–Israeli wars on over 900 000 Palestinian refugees who lost their homes, villages, land and water resources. In 2009 the large majority of those alive are still refugees whose number, with descendents, is around four million. In terms of numbers and duration of separation from homeland, this is one of the largest forced removals of people since the end of the Second World War. Its causes, the impacts on those involved and the refugees' responses to those impacts require analysis.

The origin of the two wars lies in two closely related Semitic people – Jews and Palestinian Arabs – fighting for political and ideological control of the same homeland. In that sense, the fighting has background similarities to the conflict in Sri Lanka between Sinhala-speaking Buddhists and Tamil-speaking Hindu who both claim rights to the same country. In both cases the nature, duration and violence of the conflict also has been exacerbated by religious and political fundamentalism.

Religious fundamentalists in Israel have supported government policies to impoverish and politically marginalize the Palestinian population. They have also succeeded in restricting in-country benefits of Israel's Arab citizens (roughly 20 per cent of the population)[20] and in dominating social legislation and budgets at the expense of the majority of Jewish nationals.[21]

The analysis that follows draws on my own experience and research, on the statements of Israeli human rights organizations[22] and members of the Jewish Diaspora, on the writings of water resources consultant Harald Frederiksen and on World Bank, UN and other reports. Regarding the impacts of fundamentalism on the Palestinian population, I focus on the refugees, due to my own 55 years of global research on involuntary community resettlement. The evidence presented shows that the policies of the Israeli government were intentionally to impoverish and politically marginalize the Palestinian population. Two conclusions are clear. The first is that the future of both Israel and the Palestinian people are jeopardized by the continuing emphasis on warfare. The second is that equity and peace require a two sovereign state solution.

One effect of ongoing warfare is to increase relative poverty and animosity against Israel among Palestinian youth, many of whom, though relatively well educated, are unemployed and unable to contribute to the development of Palestine's political economy. That is especially the case in Gaza, where Israel has restricted the ability of students to leave Gaza to further their education elsewhere, and at times stopped them from doing so. According to Israeli human rights organization Gisha, 'even when Gaza's borders are open, Israel does not allow Gaza residents to study in the West Bank, where most of the Palestinian universities are located, and does not allow foreign lecturers and experts, especially from Arab countries, to enter the Gaza strip.' Gisha's Executive Director adds, 'Allowing these talented young people to access education is vital to Gaza's future – and to Israel's future, too.'[23]

Members of Israel's parliament have stated similar concerns. On 28 May 2008 Rabbi Michael Malchior, chair of the parliament's education committee, said that 'trapping hundreds of students in Gaza is immoral and unwise . . . this could be interpreted as collective punishment.'[24] As such, the situation is just one example of Israeli collective punishment policies that can be expected to be counterproductive in terms of eventual peace because, as op. ed. journalist Roger Cohen recently wrote, 'The only changed equation I see over time is more entrenched hatred for Israel in Gaza: those myriad dead and wounded have relatives, some of whom may one day strap on suicide belts.'[25]

Cohen's viewpoint is hardly unique. Thoughtful and well-informed UN officials within Palestine, Israeli citizens and members of the Jewish Diaspora increasingly are speaking out against 'the military solution.' Referring to the travel ban into and out of Gaza and the West Bank, the senior UN official in the region stated in December 2000 that it was counterproductive: 'It's fueling the fury and anger and the radicalization on the Palestinian side . . . There is a real danger of a new generation of Palestinians whose anger is growing by the day.'[26]

Concerns of Israeli citizens are reflected in Carey and Shainin's 2002 *The Other Israel: Voices of Refusal and Dissent*. Included in the edited volume are essays and articles by former Israeli officials, journalists who write for *Ha'aretz*, and reservists who refuse service in the occupied territories. In a review of *The Other Israel*, *The Economist* notes that:

> The effect on Israel of Mr. Sharon's policy of massive reprisal, his preference for force over diplomacy, is what concerns writer after writer. They see a new arrogance and a new cruelty. Michael Ben-Yair, a former attorney-general, writes that occupation has transformed Israel from a just society to an unjust one. The steps taken to prolong the occupation – killing the innocent, executing wanted men without trial, the encirclements, closures and roadblocks – 'are causing us to lose the moral base of our existence as a free, just civilization.'[27]

A two-state solution was decreed by the 1947 UN Resolution 181 just prior to Israel's independence and is accepted today as a solution by the international community. Periodically Israeli and Palestinian government officials also have accepted the concept of a two-state solution, though currently that is not the case with either Hamas (which became the dominant power in Gaza after the January 2006 parliamentary elections)[28] or Israel's current coalition government. Both need to approve the formation of two independent states for peace negotiations to proceed.

**Religious and Political Fundamentalism**

Religious fundamentalists in Israel and throughout the Diaspora interpret Jewish sacred texts literally in regard to God's decreeing Jews as a special people who have a divine right to the land of Israel. Though a minority among Jews, there is great diversity, and much argument, among Jewish fundamentalists in regard to what political actions should be taken, if any, not just to speed up, but also to facilitate, the coming of the Messiah and the rising up of the Jewish people.

Jewish fundamentalists are a threat to the peace process with Palestinians because they oppose a return of the occupied territories.[29] The threat posed has increased in recent years after the formation of fundamentalist political parties which support influential secular and religious politicians who oppose a return of the occupied territories and a two-state solution. One example is the National Union, which was formed in 1999 to contest, that year, the Israeli elections.

The National Union's 2003 political platform rejects a two state position and supports Jerusalem as 'the undivided eternal capital of the Jewish people in the land of Israel', contrary to the requirement of UN Resolution 181 under which Jerusalem was to be under international administration for the joint benefit of the Israeli and Palestinian population and open to all religions. Moreover, settlement expansion was supported by the National Union throughout Palestine as well as on the Golan Heights.[30]

Another fundamentalist party is Yisrael Beiteinu, dominated by Jewish immigrants from Russia, which was also founded in 1999 to contest the election. Subsequently the party joined the National Union, but separated after the 2003 election. Though antagonistic to the power of ultra-conservative Orthodox rabbis over such issues as marriage and definition of who is a Jew, Yisrael Beiteinu 'believes that the state of Israel must be a Jewish state . . . To be a Jewish state, it must remain loyal to the faith of its forefathers . . . Yisrael Beiteinu strenuously opposes the separation of religion from the state . . . The uniqueness of the Jewish people is that there is no distance between state and religion.'[31]

Though fundamentalist political parties rarely received more than 4 or 5 seats in the 120-member Israeli parliament, in recent years their influence has grown in coalitions which are formed to govern when no single party receives a majority. That was especially the case after the 2009 elections, when Likud, which was unwilling to accept a two-state solution in its platform, turned to Yisrael Beiteinu (which received 15 seats), National Union (4 seats) and other fundamentalist parties. Even before the new government was formed, the National Union's leader declared on leaving a coalition-forming meeting that the 2009 government 'would be more Jewish and more Zionist.'[32] Prime Minister Netanyahu subsequently appointed Avigdor Lieberman, founder of Yisrael Beiteinu, as Deputy Prime Minister and Foreign Minister.

**Distributions of Palestinian Refugees**

In 1948–49, 750 000 Palestinians became homeless, followed by another 200 000 in 1967. Since then, the number of Palestinian refugees has increased to about four million. Approximately 40 per cent now live in Jordan, a fifth of whom still live in refugee camps there 60 years after the first became refugees in 1948. A further 37 per cent of Palestinians live in Gaza and the West Bank. In Gaza they make up nearly 60 per cent of the Palestinian population while 53 per cent still live in refugee camps. The remaining 23 per cent of refugees are scattered throughout the world, with the largest numbers in Syria and Lebanon.

**Palestinian Impoverishment in Gaza and the West Bank**

According to the World Bank's West Bank and Gaza Office, poverty increased in Gaza from 48 per cent in 2006 to 52 per cent in 2007. Moreover, 'If remittances and food aid are excluded and poverty is based only on household income, the poverty rate in Gaza and the West Bank would soar to 79.4 per cent and 45.7 per cent respectively.'[33] Furthermore as the years go by, more and more families no longer have valuables to sell or the ability to obtain credit.

There are two major theoretical approaches that attempt to improve our understanding of communities like those in Palestine that are forced to leave their homes. Together they provide a more objective framework for examining Palestinian impoverishment in Gaza and on the West Bank. One is based on my own comparative and worldwide research.[34] Especially applicable is the multidimensional stress that affects a majority of those who are forced to move, or having fled warfare, are unable to return home. Three stress components are synergistically interrelated. They are stress arising from increased morbidity and mortality rates, increased psychological stress that involves grieving for a lost home and anxiety about the future, and social, political and cultural stress due to loss of control over individual and family wellbeing and economic and political independence.

The second framework was formulated by Michael Cernea[35] while serving as Senior Adviser for Sociology and Social Policy at the World Bank. It is based on eight interlinked impoverishment risks and has been applied by Cernea to both development-induced resettlers and to refugees. The eight risks are landlessness, loss of access to common property resources, joblessness, homelessness, marginalization, food insecurity, increased morbidity and mortality, and social disarticulation.

Alone, any one of Cernea's impoverishment risks can be stressful. Though no one to the best of my knowledge has applied them to the Palestinian case, they are especially useful in assessing the desperateness of the situation since all eight apply. That is an uncommon situation that I believe needs to be brought more to the attention of policy makers on all sides, to the Jewish Diaspora and to the Jewish population in Israel. In the paragraphs that follow, I wish to relate each risk to the current Palestinian situation.

**Landlessness**
Fifty-five per cent of Palestine was to be allocated to Israel when the UN General Assembly approved Resolution 181 in November 1947. Victory in the 1948–49 and 1967 wars led to Israeli control over 78 per cent of the land. Hundreds of Palestinian villages were literally obliterated. In the 4 April 1969 issue of the Israeli newspaper *Ha'aretz*, Israeli Minister of Defense Moshe Dayan was quoted as saying:

> Jewish villages were built in the place of Arab villages. You do not know the names of these Arab villages, and I do not blame you because geography books no longer exist; not only do books not exist, the Arab villages are not there either . . . There is not one single place built in this country that did not have a former Arab population.[36]

Palestinian access to, and economic activity within[37] their 22 per cent has become increasingly difficult over the years due to Israeli road closures, checkpoints, permit requirements and other restrictions. That is especially the case on the West Bank, where Israel had built 120 settlements by 2008 and allowed settlers to build and occupy another 100 'outposts' which are also under military protection. Scattered throughout the West Bank, these settlements, and restricted roads between them, make access difficult between Palestinian communities that may have been only a few kilometers apart in the past.

The security barrier that Israel began building in 2002 is causing additional landlessness and difficulties of access:

> In some places, the barrier cuts as deep as six kilometres into Palestinian land, enveloping (so far) 18 000 settlers in ten settlements. And for the 'defense' of these settlers, Israel has requisitioned some of the best farmland and water resources in the northern West Bank . . . [Two Palestinian settlements] are now hemmed in on three sides by the barricade. Much of their best agricultural land has been declared off-limits to farmers. Unemployment has soared . . . Some 20 000 people who live on the Palestinian side of the barricade have become separated from their orchards, farms and groves on the Israeli side.[38]

**Loss of common-property resources**
Water, along with land, is the most important Palestinian common-property resource. In February 1996 while preparing a talk in Jerusalem on water resources for a group of visiting Caltech alumni that I was

accompanying, I was appalled by the extent to which Israel had 'captured' Palestinian water supplies. Even before Israel's independence, Jewish leaders were emphasizing the importance not only of controlling water resources in Palestine but also the headwaters of the Jordan River where they originated on the slopes of Mount Hebron in Lebanon. With British assistance the boundary between Palestine and Jordan became the east bank of the Jordan River rather than the middle of the channel. By the end of the 1967 war Israel had secured all such waters plus those originating on the Golan Heights. An attempt by Syria to build a large dam on the Yarmuk tributary of the Jordan outside Israeli control was bombed and stopped. International reactions to such water grabbing were few except for UN reports which periodically complained about Israeli water grabbing and insisted on restoration of water resources captured since 1947.[39]

Following the 1967 war, 'Israeli military decrees nationalized the water of all the occupied lands, classified all water-resources data as Israeli state secrets, and extended its control of the Upper Jordan Basin to include the Golan Heights' groundwater.'[40] Also that year no expansion of Palestinian irrigation was allowed. Israel subsequently uprooted 'over 99 000 Palestinian fruit trees between 1987 and 1991 within the occupied lands.'[41] Planting of new fruit trees was prohibited without a permit from the military. Farmers were not allowed to build new wells or deepen old ones if they dried up because of Israeli offtake from their new deeper wells.[42]

Between 1953 and 1964 Israel built the National Water Carrier, which now diverts 75 per cent of Jordan River water.[43] Palestinian cities are connected to it so as to increase Israeli control. Water prices are higher than for Israeli nationals. The West Bank's Mountain Aquifer[44] is also connected to the National Water Carrier by a system of deep tube wells and interconnecting pipelines. Palestinians have also lost their control of the Gaza aquifer, whose water quality is worsened by saline intrusion due to over-pumping. Having 'lost control of their aquifers . . . and their equitable allocation of the Jordan River,'[45] Palestinians are left with under 5 per cent 'of the fresh water available to historic Palestine.[46] Meanwhile, Israel uses 60 per cent of its supplies for 'highly subsidized agriculture,' which provides only '1.6 percent of Israel's GDP, employs 3 percent of its workforce and contributes only 2.2 per cent of its exports.'[47]

**Joblessness**
According to the World Bank:

Unemployment in the West Bank rose from 17.7 per cent in 2007 to 19 per cent in the first quarter of 2008, while unemployment in Gaza has increased from 29.7 per cent to 29.8 per cent. In the second quarter of the year, unemployment in the West Bank fell to 16.3 per cent, but unemployment falls almost every year in the second quarter and probably reflects increased agricultural employment . . . These figures do not give an accurate picture of the full impact of the economic crisis, because they do not take into account underemployed workers such as the large number who have turned to unpaid family labor or seasonal agriculture. The figures also do not include the many discouraged workers who have left the labor force. Labor force participation rates are low and dropping. In the West Bank it fell from 44 per cent at the end of 2007 to 43.5 per cent in the first quarter of 2008 and in Gaza it held steady at 38 per cent. Adding discouraged workers would increase the unemployment rate to 23.2 per cent in the West Bank and 49.1 per cent in Gaza.[48]

The World Bank's report also states that:

> The economic blockade has devastated the Gaza private sector and driven almost all industrial producers out of business. Gaza businesses are not only unable to export but because the blockade only allows in humanitarian goods, they are unable to import intermediate inputs. In addition, fuel and power shortages significantly hamper production. According to recent estimates by local business associations, only about 2 per cent of industrial establishments are still functioning. They are mainly food processors who can obtain local inputs or who use inputs that are allowed to be imported on humanitarian grounds. Industrial employment has fallen from about 35000 before the Israeli disengagement in 2005 to about 860 at the end of June, 2008. In addition, the business associations estimate that another 70000 workers have been laid off from other sectors. The damage has been so severe, that it is unlikely that many establishments will be able to recover once the blockade is lifted . . . The halt in exports and the prohibition on importing fertilizer, pesticides, packaging materials and other inputs has led to the loss of more than 40000 jobs in the agriculture sector.[49]

### Homelessness

Grieving for a lost home is a universal characteristic of involuntary resettlement. In the Palestinian case the numbers of people involved have remained high because Arab and other Muslim countries have been disinclined to accept Palestinian refugees as citizens in the absence of an equitable resolution of the Israeli–Palestinian conflict. Homelessness is especially serious where refugee camps exist in other countries. In Lebanon, for example, over 360000 Palestinians live a marginal life in 12 Lebanese refugee camps, outside of which they are not allowed to work.

### Marginalization

According to Cernea,

> Marginalization occurs when families lose economic power and spiral on a 'downward mobility' path . . . Economic marginalization is often accompanied

by social and psychological marginalization, expressed in a drop of social status, in resettlers' loss of confidence in society and in themselves, a feeling of injustice, and deepened vulnerability.[50]

Curfews and travel restrictions imposed by the Israeli authorities are especially stressful. According to the March 1990 UN report, the *Situation of Palestinian Women in the Occupied Territories*, during curfews:

> There is a deterioration of the psychological well-being of mothers in particular. During prolonged periods of curfew, women are fully responsible for finding food to feed the large Palestinian family. They must also ensure that the children stay within the family home, which is often overcrowded. Women must also deal with their husband's frustration at his inability to go out and earn an income . . . the combined effect of this stressful situation is linked to an increase in cases of high blood pressure, miscarriages, diabetes, headaches and psychosomatic illnesses among women.[51]

On the West Bank, Israeli settlements and outposts, with their security roads, checkpoints, and other obstructions to free passage, have broken up Palestinian lands into '227 separate, non-contiguous patches of land.'[52] Nearly 60 per cent of the West Bank remains:

> [U]nder full control of the Israeli military for both security and civilian affairs relating to territory, including land administration and planning . . . Where village master plans are available, they are prepared by the Israeli Civil Administration without community participation and limit development primarily to filling in existing developed areas. Building permits are rare and difficult to obtain.[53]

Resident Palestinians are mainly farmers and herders who 'tend to fare worse than the general population in terms of social indicators, being underserved in public services and infrastructure, and being denied permits to upgrade their homes or invest in agriculture and other businesses.'[54]

**Food insecurity**
The World Bank's 2008 report refers to surveys of the World Food Programme (WFP); these report that food insecurity in Gaza and the West Bank 'is estimated to have increased from 34 per cent in 2006 to 38 per cent in 2007.' It is most pronounced in Gaza, 'reaching 56 per cent of households.' According to another WFP survey, 75 per cent of Palestinians surveyed reported that they were eating less purchased food, with 89 per cent also buying food of lower quality. Many have also decreased their consumption of fresh foods, including vegetables and meat. The World Bank sums up the situation by stating, 'The lack of protein and vitamins

has increased the prevalence of anemia and other nutrient deficiencies and is likely to have long term health consequences on children.'[55] Israeli bulldozing of orchards in Gaza and on the West Bank has contributed to the food insecurity issue, as has the loss of agricultural lands throughout the occupied territories, the desiccation of other orchards due to Israeli 'capture' of shared aquifers and Israeli prohibition of new Palestinian irrigation.

### Increased morbidity and mortality

I first became aware of the existence of stress-related morbidity and mortality among Palestinian refugees during my 1979 work in Jordan. During a visit to a Jordanian university whose faculty contained a large number of Palestinian exiles, I asked if they knew of any Palestinians in their 20s and 30s who had died from heart attacks and strokes. With surprise, they asked, 'How did you know?' They then mentioned the names of young people whose deaths they believed, as did I, were premature due to the stressful humiliation and despair of being members of a population that, as of now, has been marginalized over three generations.

According to pediatrician Adnan Al-Wahaid 'a nutrition survey carried out in August 2002 found 13.2 per cent of children in the Gaza Strip suffering from acute malnutrition. This compares unfavorably with survey figures from 1995, where only 5.7 per cent of children under 5 years were acutely malnourished.'[56]

Though the current conflict is only one reason why 'Palestinian infant mortality rates . . . are almost five times higher than those of Israel' in 2001,[57] directly related to the current conflict is the disproportionate number of civilian deaths among the Palestinian population as Israel continues to seek a military solution. According to the 2002 annual report on human rights of the U.S. State Department, 'Israeli security forces killed at least 990 Palestinians and two foreign nationals and injured 4382 Palestinians and other persons during the year, including innocent bystanders.'[58] Human Rights Watch refers to Gaza Ministry of Health data that 910 Palestinian civilians and combatants have been killed and 4250 wounded between mid-2007 and mid-January 2009. Based on a UN report Human Rights Watch adds that, 'more than 40 per cent of the dead and 50 per cent of the wounded are women and children.'[59]

### Social disarticulation

Cernea defines social disarticulation as tearing 'apart the existing social fabric. It disperses and fragments communities, dismantles patterns of social organization and interpersonal ties; kinship groups become scattered as well.'[60] As the conflict drags on, social relations within Palestine are breaking down. According to a 13 December 2002 article in the *Los Angeles Times*:

> In Palestinian cities, social workers face a wave of women who were beaten or abused at home and a rash of intra-clan murders. Everywhere, children are learning about hate . . . Palestinian men trapped at home by Israeli-imposed closures and curfews feel diminished self-worth and often take it out on the family, experts say. They've been humiliated at check points in front of their children; they are unable to provide for or even protect their families.[61]

The breakdown of the social fabric is also affecting Israeli communities:

> The basic fabric of the family, in two societies where family ties are strong, is being shredded by the trauma of war . . . Extremism and a tolerance of brutality have spread. Despair over the future – over whether there even *is* a future – dominates the thinking of youth as well as their parents . . . Unemployed Israeli men have seen their traditional role as breadwinner threatened. Nearly one in five Israelis now lives below the poverty line; three in five Palestinians are similarly impoverished. [The *Los Angeles Times* article then quotes Zvi Eisikovits, Dean of the College of Social Welfare and Health of the University of Haifa, as saying] 'Attitudes toward violence are changing to the point where violence is an acceptable means to solve problems. There is an overall desensitization to human life and desensitization to suffering as a way to survive suffering.'[62]

# UNITED STATES

### Government Implemented Political and Cultural Fundamentalism

U.S. governments have tried to export American values and democracy since the founding of the republic in 1776. Government efforts have been episodic, although efforts by other Americans have been a constant theme in American history. Paul Carrington, former Dean of the Duke University Law School, analyzes the international activities of those he labels lawyer-missionaries in his 2005 *Spreading America's Word*.[63] He also refers to human rights advocates and evangelical economists from the United States who 'shared the aim of making more of the world more like the United States.' Carrington's emphasis on the efforts of lawyers is an especially relevant example of government-supported political fundamentalism. Indeed, many American presidents, trained and practicing as lawyers before running for public office, were so involved.

Carrington traces the stimulus for, and commitment to efforts 'to make the governments and laws of other peoples more like their own,' back to the Declaration of Independence and Abraham Lincoln's 1883 Gettysburg

Address. Influential was the Declaration's emphasis on self-evident rights that governments 'with the consent of the governed' are formed 'to secure.'[64] Thomas Jefferson, who subsequently became the third president of the United States, was the Declaration's main author. Carrington labels him the first American lawyer missionary, for subsequently he was instrumental in the drafting and co-authorship of the French Declaration of the Rights of Man and the Citizen. In Carrington's words, Lincoln's prayer a hundred years later that 'government of the people, by the people, and for the people shall not perish from this earth reaffirmed that the American dogma is by its terms applicable to all human beings at all times.'[65]

Efforts by influential Americans to propagate American values and democracy around the world were fewer during the 19th century, when U.S. history was dominated by westward expansion at the expense of Native Americans as well as by internal disagreements that led up to the civil war. During those years Carrington notes how otherwise pro-America writers like the Frenchman Alexis de Tocqueville were concerned that the new republic might attempt to expand at the expense of other countries and to export its own democratic institutions and values.

Government and other efforts to export American values expanded significantly during the twentieth century, a trend that continues today. Following the First World War, President Wilson's emphasis on making the world safe for democracy was institutionalized through his strong support for the League of Nations. His Secretary of State, William Jennings Bryan, believed 'that God had ordained that America should establish an era of peace and justice throughout the world.'[66] During, and following the Second World War, every U.S. President has urged the world not just to accept American values and democracy, but also economic ideologies that, at the same time, would favor the U.S. business community. President Bush's Operation Iraqi Freedom in 2003 is the most recent example of that trend, which Carrington illustrates with the following quote from the President's 2002 *National Security Strategy of the United States of America*: '[T]he United States will use this moment of opportunity to extend the benefits of freedom across the globe. We will actively work to bring the hope of democracy, development, free markets, and free trade to every corner of the world.'[67]

U.S. efforts 'to propagate the American ideology is replete with failures, and marked by few successes.'[68] Two main reasons for failure stand out. The first was the failure of American political evangelists to understand the complexities involved in changing the cultures, systems of governance and laws of other societies. Even where leaders and the public might be interested in the American experience, the process of political change should be primarily fostered from within. As with development, people want cultural and political change to be implemented on their own terms rather than imposed upon them. That generalization especially applies to elites who dominate a nation's political economy.

U.S. lawyer missionaries were attracted to the Philippines and Latin America as willing subjects for their ministrations because they assumed such newly independent countries would be eager to accept American values and democracy. But those were countries whose feudal elites, with the help of Spain, had entrenched themselves and who, with the Church, often controlled – as in Mexico and the Philippines – over 50 per cent of the arable land. While the more astute American lawyers understood that land reform would be necessary if American democracy was to function,[69] not only were their efforts resisted, but the need for land reform, and internal opposition to it, remains a major equity problem in those countries, as well as throughout Latin America.

As for the second reason, U.S. lawyer missionaries also underestimated opposition to their activities from the business community, politicians and government officials within the United States. As more and more U.S. businesses invested internationally, successive U.S. governments tended to protect their interests as opposed to those of local citizens pushing for a more participatory form of government. Central America was especially victimized in that regard, with the United States willing to use its armed services to protect U.S. companies 'from unfavorable regulation, or indeed from taxation.'[70]

More recently, Carrington refers to the U.S. government's willingness to use the CIA and other resources 'to organize and aid local attempts to overthrow governments displeasing to the administration.'[71] Included were governments with elected leaders, as was the case in Iran under Mohamed Mossadegh in the early 1950s, the Congo under Patrice Lumumba in 1960 and Chile's Salvador Allende during the first half of the 1970s. In other words, America's export of democracy did not apply to situations which the administration perceived as being contrary to short-term national interests.

## The Impact of Christian Fundamentalism under the Second Bush Administration on U.S. Government Policies in Relation to Science and Health

### Introduction

Adopted on 17 December 1791, the First Amendment to the U.S. Constitution starts off by stating that 'Congress shall make no law respecting an establishment of religion, or prohibiting the free exercise thereof.' Over the years, the courts have expanded the context of the first amendment to include the Executive and Judicial branches of government. They have also interpreted the amendment to mean that government must not actively propagate religion; hence the separation of Church and State doctrine since Christianity was, and remains, the religion of the majority.

The United States not only has the largest number of church-going Christians in higher income countries, but also has produced the largest number of fundamentalist missionaries who have fanned out around the world, including within the United States, to convert non-Christians or save backsliders. I have met such missionaries in Zambia where, without question, they have played a key role in bringing western education and medicine to areas without either. But in the process they have too often denigrated local cultures and stand accused of being a major force that has left millions of poor people between two worlds – no longer participants in their birth cultures but also unable to participate fully in the culture and society to which they now aspire as a result of their missionary education.

Currently approximately 50 per cent of the U.S. population claims to be Protestant, 25 per cent Catholic, 15 per cent secular, and the remainder affiliated with a range of belief systems.[72] I divide the Protestant majority into liberal Christians and fundamentalists – here defined as a broad category that also includes Evangelicals and Pentecostals. Numbers of fundamentalists have been increasing significantly in recent years so that today they constitute a slight Protestant majority and total approximately 25 per cent of the American population.

Innumerable polls show that U.S. Christians are more religious than the citizens of other highly industrialized, literate and upper income countries. In 2006, 78 per cent of Americans believed the Bible to be the word of God. Though 65 per cent have a favorable attitude toward science, 42 per cent reject evolution, believing that humans have 'existed in present form only.'[73] Though I lump them together, there are major differences between and among fundamentalists. But as voters on public policy issues, the majority require believers to acknowledge their sinful nature, accept Christ's sacrifice as essential for salvation, believe in the second coming of Christ and other biblical prophecies, and reject, because of original sin, the liberal Christian belief that good works can produce a better world.[74]

While fundamentalist beliefs concerning the origin of the universe and of humankind are contrary to scientific explanations, until recently fundamentalists were not organized as a voting block to influence U.S. government policy. That began to change during the 1990s, and in the 2000 presidential election 68 per cent of white fundamentalists voted for George W. Bush, with an increase to 78 per cent in the 2004 election, at which time they provided approximately 40 per cent of those who voted for the President.[75]

A born-again Christian, President Bush and his advisers for the first time in American history systematically recruited like believers into the inner circle, government positions and innumerable committees dealing with public interest issues. Together they began pushing fundamentalist policies, often through a supportive Congress, in a wide range of domestic and foreign policy areas including the environment, public health, pollution and contamination and national security.[76] If they could not get the support of Congress, the President issued executive orders.[77]

**Bush administration and science**
In February 2004, the Union of Concerned Scientists issued a report called 'Scientific Integrity in Policy Making: An Investigation into the Bush Administration's Misuse of Science.' It was signed by 62 scientists, including 20 Nobel Laureates, ten recipients of the national Medal of Science, the administrator of the Environmental Protection Agency in the Nixon and Ford administrations and several science advisers to previous Democratic and Republican presidents. According to the report, to support its fundamentalist policies the administration was willing to suppress and distort scientific analyses by government agencies. It was also willing to upset the balance of scientific advisory committees by appointing a disproportionate number of advisers holding administration views. Otherwise qualified scientists were rejected even though recommended by the heads of the agencies over which the committees had oversight.

Four major findings were reported:

1.  There is a well-established pattern of suppression and distortion of scientific findings by high-ranking Bush administration political appointees across numerous federal agencies. These actions have consequences for human health, public safety, and community well-being. . . .
2.  There is strong documentation of a wide-ranging effort to . . . prevent the appearance of advice that might run counter to the administration's political agenda. . . .
3.  There is evidence that the administration often imposes restrictions on what government scientists can say or write about 'sensitive' topics. . . .
4.  There is significant evidence that the scope and scale of the manipulation, suppression, and misrepresentation of science by the Bush administration are unprecedented.

One of the signatories was Nobel Laureate David Baltimore, who was president of Caltech at the time. A microbiologist, Baltimore's research on the polio virus and subsequently on retroviruses led to his involvement in public policy issues relating to stem cell research and HIV/AIDS. At the 28 May 2004 annual meeting of the Fellows of the New York Academy of Medicine he elaborated on his concerns, stating that '[n]ever until now has (government) banned a direction of research. Right now there is an effective ban from the Executive on government-funded work leading to development of new human stem cell lines. The rationale is not safety . . . but a moral judgment about what type of research is proper.'[78]

More specifically, Baltimore mentioned that the Bush administration had disallowed, against the advice of an advisory panel, over-the-counter sale of day-after conception pills and replaced information from the website of the Centers for Disease Control on condom use to prevent pregnancy and HIV/AIDS transition with incorrect information on condom failure and invalid information on the effectiveness of abstinence.

The Bush administration's policies also led to a major cutback in financing international family planning. By 2005, for example, congressional appropriations for family planning were 'below 70 per cent of 1995 levels (calculated in constant dollars).'[79] Worldwide, family planning has played an important role in empowering women[80] and in reducing population increase and the 'youth bulge' problem in late industrializing countries, where 90 per cent of future increase is expected to occur.[81]

Access to family planning is a crucial means for improving female empowerment. According to *Return of the Population Growth Factor* (Return Report) 'Evidence shows that when family planning is easy to obtain, and free of barriers, both educated and uneducated women use contraception at the same rate, opening the door to a reduction in poverty.'[82] I have observed such evidence among one of the poorest ethnic minorities in Laos, itself one of the poorest countries in Asia. Without exception, uneducated Lao women from different ethnic minorities to whom I have talked not only want to control family size but prefer injections which give them control over the means used.

Throughout Sub-Saharan Africa, the Return Report notes that unwanted pregnancies result in between 8 per cent and 25 per cent of girls dropping out of school. More general information submitted by the International Council on Management of Population Programmes notes that 'countries with high contraceptive use have a higher proportion of girls in secondary school.'[83] As for child mortality, the UN Economic Commission for Africa provided a graph based on 2005 data showing that high fertility and child mortality are strongly associated, while increasing literacy of women is associated with reduced infant mortality.[84]

What has been labeled 'the youth bulge' refers to a disproportionate number of young men aged 15 to 29. Such a surge has increased relative poverty in low-income countries, since it 'virtually guarantees that the number of schooled youths will outpace job growth, leaving even educated young men underemployed, frustrated and resentful of those who enjoy the opportunities they lack.'[85] By 2007, 67 countries had youth bulges which are a contributing factor to conflict in 60 of those 67 nations 'experiencing social unrest and violence.'[86] Aside from Sub-Saharan Africa and the Middle East, other areas with youth bulges and civil conflicts include countries in South America, Central Asia and the Pacific Islands.

## SUMMARY

Fundamentalism of any kind becomes especially dangerous when it becomes the accepted ideology of a national government or revolutionary movement. Fundamentalist revolutionary movements can topple and install national governments as in contemporary Iran or they can ignore national boundaries. A major goal, for example, of Muslim Brotherhoods, and more recently Al Qaeda, is to restore the Caliphate under Sharia law from Indonesia to Spain. But I have purposely not included Islamic cases in order to emphasize the threat posed by all of the great world religions. In Sri Lanka and Israel, Buddhist and Jewish fundamentalism, coupled with the political fundamentalism of the state, continue to pose globally significant threats to a peaceful solution to the ongoing conflicts between the government of Sri Lanka and the Tamil-speaking minority and the government of Israel and the Palestinian people.

In the Sri Lankan case, with the army's victory over the Tamil Tigers, the government has the opportunity to address legitimate Tamil complaints of exclusion from the country's national culture and political economy – exclusion which led to a civil war in which over 70 000 people died.[87] In Israel the 2008 election of a more fundamentalist government is disheartening. On the other hand, as with the United States' rapprochement with China in the 1970s and with Russia in the 1980s under the Nixon and Reagan administrations, the opportunity to make peace is apt to be less susceptible to criticism from ultra-orthodox and nationalistic citizens.

A broad definition of fundamentalism to include religious, political, economic and cultural features invites not only comparison, but throws into relief the risks imposed by any national government that attempts to use its influence to propagate a fundamentalist ideology among its citizens and/or to export it internationally. In the case of Western colonialism, the empire building of England, France, Spain, Portugal, Germany and the Netherlands was backed by the force of the state but fueled by a combination of political, religious, economic and cultural fundamentalism at the expense of the societies colonized. Indian sociologist Susan Visvanathan refers to British colonization in nineteenth century India, for example, as 'The Homogeneity of Fundamentalism.' She goes on to state that 'the moral tones of a "civilizing mission" are present everywhere, and with

Victorianism this gets compounded in the strident tones of missionary and evangelical zeal.'[88]

Today fundamentalist economic policies of the governments of the United States and China risk destabilizing the world in regard to actions taken or not taken. As the leading emitters of greenhouse gases, unless the U.S. and China take strong action such as the enforcement of a carbon tax, it is unlikely that an effective international attack on global warming will occur. Yet economic fundamentalism in both countries is opposed to such strong measures. In China it is also a cause of serious environmental degradation as discussed in Chapter 5, while recent U.S. efforts to export political fundamentalism have destabilized the Middle East and adversely affected the U.S. international reputation.

# NOTES

1. The American Academy of Arts and Sciences' Fundamentalism Project produced five volumes from the multi-author international effort during 1987–1995.
2. The worst example since the end of the Second World War occurred during and following the religiously motivated partition of India, when hundred of thousands were killed and over ten million refugees migrated between India and Pakistan. Thousands of women were raped and abducted.
3. See E.O. Wilson (2006). *The Creation: An appeal to save life on earth*. New York: W.W. Norton and Company, and Gary T.Gardner (2006). *Inspiring Progress: Religion's contribution to sustainable development*. New York: W.W. Norton and Company.
4. See Princeton emeritus anthropology professor Gananath Obeysekera's 1984 'Political Violence and the Future of Democracy in Sri Lanka.' In *Sri Lanka: The ethnic conflict: Myths, realities and perspectives*. New Delhi: Navrang. A Sinhala-speaking Buddhist, Obeysekera's chapter was written after he witnessed the riots of 1983, when thousands of Tamils were killed by Sinhalese mobs, with many thousands more fleeing as refugees.
5. *Ibid.* Page 72.
6. The phrase Sri Lankan Tamils distinguished those Tamils from so-called Indian Tamils who were imported by the British to work their tea estates in the inland hill country.
7. 1951 Sri Lankan Census of Population.
8. Sinhala mobs and high-level governmental officials have been accused, with justification, of involvement in ethnic cleansing of Tamil-speaking Hindus as have the Tamil Tigers in regard to both Buddhists and Muslims. A recent example of ethnic cleansing involving the government was the June 2007 forcible eviction of several hundred Tamils from Colombo. In that case, the Supreme Court stopped the evictions with a stay order the next day 'in response to a fundamental rights case filed by the Colombo-based think tank, the Centre for Policy Alternatives' – see Lasantha Wickrematunge (11 June 2007). '"Ethnic Cleansing" in Sri Lanka?' *Time*.
9. See, for example, Obeyesekere. Op. cit.
10. World Bank (June 1998) *Experience with Post-conflict Reconstruction*. Report No. 17769. Page 128.
11. *Ibid.*
12. S.J. Tambiah(1986). Sri Lanka: Ethnic fratricide and the dismantling of democracy. London: I.B. Tauris. Page 15.
13. World Bank. Op. cit. Page 128.

14. Gamini Dissanaake's inaugural speech at the April 1981 Conference on Land Settlement Experiences in Sri Lanka, published in May 1982 under the same title in Kapila P. Wimaladharma (ed.). *Land Settlement Experiences in Sri Lanka.* Colombo: Karunaratne & Sons, Ltd. for Kapila P. Wimaladharma.

15. Malinda H. Gunaratna (1988). *For a Sovereign State.* Ratmalana: Sarvodaya Book Publishing Services. One of the planners within the Ministry of Mahaweli Development, Gunaratna discusses in detail his involvement within the cabal.

16. Throughout *For a Sovereign State* Gunaratna justifies the land invasion as necessary to stop large-scale settlement of Tamils in the Madura Oya basin under the auspices of Tamil separatists. Concurrent official government reports by senior district officials, however, as well as subsequent reports, make no mention of such settlement (see especially Gunaratna, page 87).

17. I subsequently learned that attacks and counterattacks involving massacres occurred in villages that I had listed at risk. In our two Hindu study villages at least 20 people were killed. In another attack, this time on Sinhalese villages, 74 settlers were killed.

18. Thayer Scudder (1985b). 'Memo on Mahaweli Report Number 6' to USAID's Colombo Office'. December.

19. Atrocities committed by the security forces were even worse during the time of the 1985–1987 JVP (People's Liberation Front) rebellion of Sinhalese youth. The Accelerated Mahaweli Project, as the government's largest national project, was a special JVP target. In 1985 Wimaladharma and I heard that a landmine had killed five security personnel in a nearby area. We reached the spot after going through two road blocks. Standing by the road was an elderly Mahaweli settler whose house had been burned by retaliating security forces simply because he lived next to the landmined site. He told us that they arrived in the middle of the night, told him and his wife to pile their furnishings in one room and then torched their house. Their house was not the only one burnt. On walking about the area I noted that at least 20 houses had been incinerated. We were also told that the security forces had incinerated a number of youth at a nearby crossroads so as to terrorize any Mahaweli settlers who might consider aiding the rebellion. The procedure was to arbitrarily select detained youth, cut off their heads to avoid identification, necklace them with tires, soak them with gasoline and set them on fire. We inspected one such site the following morning and found only ashes, some bones and metal used as tire reinforcing. I totaled the number killed by counting the hip bones.

20. Anthropologist Roselle Tekiner explains how nationality, rights to which are granted 'by the law of return,' apply only to Jews. See Roselle Tekiner (January 1990). 'Israel's Two-Tiered Citizenship Law Bars Non-Jews from 93 per cent of its Lands.' See also Harald Fredriksen (2007b). 'A Federation of Palestine and Jordan: A chance for peace?' *Middle East Policy.* **XIV** (2). Page 32. Palestinian citizens in Israel cannot lease and, to an extent, work on Israeli stipulated land, which constitutes over 90 per cent of the country's land. Arab citizens also are not welcomed in the military, which restricts them from various educational and other benefits. Arab villages are not allowed to expand nor can new villages be built (page 33).

21. New Israel Fund (no date). 'Religious Pluralism and Tolerance: Why is religion Israel's touchiest issue?' Available at http://www.nif.org/issue-areas/religious-pluralism/.

22. These include B'Tselem, the Israeli Information Center for Human Rights, founded in 1989 'primarily to change Israeli policy in the Occupied Territories and ensure that its government . . . protects the human rights of residents there and its obligations under international law.' Available at http://www.btselem.org/english/About_BTselem/Index. asp. Also included are Gisha, 'founded in 2005, whose goal is to protect the freedom of movement of Palestinians, especially Gaza residents' (Available at http://www.gisha. org/index.php?intLanguage=2&intSiteSN=137&intItemId=107) and Peace Now.

23. Gisha (January 2008). 'Israel Still Preventing at least 625 students from Leaving Gaza.' Available at http://www.gisha.org/index.php?intLanguage=2&intItemId=930&intSite SN=113&OldMenu=113.

24. Quoted in Human Rights Watch 3 June 2008 in a letter, co-signed by the Middle East Studies Association and the American Anthropological Association, to the US State Department urging the US government to request Israel to cancel its ban on preventing Gaza students seeking further education elsewhere. Available at http://campus-watch.org/article/id/5201.
25. Roger Cohen (12 February 2009). 'Eyeless in Gaza.' *The New York Review of Books.* **56** (2).
26. As posted on the CNN Website 5 December 2000 under the title 'Israeli Ban Tripled Palestinian Unemployment, says UN Report.'
27. *The Economist* (29 March 2003a) 'Book review. "The Other Israel. Voices of refusal and dissent"'. Page 78.
28. The similarities between Hamas and the Tamil Tigers are too many to be a coincidence. Relative poverty was a factor in the rise of both movements. Both tried to provide social benefits to the areas under their control. On the other hand, both movements increasingly used unacceptable military tactics including suicide bombing, targeting civilians including women and children and putting their own civilians at risk by launching attacks and seeking protection in their midst.
29. I deal only with the threat of Jewish fundamentalism to the Palestinians. Various Israeli human rights groups believe Jewish fundamentalism also is a threat to Israel's democracy. For example, 'The ultra-orthodox establishment that controls Israel's civil sphere continues to exclude other streams of Judaism on issues ranging from marriage to conversion . . . Moreover, religious extremism too often joins forces with extreme nationalism, to the detriment of democracy and to the pursuit of peace.' New Israel Fund. Op. cit.
30. Elections for the 16th Knesset (28 January 2003). 'National Unity (halchud HaLeumi): Platform.' Available at http://www.knesset.gov.il/elections16/eng/lists/plat_27-e.htm.
31. *Ha'aretz* (February 15, 2009). 'A New Jewish State' by Anshel Pfeffer. Available at http://www.haaretz.co.il/hasen/spages/1063791.html.
32. *Ha'aretz* Service and Reuters. 'Israel's Next Government Will Be "More Jewish and More Zionist."' Available at http://Einyurl.com/nsj4nq.
33. World Bank (2008). *West Bank and Gaza Update.* Washington DC: The World Bank. Page 16.
34. Thayer Scudder (2005). *The Future of Large Dams: Dealing with social, environmental, institutional and political costs.* London: Earthscan.
35. Michael M. Cernea (2000). 'Risks, Safeguards, and Reconstruction: A model for population displacement and resettlement'. In Michael M. Cernea and Christopher McDowell (eds). *Risks and Reconstruction: Experiences of resettlers and refugees.* Washington DC: The World Bank.
36. As quoted by Harald Frederiksen (2003) in 'Water: Israeli strategy, implications for peace and the viability of Palestine.' *Middle East Policy.* **X** (4). Page 79.
37. See *West Bank and Gaza Update* (2008). 'West Bank and Gaza: The economic effects of restricted access to land in the West Bank.' A Quarterly Publication of the West Bank and Gaza Office. Washington DC: The World Bank. Pages 4–9.
38. *The Economist* (29 March 2003b). 'Walling them in. Israel's security barrier.' Pages 42–43.
39. According to the United Nations' 1992 'Water Resources of the Occupied Palestinian Territory', water resources 'are being diverted and used at an alarming rate by Israel, the occupying Power, at the expense of the Palestinian people. Severe restrictions on drilling for water, planting and irrigation and such Israeli practices as the felling of productive trees and the destruction of crops have diminished or maintained at a low level the amount of water made available to the Palestinian population' (page 6). See also Harald Frederiksen (June 2007a). 'Water in the Israeli/Palestinian Conflict: A history that leaves few options.' Presentation at the *Fifth International Water History Association Conference.* Tampere, Finland. Page 9; and (no date) 'Return of Water: One component for attaining an Israel-Palestine peace and a more secure Middle East.'

Presentation at the *Third Annual Conference of the Center for Macro Projects and Diplomacy*. Roger William University, Bristol, RI. Pages 6–7.

40. Harald Frederiksen (2003). Op. cit. Page 81.
41. *Ibid.*
42. *Ibid.*
43. *Ibid.* Page 79.
44. The Coastal or Eastern Aquifer provides groundwater to Israel and Gaza. The eastern portion of the Mountain Aquifer underlies the West Bank while the western portion extends into Israel.
45. Harald Frederiksen (2007b). 'A Federation of Palestine and Jordan: A chance for peace?' *Middle East Policy*. **XIV** (2). Page 35.
46. Harald Frederiksen (2009). 'The World Water Crisis and International Security.' *Middle East Policy*. **XVI** (4). Page 82.
47. *Ibid.* Page 38.
48. *West Bank and Gaza Update* (October 2008a). Op. cit. Page 16.
49. *Ibid.* Pages 14–15.
50. Cernea, Michael M. (2000). 'Risks, Safeguards, and Reconstruction: A model for population displacement and resettlement.' In Michael M. Cernea and Christopher McDowell (eds). *Risks and Reconstruction: Experiences of resettlers and refugees*. Washington DC: The World Bank. Pages 11–55.
51. United Nations, Commission on the Status of Women (March 1990). 'The Situation of Palestinian Women in the Occupied Territories.' New York: United Nations; also quoted in Suha Sabbagh (March 1991). 'Behind Closed Doors: Palestinian families under curfew.' *Washington Report on Middle East Affairs*. Page 15. Available at http://www.wrmea.com/backissues/0391/9103015.htm.
52. Kathleen Christison (2 May 2002). 'Before There Was Terrorism.' *Counterpunch*.
53. *West Bank and Gaza Update*. Op. cit. Pages 4–5.
54. *Ibid.* Page 5.
55. *Ibid.* Page 16.
56. Al-Wahaid (no date). 'Border closure and Nutrition in Gaza.' Page 2.
57. Quoted from the Population Resource Center's *Executive Summary: Israel and the Palestinian Territories* (February 2003).
58. U.S. Department of State (31 March 2003). 'Israel and The Occupied Territories.' Page 25.
59. Human Rights Watch (13 January 2009). Israel: End Gaza's humanitarian crisis at once. Available at http://www.hrw,org/en/news/2009/01/12/israel-end-gaza-s-humanitarian-crisis-once.
60. Cernea (2000). Op. cit.
61. Tracy Wilkinson (13 December 2002). 'Mideast Violence Moves to the Home Front.' *Los Angeles Times*.
62. *Ibid.*
63. Paul D. Carrington (2005). *Spreading America's Word: Stories of its lawyer-missionaries*. New York: Twelve Tables Press.
64. Carrington notes that all but three U.S. Presidents before 1920 had been lawyers.
65. Carrington (2005) Op. cit. Page 3.
66. *Ibid.* Page 171.
67. United States (17 September 2002). 'The National Security Strategy of the United States of America.' Page 4.
68. *Ibid.* Page 6. The main exceptions are Germany and Japan following the end of the Second World War. Unlike other countries that America tried to influence, both were already highly industrialized countries with a well-educated citizenry.
69. *Ibid.* Page 149. President Wilson believed that land reform in Mexico should be 'a pre-condition to democratization and diplomatic recognition.' Not only did the necessary land reform not occur but efforts to export America's experience with governance were 'not merely a failure but a disaster' (page 51).

70.  *Ibid.* Page 135.
71.  *Ibid.* Page 273.
72.  Pew Research Center (23 June 2008). 'Religion in America: Non-dogmatic, diverse and politically relevant.' Religious Beliefs and Practices/Social and Political Views: Report 2.
73.  The Pew Research Center for the People and The Press/The Pew Forum on Research and Public Life (24 August 2006). 'Many Americans Uneasy With Mix of Religion and Politics.' Pages 15 and 19.
74.  Taken from Walter Russell Mead (2006). 'God's Country?' *Foreign Affairs.* **85** (5). Pages 24–43.
75.  *Ibid.* Page 36.
76.  See the Union of Concerned Scientists (no date) 'The A to Z Guide to Political Interference in Science.' Available at http://www.ucsusa.org/scientific_integrity/abuses_ of_science/a-to-z-guide-to-political.html.
77.  See Garry Wills (16 November 2006). 'A Country Ruled by Faith.' *The New York Review of Books.* Pages 8–11.
78.  New York Academy of Medicine (28 May 1982) Newsroom. 'Baltimore Criticizes Bush Administration's Restrictions on Scientific Research at Annual Spring Stated Meeting.'
79.  Richard Cincotta (1 March 2005). 'Youth Bulge, Underemployment Raise Risks of Conflict.' State of the World 2005 Global Security Brief #2 Washington DC: Worldwatch Institute. Available at http://www.worldwatch.org/node/76.
80.  See All Party Parliamentary Group on Population, Development and Reproductive Growth (January 2007). 'Return of the Population Growth Factor.' London: APPC. Page 32.
81.  *Ibid.* Page 4.
82.  *Ibid.* Page 59.
83.  *Ibid.* Page 33.
84.  *Ibid.* Page 195.
85.  Richard Cincotta. Op. cit.
86.  Lionel Beehner (27 April 2007). 'The Effects of "Youth Bulge" on Civil Conflicts.' New York: Council on Foreign Relations.
87.  CBC News (10 June 2009). 'Rae "dumbfounded" after Sri Lanka denied him entry.'
88.  Susan Visvanathan (2000). 'The Homogeneity of Fundamentalism: Christianity, British colonialism and India in the nineteenth century.' *Studies in History.* **16** (2) (n.s). Page 221. The phrase 'a civilizing mission' she takes from Erik Stokes (1959). *The English Utilitarians and India.* Oxford: Oxford University Press. Page xiii.

# 3. The threat of environmental degradation

## INTRODUCTION

Environmental degradation involves a daunting range of issues. I will start with a case history of the complex interrelationship between development, increases in population and population density, poverty and environmental degradation. I will then concentrate on threats to ecosystems, ecosystem services and biodiversity. Special attention will be paid to river basins, coastal ecosystems, decreasing water availability due to melting of mountain glaciers and snowfields and threats to bird species and numbers. Discussion of the state of global ecosystems and biodiversity will be informed in part by the 2005 synthesis reports of the Millennium Ecosystem Assessment's *Ecosystems and Human Well-Being: General Synthesis* and *Ecosystems and Human Well-being: Biodiversity Synthesis*.

A credible argument can be made that global climate change alone will be sufficient to reduce the living standards and quality of life of future generations. Rich and poor will be affected although the poor will be the most vulnerable, since they tend to live in more marginal areas, have access to a narrower range of options and resources (including less government assistance, as illustrated by the weak U.S. responses in 2005 to the poor in New Orleans following hurricane Katrina) and, as in the case with many ethnic minorities, have already lost what resilience they had prior to their incorporation into 'the modern world.'

## A CASE HISTORY: GWEMBE TONGA RESETTLEMENT AND ENVIRONMENTAL DEGRADATION

The environmental degradation caused by the development-induced resettlement of 57000 Gwembe Tonga may strike readers as an extreme case. It is especially important, however, because it illustrates what I am convinced is happening at a slower rate throughout Africa due to the interplay of growth-based development policies, poverty, increases in consumption and population, and degradation and depletion of natural resources.

Dam-induced resettlement provides a quasi-laboratory setting for examining through the use of research on the ground and remote sensing the impact of increasing population numbers and density on land use and land cover change. In most cases planners use resettlement to consolidate people into larger communities where it is cheaper to provide physical infrastructure and social services along with tighter policing and other administrative controls. The problem is that more often than not the natural resource base is inadequate to support the resettlers, with the result that poverty and environmental degradation follow as does, in some cases, conflict with the host population. The 'hot spots' that result can be used as models for forecasting adverse environmental changes that are occurring at a slower rate elsewhere.

Resettlement during the late 1950s in connection with the Kariba dam has produced such 'hot spots.' Remote sensing combined with our long-term research was used to assess the environmental impact of resettling 6000 people in a 22 000 hectare area close to the Zambezi below the dam.[1] Figure 1 shows land cover in 1954 before resettlement occurred. The cleared areas are fields of the small host population. The numbers 1 and 2 indicate where two of our study villages were resettled. Figures 2–3 show what happened during the 1980s and 1990s as population and impoverishment increased. Over a 12-year period (1986–1997), that area's woodland savanna was reduced by 44 per cent, at an average annual rate of 4 per cent.

Land clearance for agriculture was the main change factor. While the natural resource base was sufficient to support the first generation of resettlers along with a host population of about 1000, it was insufficient to support a rate of population increase of over 3 per cent among 7000 people. Erosion of arable land increased and soil fertility and crop yields dropped. Especially obvious was the dry season expansion of bare land around villages. In some cases surface erosion removed top soil to the extent that root exposure caused giant baobab trees to topple over (Figure 4). Close to villages, most topsoil has been removed because of gully, sheet and wind erosion. When the wind blows toward the end of the dry season, as it frequently does, the area takes on a Sahel-like appearance, with dust obscuring the sun or turning it a deep red.

Grazing was also adversely affected, with increased mortality of cattle either requiring villagers to practice transhumance for the first time by annually moving their herds to graze elsewhere, or to relocate themselves to a less degraded habitat. Increasing poverty has required villagers to increase use of natural resources other than arable land and pasture.

Hunting has reduced the wildlife, and poaching occurs across the river in Zimbabwe, in spite of the risk of being shot by game rangers. Thatching grass, a common-property resource formerly available to all, has become so scarce that it has taken on cash value, which encourages exploitation farther and farther away from the villages.

While the rate of land cover change has lessened in recent years, that is largely because of the voluntary out-migration of people to less degraded areas elsewhere in the Middle Zambezi Valley and especially to the adjacent Zambian Plateau, where the government has opened up a Game Management Area for human settlement – hence accelerating the process of national deforestation in a new area.

I have watched since 1956 the area deforested by agriculture and charcoal production expand outward from Zambia's capital as population and urbanization increased. Today deforested areas extend into the Middle Zambezi Valley over 100 km distant. Charcoal production kilns are made by covering cut wood with earth. Approximately 95 per cent of the charcoal produced is consumed as fuel by households. Average annual consumption was about 1046 kg per urban household and 100 kg per rural household during 1983–1994. Total consumption increased from 0.32 million tons in 1969 to 0.66 million tons in 1990.[2]

Kammen and Lew estimate in a 2005 paper that biomass fuels such as wood, crop residues, dung and charcoal are used for cooking by half of the world's population. More available as a common-property resource, the first three fuels are preferred by the rural poor while charcoal is preferred by the urban poor because of its higher efficiency and better storage characteristics. Finding sufficient fuel for rural use normally is not a major cause of deforestation and land degradation since use of green wood is largely avoided. It is, however, a major inconvenience for women in many countries, who have to extend their search further and further from their homes as the years go by.

Charcoal production has more serious impacts both because green wood is used and because the production process is a source of greenhouse gases. Using Food and Agriculture Organization data, which indicates that about half of charcoal production occurs in Africa, Kammen and Lew estimate that global charcoal production 'increased by about a third from 1981 to 1992,'[3] when 24 million tons were consumed. Further increases were expected. A relatively low cost in comparison to other urban fuels is one reason. Another is that health problems and greenhouse gas emissions can be significantly reduced by use of relatively low-cost and more efficient charcoal stoves.[4]

Globally, charcoal production is not a major cause of deforestation, unlike commercial logging and land clearance for large commercial cattle

ranches and agribusinesses as in Brazil and Indonesia. But it is a cause of
deforestation in various developing countries. African examples include
Zambia, where over 50 per cent of the population is urban, Somalia, the
Sudan and the Sahelian countries in West Africa. Charcoal production
is especially damaging in Somalia due to export to towns and cities in
Saudi Arabia and elsewhere in the Middle East.[5] In all of those African
cases, land clearing for extensive systems of agriculture and charcoal
production are the most prominent forms of deforestation. The two
may be combined. In Zambia, some Gwembe Tonga emigrants from the
Middle Zambezi Valley to the Plateau combine agriculture and charcoal
production on the farms they have received in previously uncultivated
areas.

# LOSS OF ECOSYSTEM SERVICES

## Introduction

According to the 2005 *Millennium Ecosystem Assessment*, 15 (approximately 60 per cent) of the 24 ecosystem services examined, 'are being
degraded or used unsustainably, including fresh water, capture fisheries,
air and water purification, and the regulation of regional and local climate,
natural hazards, and pests.'[6] What evidence is available indicates that
losses and degradation 'are substantial and growing.' That is the first of
three major conclusions of the four-year assessment. The second conclusion is that 'there is *established but incomplete* evidence that changes being
made in ecosystems are increasing the likelihood of nonlinear changes in
ecosystems (including accelerating, abrupt, and potentially irreversible
changes) that have important consequences for human-wellbeing.' The
third conclusion, pointing up again how various threats to global living
standards are interrelated, is that 'the harmful effects of the degradation
of ecosystem services . . . are being borne disproportionately by the poor,
are contributing to growing inequalities and disparities across groups of
people, and are sometimes the principal factor causing poverty and social
conflict.'[7]

Ecosystems are defined as communities, composed of animals, flora and
micro-organisms that interact with their chemical and physical environment and are interlinked through complex processes of nutrient cycling.
Animals include people, who today are the most dominant species in
regard to how they influence ecosystems. That definition of ecosystems
includes even small isolated ponds far removed from direct human activities as well as the global ecosystem that is the subject of this book. My wife

Eliza and I visited such a pond close to the border of the United States and Canada in July 2007. Both of us having been born in New England, we wanted to visit the origin of the largest river – the Connecticut – in the region. To get there we drove to the unpopulated border, parked across from the U.S. customs and immigration station and hiked several miles uphill through a dense temperate forest. Our trail most recently had been used by a moose that had crossed and recrossed the border. The small pond we reached was only a couple of acres in size. Its dominant feature was a beaver dwelling made of branches and earth. There was no obvious sign of human life. Yet the ecology of that pond and the surrounding area was undergoing change because of industrial activities causing, for example, acid rain and mercury pollution.

Ecosystem services are defined as the benefits that humankind receives from ecosystems. The Millennium Assessment divides them into four categories. The first includes such provisioning services as fresh water, food, fiber (including timber, cotton and fuel wood), genetic resources (especially important for engineering improved crops) and a wide range of natural products such as medicinal plants. The second category involves a wide range of regulating services, most of which have undergone decline. Examples include maintenance of acceptable air quality, pollination of flora, protection against hazards, water purification and treatment of wastes, and regulation of erosion and pests. The third category involves cultural services that relate to spiritual and religious values and to recreation and tourism. Supporting services, such as soil formation, form the fourth category.

**Assessment of Human Influence on Ecosystems and Ecosystem Services**

Indicating our cavalier attitude toward humankind's dependence on its encompassing global ecosystem, the first major attempt to assess the state of global ecosystem services was delayed until 1999. The results were presented in a 2000 report published by two UN agencies, the World Bank and Washington's World Resources Institute.[8] Two goals were emphasized. The first was to report what was known and what was not known about the current state of global ecosystems. Unique was the report's pilot analysis of global ecosystems. Five of those systems – coastal, forest, grassland, freshwater and agricultural – were assessed against a global background in which, 'since 1980 the global economy has tripled in size and the population has grown 30 per cent to six billion people . . . all at a cost to ecosystems.' With pressures expected to increase during the next five decades, the report, to which over 175 scientists had contributed over a two-year period, concluded that '[t]he current rate of decline in the long term productive capacity of ecosystems could have devastating implications for human development and the welfare of all species.'[9]

The second goal was 'to motivate nations, local communities and individuals to adopt an ecosystem-oriented approach to managing the environment.' The problem was that in the year 2000 relatively little was known about 'ecosystem conditions on a global, regional, or, in many instances, even a local scale.'[10] That situation remains the case today in regard to long-term research on global and regional ecosystems and, more specifically, on research on the dynamics of how people impact upon such ecosystems.

In the United States it was not until the 1970s that the National Science Foundation played a key role in pushing the importance of long-term ecological research. The first projects started in 1980. By 2005 there were 26 U.S. sponsored projects involving over 1800 scientists and students. But none dealt with global ecosystems or even broad regional ecosystems. Rather they dealt largely with specific locales which might be restricted to a small area.

The international program to study ecosystems only began in 1993, with 32 member countries by 2006, but there is still insufficient focus on global and regional ecosystems. The situation, however, is much worse for equivalent long-term research on how people, and, more specifically, current national and international development policies, impact upon global and regional ecosystems. Again, as with our own long-term research in the Middle Zambezi Valley, the emphasis is primarily on sub-regions. In both ecological and socio-economic research, the necessary methodologies and technologies (remote sensing in particular) have been, or are being, developed but government support and financing are not present.

The 2005 Millennium Assessment (MA) arose from a 2000 request from the UN Secretary-General during a report to the General Assembly. Assessment involving over 2000 authors and reviewers began under UN auspices in 2001. As with the Intergovernmental Panel on Climate Change, the purpose of the assessment reports was not to make recommendations for implementation but only to present a careful scientific assessment of the current situation which then would be summarized for non-responsive decision makers.

**The Current Situation**

**Introduction**
The purpose of the sections that follow is to illustrate in more detail the severity of the current threat to ecosystems and to ecosystem services and by implication the inaction of politicians and other decision makers.

The first section shows how human activities are adversely affecting river basins. The second emphasizes how the destruction of coastal ecosystems is threatening the welfare of coastal communities, while the third section deals with the threats posed by reduction of glaciers and snowpack.

### River basins

River basins frequently are national heartlands. They are especially important for food production. The rivers that serve them, however, are in trouble. The major reasons involve human activities, of which large dams and intensive systems of agriculture have had the most adverse impacts. Dams, inter-basin transfers and water withdrawn for irrigated agriculture 'have fragmented 60 per cent of the world's rivers.'[11] Today reservoirs behind dams contain more water than do natural rivers, with withdrawals for human activities from rivers and lakes doubling between 1960 and 2005.[12]

Approximately 70 per cent of all water withdrawn for human use from subsurface aquifers and from lakes and rivers is used for irrigated agriculture. Only 30–60 per cent of water withdrawn from rivers returns for downstream use.[13] Run-off from intensive systems of agriculture also degrades water quality, as do industrial and urban wastes, and are a major cause of offshore dead zones such as the one beyond the mouth of the Mississippi River. Resulting from the combined impact of agriculture and dams, approximately 20 per cent of species of freshwater fish are either extinct or under threat.

Currently approximately 50 000 large dams are operational throughout the world. By definition they are at least 15 meters tall or if between 5 and 15 meters in height have a storage capacity of over 3 million cubic meters. China, with over 20 000 large dams, has the largest number as well as being the most involved currently in dam construction at home and abroad. Second to China, the United States has over 6000 large dams, followed by India with over 4000 and many more on the drawing board, and Japan and Spain – each with over 1000. Then there are the many smaller dams, with the total number of all sizes in the United States exceeding 70 000.

Large dams are not sustainable development. Though their short- and medium-term benefits as generators of electricity and water for irrigation and residential, industrial and urban use are substantial, eventually the large majority of dam reservoirs will silt up. Exceptions exist mainly in rock-solid mountainous areas, but on average reservoirs silt up by 0.5 per cent per annum. How to decommission them, let alone remove them to restore natural flows, is not built into the cost-benefit analysis that justifies their initial construction. Nor, in the majority of cases, does the engineering and science exist on how to flush out the silt that backs up behind dams in large and broad reservoirs or to deal with the heavy metals and industrial wastes that have been deposited.

Not only will large dams continue to be built to capture their short-term benefits, but they continue to occupy a major place in national development plans and funding provided by international financial institutions. In many developing countries, large dam-driven development tends to exceed other projects in scale and in financing. The World Bank, for example, has once again become a leader in financing 'high risk, high return' projects.

I have been studying for over 50 years the socio-economic and environmental impacts of large dams on people living beside or near some of the great rivers of the world. Adverse environment impacts to river basin and coastal ecosystems are huge, as are impacts to the livelihoods of hundreds of millions of people.[14] Capture of silt behind reservoirs has several negative impacts. Downstream farmers must use expensive and polluting fertilizers as opposed to past reliance on flood-deposited silt. Downstream erosion is increased by silt-free waters. Abutments of bridges may be endangered, as was the case following the completion of Egypt's Aswan High Dam. Erosion can also increase dramatically within the reservoir basin due to wave action and slope instability, as is currently the case with China's Three Gorges Dam.

The overall deficit in river silt loads due to reservoir deposition behind mainstream dams can be sufficiently great to cause coastal erosion. Examples include Ghana's Volta dam, where up to 10 000 people were displaced from one coastal town while coastal erosion accelerated in the neighboring countries of Benin and Togo. In Southern California, the construction of hundreds of small check dams in coastal ranges has reduced sediment flows into the Pacific Ocean to the extent that coastal erosion is occurring.

Even more serious are the adverse impacts of reduced natural river flows and silt deposition on deltas. Deltas are highly productive ecosystems formed by silt accumulation that are colonized by freshwater and salt-tolerant grasses, shrubs and trees according to the mix of fresh and saline waters. Because of dams, a number of major rivers no longer reach the sea for extended periods, or deliver water to only a fraction of the area previously flooded. Examples include the Colorado River in the Western United States and the Indus in India and Pakistan. Because of 22 upstream dams, Indus flows today seldom cover more than 25 per cent of its historic floodplain, while water extraction and flood levees have restricted the delta to 'only 10 per cent of its original area.'[15]

Because of two large upstream dams, reduced Zambezi River flows have adversely affected the extent of delta flooding. Wetlands have been reduced while smaller channels are apt to be clogged with aquatic vegetation.

Desiccation caused by reduced flooding has led to wildfires and opened the delta to poaching, with one zoologist reporting more than a 95 per cent reduction of large mammals such as buffalo and hippopotamus.[16]

While erosion is also a problem in the Nile Delta, still more serious is saline intrusion and seepage from the Mediterranean, which threatens the agricultural productivity of Egypt's main breadbasket. In other major rivers, the Indus and the Yangtze, for example, saline intrusion is an increasing problem, with saline waters intruding up to 30 km inland along the Indus.

Dams also cause a serious reduction in the productivity of downstream fisheries, which are the main source of protein for hundreds of millions of people in developing countries like Laos and Nigeria. Research following the construction of Nigeria's Kainji Dam documented catch declines exceeding 50 per cent, while Adeniyi documented income from fishing dropping 47 to 73 per cent in three villages, one of which was located 200 km downstream.[17] Because large dams replace a river's natural flood regime with a regularized flow within a river's primary channel, the extent and productivity of wetlands is also seriously reduced.

While the flood control benefits of large dams can be a major benefit, with Egypt's Aswan High Dam being an excellent example, realization of that benefit requires sophisticated operations and management, which too often are lacking. In addition to staff capacity, two requirements are essential. One is availability of an above-dam network of rainfall and river flow stations that can promptly deliver information on river flows to dam site operators. The other, especially crucial in climates with alternating annual dry and rainy seasons, and influenced by monsoons, hurricanes and typhoons, is drawing down reservoirs before a rapid rise due to heavy and unexpected rainfall.

Too often operators are under pressure to keep reservoir levels as high as possible to retain water for hydropower generation and irrigation. When miscalculations occur and excessive flood waters arrive, flood gates are opened to protect the dam before adequate downstream warning occurs. Unfortunately because people, towns and cities believe that dams protect them, they tend to move onto former flood plains after construction. The resulting dam-related floods have caused loss of life and damage to crops, buildings and communities in recent years in Ghana, Nigeria, Zambia, Mozambique, India, Cambodia, Vietnam and elsewhere. Unannounced releases from the Kariba Dam in 2001 eliminated the crops of thousands of downstream farmers, including in one of Colson's and my research villages. After maize was destroyed on a field belonging to Adam Sikaguma Senete he wrote 'I can't express the anger that came into our family as a result of the flooding.'

**Coastal ecosystems**

Approximately one-third of the world's human population lives in coastal regions that cover about 4 per cent of the world's land area.[18] Their number and percentage is expected to increase significantly due to ongoing urbanization. Especially relevant to their wellbeing are coastal and marine ecosystems. The dividing line between the two ecosystems is arbitrary, with coastal ecosystems defined as extending from marine waters above 50 meters depth at low water to 100 km inland or an elevation rise of 50 meters.[19] In my analysis, coastal ecosystems include estuaries, vegetation (especially mangroves and salt marshes) that tolerate saline conditions, tidal zones and coral reefs. The Millennium Ecosystem Assessment of marine ecosystems focuses on fish. Interconnections are crucial and must not be ignored. The life history of many marine fish, for example, starts in coastal waters.

Especially important for the wellbeing of coastal people are the inter-connections between mangroves, sea grasses and coral reefs. When healthy, those ecosystems protect coastal regions from wave surges due to hurricanes, typhoons and other major storms and to tsunamis (tidal waves) caused by earthquakes and volcanic eruptions. In 2005, 'the Asian tsunami did far less damage in coastal areas where mangrove forests and coral reefs were intact than where they had been stripped away by shrimp aquaculture and other development.'[20] Much of the devastation caused by hurricane Katrina in the United States was due to human activities, which had played a major role in the removal in Louisiana of '1900 square miles of protective coastal mangroves . . . since the 1930s.'[21]

Mangroves are a vegetation complex of nearly 70 species, including trees over 40 meters high, that are adapted to saline conditions in the tropics and subtropics, where formerly they occupied millions of hectares along shorelines, in estuaries and in the lower reaches of rivers affected by saline intrusion. Mangrove forests provide a range of important services. They provide nurseries for important crustaceans (including shrimp) and fish to the extent 'that 80% of global fish catches are directly or indirectly dependent on mangroves.'[22] They also protect coastal areas from erosion, facilitate nutrient recycling and 'enhance water quality by filtering sus-pended particles and anchoring sediments on the banks and to the sea-floor'[23] – a service that is especially important for protecting coral reefs from suffocating siltation.

Sea grasses live underwater in saline habitats. Dependent on sunlight, the depth at which they live is related to water clarity. Like mangroves they include many species, stabilize bottom areas, maintain water clarity and provide sanctuary and/or food for innumerable fish, crustaceans, shellfish, sea turtles and marine mammals. While scuba diving at night,

I was overwhelmed by the vast assemblage of life in the kelp forests off Catalina Island in California. Our flashlights picked up red crustaceans including crabs and lobsters on the ocean floor and many species of fish swimming and feeding in and around the kelp. When we turned off our lights, we were surrounded by countless tiny phosphorescent diatoms.

Coral reefs occur in warm waters at temperatures 16°C and higher, and at depths down to about 30 meters. They are made of the calcium carbonate skeletons of a variety of marine organisms, including the many species of coral that build up over the years. Their formation requires clear waters, hence the importance of coastal mangroves and sea grasses to filter out sediments and industrial and human wastes. Each reef is a vibrant community of many species, including the algae that maintain a symbiotic relationship with coral organisms, other types of algae, sea grasses, worms, echinoderms (including starfish and sea cucumbers), sponges, crustaceans, mollusks, moray eels, sea snakes and innumerable species of fish. Because of this range and quantity of species, coral reefs support more biodiversity than any other marine ecosystem. They occur in many different forms. In addition to their fisheries productivity, they serve humankind by protecting continental and island coastlines and providing a major environment for tourism. The Great Barrier Reef, for example, 'contributes $6.9 billion annually to the Australian economy – $6 billion from the tourism industry, $544 million from recreational activity and $251 million from commercial fishing. This economic activity generated more than 65 000 jobs.'[24]

Scientific report after report has warned about the seriousness of the threats posed by human activities to coastal ecosystems. The authors of *World Resources 2000–2001* stated that '[p]opulation increase and conversion for development, agriculture and aquaculture are reducing mangroves, coastal wetlands, seagrass areas and coral reefs at an alarming rate.'[25] Mangrove forests, salt grasslands and other saline marshes are threatened by coastal development and especially by logging, oil and natural gas extraction and land clearing for agriculture and shrimp aquaculture. According to the Millennium Ecosystem Assessment, 'Approximately 20 per cent of the world's coral reefs were lost and an additional 20 per cent degraded in the last several decades of the twentieth century, and approximately 35 per cent of mangrove area was lost' in countries where sufficient data were available for analysis.[26]

Following the October 2007 National Forum on Coral Reef Futures, 50 scientists unanimously endorsed a statement that without targeted reductions in greenhouse gas emissions, 'the ongoing damage to coral reefs from global warming will be irreversible.'[27] Major reasons for decline included acidification of the oceans by carbon dioxide (which interferes with the skeletal growth of coral reef organisms) and fatal coral bleaching 'which has greatly increased in frequency and magnitude over the past 30 years due to global warming.'[28]

Other threats to coral reefs are caused by 'increases in diseases and plagues of coral predators that are increasingly linked to human disturbances in the environment.'[29] Especially destructive are increased populations of crown-of-thorns starfish, which feed on coral polyps, and of algae blooms due to increased seawater pollution from human, agricultural and industrial wastes. Overfishing, and especially fishing with dynamite and cyanide, is another threat. Other more general threats are deforestation, including cutting of mangrove forests, and rural and urban land development to serve increasing coastal populations.

Shrimp aquaculture has been especially destructive to mangrove vegetation in Latin America and Asia. From the 1970s, shrimp aquaculture has grown from a small-scale village industry to a multi-billion dollar commercial enterprise that has become an important source of foreign exchange for over 50 countries. Public and private international financial institutions and foreign aid programs provided financing which enabled entrepreneurs to intensify pond output to thousands of kilos per hectare, with an annual production of nearly 800 000 tons per year by 1996.[30]

Rapid development of shrimp aquaculture has come at a major cost, however, since large areas have been clear-cut of mangroves and replaced with shrimp ponds. The extent of mangroves in the Philippines, for example, had been reduced from 1700 km² in the 1920s to 540 km² by 1991, while 'Thailand had lost more than half its mangroves since 1960' and 'Ecuador has lost 162 square miles out of 788 square miles of mangroves from 1969 to 1991.'[31] By the end of the 1990s, at least a million hectares of coastal lowlands had become shrimp ponds, with shrimp farmers producing in 1998 'an estimated 840,200 metric tons of whole shrimp in an operating area of 999,350 hectares.'[32] By 2006, shrimp aquaculture produced approximately 25 per cent of total shrimp production,[33] with exports going primarily to the United States, Europe and Japan.

Major social costs have also been involved due to shrimp aquaculture causing involuntary displacement and occupying communal lands of value for providing food and a wide range of natural products on which local villagers are dependent. As in Brazil's tropical forests, conflicts have developed between local communities and commercial operators over property rights, during which community protesters have been murdered in a number of countries, including Thailand (currently the largest producer of farmed shrimp with the possible exception of China), India, Indonesia, Honduras and Guatemala.[34]

**Mountain glaciers**

When I was a child and a young adult, the study of birds and mountaineering were my first two career choices. In 1952, while president of the Harvard Mountaineering Club, I led a small expedition to the Alaska Range in Denali National Park. Our base camp had only recently been covered by the retreating and thinning Muldrow Glacier, which flowed off Mt McKinley. Retreat and thinning have since accelerated, with measurements taken several kilometers up the glacier showing that the Muldrow had thinned about 20 meters in depth between 1979 and 2004, while photographs showed the loss of the beautiful hanging glaciers on Mt Brooks which we had traversed during our first ascent of that peak.[35]

The accelerating retreat of the large majority of mountain glaciers due to global warming threatens the future water supply of hundreds of millions of people over the next hundred years. Satellite imagery shows significant glacial retreat in recent years around the world including in the South American Andes, the European Alps and the Asian Himalayan region.[36] According to W. Haberli and M. Hoelzle of the World Glacier Monitoring Service, measurements indicate an accelerating decline since the 1980s at a rate 'beyond the range of pre-industrial variability.'[37]

Aside from the polar ice caps, the concentration of glaciers is highest on the international Tibetan Plateau, where glaciers cover 104 850 km², 'including 40 000 km² in India and Pakistan and 49,873 km² in China.'[38] Over 6600 km² have been deglaciated over a 40-year period, 'with the greatest retreat occurring since the mid-1980s. With strong retreat since the 1990s, all glaciers, except some large glaciers in the Tibetan Plateau, have begun shrinking'.[39] The significance of this retreat is that '[t]he Tibetan Plateau is the headwater of rivers that flow down to half of humanity',[40] much of which is at risk.

Roughly one-third of the Tibetan Plateau glaciers are located in the Himalayas. By 2005, 67 per cent of those Himalayan glaciers were 'retreating at a startling rate.'[41] If current rates of decline continue, initially creeks, streams and rivers will contain more water but over a hundred-year period, flows will decline in the great rivers of Asia that originate on the Tibetan Plateau. They include the Indus, serving the downstream countries of India and Pakistan, the Ganga, serving India and Bangladesh, the Salween, serving Burma, the Mekong, serving Thailand, Laos, Cambodia and Vietnam and the Yangtze and Yellow Rivers, serving China.

It is estimated that glacial melting eventually could reduce July–September flows in the Ganga by two-thirds and cause water shortages for '37 per cent of India's irrigated land.'[42] Such declines there and in the Indus and Brahmaputra could adversely affect 500 million people living in the three river basins.[43] Poor farmers, and women and children, are expected to be especially vulnerable, with increased family migration in search of work to already overwhelmed cities.[44] Similar impacts can be expected in China although the effects of slower retreat of glaciers serving the Yangtze and Yellow Rivers (6.3 per cent over the past 40 years[45]) will postpone adverse impacts.

**Snowpack reduction in the Western United States**
In the Northern Hemisphere, the maximum area normally covered by snow in winter is 45.2 million km².[46] Worldwide snow cover provides major services. In mountainous areas snow melt provides the major source of fresh water – up to 75 per cent in the Western United States.[47] Snow also reflects heat back into the atmosphere and provides insulation to the underlying ground. Yet snow-cover extent is decreasing, especially in the Northern Hemisphere, where a reduction rate of 1.3 per cent per decade has occurred over the past 40 years.[48]

The extent of decline varies greatly between regions, being worse in areas threatened by both drought and global warming. That includes the Western United States, with over 65 million people who are dependent on stream run-off from the various mountain ranges for agriculture (70 per cent of water use) and hydropower generation,[49] as well as urban residents and industries. Already snow cover in the mountains is being reduced due to increasing spring temperatures. As a result stream flow from snow melt is increasing earlier than in the past. It is also flowing in more irregular amounts due to a greater proportion of spring participation in the form of rain. That change requires dam operators to release more water in the spring, as a flood management requirement, as opposed to the hotter summer and fall months when more water is needed for irrigation and electricity generation. Such a changing regime is also a factor increasing the risks of wildfires since snowpacks in semi-arid western mountains reduce fire danger. With earlier reduction of snow cover, 'the forests can become combustible within 1 month because of low humidity and sparse summer rainfall.'[50]

A majority of the West's population lives in California, which receives most of its run-off from the Sierras. According to a more optimistic climate change model, expected snow cover decline during the current century will vary from 30–70 per cent versus 73–90 per cent in a more pessimistic model. At a September 2006 forum at Stanford University, Steve Chu, Nobel Laureate and Secretary of Energy in the Obama government, told the audience and scientific colleagues that '[i]f the Sierra snowpack declines by even 50 per cent, this will have a profound impact on our water supply because the combination of dams and snowpack provides us with the water supply for the summer and late, early fall and even spring.'[51]

When interviewed during 2007 by *New York Times* writer Jon Gertner, Chu added, 'There is a two-thirds chance there will be a disaster and that's in the best scenario.' Southern California, and the metropolitan zone that includes San Diego and Los Angeles, will be most at risk since most of its water comes by canal and tunnel from central and northern California's dams and rivers, the Owens Valley that drains the eastern Sierras and the Colorado River. Conflict and lawsuits have already involved Los Angeles and the residents of the Owens Valley. If present snowmelt trends continue, conflict and lawsuits can be expected also to include Northern California and the six other states that share the Colorado River with Los Angeles and other areas in Southern California.

Peter Gleick, Director of the Pacific Institute, refers to the Colorado River as 'the most complicated water system in the world'.[52] Flowing through semi-arid and arid lands, the much-dammed Colorado no longer carries enough water to support a formerly biodiversity-rich delta ecosystem. Its headwaters lie in the Rocky Mountains. Though snowpack reduction there has not been in decline during most of the past 50 years, except in the Northern Rockies where decreases range between 15 and 30 per cent,[53] decreases 'in 2002, 2004, and 2006 . . . were quite significant, and were caused in part by substantial spring time warm periods without precipitation.' Summing up the situation in a June 2007 testimony to a Senate subcommittee, Bradley Udall, Director, NOAA–University of Colorado Western Water Assessment, stated that the two major dams on the Colorado were 'now approximately half full. Lake Mead is currently losing 1.4 million acre-feet per year, and contains only 10 years of water at this rate of loss.'[54]

# LOSS OF BIODIVERSITY

## Introduction

Within our global ecosystem, 'biodiversity provides the conditions and drives the processes that sustain the global economy – and our very survival as a species.'[55] Provision of food security is one such benefit, with biodiversity providing 'the vast majority of our foodstuffs' as well as essential pollination of many flowering plants and pest control. Other essential benefits and services include soil formation and maintenance, and maintenance of air and water quality. Biodiversity also has cultural value for improving people's quality of life.[56]

Following the 1992 UN Earth Summit conference in Brazil, scientists increasingly have been warning an unaware human population and largely uncomprehending and unconcerned government leadership of an impending catastrophic decline in global biodiversity. At the same time the concept of a sixth global extinction has gained currency. In April 1998 the American Museum of Natural History and Louis Harris and Associates released their 'Biodiversity in the Next Millennium' survey, which reported that seven out of ten biologists in the United States believed 'that we are in the midst of a mass extinction of living things, and that this loss of species will pose a major risk to human existence in the next century.' Of the 400 scientists polled, 70 per cent estimated that up to one-fifth of living species could die out within the next 30 years while the estimate of one-third of the scientists was as high as 50 per cent. Furthermore, they emphasized that 'this so-called "sixth extinction" is mainly the result of human activity and **not** natural phenomena' as in the past.[57] In government circles their concerns and recommendations for immediate action fell largely on deaf ears.

Also in 1998, the United Nations issued its 'Troubled Water: A Call for Action', which was endorsed by over 1600 marine scientists and conservation biologists representing 65 countries. In this case the call for immediate action was an international one coming from research institutions, such as Australia's Institute of Marine Sciences, Russia's Academy of Sciences and the United States' Woods Hole Oceanographic Institute, and from conservation agencies, the private sector and individual scientists. The call, also largely unheeded by national leaders, was made based on major threats to marine species and ecosystems due to overfishing and destruction of indigenous species, invasion of alien species, alteration and pollution of ecosystems and global atmospheric change.[58]

In 2000, UNDP, UNEP, the World Bank and the World Resources Institute released *World Resources 2000–2001: People and Ecosystems: The Fraying Web of Life*.[59] Though dealing more with ecosystem services than biodiversity, the report updated information on some categories of biodiversity decline. It was estimated, for example, that 9 per cent of global tree species risked extinction, 20 per cent of freshwater fish were at risk or extinct and 70 per cent of major marine fish stocks were either 'overfished or being fished at their biological limit.' The need for major changes in government policy was emphasized, with the then World Bank president James D. Wolfensohn stating that '[g]overnments and businesses must rethink some basic assumptions about how we plan and measure economic growth.' Again the necessary policy responses from national leaders were not forthcoming.

At a March 2006 UN meeting in Brazil, the Secretariat of the UN Convention on Biological Diversity released its *Global Diversity Outlook*

*2* report, which stated, 'in effect, we are currently responsible for the sixth major extinction event in the history of the earth, and the greatest since the dinosaurs disappeared 65 million years ago.'[60] Several months later, in July 2006, the premier journal *Nature* published a commentary in which 19 influential scientists reported that 'there is clear scientific evidence that we are on the verge of a major biodiversity crisis.' Currently threatened with extinction were 12 per cent of the world's 8000 species of birds (a decline which I have singled out for more detailed discussion), 23 per cent of mammals and 32 per cent of amphibians. Among trees, 25 per cent of conifers and 52 per cent of cycads (including palm trees) are at risk. Climate change might accelerate the decline by subjecting 'an additional 15 to 37 per cent of extant species to premature extinction within the next 50 years.'[61]

The scientific community is especially concerned about threats to biodiversity in the naturally alkaline oceans due to increasing acidification. Policy makers and the public should be equally concerned since acidic oceans produce less food and assimilate less greenhouse gases. As with the impact of acid rain on terrestrial ecosystems, again the culprit is global increases in atmospheric carbon dioxide, approximately one-third of which ends up in the oceans, where it 'lowers the concentration of carbonic ion, a building block of the calcium carbonate that many marine organisms use to grow their skeletons and create coral reef structures.'[62] In addition to corals (and the ecosystem services provided by coral reefs throughout the world), also threatened are innumerable calcifying species of plankton at the bottom of the food chain that nourish marine fisheries and mammals. According to one author of the July 2006 report, 'Impacts of Ocean Acidification on Coral Reefs and Other Marine Calcifers,' acidification 'is leading to the most dramatic changes in marine chemistry in at least the past 650 000 years.'[63]

Initiated in 1963, IUCN correctly advertises its Red List of Threatened Species as 'the world's most authoritative assessment of the Earth's plants and animals.'[64] IUCN's news release on the 2007 Red List emphasizes that the '[e]xtinction crisis escalates.' Summing up major analyses in 1996, 2000 and 2004, the 2007 report states that though estimates vary greatly, 'current extinction rates are at least 100–1000 times higher than natural background rates' and that though the 'vast majority' of extinctions since 1500 were on oceanic islands, 'over the last 20 years, continental extinctions have become as common as island extinctions.'[65]

There is little evidence of concern on the part of national governments. True, individual country presidents like France's Jacques Chirac have spoken out about the need to take action. But the passage and implementation of the necessary legislation has yet to occur. The 19 authors of the

94        *Global threats, global futures*

above-mentioned article in *Nature* believe that it is even harder to get significant action on biodiversity than on global climate change. 'By definition,' they argue, 'biodiversity is diverse; it spans several levels of biological organization (genes, species, ecosystems ); it cannot be measured by simple universal indicators such as temperature or atmospheric $CO_2$ concentration; and its distribution and management are more local in nature.' They illustrate their argument by noting that while the UN Framework on Climate Change led to setting up the influential Intergovernmental Panel on Climate Change, efforts based on the UN Convention on Biological Diversity have failed to establish a similar Intergovernmental Panel on Biodiversity to be linked to and funded by governments and, hopefully, to influence government policy.

**Bird Decline: Its Significance, Magnitude and Causes**

**Introduction**
Birds have been studied in greater detail that any other category of fauna including mammals. Bird guides now cover the birds of the world for the hundreds of thousands of people, including myself, for whom birdwatching is a hobby. Thousands keep life lists of birds seen, many of whom are willing to travel at considerable cost to add rare birds. I was present in the Pribilof Islands between Alaska and Siberia when a wind-blown Chinese mud heron arrived. Because it was the first of its kind identified in North America, within days serious birdwatchers arrived from the continental United States.

The most detailed information on bird decline comes from the United States, where the Audubon Society's Christmas Bird Count is called 'the longest running wildlife census in the world.' The Count began at the turn of the twentieth century and currently involves over 50 000 birdwatchers who enumerate from over 2000 locales all birds seen or heard during a 24-hour period. Data accumulated are combined with the North American Breeding Bird Survey, which was launched in 1966 as a joint effort of the U.S. Geological Survey and the Canadian Wildlife Service. Over 400 breeding species are counted during a June census, during which 3-minute counts of birds seen or heard are completed at half-mile intervals along 24.5-mile fixed roadside routes. Data are analyzed using statistical measures which the Audubon Society has begun to use.

The Audubon Society has also published a 2007 list of common birds in decline, a 2004 Habitats and Birds List and a 2002 Watch List. The 2007 list includes 20 common U.S. and Canadian species that have lost between 54 per cent and 82 per cent of their population since the mid-1960s. Included are species that have figured prominently in art and literature. The 2004 list assesses the status of 654 continental U.S. species, while the 2002 list deals with hundreds of species at risk in Continental North America, in Hawaii and the Pacific and in Puerto Rico and the Virgin Islands.

I have a very personal concern about the escalating global decline of the world's birds. By age ten I wanted to become a professional ornithologist, a decision that remained in force until I was 21. When I was 11, I began keeping a bird diary in which I carefully recorded each day the name and number of every bird species seen. While in secondary school, bicycle camping allowed me to expand my birding throughout New England, while my hitchhiking over 20 000 miles between the ages of 14 and 21 opened up the entire United States. On enrolling at Harvard I got a part-time job dusting the thousands of bird specimens in the laboratory of world-famous ornithologist James Lee Peters, who, at that time, was working on his monumental many-volume *Check List of Birds of the World*. By then, I was a proficient amateur ornithologist who could identify most birds in the Northeastern United States by song.

Professor Peters taught me how to prepare bird skins for study. To get specimens I remember shooting sparrows and pigeons by leaning out the third floor window of the Museum of Comparative Zoology. Peters wanted me to collect specimens of rosy finches and Louisiana water thrushes during the summer of 1951 when my wife Eliza, I and several mountaineering colleagues were planning an expedition in the then well-glaciated Selkirk Mountains of British Columbia. He helped me get the necessary collector's permit from Canadian museum authorities, and equipment including a 410 shotgun to be used with dust shot.

We established base camp at about 6000 feet and to hone my skills, I shot and prepared the skin of a Wilson's warbler. That experience ended my career as a professional ornithologist for I realized that it was one thing to enjoy watching birds in their natural environment but another to collect and study specimens. Peters, of course, was disgusted with my performance and hit the nail on the head by derogatively calling me just 'another bird golfer' – meaning a hobbyist whose enjoyment is to count as many different birds as possible during each outing.

But in my case, my love of wild birds was intricately related to their being a major part of whatever environment I was exploring. Hence Eliza's and my visit to the Pribilof Island of Saint Paul in the Bering Sea was not just for birding but also to explore the bio-cultural diversity of the island, which housed the largest community of Aleut Eskimo, whose ever-changing culture was adapted not just to the world's largest community of fur seals but also to the herding of introduced reindeer and the hosting of a large cannery with laborers from many countries of the Western Pacific and the Indian Ocean. Similarly our visit to Midway Island was not just to see nesting albatrosses and other sea birds but also to explore World War II history and the ecology of a mid-Pacific atoll.

It was in June 1994, four years before the risk of a human-initiated sixth world extinction was muted, that I first realized the magnitude of the accelerating decline in America's songbirds. I was in Montreal during a consultancy. Having been impressed in the mid-1980s by the variety of migrating birds on Mount Royal, whose wooded slopes rose 764 feet in the middle of the city, I started my early morning walk in anticipation of a repeat performance, during which I expected to hear and see a variety of warblers and thrushes as well as rose-breasted grosbeaks, scarlet tanagers and Baltimore orioles. But the woods were virtually silent and I saw few migratory birds. That experience I have since repeated on several occasions during spring visits to Washington DC, where I can no longer count on hearing the song of previously common wood thrushes and red eyed vireos.

The summer of 2008 was the first during which I saw no returning white-throated swifts from our home overlooking Eaton Canyon in Southern California. That puzzled me. This had been a previously common bird well-protected from predators by roosting and nesting in openings on cliffs and other exposed surfaces. Yet the white-throated swift was now on the Audubon Society's watch list following 'a significant long term decline across its U.S. and Canadian breeding grounds', with a total estimated population size of under 500000 birds. Why the decline? Rather than nesting site disturbance, 'a more likely broad-scale threat is from decreases in aerial insect abundance from habitat loss and use of pesticides.'[66] I was also troubled to find that the watch list also contained the Wilson's warbler – one of which I had killed in the Selkirks during my short career as a professional ornithologist.

### The significance of bird decline

Of the world's approximately 10000 species of birds, there are some to be found everywhere. There are, for example, penguins in Antarctica and ivory gulls in the Arctic. A minority of birds are also adaptable. English sparrows have thrived in cities for millennia, while kites and vultures have learned to find carrion in urban environments. White storks build their nests on housetops in villages, while migrating swifts seek protection in chimneys at night. Once rare, falcons nest on high-rise buildings. By pecking through foil caps, tits had learned by the 1960s to sip milk from bottles in English cities, a trait which they subsequently spread across the English Channel to Europe.

Many of the common birds in middle-class gardens, and even some not so common ones such as pileated woodpeckers in the United States, have expanded their range from other habitats. Included are thrushes in both tropical and temperate zones, and nectar feeders such as sunbirds in the tropics and humming birds in temperate habitats. Formerly uncommon white-tailed kites hunt small rodents that live in the grass fringes of North American highways.

Birds are significant indicators of environmental health or decline just because they exist everywhere. They are found in forests, coastal and inland scrub habitats, grasslands, marshes, marine and freshwater habitats and transitional habitats. Like a miner's caged canary to detect declining air quality, decline of birds is a warning signal that something is amiss with the habitat or habitats where they are found or that they are being over-harvested by people.

Birds also perform a variety of important services. They propagate fruit and other trees by scattering seeds at the time of eating or when they defecate. Nectar feeders pollinate a wide variety of flora – an increasingly important service today due to the decline of honey bees. They consume quantities of destructive insects, a service expected to become increasingly important as malaria-carrying mosquitoes and other disease-carrying insects expand their habitat because of global warming and as drought-weakened trees become more susceptible to insect damage. Birds also consume rodents and carrion – hence concern in India over the dramatic recent decline of vultures. Because birds are so easily seen or heard when present, their absence from previously inhabited areas may provide the first or early indication of polluting agents and disease. For example, cracking of eggs of nesting species alerted scientists to the risks of DDT, while the death of birds in the Northeastern United States signaled the introduction of West Nile virus.

### The magnitude of bird decline

People throughout history have been responsible for declining bird diversity in isolated habitats and for the extinction of individual species. Jared Diamond notes how the activities of Polynesian settlers were responsible for the extinction of five of the nine species of land birds (including three species of large pigeons) on Henderson Island as well as for exterminating 'colonies of about six of its species of breeding seabirds.'[67]

Based on archaeological excavations, it is estimated that Polynesian settlers had exterminated New Zealand's moas – large flightless birds double the weight of ostriches – approximately 700 years ago. More recently the activities of European sailors and settlers (including importation of rats and domestic animals) exterminated during the second half of the 17th century a large flightless land bird related to pigeons – the Dodo – that lived on Mauritius in the Indian Ocean. Still more recently, European settlers in Eastern North America were responsible for the extinction of the passenger pigeon; the last one of what had been one of the commonest birds in North America died in a zoo in 1914.

Today decline in birds is on a much larger scale and is global. According to Birdlife International's *State of the World's Birds 2004*[68] one of every eight bird species (12 per cent), totaling 1213 species, is globally threatened. Of these 179 face 'imminent extinction,'[69] with IUCN's Red List showing a more threatening trend since 1988. While the large majority of most threatened birds in the past were island species, birds in all global habitats are threatened today. The tropics contain the largest number simply because there are more species there than in the temperate and other global zones.[70]

Not all species are declining. The exceptions include generalist species which have been able to adapt to human-caused habitat change. Hence while European farmland birds have declined 28 per cent from 1980 to 2003 and forest birds 13 per cent during the same period, generalist species increased 28 per cent.[71] But such species are a small minority of the nearly 10 000 species identified throughout the world.

In his 2003 *Winged Messengers: The Decline of Birds*, Howard Youth pulls together a list of 'regional estimates of bird declines.' They include a 1994 study that 195 of 515 (38 per cent) of European birds were at risk; a 2002 study that estimated that 65 per cent of birds in the United Kingdom 'fell under some category of conservation concern,' and that 28 per cent of 403 species in North America 'showed statistically significant negative trends' and a 2001 study of Asian birds that showed that one-fourth (664) of the region's birds were 'in serious decline or limited to small, vulnerable populations.'[72] Declines are especially serious for certain families and categories of birds. All species of albatross 'are in alarming decline,' while a third of 346 species of the family Anatidae (which includes ducks, geese and swans) 'are in decline.'[73] In recent years seabirds 'have deteriorated dramatically compared to other groups.'[74]

**Causes of bird decline**

Major causes of bird decline include habitat loss, predation by invasive and native species, capture by people, the use of pesticides, pollution, disease and collisions especially during migration. Habitat loss is unquestionably the most serious threat, with Birdlife International estimating that 'bird populations have declined 20–25 per cent since pre-agricultural times as a result of conversion of natural habitats by humans.'[75] Especially significant is deforestation in the tropics. This not only removes the incredible floral and faunal biodiversity of forests, but replaces it with low-diversity private or public sector production systems or, in the case of illegal logging of parks and reserves, areas of disturbed and reduced biodiversity.

Examples of tropical deforestation are global. Four analyses of the IUCN Red List between 1988 and 2004 document that 'Asian birds have undergone the sharpest declines since 1988. This is largely due to rapid forest destruction in the lowlands of Borneo and Sumatra through the 1990s.'[76] In Malaysia, Papua New Guinea and Indonesia, species-diverse forests are replaced by single species oil palm and rubber plantations.

During 2005 I noticed how dry forests in China's Yunnan Province were being replaced by extensive rubber plantations, while Chinese and Vietnamese interests are clearing forests in Laos to grow still more rubber to supply their rapidly expanding economies. In Brazil, grasslands and forests are being converted to mono-cropping of soybeans and cattle ranching for export, and of sugar cane for fueling the country's demand for ethanol, which already fuels 30 per cent of the country's vehicles. In Middle America, deforestation accompanies coffee, banana and other fruit crop plantations.

In the United States habitat loss is primarily due to agricultural intensification and urban expansion. While the dwindling number of family farms was more apt to grow a variety of crops, agribusiness is more oriented toward mono-cropping. In California, agricultural intensification and urban expansion have been responsible for the loss of 90 per cent of the state's wetlands as well as for groundwater, surface water and atmospheric pollution.

Habitat fragmentation has also been a major cause of declining birdlife. Though best documented for forests, research during 2001 in Uganda indicates that fragmentation of papyrus wetlands is also associated with the decline of endemic species of birds.[77] The ratio of forest boundary area to the total forest area increases as forested areas are split into parcels by power lines, roads and suburban housing projects. Such increases open the smaller parcels to drying wind and sun effects, which increase the risk of fire. They also give predators more access to forest birds of all types.

While ground foraging and nesting species are the first to decline, other species are also at risk from climbers like raccoons and feral cats, while their nesting sites, eggs and young are at risk from cowbirds that lay their eggs in other birds' nests, and crows that devour eggs and young alike. In Washington DC, predation in fragmented woodlands most likely is responsible for the decline of wood thrushes that I have noticed over the years.

Accidentally or intentionally introduced alien predators include cats, rats, pigs and snakes. House and feral cats and rats have been the most destructive. It is estimated that cats, for example, are responsible for killing a billion birds a year in the United States.[78] Capture of rare and common cage birds for song, beauty and distinctive characteristics (as with parrots) has been a major cause of bird decline in China and in the tropics. South European villagers using nets catch and eat quantities of birds of all sizes as they migrate through mountain passes. Throughout the world, small boys can be found using sling shots and various types of snare to kill anything that flies or moves.

As poverty increases, bird life may vanish over large areas, especially during conflicts where hunger and guns co-exist. Among my lasting impressions since visiting war-ravished areas in Mozambique and Laos was the absence of bird life. Organized sport hunting, on the other hand, can play a major role in the conservation of game birds, as is the case in Canada and the United States through the activity of Ducks Unlimited, whose members play an important role in conserving and creating reserves for resident and migrating waterfowl. On the other hand, use of nets and long lines with thousands of baited hooks by commercial marine fisheries continues to kill unknown numbers of diving birds.

Use of agricultural and other pesticides, and of poisoned baits to kill predators of domestic animals, also continues to kill quantities of birds. DDT, which was taken off the U.S. market in the 1970s, is a well-known and controversial pesticide example (due to use for low-cost control of mosquito carriers of malaria). A more recent example concerns use of the crop pesticide carbofuran, which was removed from the market in 2006 by the U.S. Environmental Protection Agency and was believed to be responsible for the death of millions of birds since its introduction in 1967. Deaths included eagles and hawks, water fowl and migratory song birds. According to one EPA prediction, if a flock of mallard ducks was to feed in an alfalfa field treated with carbofuran, 92 per cent would die shortly.[79]

Oil spills are the most frequently quoted pollution source causing bird declines, while the West Nile disease is a recent example of a virus that kills large numbers of birds and can also prove fatal to vulnerable people such as these who are elderly or ill. Howard Youth mentions two major oil spills that together were estimated to have killed at least 350 000 birds and perhaps over 450 000.[80] One was the 1989 spill near Anchorage, Alaska, and the other a 1999 spill off the coast of France. Ten major spills are also mentioned along the South African coast, including one near a World Heritage Site.

The West Nile virus arrived in New York City in 1999. Since then it has spread across the United States to the Pacific Ocean. Research released in 2007 dealt with 21 species of birds that previous research had indicated were most susceptible to infection. Trends in their abundance were then analyzed over the 1980–2005 period. Results indicated that several of the species had declined 'almost 50 per cent across entire regions' and that only two of seven species 'showed signs of recovering after the intense epidemics in 2002 to 2003.'[81] One of the three study authors stated that

'with increasing globalization often come dire consequences for our native wildlife and their dependent ecosystems, including unprecedented movement of invasive pathogens around the world.'[82]
Tall buildings, lighthouses and transmission lines and towers are responsible for the death of unknown millions of birds, especially those that migrate at night and are attracted to or confused by bright lights or crash into structures under cloudy or foggy conditions. Howard Youth refers to one study's estimate that communications towers in the U.S. may be responsible for 40 million bird deaths a year, while another study documented a single case where 121 000 birds representing 123 species were collected dead under a single 960-foot high television tower between 1957 and 1994.[83]

## SUMMARY

Unfortunately throughout the world short-term economic profitability continues to trump long-term environmental security. Prior to its annual meetings in Davos, Switzerland, the World Economic Forum supports 'a series of public-private and multi-stakeholder projects to catalyze action on key global challenges.' One project involved the Global Governance Initiative (GGI) which submitted three annual reports (2004–2006). Their purpose, in the words of the Forum's Managing Director, was 'to assess the level of effort around the world on a range of internationally agreed goals in six areas,'[84] one of which was the environment. Over 40 experts, grouped into six task forces, were involved each year with support from the Swiss Agency for Development and Cooperation, the UN Foundation, Canada's Centre for International Governance Innovation and Nike Inc.
Each Task Force was instructed to assess progress in regard to two to four goals. The three environmental ones were to 'stabilize greenhouse gas concentrations in the atmosphere at a level that would prevent dangerous anthropogenic interference with the climate system,' 'reverse the loss of biological resources', and 'halve, by 2015, the proportion of people without sustainable access to safe drinking water and sanitation.'
The most recent sources of information were reviewed by the Global Governance Initiative, including the analysis of global ecosystem services and biodiversity in various Millennium Assessment reports. Their conclusion was that the world's effort during 2005 to deal with the three goals was given a low score of two on a zero to ten scale[85] versus three the previous year. On efforts to reverse the loss of biological resources, the world was given a score of zero. Low scores were due primarily to 'lack of serious high-level political commitment to global environmental goals.'[86] Efforts to significantly reduce greenhouse gases were 'uncertain at best' while no

serious frameworks were 'in place to ensure the integrity of the ecosystems
that human societies ultimately depend upon.'[87]

# NOTES

1.  See C. Petit, T. Scudder and E. Lambin (2001). 'Quantifying Processes of Land-
    Cover Change by Remote Sensing: Resettlement and rapid land-cover changes in
    south-eastern Zambia.' *International Journal of Remote Sensing.* **22** (17). Pages 3435–
    3456.
2.  Emmanuel N. Chidumayo (no date). 'Inventory of Wood Used in Charcoal Production
    in Zambia'. Available at http://www.worldwildlife.org/bsp/publications/africa/inven-
    tory_wood/inventory.html.
3.  Daniel M. Kammen and Debra J. Lew (1 March 2005). 'Review of Technologies for
    the Production and Use of Charcoal.' Renewable and Appropriate Energy Laboratory
    Report. Berkeley, CA: University of California, Berkeley.
4.  Robert Ballis, Majid Ezzati and Daniel M. Kammen (1 April 2005). 'Mortality and
    Greenhouse Gas Impacts of Biomass and Petroleum Energy Futures in Africa.'
    *Science.* **308**. Pages 98–103.
5.  Feysal Ahmed Yusuf (no date). 'Environmental Degradation in Somalia.' Available at
    http://www.cru.uea.ac.uk/tiempo/floor0/archive/issue26/t26art1.htm.
6.  Millennium Ecosystem Assessment (2005). *Ecosystems and Human Well-Being: Synthesis:
    Summary for decision-makers.* Washington DC: World Resources Institute. Page 1.
7.  *Ibid.* Page 2 (original emphasis).
8.  World Resources Institute (2000). *A Guide to World Resources 2000–2001: People and
    ecosystems: The fraying web of life.* Washington DC: World Resources Institute.
9.  *Ibid.* Page 6.
10. *Ibid.* Page 9.
11. World Commission on Dams (2000). *Dams and Development: A new framework for
    decision-making.* London: Earthscan. Page 73.
12. Millennium Ecosystem Assessment (2005). Op. cit. Page 2.
13. World Resources Institute. Op. cit. Page 11.
14. Examples which are not footnoted are taken from my 2005 *The Future of Large
    Dams.*
15. Asiatics Agro-Dev, International (Pvt) Ltd (2000). 'Tarbela Dam and related aspects
    of the Indus River Basin Pakistan.' A case study prepared as an input to the World
    Commission on Dams. Available at http://www.dams.org/docs/kbase/studies/cspk-
    main.pdf. Page 107.
16. K. Tinley (1994). 'Description of Gorongosa-Marrameu Natural Resource Management
    Area, Section 2: Ecological profile of the region (form, content, process).' Harare:
    IUCN Regional Office for Southern Africa.
17. E.O. Adeniyi (1973). 'Downstream Impact of the Kainji Dam.' In A.L. Mabogunje
    (ed.). *Kainji: A Nigerian man-made lake, socio-economic conditions.* Kainji Lake Studies.
    2. Ibadan: University of Nigeria Press for Nigerian Institute of Social and Economic
    Research.
18. Millennium Ecosystem Assessment (2006). *Marine and Coastal Ecosystems and Human
    Well-being: A synthesis report.* Nairobi: UNEP. Page iii.
19. *Ibid.* Page v.
20. World Economic Forum, Global Governance Initiative. 'Annual Report 2006'. Page
    31.
21. *Ibid.* Page 32.
22. UN Atlas of the Oceans (updated online). 'Mangroves.' Page 1. Available at http://
    www.oceansatlas.com/servlet/CDSServlet?status=ND0xMjczMCY2PWVuJjMzP.

23. UN Atlas of the Oceans (no date). 'Affiliated Ecosystems. Mangroves.' Page 1.
24. *Science Daily* (22 October 2007). 'Coral Reefs on Brink of Disaster.' Available at http://www.sciencedaily.com/releases/2007/10/071021225256.htm.
25. World Resources Institute. Op. cit. Page 12.
26. Millennium Ecosystem Assessment (2005). Op. cit. Page 2.
27. *Science Daily*. Op. cit.
28. *Ibid.*
29. Wilkinson, C. (ed.) (2004).'Status of Coral Reefs of the World: 2004.' Australian Institute of Marine Science. Executive Summary. Page 19.
30. See Will Nixon (1996). 'Rain Forest Shrimp.' *Mother Jones*. March/April. Available at http://www.motherjones.com/politics/1996/03/rainforest-shrimp.
31. *Ibid.*
32. Federico Páez-Osuna (2001). 'The Environmental Impact of Shrimp Aquaculture: Causes, effects and mitigating alternatives.' *Environmental Management*. 28 (1). Pages 131–140.
33. Helga Josupeit (January 2006). 'Aquaculture Production and Markets.'
34. Susan C. Stonich (2002). 'Farming Shrimp, Harvesting Hunger: The costs and benefits of the blue revolution.' *Backgrounder*. 8 (1).Winter. Available at http://www.foodfirst.org/en/note/54.
35. Guy W. Adema, Ronald D. Karpilo, Jr. and Bruce F. Molnia (no date). 'Melting Denali: Effects of climate change on the glaciers of Denali National Park and Preserve.' Our four-person expedition made first ascents of 12000 ft Mt Brooks, which is situated next to Mt McKinley (hence explaining why it had not been previously climbed) and 14000 foot Mt Mather. The Muldrow Glacier drains Mt McKinley (Denali in the Athabascan language) in what was renamed Denali National Park and Preserve after boundaries were expanded in 1980.
36. Except where otherwise indicated, the analysis that follows is taken from 'An Overview of Glaciers, Glacier Retreat, and Subsequent Impacts in Nepal, India and China.' WWF Nepal Program. March 2005.
37  Quoted in WWF Nepal Program (March 2005). An Overview of Glaciers, Glacial Retreat and Subsequent Impacts in Nepal, India and China. Page 2.
38. WWF Nepal Program. Op. cit. Page 39.
39. *Ibid.*
40. *Ibid.*
41. *Ibid.* Page iii.
42. *Ibid.* Page 3.
43. *Ibid.* Page 29.
44. *Ibid.* Page 38.
45. *Ibid.* Page 56.
46. United Nations Environment Programme (2007). 'Global Outlook for Ice and Snow.' Page 40.
47. United States Geological Service (March 2005). 'Changes in Stream Flow Timing in the Western United States in Recent Decades.' Fact Sheet 2005-3018.
48. United Nations Environment Programme (2007). Op. cit.
49. Washington and Oregon are the major producers of hydropower. Over a 50-year period during which Hamlet *et al.* modeled trends in snow water equivalent, the greatest decreases were in those two states as well as in Northern California; see A.F. Hamlet, P.W. Mote, M.O. Clark and D.P. Lettenmaier (2005). 'Effects of Temperature and Precipitation Variability on Snowpack Trends in the Western United States.' *Journal of Climate*. 18. Pages 4545–4561.
50. Steven W. Running (18 August 2006). 'Is Global Warming Causing More, Larger Wildfires?' *Science*. 313. Page 927.
51. Steve Chu at Stanford's second annual research symposium hosted by the Global Climate and Energy Project, 18 September 2006 as reported by Dawn Levy (25 October 2006). 'Forum Examines Technologies Aimed at Reducing Greenhouse Gasses.' Stanford Report. Stanford News Service.

52.  Peter Gleick as quoted by Jon Gertner (21 October 2007) in 'The Future is Drying Up.' *New York Times Magazine.*
53.  Bradley Udall and Gary Bates (January 2007). 'Climatic and Hydrologic Trends in the Western U.S.: A review of recent peer-reviewed research.' *Intermountain West Climate Summary.* Pages 2–8.
54.  Bradley Udall (6 June 2007). 'Written Testimony.' Hearings on Impacts of Climate Change on Water Supply and Availability in the United States before the Sub Committee on Water and Power. US Senate.
55.  United Nations Development Programme (no date). 'The Importance of Biodiversity.' Available at http://www.undp.org/biodiversity/biodiversitycd/bioImport.htm.
56.  *Ibid.*
57.  American Museum of Natural History (20 April 1998). Press Release (bold in original). The 400 scientists surveyed were members of the American Institute of Biological Sciences and belonged to a wide range of relevant disciplines. Five previous extinctions are believed to have occurred some 65 million, 208 million, 245 million, 354 million and 438 million years ago. Causes emphasize such natural phenomena as global freezing, volcanic eruptions and meteor collisions with the earth.
58.  Global Development Research Center. News Release (6 January 1998). 'Troubled Waters: A Call for Action.' Available at http://www.gdrc.org/oceans/troubled.html.
59.  Available at http://www.wri.org/wr2000.
60.  Secretariat of the UN Convention on Biological Diversity (March 2006), 'Global Biodiversity Outlook 2.'
61.  M. Loreau *et al.* (20 July 2006). 'Diversity without Representation.' *Nature.* **442**. Pages 245–246.
62.  UCAR – The University Corporation for Atmospheric Research (5 July 2006 Press Release). 'Report Warns about Carbon Dioxide Threat to Marine Life.'
63.  Richard Feely in UCAR (5 July 2006). *Ibid.* Page 1.
64.  IUCN (12 September 2007). 'Extinction Crisis Escalates: Red List shows apes, corals, vultures, dolphins are in danger.' see References for web address. The 2007 Red List contains 41 415 species. Of those, 16 306 'are threatened with extinction,' an increase of 188 species since the previous year. Reflecting the concern of marine biologists, species of corals were added for the first time.
65.  *Ibid.*
66.  Available at http://www.audubon2.org/watchlist/viewSpecies.jsp?id=216.
67.  Jared Diamond (2005). *Collapse: How societies choose to fail or succeed.* New York: Viking. Page 133.
68.  Birdlife International defines itself as 'a global partnership of conservation organizations that strives to conserve birds, their habitats and global biodiversity, working with people toward the sustainability in the use of natural resources.' Available at http://wwwbirdlife.org/worldwide/index.html. Currently the partnership operates in over 100 countries. Its information data base contains information on approximately 10 000 bird species.
69.  Available at http://www.birdlife.org/action/science/sowb/state/index.html.
70.  Columbia, with 1815, has the largest number of species, following by Peru (1703), Brazil (1622), Ecuador (1559) and Indonesia (1531). See Howard Youth (2003). 'Winged Messenger: The Decline of Birds.' Worldwatch Paper #165. Page 14.
71.  Available at http//www.birdlife.org/action/science/indicators/pdfs/2005_pecbm_indicator_update.pdf.
72.  Howard Youth (2003). Op. cit. Page 12.
73.  Available at http://www.birdlife.org/action/science/sowb/state/10.html.
74.  Available at http://www.birdlife.org/action/science/sowb/state/16.html.
75.  See Note 72. Op. cit.
76.  See Note 73. Op. cit.
77.  Ilya Maclean (no date). 'Effects of Edge Habitat Type on the Density of Papyrus Endemic Bird Species.' Available at http://www.britishecologicalsociety.org/articles/grants/reports/SEPG1925.

78. Howard Youth. Op. cit. Page 23.
79. American Bird Conservancy and Defenders of Wildlife Press Release (August 2006). 'Pesticide Ban Follows Millions of Bird Deaths.' Available at http://www.abcbirds.org/newsandreports/releases/060803.html.
80. Howard Youth. Op. cit. Page 30.
81. *Science Daily* (17 May 2007). 'West Nile Virus Threatens Backyard Birds.' Available at http://www.sciencedaily.com/releases/2007/05/070516161231.htm.
82. *Ibid.*
83. Howard Youth. Op. cit. Page 34.
84. The six major areas were Peace and Security, Poverty and Hunger, Education, Health, Environment and Human Rights.
85. The two lowest scores (2 in both cases) were given to Environment and Human Rights.
86. Global Governance Initiative (2006). Op. Cit. (note 20). Page 29.
87. *Ibid.*

*Source:* Fairey Air Surveys of Rhodesia

*Figure 1    Lusitu area land cover in 1954*

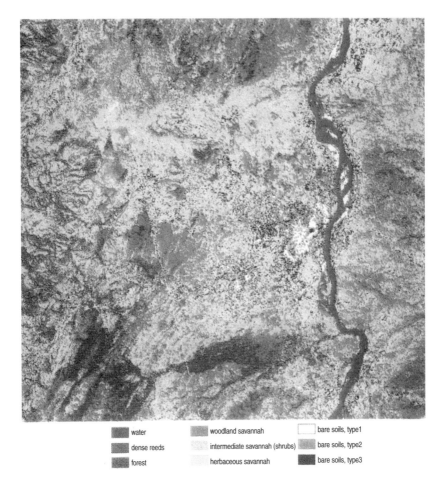

| water | woodland savannah | bare soils, type1 |
| dense reeds | intermediate savannah (shrubs) | bare soils, type2 |
| forest | herbaceous savannah | bare soils, type3 |

*Source:* Courtesy of Carine Petit and Erik Lambin

*Figure 2   Lusitu area land cover in 1986*

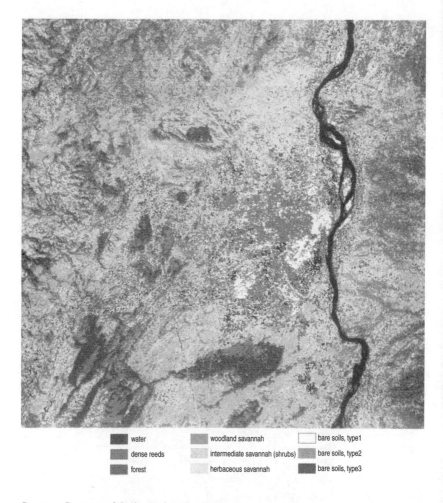

| | | |
|---|---|---|
| ■ water | ■ woodland savannah | □ bare soils, type1 |
| ■ dense reeds | intermediate savannah (shrubs) | bare soils, type2 |
| ■ forest | herbaceous savannah | ■ bare soils, type3 |

*Source:*   Courtesy of Carine Petit and Erik Lambin

*Figure 3    Lusitu area land cover in 1992*

*Source:* Scudder archives

*Figure 4   Toppled baobab tree and exposed roots*

109

Source:   National Regulatory Authority for UXO/Mine Action Sector in Lao PDR and the Nam Theun 2 Power Company Ltd

*Figure 5    U.S. bombing data (1965–1975): Nakai Plateau*

# 4.  United States

## INTRODUCTION

For the first time in human history, threats such as global warming have arisen that require global attention. The United States and China must take the lead as the leading old and new industrial countries. The United States remains the world's only super power, with China expected to reach super power status by mid-century. China also is leading late-industrializing countries such as India and Brazil to embrace equally destructive forms of capitalism.

The United States' and China's role in degrading the globe's natural resources is just one reason requiring their primary involvement. The characteristics of their institutions and citizens also mean that they have the potential to provide the necessary leadership. No other country rivals the United States' scientific and technological capacity and the drive of its citizens, a disproportionate number of whom are immigrants, to experiment with new ideas and to develop new enterprises. In China, science and technology were the keys to the four modernizations that were emphasized by Premier Deng Xiaoping in the late 1970s. By 2008 China had become 'the world's fastest-growing supporter of scientific R&D' with a budget surpassed only by that of the United States and Japan.[1] As for China's citizens, once their initiative was released by Deng's support for the household responsibility system (Chapter 5), the rural and small-town majority set a record yet to be surpassed in moving household economies in a single generation from subsistence agriculture to cash cropping and industry.

Since the 1970s both science communities have been linked through cooperative agreements. The first was the US–China Agreement on Cooperation and Technology, which was signed in 1979 by President Carter and Premier Deng Xiaoping. More recent are cooperative agreements in 2007 between the American Association for the Advancement of Science and Chinese scientists 'to address challenges that trouble the entire global research enterprise.'[2] Harnessing both countries' scientists in this way is an important start. This chapter deals with the United States and the next with China.

Many admirable characteristics contribute to the greatness of the

112          *Global threats, global futures*

United States. But this book deals with global threats that must be addressed and so dwells upon current weaknesses that make it difficult for the United States to play the necessary constructive role in living with, and addressing, global challenges. Weaknesses analyzed include political corruption of American democracy and the weakened economic position of its citizen majority, anti-intellectualism and fundamentalism, educational deficiencies starting at the preschool level, inadequate construction and maintenance of essential infrastructure, inadequate agricultural policies and an overemphasis on global domination through military preparedness and use. Taken together such constraints make America look increasingly like an inept third world country.

Nobel Prize winner in economics Amartya Sen links political freedoms, economic facilities, social opportunities, transparency guarantees and protective security in presenting a well-argued case for Development as Freedom. He gives pre-eminence to political freedoms and democracy, and while his audience is primarily late-industrializing nations, he emphasizes how inadequacies of practice apply 'also to some failings in more mature democracies as well.' His examples are American. Criticized are the 'exceptionally high' mortality of African Americans due to 'the extraordinary deprivation in health care, education and social environment' and the 'apathy and alienation' associated with 'the low percentage of voting in American elections.'

Sen wrote those words in 1999 in his aptly named *Development as Freedom*. Ten years later American democracy has weakened further. Political weaknesses include the increasing domination of corporate America's multinational corporations and associated lobbies at the expense of civil society and unions. It is significant that the American Academy of Arts and Sciences held its first joint meeting in 2007 with the American Philosophical Society, with attending members from the National Academies of Science, to remind Americans that knowledge for the foundation of a democratic society is a public good.[3] That something needed to be done became part of public debate during the 2008 presidential election and contributed to Barack Obama's election. Dealing with current fiscal, economic and political crises, however, continues to dominate the government's agenda and it remains to be seen if the current administration has the ability, influence and foresight to unify a partisan public to address the type of transformational changes required to deal with a wider range of global threats.

Economic weaknesses continue whereby the United States' government favors policies, including globalization, that benefit corporate America rather than the majority of its citizens. Social opportunities are weakened by a defective system of education and the decreasing social security of the

American public. The public's right to information is voided when government misuses statistics or lies about its actions as the George W. Bush administration did when justifying the pre-emptive war in Iraq.

## PERSONAL REFLECTIONS

Let it be understood from the start that despite my strong criticism of, and anger about the contemporary United States' failure to live up to its potential, I respect this country and its people. How that respect came about needs explanation for it influenced my choice of career and my ongoing belief that the U.S. and the world's greatest single resource is the variety and enterprise of people within each of many cultures.

I was fourteen when I began hitchhiking around New England. While birdwatching and mountaineering led to my love of the American landscape, it was hitchhiking that brought me in touch with the variety of American citizens and probably played a major role in my decision to switch from being a naturalist to the social sciences. My first major hitchhiking outside New England was two years later to visit a friend who lived near the Mississippi River.

The next two years I hitchhiked over 15 000 miles through more than 40 of America's 50 states. The summer of the first year, three of us worked in blister rust control in California's Yosemite National Park only long enough to enable us to finance more hitchhiking up and down the West Coast between Canada and Mexico. I also hitched back to the Midwest via the Grand Canyon and then back to Wyoming to lead a classmate up the Grand Teton. That December two of us hitched from Harvard Square to Florida. We were en route to Cuba for our Christmas holidays but the trip was aborted in the Florida Keys when an oil tanker ran into the pickup truck in which we were traveling. I was sitting on the floor of the truck bed when the tanker hit us a glancing blow from behind which sent me somersaulting over its cab onto the curbside with sufficient injuries to end the trip.

The next summer, I went west again and with a classmate worked for the Oregon Bureau of Public Roads. As at Yosemite, I was the youngest member of a crew of rugged individuals who taught me much about how the less privileged live. Weekends were spent hitchhiking around Oregon and Northern California, including climbs up Mount Hood and Mount Shasta.

During the summer of 1948 the content of my diary gradually changed. En route to Yosemite, experiences with new birds and landscapes dominated. Thereafter and during the summer of 1949 comments on people met and what they said, and on towns and cities increased. People of all ethnicities, classes and occupations either picked me up or accompanied me when I was not hitching. Most talked freely and often about personal concerns for they thought that they were with someone whom they would never see again. Some paid for my meals while others invited me to their homes. Their diversity ranged from criminals recently released from jail to bankers, one of whom loaned me money to get home from the Midwest when time was running out for returning to Harvard.

The sum of these experiences influenced my taking an anthropology course in my first semester at Harvard and later my shifting from the biological to the social sciences. My increasing respect for humanity every-where was especially influenced by three hitchhiking experiences. One night in August 1948 I was sleeping in a park in Needles, California, when I was awakened 'at about 1.30 in the morning by a pat on the shoulder. A Mexican stood over me, with two squatting on the grass behind him. We talked for a while until finally, putting on his hat, I entered a bar and bought with his money two bottles of cheap wine.' That entry in my diary was only one of many that made me aware of how people discriminate against each other.

In December 1948 prior to our accident on the Florida Keys, two of us were hitching near Miami, Florida when:

> a sedan crawled to a stop, occupied by a Negro family mostly sitting in the back. We clambered in front beside the driver, a lanky Negro with a hopeful face. He took great pleasure in introducing himself to us and in turn was equally happy when we gave him our names . . . We asked him about the Florida Keys; whether we would have a good time there, and about Havana. He answered in the affirmative, adding 'because you are white men.' We questioned him about his amusement facilities. No beaches, that is, public beaches, were open to him; only certain stretches along the ocean away from towns where the water was open to sharks, and the beaches were inferior. He continued to say that although freed in law from slavery, it amounted now to the same thing or worse for when the Negro tried to reap the rewards of freedom he found them few indeed.

I had a very different experience less than a week later while traveling home on a train after we were hit by the oil tanker. At the hospital where I was patched up:

> the doc said I had to get home. I caught the nine AM train out of Miami. After sitting in my seat for a while I found it hard to get up. It was that way all the way north. Sometimes it took me fifteen minutes to rise. The pus had come through my pants. In Jacksonville, I got out to buy some tangerines. The con-ductors and porters were changing here. I got back on. My wallet was gone. My ticket was gone. The [new] conductor said I had to get off the train . . . The lady behind me helped [search my seats] and gave me two dollars. The man across

the way gave me two more. Two other people supplied two more. I felt awful. They said they would pay my way if the conductor insisted on me getting off. I felt worse. I slumped down in my seat and thought and tried to go to sleep. I couldn't. It was a wonderful thing how people would help a stranger if he was in worse condition than they. Wonderful and strange . . . They helped me and I loved them for it. Yet they were ordinary people. It was heart warming. It showed a faint bond that still existed from man to man.

Moreover, one of the men who helped me was much worse off than I was. He told me how his recently deceased wife was in a coffin in the baggage car.

These various experiences occurred before I was 20. Since then they have been replicated many times over in more than 50 other countries in which I have lived for more than ten years. Such is my respect for the United States, however, that Eliza and I have no desire to live permanently in any other country. Nonetheless in recent years I have been both embarrassed and angered by the global policies and actions of the United States as well as by the inability of Democratic and Republican administrations to realize their potential for bipartisan leadership at home and abroad. The sections that follow deal with a wide range of national weaknesses that need be acknowledged and corrected.

# THE DECLINE OF AMERICAN DEMOCRACY

**Introduction**

I am not the only one who believes that U.S. democracy is in decline and that the political process is undermining the ability of citizens both in the United States and abroad to realize their potential and achieve their goals. Both political parties must share responsibility for weakening U.S. democracy over the past 30 years. Money and lobbyists have become increasingly important in influencing national elections and the voting records of individual politicians. Bipartisan leadership has suffered in part due to the shift to the right of the Republican Party since the 1960s and more recently the continuing anti-science influence of the Christian right on government policy. Polls have become more powerful in influencing politicians to devote their attention to being re-elected instead of providing national leadership. Meanwhile a confused public too often has been influenced by politicians and by pundit use of the media to vote against their own interests.

I have been especially influenced by two books in writing this section. One is Larry M. Bartels' 2008 *Unequal Democracy: The Political Economy of the New Gilded Age.* Bartels is a political scientist and the Donald E. Stokes Professor of Public and International Affairs at Princeton University. Bartels' conclusions that economic inequality has increased significantly over the past 30 years under Republican administrations is based on a six-year study involving statistical analysis where adequate data were available. When he began the study, his approach was 'as an unusually apolitical political scientist'[4] who had voted for Republican presidential nominee Ronald Reagan in 1984. By the end of the study he noted his surprise 'to discover how often and how profoundly partisan differences in ideologies and values have shaped key policy decisions and economic outcomes.'[5]

The second book is Peter Gosselin's 2008 *High Wire: The Precarious Financial Lives of American Families.* Gosselin is the national economics correspondent of the *Los Angeles Times.* Twice his writing has received journalism's annual George Polk Award. *High Wire* is a searing commentary, packed with family and individual case histories, of the toll on U.S. households in recent decades of the erosion of previous safety nets. The two books complement each other exceptionally well. Gosselin describes in detail the damage done to America's households while Bartels provides the analysis of why that damage is occurring and how it is adversely affecting U.S. democracy.

**The Corrupting of U.S. Democracy**

Corrupting the political process with money is legal in the U.S. and very influential in regard to policy making and policy implementation. It characterizes both the Democratic and Republican parties. The sums involved are astronomical. During the nominating phase of the 2004 presidential election, Republican candidate George W. Bush raised $274.7 million and the Democratic candidate raised $253 million. In the 2008 campaign, Democratic candidate Barack Obama raised $744.9 million and Republican candidate John McCain $346.6 million. Millions are also necessary for election to the Senate and the House of Representatives. In the 2008 election the total sum for all candidates for the Senate raised nearly $437 million and for the House of Representatives nearly $992 million.[6]

The money comes from companies, labor unions, other organizations and individuals for the purpose of gaining influence with candidates, political parties and federal agencies on issues of concern. Amounts spent by the hundred largest donors between 1989 and 2008 ranged from nearly $40 million to over $5 billion. Though each donor tends to prefer one party or another, in the large majority of cases funds are given to both parties with the amount reflecting which party is favored to win. The wealthiest donors use lobbyists to gain influence with candidates, Congress and federal agencies. Between 1998 and 2008 the number of lobbyists increased from 10 689 to 12 741 and the amounts they spent increased from $1.44 billion in 1998 to $2.81 billion in 2007.[7]

Convention costs for Democratic and Republican presidential nominees have been increasing much faster than inflation. In 1980 they were $1 million, in 1992 $8 million, in 2000 $56 million and in 2004 $142 million.[8] A major source of the money to cover expenses will be the business community. There were 52 corporations lined up to support the Republican 2008 convention and 80 for the Democrats'. Twenty-five of the 107 donors contributed to both conventions. A total of 107 donors has made over $98 million of federal election contributions since 2005 and spent over $721 million on lobbying the federal government.[9]

The nature of corporation contributions for the two conventions shows the dependence of each party on corporate America. Democrats attending their convention could expect reduced fare tickets from United Airlines and to be delivered to the convention from the airport by 'plush new vehicles donated by General Motors that run on fuel made from "waste beer" donated by Molson Corp Brewing Company.'[10] Microsoft's contribution of $4 million was divided between both conventions. AT&T also contributed to both conventions as did Northwest Airlines through a 15 per cent discount to all convention goers.[11]

**Unequal Democracy[12]**

Bartels starts his book on *Unequal Democracy* by referring to political scientist Robert A. Dahl's *Who Governs? Democracy and Power in an American City*. The city was New Haven in the late 1950s and Dahl concluded that political power was well dispersed. Since then Bartels' research shows that 'Economically, America has become vastly richer and vastly more unequal.' No question that technology has contributed to higher productivity and globalization has extended the economic reach of the U.S. Meanwhile the strength and clout of unions has weakened. But Bartels, after noting such factors, concludes that 'economic inequality is, in substantial part, a political phenomenon' since policies made and implemented under Republican administrations played a major role in how wealth was allocated.

Bartels' data show that the income growth of Americans in all percentiles improved significantly during 1947–1974 while the main gainers during 1974–2005 were more affluent Americans. The proportion of total income of the top 1 per cent more than doubled from Dahl's time from 10.2 per cent to 21.8 per cent. During the same period, the share of the top 0.1

per cent 'more than tripled from 3.2 per cent in the late 1950s to 10.9 per cent in 2005.'[13]

Income inequality grew much faster under Republican presidents between 1947 and 2005. As to who does not benefit, Bartels' analysis suggests that 'middle-class and poor families in the post-war era have routinely fared much worse under Republican presidents than they have under Democratic presidents. By this accounting, economic inequality in contemporary America is profoundly shaped by partisan politics.'[14] Conversely, 'the real incomes of middle-class families have grown twice as fast under Democrats as they have under Republicans.'[15]

The wealthy are more apt to be Republicans, and Bartels, based on a 1995 survey,[16] noted that 'almost three-fourths of the total value of campaign contributions reported . . . came from people in the top quarter of the income distribution.'[17] Such data, Bartels concluded, are 'consistent with the hypothesis that senators represented their campaign contributors to the exclusion of other constituents.'[18] Certainly senators have considerable leeway on deciding the values and issues they represent. Otherwise, how to explain the different voting records of two senators, one a Democrat and the other a Republican, who represent the same state? Moreover, Bartels' case for politicians being 'consistently responsive to the views of affluent constituents', and for an increasingly 'unequal democracy' over the past thirty years, is also supported by his conclusion that senators of both parties 'are entirely *un*responsive' to the views of 'those with low incomes'[19] in spite of the fact that significant numbers vote.

## The Erosion of Safety Nets for the U.S. Majority

### Introduction

In *High Wire*, Peter Gosselin writes about the increasingly precarious financial lives of U.S. families due to 'a shift of economic dangers from the broad shoulders of business and government . . . to the backs of working families.'[20] Those families include not just those without a primary and secondary school education but also college graduates with advanced degrees. All but the most affluent 'are in danger of taking steep financial falls from which they have a terrible time recovering; . . . the fraction of Americans facing this danger is on the rise and now constitutes a majority.'[21]

Increasingly at risk are jobs and employer-provided benefits such as pensions for retirement and health insurance. Government unemployment insurance is only short term and is available to a decreasing proportion of the unemployed. Causes of increasing financial insecurity are varied. Globalization is one cause, with the corporate sector in the U.S.

reducing employee benefits to remain competitive. Other causes include longer periods of retirement due to longer life spans, Bartels' increasingly unequal democracy and the weakening of labor unions.

**Jobs and income**
Job uncertainty is associated with globalization in part because expected employment benefits in the U.S. and elsewhere have not occurred. In the United States, 'there's a slowly growing consensus that yes, job tenure is declining; yes, the fraction of Americans with the same employer for ten or twenty years or more is going down; and yes, these changes have increased the chances that what once would have been a modest setback can now send a working person's fortunes plunging.'[22] On declining job security, Gosselin refers to a study by labor economist Henry Ferber that shows that those starting work in the 1990s spent half the time with the same employer as those whose working lives began in the 1940s and 1950s.[23] Not only has job loss increased since the 1980s, but job loss 'can occur not just in bad economic times but also in good ones.'[24]

Part of the problem is increased income volatility, with poor families 'subject to considerably larger fluctuations in income growth rates.' The real incomes of the poorest fifth of U.S. families declined in 20 of the 55 years between 1947 and 2005. Since 1951 the richest 5 per cent of families 'have experienced only one decline of 3 per cent or more in their real incomes.'[25] For the poorest of the poor, especially damaging has been a 45 per cent decline in the real value of the minimum wage between 1968 and 2006.

**Retirement pensions**
Approximately 10 per cent of the U.S. labor force has government jobs at federal, state, municipal and other levels. Ninety per cent have defined benefit plans from their employer that provide major health and retirement benefits. The percentage of private sector employees with defined benefit plans covering both health and retirement is much smaller. The percentage has also declined significantly during the past three decades because of 'a rapid shift from saving through employer-managed defined benefit (DB) pensions to defined contribution (DC) retirement savings plans that are largely controlled by employees.'[26] Thirty years ago approximately 40 per cent of private sector employees had defined benefit programs. By 2006 only 19 per cent had them.[27] Even some of America's largest companies are dropping DB programs and encouraging employees to take on responsibility for funding their own defined contribution plans, either by themselves or though their employer.

It is unrealistic and unfair to expect employees to have the interest and ability to invest on their own sufficient income to provide for a secure retirement. Even those who attempt to diversify and regularly review their portfolio may come up short. While researching *High Wire*, Gosselin asked a majority of Nobel Prize-winning, U.S.-based economists about their own retirement planning. He reports that many 'acknowledged slipping up, either by making faulty decisions or by failing to pay attention to their own retirement arrangements.' They included Harry Markowitz, who did the initial research showing the importance of asset diversification. Nobel Laureate Joseph E. Stiglitz, a former chief economist at the World Bank, told Gosselin 'If I only listened to myself . . . I would be considerably better off than I am today.'[28] The record for intelligent investment is even worse for other educated people, with Gosselin discovering that 'roughly half' of university academics and staff surveyed, including those at Harvard and Stanford, 'failed to make any decision about retirement at hiring.'[29]

**Health insurance**
As Americans live longer and medical expenses continue to rise faster than the cost of inflation, health insurance for all Americans has become a necessity which figured prominently in the speeches of Democratic and Republican candidates seeking the presidency in the 2008 election. According to the National Coalition on Health Care, 16 per cent (47 million) had no health insurance in 2005, while 'nearly 90 million people . . . spent a portion of either 2006 or 2007 without health insurance.'[30] Part of the problem is a reduction in health insurance by employers, with Gosselin noting a decrease from 68 per cent with medical insurance to 62 per cent since the year 2000. The situation is worse with smaller firms, where about 40 per cent provide no health insurance.[31] The proportion of such firms is growing so that in 2006 'a third of firms in the U.S. did not offer coverage.'[32] Even large firms are cutting back, with corporate leaders arguing that 'they can no longer compete with foreign firms that don't bear such costs.'[33]

Households without employer-sponsored health insurance are finding it increasingly difficult to afford or qualify for individual or family private health insurance policies. Premiums have recently been rising much faster than inflation. Health insurance companies also have become more selective in accepting who they will cover. In California, the state sued several of America's largest health insurance providers for dropping coverage on patients after they had been billed for major medical expenses.[34] In July 2008, for example, WellPoint Inc agreed 'to pay $11.8 million to settle claims from about 480 California hospitals that it failed to cover the bills of patients it dropped after they were treated.'[35]

**Unemployment insurance**

Government unemployment insurance currently is only for 37 weeks. It is a federal and state benefit program managed by the states. In 1999, before the 2000–2002 and 2007–2010 economic downturns, unemployment insurance only 'replaced 33 per cent of the average workers' lost earnings' according to a 2001 Issue Brief from the Economic Policy Institute. Hence 'benefits for a typical, or median, worker with children fall short of what a family needs to meet its living expenses.'[36] The situation was especially serious for single-parent families with two children under twelve. The authors calculated basic family monthly budgets in one metropolitan statistical area in all 50 states and Washington DC. The monthly income gap exceeded the monthly benefit in 47 of those 51 cities.[37] The situation is much worse, of course, for the majority of unemployed, who receive no unemployment benefits. That figure has increased over the years to 67 per cent in 2007.

# AMERICAN FUNDAMENTALISM

### Introduction

Chapter 2 included examples of efforts by the United States since its 1776 origin to export American values and democracy.[38] That approach was pursued at the expense of other cultures not just in other countries, but in the United States as well. Walter Russell Mead extends this characteristic to all Anglo-Saxons in his 2007 *God and Gold*, which analyzes why Britain and the U.S. have played the key role in the making of the modern world over the past three centuries. Chapter 2 also examined the increased influence of Christian fundamentalism on government policies in science and health under the George W. Bush administration. This section explores further American economic fundamentalism as well as fundamentalism in relation to ethnic minorities within the United States and to governments in other countries. The negative portrayal applies more to the political leadership of Democratic and Republican administrations than to the American public.

### Economic Fundamentalism

America's global, unregulated, free-market capitalism to a large extent underlies the current (2009) global economic and financial crisis. Too polite to be more specific, the November 2008 communiqué of the G-20 financial ministers and governors referred to advanced economies 'where the crisis came into being.' They also noted 'deficiencies in financial regulation and supervision in some advanced countries' as contributing to a crisis caused by 'excessive risk taking and faulty risk management practices in financial markets' and inconsistent economic policies.[39] The U.S. would have been the number one culprit if those economies and countries had been named.

A July 2008 issue of *The Economist* referred to the 'sorry state of American capitalism . . . The "Washington consensus" [Chapter 1, this volume] told the world that open markets and deregulation would solve its problems. Yet American house prices are falling faster than during the depression, . . . banks are collapsing, . . . credit is scarce, recession and inflation both threaten the economy.'[40] But because of globalization, that threat to the economy soon spread worldwide.

**Cultural and Political Fundamentalism within the United States**

Throughout U.S. history, dominant Anglo-Saxon politicians have ignored and denigrated the cultures of resident and immigrant ethnic minorities as well as their poverty. Treatment of Native Americans is a well-known example, as is treatment of African Americans and Chinese Americans, and, during the early stages of their assimilation, Irish and Italian Americans. Then there is the current 'fortress America' hysteria over illegal Hispanic immigrants. I have had ample opportunity to observe these characteristics during consultancies among the Navajo – America's largest population of Native Americans and one of its most impoverished ethnic minorities, with a current unemployment rate exceeding 30 per cent.

During the nineteenth century, Native Americans were forced onto inadequate reservations with no consideration of their cultural requirements; for the majority, high levels of unemployment remain there today. Many children were forced to attend government boarding schools where they were punished for speaking their indigenous languages. During the twentieth century, development-induced and other types of involuntary resettlement have disproportionately removed ethnic minorities from their rural and urban homes. The policy assumption that all they needed in compensation was the decent, safe and sanitary housing that the middle-class majority desires illustrates how little consideration was given to impacts on their different living standards, quality of life and cultures.

Examples include Native Americans displaced during the construction of dams. The U.S. Army Corps of Engineers commenced construction of the Garrison Dam on the Missouri River even before informing the Sioux Indians who lived in the future reservoir basin. The Corps also attempted to illegally acquire their reservation land; 90 per cent of it was inundated, with the reservoir splitting the Sioux into four different segments. No funds were provided for tribal development. Unemployment rates subsequently rose as high as 79 per cent, while 'many tribal members were driven into a life of despair in nearby urban centers.'[41]

Similar outcomes characterized the resettlement record of the U.S. Bureau of Reclamation. During the construction of the Grand Coulee Dam on the Columbia River, no proper census of the two affected tribes was completed. Subsequently that dam stopped the migration of salmon which were central to each tribe's cultural and economic welfare in addition to providing the basis of the people's diet.[42] Two towns required relocation but received no services 'because Congress did not provide Reclamation with the authority to finance new water, electrical or telephone services.'[43] As for resettlement required by Tennessee Valley Authority dam construction, that disproportionately dis-benefited Black Americans.[44]

Forced resettlement of Native Americans was legislated by the U.S. government as recently as the 1970s as the solution to a land dispute between the Hopi and the Navajo Indians in spite of more culturally and developmentally appropriate options.[45] Between 1974 and 2005 that decision forced over 11 000 Navajo and several hundred Hopi to move; the largest forced removal of rural Americans since Japanese Americans were incarcerated during the Second World War.

As I had predicted, the magnitude of the task, the number of Navajo involved, the expected suffering, the higher death rate and the financial costs were greatly underestimated. Numbers moved were three to four times initial estimates and a program that was supposed to be implemented over several years at a cost of $40 million had cost $483 million by 2005.[46] Yet, with the exception of several hundred Navajo resettled as a group in a new Navajo administrative unit, the large majority of families are worse off today because emphasis was on replacement housing as opposed to a culturally relevant development program for both tribes. In 2005, as resettlement dragged on, Senator John McCain, subsequently the Republicans' 2008 nominee for the U.S. Presidency, introduced a bill to terminate the resettlement process. No funding was included to address the economic and cultural impoverishment that the federal program had caused up to that date.[47]

Urban renewal throughout the United States also is often at the expense of ethnic minorities. Herbert Gans describes such a situation when urban renewal in Boston displaced an Italian community in the late 1950s.[48] Again the emphasis of government-approved resettlement policies was on housing for individual families with virtually no attention paid to rebuilding former neighborhoods or helping households re-establish previous businesses or economies.

124 Global threats, global futures

## International Cultural and Political Fundamentalism

In his book *Spreading America's Word*, Carrington gives example after example of attempts by the U.S. government to export American values and democracy overseas. The worst cases involved efforts by the CIA and other government agencies to destabilize other governments. Examples from the 1950s included Guatemala and Iran. In neither case were the long-term interests of the United States served: 'In Guatemala, class lines became more harshly drawn. In Iran, religious lines hardened.'[49] One case not covered but with which I am familiar involved the U.S. 'illegal' or 'secret' war in neutral Laos, which, if carried out by a weaker government, could have been considered a crime against humanity. Between the second half of the 1960s and the early 1970s, more U.S. bombs were dropped on Laos than in the Pacific and European theatres during the Second World War. According to one estimate, around 3500 villages in areas controlled by 'the enemy' 'were partly or totally destroyed.'[50] The large majority were inhabited by ethnic minorities.

Since 1997 I have been visiting Laos as a member of a World Bank-required independent panel that advises the government on the environment, resettlement and other socio-economic issues associated with the country's premier national development project. This is the multipurpose Nam Theun 2 (NT2) Dam that affects two major river basins in the central portion of the country. Ninety-five per cent of the power generated will be sold to Thailand, with the foreign exchange received placed in a special fund for national poverty alleviation in Laos.

The project area extends from the mountainous border with Vietnam to the Mekong River, which is the border between Laos and Thailand. Completed in 2008, the NT2 dam is sited on a high plateau within 40 kilometers of the Vietnam border. During the Vietnam War (mid-1950s to 1975), the plateau included over 50 kilometers of the Ho Chi Minh Trail that the North Vietnamese used to transport supplies and troops into South Vietnam. On our first visit in January 1997, the absence of singing birds, similar to what I noted at the end of the civil war in Mozambique, was an eerie reminder of the war.

The area bombed day and night included over 100 villages and one small town inhabited by thousands of people belonging to over ten different ethnic minorities (Figure 5). The concentration of bomb data traces the Ho Chi Minh Trail. Where it crossed the Nam Theun River in the upper left-hand corner, two villages were obliterated.

Though U.S. policy was supposed to minimize civilian deaths, little effort was made to implement that policy. Reminders of the war were everywhere. They included bomb craters and bomb casings as well as unexploded ordinance. Villagers still collect war debris to sell as scrap. Some have used the casings of 500 pound bombs as containers for planting onions and flowers, while the casings of cluster bombs, called bombies in Laos have been fashioned into paraffin burning lamps. Laos's National Unexploded Ordinance Programme (UXO Lao) estimates that 270 million cluster bombs were dropped by American aircraft. One-third are estimated not to have exploded. They remain a major threat to villagers today.

On arrival at the NT2 project guest house we were shown an unexploded bombie at the base of a nearby tree. On another occasion I was invited to detonate one from a distance since the casing is designed to fragment into sharp pieces of shrapnel intended to travel hundreds of yards. Because the danger continues indefinitely, the main victims, as with landmines, are civilians. For that reason in May 2008, 111 nations signed a treaty outlawing manufacturing of cluster bombs and stipulating stockpile destruction within ten years. The United States was not a signatory, with a State Department spokesman reported to have said that cluster bombs are 'absolutely critical and essential' for continued U.S. use.[51]

UXO removal has become a major financial cost of preparing NT2 project areas, including all areas that will be used by resettled and other affected villages. In April 2008, for example, a $451 200 contract was signed to remove UXO from 7900 hectares of reservoir drawdown area that would be used for resettler agriculture and livestock management.

How did such unacceptable U.S. military involvement in a neutral Laos come about? Laos, under the Royal Lao Government, was unfortunate in receiving its 1953 independence from France at the time of the Cold War between the United States and the USSR. 1953 was also the year that John Foster Dulles, 'who brought an almost religious fervour to his task of saving the Free World from Communism,' became U.S. Secretary of State.[52] The U.S. soon became Laos's principle international donor, with development aid causing 'corruption and unwarranted growth in the power of the military.'[53] That increasingly alienated the Lao Communist Party (the Pathet Lao), which was one of three Lao factions competing for dominance, the other two being the Royalists and, in between, the neutralists.

Failing efforts during the next ten years to form a viable coalition government periodically led to civil war. United States support for the Royalists, and especially their strongest general, Phoumi Nasavan, who had his own political ambitions, undercut efforts to form coalition governments due to strong U.S. opposition to including, in any fashion, the Pathet Lao.[54] Throughout the 1950s and early 1960s, U.S. military assistance to the Royalists, a Hmong militia and Thai mercenaries, was provided through the CIA and military advisers in civilian clothes with air support from the CIA-funded Air America.[55] The Pathet Lao were supported by supplies and troops from North Vietnam.

In July 1963 international pressures led to the Geneva Treaty that declared Laos's neutrality and stipulated that all foreign troops be withdrawn. The United States largely complied. The civil war soon resumed, however, with the U.S. State Department's March 2008 Profile on Laos stating that 'a growing American and North Vietnamese military presence drew Laos into the second IndoChina war . . . For nearly a decade, Laos was subjected to extremely heavy bombing as the U.S. sought to interdict the portion of the Ho Chi Minh Trail that passed through eastern Laos.'[56]

Since that time the United States has never offered an apology to the government and people of Laos or funded a major program of reparations. Indeed, inter-government relations remained cool until 1982, with full diplomatic relations delayed until 1992. Largely through the effort of the then U.S. Secretary of State Colin Powell, normal trade relations were finally established by both governments in 2004 with a Bilateral Trade Agreement initiated in 2005. In 2007, U.S. financial assistance to Laos was less than $12 million, with the emphasis on the search for Americans Missing in Action (MIAs) in Laos and counter-narcotics activities – both programs of primary interest to the United States rather than Laos.[57] Clearance of unexploded ordinance is also mentioned along with other activities. The U.S., however, is not a major UXO donor and to the best of my knowledge no U.S. funds have been involved in the NT2 project, including in the multi-million dollar UXO removal program.

# AN INADEQUATE SYSTEM OF EDUCATION STARTING AT THE PRESCHOOL LEVEL

**Introduction**

The U.S. system of higher education is by far the world's best. Eight U.S. universities are ranked among the world's top ten, 17 among the top 20 and 37 among the top 50. The United Kingdom, the second ranked country, has five while Canada and Japan each have two. Russia has one university in the top 100 and China, India and Brazil none.[58]

Formal education, however, does not start in universities and colleges. It starts with the presence or absence of preschool education. The United States, like most countries, does not have a national policy for preschool education in spite of a growing public awareness of the developmental importance of the first few years of childhood and research that shows early childhood education to be economically and socially cost-effective.[59]

**School Infrastructure**

The American Society of Civil Engineers (ASCE) is the country's premier organization of civil engineers who 'build the nation's infrastructure.'[60] In 2005 and again in 2009, ASCE's Infrastructure Report Card gave America's school infrastructure a grade of poor (D). The 2009 report stated that according to the best estimate of the National Education Association, the cost 'to bring the nation's schools into good repair is $322 billion.'[61] That is a shocking commentary on the state of America's schools.

Funding school infrastructure is largely a state responsibility, with conditions varying from one state to another and within states from one school district to another. That situation makes assessment difficult. Though the public is generally supportive of bond issues to fund school facilities, 'without a clear understanding of the need, it is uncertain whether schools can meet increasing enrollment demands.'[62]

**Preschool Education**

For over 60 years my wife has pursued her career in early childhood education as a preschool and college teacher, a researcher in Egypt and Zambia and, more recently, working one-on-one with special needs children. Her interest and knowledge has been a major influence on my thinking about why a global approach to preschool education is necessary. More specifically, her interest led to our joint support of Caltech's pioneering Children's Center at Caltech, which I describe as a model for international replication in Chapter 7.

The Rand Corporation published results in 2005 of a study of early childhood interventions (2–5 years) based on a detailed analysis of 15 soundly evaluated programs which followed children at least until they began kindergarten. Some followed preschool students into adulthood and had sufficient time-series data to allow scientific analysis of longer-term impacts.[63] The study produced several important conclusions. One was that 'a sizeable fraction of children face risks that may limit their development in the years before school entry.'[64] Four risks were emphasized for children: living in poverty, living in single-parent homes, having a mother without a high school education and having parents who don't speak English at home.

Nearly 50 per cent of U.S. children have one of those four risk factors: 20 per cent of those under six live in poverty as do 53 per cent of those 'living in a female-headed household, 39 per cent for African-American children, and 32 per cent for Latino children.'[65] Overall 16 per cent of U.S. children under six have two or more risk factors.

A second conclusion was that early childhood disadvantages not only adversely affect school readiness but can persist thereafter. School readiness was broadly defined to include cognitive skills as well as skills associated with 'socialization, self-regulatory behavior, and learning approaches.'[66] Again it was the children from disadvantaged households whose knowledge and social capacities were lower, and again longer-term studies indicated that such liabilities 'persist and even widen as children progress through school.'[67]

Third, early childhood education in a few studies also had benefits for parents, especially when specifically targeted. Benefits for their children included 'cognition and academic achievement, behavioral and emotional competencies, educational progression and attainment, . . . social welfare program use, and labor market success' as well as dealing with child maltreatment, health, delinquency and crime.[68] In each category, except social welfare program use, the resulting benefits in a majority of the programs were statistically significant. Though some benefits were found to fade with time, others can be 'longer lasting gains in educational progress and attainment, labor market outcomes, dependency and pro-social behaviors.'[69]

Fourth, and important for national policy makers, favorable impacts of such programs on children can provide economic benefits not just to the participants but also to government and society. Seven of the 20 studies had sufficient time-series data for cost-benefit analysis – 'the returns to society for each dollar invested extended from $1.26 to $17.07.'[70] Programs targeted at the most vulnerable were 'likely' to have greater economic benefits. Though few in number, they were more cost-effective than those dealing with less disadvantaged children – a critically important point for future educational policy. One home visiting program, for example, had greater benefits for more vulnerable mothers. In that case 'the return for each dollar invested was $5.70 for the higher-risk population served but only $1.26 for the lower-risk population.'[71]

**Child Wellbeing**

The United Nations Children's Fund (UNICEF) believes that '[t]he true measure of a nation's standing is how it attends to its children – their health and safety, their material security, their education and socialization, and their sense of being loved, valued and included in the families and societies into which they are born.'[72]

According to UNICEF's 2007 overview of child wellbeing, the United States ranked next to last among 20 rich countries.[73] The UNICEF study involved six themes for measuring and evaluating child wellbeing. They were: material wellbeing; health and safety; education; peer and family relations; behaviors and risks; and young people's subjective sense of their own wellbeing. The United States ranked 12th on educational wellbeing, 17th on material wellbeing and last on health and safety, family and peer relations and behaviors and risks (subjective wellbeing was not measured). Included in the shocking record of the U.S. on children's health and safety is the inadequate training and numbers of teachers to deal with special needs children and the tendency – with uncertain but worrisome long-term impacts – to over-medicate disruptive behavior in children rather than to deal with its causes.

While child mortality rates range from under three per thousand in Iceland and Japan at the top of the list, in the United States, as in Hungary and Poland, they are over six per thousand. UNICEF assumes that a society that reduces child mortality below five per thousand, 'is clearly a society that has the capacity and commitment to deliver other critical components of child health.'[74] In UNICEF's and my opinion, the U.S. does not. Moreover, among 25 OECD countries, the U.S. is second from the bottom in regard to infant mortality rate and, for those under the age of 19, deaths and accidents per 100 000, as well as fourth from the bottom in regard to low birth weight.

As for the educational achievement of 15 year olds in reading, math and scientific literacy, the U.S. is fifth from the bottom of the 25 richer countries; it is third from the bottom in the percentage of OECD children aged 15–19 who remain in full- or part-time education. As for family and peer relations, OECD data on 21 countries has the U.S. second from the bottom, and it was at the bottom for 'percentage of young people living in single-family homes.' Also at the bottom is the percentage of young people aged 11, 13 and 15 'living in stepfamilies,'[75] a situation reflecting America's high incidence of single-mother pregnancies and high divorce rate.

A major problem with the U.S. public school system is that too little attention is paid to primary and middle school and too much attention to trying to play catch-up with twelfth grade seniors. By 2007, 24 states required secondary school exit exams and more were planning to phase them in. My state of California was one of the 24. In 2006, 91 per cent of California students passed the exit exam. That looks pretty good except that the exam is 'pitched at a grade 8 level in math and a grade 10 level in English Literature.'[76] Furthermore while students begin taking the exam in 10th grade, at that time only 74 per cent of the total number of students passed math and only 49 per cent of those for whom English was a second language.

To improve results, the California legislature passed two recent laws which target funding only on 12th grade students who have yet to pass the exam and on two further years of help for those who did not graduate because they failed the exam. A 2008 report based on a study of the San Diego school system emphasized why that approach is a mistake. The study notes, for example, that very few seniors who failed in 2005–2006 're-took the exam in 2006–2007, and only 3.1 per cent passed.' The most important finding, however, was that how students perform in the fourth grade can predict whether they will pass or fail the exit exam. Academic grade point average in grade 4 and especially grade 9 is the best predictor of results on the exit exam. In grade 4, English language learners (EL) such as Hispanics 'are just as likely as others to pass the exam – but grade 9 EL students are not.'[77]

Clearly far more emphasis on both mathematics and English literature should be required in pre-primary, primary and middle school. As for mathematics alone, special emphasis on algebra is essential in middle school according to an expert panel assembled by the Department of Education in 2007. One conclusion was that 'algebra is a gateway course for high school mathematics; without mastering algebra, a college degree in science or engineering is impossible.'[78]

# INADEQUATE CONSTRUCTION AND MAINTENANCE OF ESSENTIAL INFRASTRUCTURE

## Introduction

The U.S. is a failing third world country as far as its infrastructure is concerned. Periodically the American Society of Civil Engineers (ASCE) monitors the condition of 16 types of infrastructure. Those dealt with in this section are dams and roads.

In its 2009 report card the ASCE gave the U.S. an overall grade of D for the condition of its infrastructure. The grade for dams was D in both 2005 and 2009 and the grade for navigable waterways D− in both 2005 and 2009. The grade for roads dropped from D to D−. ASCE's 2009 update estimated total investment needs over a five-year period at $2.2 trillion.[79] In my state of California, the *Los Angeles Times* reported in June 2008 that more than 25 per cent of the state's nearly 50 000 miles of road were 'considered in disrepair,' while in Los Angeles county and the Inland Empire the records of the California Department of Transportation showed that 'about 30 per cent of the highways are in disrepair – most suffering from major structural distress.'[80]

**Dams**

Estimates of the number of dams within the United States vary according to their height and storage capacity. The National Inventory of Dams estimates that there are 75 000 that have 'an environmental consequence'[81] in that together they alter the natural flow of all of America's major rivers. Many, perhaps over 50 per cent, were built at least 50 years ago. ASCE estimates the total number of dams of all sizes at over 85 000, of which over 4000 are deficient and include '1,819 high hazard potential dams.'[82]

No one knows how many of the tens of thousands of smaller dams are unsafe. Part of the problem is that monitoring the condition of, and relicensing 95 per cent of the nation's dams is a state rather than federal responsibility.[83] Unfortunately many states have inadequate technical and financial capacity to do the job. Moreover, no federal organization in the United States has the scientific, engineering and technical capacity to remove dangerous dams. In 2002–3 I served on a U.S. Natural Research Council Committee to assess for Congress the U.S. Army Corps of Engineers' methods of analysis and peer review for water resources project planning. My suggestion that the Corps' future should focus more on dam safety and the science and engineering of dam removal than on new construction never made it into the final report.

The destructive capacity of a large dam is awesome. Between 1900 and 1995 five large dams have burst in the United States.[84] I live within 50 kilometers of where the one causing the most fatalities, California's St Francis dam, collapsed about midnight in 1928. That dam was nearly 60 meters high with a storage capacity of up to 47 million cubic meters. The flood released was estimated to be over 35 meters high as it swept down the San Francisquito Canyon and then widened to approximately three kilometers before reaching the ocean over 100 kilometers away. The number of people killed is unknown since bodies were swept out to sea and because there were an unknown number of immigrant farm workers living in the canyon. Estimates range from 400 and to over 650. En route to the ocean the flood swept through five towns.

The ASCE report card only deals with the state of current dams. It is not intended to cover such issues as the adverse impact of dams on U.S. river systems including wetlands and deltas, the research and literature on how such infrastructure as dams and levees increases the risks of downstream flooding and destruction, and government policies.

The United States has no comprehensive water resources policy. Rather, water resource development is dominated by the Army Corps of Engineers and the Congress. The Corps, though under the Department of Defense, in effect reports to the Congress, which allocates its annual budget. The relationship is close since the Corps' activities are largely funded as 'pork barrel' water projects of individual members of Congress. 'Pork barrel' projects are intended to benefit each member's home constituency and are attached as usually unrelated 'earmarks' to other legislation. The emphasis of both Congress and the Corps is on the construction of individual and largely unrelated projects to provide jobs and political capital, and is often at the expense of the environment.

### Roads

As with water resources, the United States has no national road policy in spite of having the largest road network in the world. The major exception is the Inter-State Highway System, which connects cities in 49 of America's 50 states. At the time of its 50th anniversary in 2006, it was 75 000 kilometers long and it contributes a very small fraction to the total length of the nation's roads.

Notwithstanding the inter-state system's national importance, it took exceptional circumstances and efforts to legislate and fund it. The key backer was Republican President Dwight D. Eisenhower, who wanted a road system which could 'meet the demands of catastrophe or defense, should an atomic war come.'[85] His difficulties in getting a Democratic Congress to legislate the system were solved only after a Democratic congressman proposed 'a dedicated highway trust fund, financed mainly by the federal tax on gasoline.'[86]

According to ASCE's Report Card 2005, 'America has been seriously under-investing in needed road and bridge repairs.' Indeed, while use increases significantly, 'the nation is failing to maintain even the current substandard conditions.'[87] Current annual spending level for improvements is $70.3 billion versus an 'estimated $186 billion needed annually to substantially improve the nation's highways.[88]

## U.S. MILITARISM

### Introduction

This section draws primarily on the writing and conversations of Chalmers Johnson and especially on his 2006 *Nemesis: The Last Days of the American Republic*, two 2004 interviews with Nic Paget-Clarke for *In Motion Magazine* and a series of interviews between 2004 and 2007 with Harry Kreisler, Executive Director of the Institute of International Studies at the University of California (UC), Berkeley. I include it to show that the unacceptable activities, impacts and reach of American militarism that I have observed in Laos are not an isolated example.

Educated at UC Berkeley, Chalmers Johnson was a member and former Chair of that university's Department of Political Science between 1962 and 1988. In 1988 he joined UC San Diego's new Graduate School of International Relations and Pacific Studies, where, as at Berkeley, he held an endowed chair. He retired in 1992 and co-founded in 1994 the Japanese Policy Research Institute in Washington DC, of which he is currently president.

While at Berkeley, Johnson considered himself a Cold Warrior who supported the Vietnam War and considered the Soviet Union a 'genuine menace.' He also gave advice as a consultant to the U.S. Central Intelligence Agency over a six-year period on the Sino-Soviet dispute and other issues. After the collapse of the Soviet Union in 1991, he expected that the United States would disarm as it did after the Second World War. As Johnson explained to Paget-Clarke in a 2004 interview, it was the Soviet Union's

> very considerable military potential that was the entire justification for our Cold War deployments, our bases spread around the world, the secret intelligence agencies, all of this . . . We should have demobilized the armed forces very considerably. We should have re-oriented the country to stress civilian needs . . . Instead our government turned almost instantly to trying to find a replacement enemy in order to continue to justify the huge Pentagon and its military-industrial complex: China, terrorism, drugs, even instability . . . This raised for me an analytic question. Was the Cold War, in fact, a cover for a more basic American imperial project, going back to World War II, to replace the British Empire as the global hegemon.[89]

Johnson concluded that the answer was 'yes'. That led to three books to warn the American public: *Blowback: The Cost and Consequences of American Empire* (2000), *The Sorrows of Empire: Militarism, Secrecy and the End of the Republic* (2004), and *Nemesis: The Last Days of the American Republic* (2006).

Basic to Johnson's concern is his conviction that empire and democracy are incompatible. In interviews he more than once refers to George Washington's farewell address, in which, in Johnson's words, Washington 'warns about the threat of standing armies to liberty, and particularly republican liberty'[90] and to Dwight Eisenhower's farewell address in which the President warned Americans about the danger posed by the 'military-industrial complex.'[91]

U.S. militarism also lends itself to corruption both in the military-industrial complex and in Congress. In Johnson's words, 'Certainly, there are huge corporate vested interests in the military-industrial complex and in the Pentagon. But these corporate interests are probably closer to state socialism than anything that is to be called capitalism because these corporations have only one customer. There is very little competition among them.'[92] In 2004, as an example, over $10 billion for missile defense in the Defense Appropriations Bill was assigned to the Missile Defense Agency in the Pentagon, which consults with four manufacturers on how the money should be spent; 'to say that this is open to corruption is just perfectly obvious.'[93]

Where Congress comes in is on how to allocate the Defense Facilities budget, which is separate from defense appropriations. Building and maintaining bases subject to Congressional oversight is expensive. Currently the ranking Democratic and Republican members of the Subcommittee for Military Construction, Veterans Affairs, and Related Agencies are from California and Texas – 'the states with the largest number of military bases.'[94] Members of the House and the Senate use earmarks, as with Army Corps of Engineers' projects, to benefit military bases in their constituencies.

### The Facts about U.S. Militarism

#### Introduction
Johnson defines American militarism as 'corporate interest in a military way of life. It derives above all from the fact that service in the military forces is, today, not an obligation of citizenship. It is a career choice . . . Standing behind it [the career choice] is the military-industrial complex.'[95] Incredible as that may seem, in support of the military the United States spends more 'than all other nations on earth combined.'[96] That money supports over half a million troops, contractors, and dependents stationed in military bases in over 130 countries.

#### The defense budget
The defense budget exceeds that for all other national expenses including social security. Though the Bush administration military budget request for fiscal year 2008 was six billion less than the $613 billion requested for social security,[97] Johnson emphasizes that the defense budget submitted to Congress is only 60 per cent of the total defense budget. The existence of the other 40 per cent, which includes intelligence budgets, is a secret kept from the public and Congress, contrary to the first Article of the Constitution, which requires an annual report to the public on how their tax money is spent. That report was stopped during the Second World War and has never been reinstated even though the Constitution 'gives Congress the power of the purse, the power to supervise.'[98] Some unlisted

bases are disguised by claiming that they are entirely staffed by personnel from the country in which they exist; some Royal Air Force bases in England, actually staffed by Americans, are an example. Not counted in 2004 were bases in Iraq, Israel, Afghanistan and Kyrgyzstan.

**Military bases**

Johnson's designation of the U.S. as an empire rests on the global existence of U.S. military bases which 'are the equivalent of what used to be colonies.'[99] Official accounting of bases outside the United States varies from 737 to 860. That accounting is 'incomplete, omitting all our espionage bases and a number of others that are secret or could be embarrassing to the United States.'[100]

Johnson's concern with U.S. international bases began in 1996 when the governor of Okinawa asked him to come after a large popular demonstration against the U.S. following the rape of a 12-year old girl by three U.S. servicemen. In a 29 May 2004 interview with Nic Paget-Clarke he was quoted as follows:

> I was shocked by the impact of 38 American military bases, including the 3rd Marine Division, on 1.3 million people living on an over-crowded island with the choicest 20 per cent of the land given over to these military bases . . . we now know that the rate of sexually violent crimes committed by American servicemen in Okinawa leading to courts martial is about two per month and this rate has been constant over fifty years . . . The actual rate is probably much higher because many women are too humiliated to come forward and make a formal complaint, and the Marine Corps depends on that . . . But still reflecting my Cold War mentality, I thought Okinawa must be exceptional. Only as I began to look at the 725 [737 by 2006] military bases we have around the world – the 101 bases in South Korea; the massive military reservation in Germany, and Britain, and Italy; the bases around the Persian Gulf, on the island of Diego Garcia . . . did I conclude that Okinawa was not unusual. It was all too typical of the kinds of incidents that are associated with our empire of military bases.'[101]

In another 2004 interview, this time with UC Berkeley's Kreisler, Johnson said:

> The base world is complex. It has its own airline. It has 234 golf courses around the world. It has something like 70 Lear jet luxury airplanes to fly generals and admirals to the golf courses, to the armed forces ski resort at Garmisch in the Bavarian Alps. Inside the bases, the military does everything in their power to make them look like Little America.[102]

Uncompensated forced removal of residents has also been used by the United States when building military bases: 'Almost always these have led to the impoverishment of those affected . . . In total there are at least sixteen documented cases of base displacement outside the continental United States.'[103] The case I am most familiar with involves Diego Garcia, in the middle of the Indian Ocean, since my Harvard classmate Jonathan Jenness has been actively involved in trying to help repatriate former residents to their homes in the Chagos archipelago, within which Diego Garcia is one of over 60 islands. In the late 1960s the United States required all residents on the inhabited islands to be removed when a long-term lease was secretly negotiated with the British in violation of 'British law and international human rights guarantees.'[104] An estimated 1500 to 2000 residents were involved. Removal was rushed so that U.S. engineers could get on with base construction. On at least one occasion, those involuntarily removed had to leave behind 'most of their possessions and all their animals.'[105] Pet dogs were killed, sometimes with their owners present. Compensation was totally unacceptable. Today the large majority of approximately 5000 refugees live marginal lives as exiles in Mauritius and the Seychelles.

## SUMMARY

Toward the end of the Second World War, the United States provided the type of international leadership that will be necessary today and in the future if global threats are to be addressed. In 1944, 44 nations formed the World Bank and the International Monetary Fund following a meeting at Bretton Woods in New Hampshire, USA. In 1945 the United Nations was formed. In 1948 the Foreign Assistance Act established the Marshall Plan for the recovery of war-devastated Western Europe. The Plan was 'a bipartisan effort – proposed by a Democratic president and enacted into law by a Republican Congress in a hotly contested presidential election year.'[106] By the end of the 1950s, with major U.S. guidance and assistance, Japan's economic and political recovery was well under way. How the United States has fallen since those times!

Seventy-six per cent of Americans polled in June 2008 believed that the United States was headed in the wrong direction.[107] In a July 2008 poll, 69 per cent believed that America's Founding Fathers would be disappointed to see 'the way the United States has turned out 232 years after declaring its independence.'[108] The United States has fallen short for many reasons. National fundamentalism is a major one which restricts the government's capacity to play what should be a mandatory role in international affairs and institution building which, inevitably, must take precedence over national interests in dealing with global challenges and threats. A particularly infamous example of counterproductive policies relates to the refusal of the United States to honor its financial commitments to the United Nations and to ratify commonsensical UN conventions. One example is the Rights of the Child. That was adopted by the General Assembly in 1989 and institutionalized as international law in 1990. To date 193 countries have signed the convention. Non-signers are the United States and Somalia.

Threatening to the neighbors and reputation of the U.S., and to U.S. democracy, U.S. militarism has increased significantly since the end of the Second World War. We have arrogantly conducted illegal wars in Laos, Cambodia, Iraq and elsewhere which could meet the definition of crimes against humanity. Chalmers Johnson estimates that the budget supporting militarism now exceeds the budgets of all other countries together and that the United States has more than 1000 bases in over 130 countries. Forty per cent of that budget is secret, being kept from the public and Congress contrary to the First Article of the Constitution. Under the George W. Bush administration the United States has waged pre-emptive war and justified, at the highest level, the use of torture.

How the United States government treats agricultural research and development are another example of counterproductive U.S. policies with adverse national and international impacts. Within the United States, government-supported agricultural research, including that funded through the country's land grant universities,[109] is underfunded and disproportionately benefits large-scale corporate agriculture as opposed to family farms and the more viable towns that serve those farms. At the international level, Congress passes laws – most recently in June 2008 – subsidizing agribusiness with billions of dollars and other benefits at the expense of the livelihood of over a billion small-scale farmers throughout the world.

The U.S. government is also dysfunctional in dealing even with such critical internal issues as public education and infrastructure at the congressional district, state and national levels. Bipartisan politics has been replaced by partisanship and the influence of single-interest groups to fund and lobby politicians and civil servants to protect their narrow interests at the expense of the broader interests of society. The point is an important one, not just because the stronger interest groups disproportionately influence government decisions but because at a broader and more critical level, it illustrates the imbalance between catering to the interests of individuals and organizations as opposed to those of society.

Money used to achieve partisan political goals is corrupting American democracy, which is also becoming increasingly unequal economically. The more affluent are the principal gainers, with the income share of the top 1 per cent increasing from 10 to 22 per cent since the late 1950s. A major conclusion of Bartels' research is that 'middle-class and poor families in

the post-war era have routinely fared much worse under Republican presidents'[110] while 'the real incomes of middle-class families have grown twice
as fast under Democrats than they have under Republicans.'[111]

Over the past 30 years, the erosion of the safety nets of the American
majority has made their lives increasingly precarious. Job uncertainty
has increased under the form of globalization pushed by the Washington
Consensus, the U.S. treasury and the Clinton and two Bush presiden-
cies. In partial response to globalization, the private sector has decreased
employee health and retirement benefits while government unemployment benefits are inadequate to cover increasingly longer periods of
unemployment.

## NOTES

1. 'Chinese Science on the Move'. Editorial. *Science* (7 December 2007a). **318**. Page
   1523.
2. 'AAAS Strikes Landmark Agreements to Build Long-Term China Engagement.'
   AAAS News & Notes. *Science* (26 October 2007). **318**. Page 586.
3. Joint Meeting of the AAAS and APS with members of the National Academies of
   Science (27 – 29 April 2007) with sponsorship by the Annenberg Foundation Trust at
   Sunnylands.
4. Larry M. Bartels (2008). *Unequal Democracy: The political economy of the new gilded
   age*. New York: Russell Sage Foundation.
5. *Ibid.* Page ix.
6. Federal Election Commission. 'Presidential Campaign Finance.' Available at
   http://www.fec.gov/DisclosureSearch/mapApp.do; United States, Federal Election
   Commission (2008) 'United States, House and Senate Campaign Finance.' Available
   at http://www.fec.gov/DisclosureSearch/mapHSApp.do?election_yr=2008.
7. The above figures are from the Center for Responsive Politics Open Secrets.org
   website. The nonpartisan, independent and nonprofit Center calls itself the 'nation's
   premier research group tracking money in U.S. politics and its effect on elections and
   public policy.' Its data is widely used, including by the campaign finance website of
   Stanford University's conservative Hoover Institution.
8. *Ibid.*
9. Figures from Tom Hamburger and Peter Nicholas (18 June 2008). 'Partying Hard on
   Soft Money'. *Los Angeles Times*. Pages A1 and A13.
10. *Ibid.* Page A1.
11. *Ibid.* Page A13.
12. Title taken from Bartels' book.
13. Bartels. Op. cit. Page 1.
14. *Ibid.* Page 34.
15. *Ibid.* Page 3.
16. Sidney Verba, Norman H. Nie and Jae-on Kim (1995). *Voice and Equality: The view
    from the top*. Cambridge, MA: Harvard University Press.
17. Bartels. Op. cit. Page 280.
18. *Ibid.*
19. *Ibid.* Page 275 (Italics in original).
20. Peter Gosselin (2008). *High Wire: The precarious financial lives of American families*.
    New York: Basic Books. Page 8.

21. *Ibid.* Page x.
22. *Ibid.* Page 115.
23. *Ibid.* Page 116.
24. *Ibid.* Page 125.
25. Bartels. Op. cit. Page 7.
26. James Poteba, Steven Venti and David A. Wise (2006). 'The Decline of Defined Benefit Retirement Plans and Asset Flows.' Paper prepared for the *Eighth Annual Joint Conference of the Retirement Research Consortium.* Washington DC. 10–11 August. Page 1.
27. Kathleen Day (17 September 2006). 'Retirement, Squeezed: As traditional plans decline, workers face a less certain future.' *Washington Post.*
28. Gosselin. Op. cit. Page 265.
29. *Ibid.*
30. National Coalition on Health Care (NCHC) (2008). 'Facts on Health Insurance Coverage.' Available at http://www.nchc.org/facts/coverage.shtml. That 90 million were 'about one-third of the population below the age of 65.'
31. Gosselin. Op. cit. Pages 235–236.
32. NCHC (2008). Op. cit. Page 2.
33. Gosselin. Op. cit. Page 236.
34. See, for example, 2007 and 2008 articles in the *Los Angeles Times* by Lisa Girion that involve Health Net, Anthem Blue Cross and Blue Shield.
35. Lisa Girion (8 July 2008). 'WellPoint Settles with California Hospitals Over Rescissions.' *Los Angeles Times.*
36. Heather Boushey and Jeffrey Wenger (30 October 2001). 'Coming Up Short: Current unemployment insurance benefits fail to meet basic family needs.' Brief. Washington DC: Economic Policy Institute.
37. *Ibid.* Page 3.
38. For a detailed analysis of this American characteristic see Paul D. Carrington (2005). *Spreading America's Word: Stories of its lawyer-missionaries.* New York: Twelve Tables Press.
39. G-20 Communiqué. Meeting of Ministers and Governors. São Paulo, Brazil. 8–9 November 2008.
40. *The Economist* (26 July 2008). 'Unhappy America.' Leaders. Page 15.
41. M.L. Lawson (1994). *The Dammed Indians: The Pick-Sloan plan and the Missouri River Sioux, 1944–1980.* Norman, OK: University of Oklahoma Press.
42. L. Ortolano and K. Cushing (2000). 'Grand Coulee Dam and the Columbia Basin Project, USA.' Case study report prepared as an input to the World Commission on Dams, Cape Town. Available at www.dams.org/docs/kbase/studies/csusmain.pdf. Page xv.
43. *Ibid:* Page 3.7–8
44. M. McDonald and J. Muldowny (1982). *TVA and the Dispossessed: The resettlement of population in the Norris Dam area.* Knoxville, TN: University of Tennessee Press.
45. See Thayer Scudder with the assistance of D. Aberle, K. Begishe, E. Colson, *et al.* (1982). *No Place to Go: The impacts of forced relocation on Navajos.* Philadelphia, PN: ISHI.
46. 'McCain Prods Tribes, Government on Tribal Land Dispute' (22 July 2005). Available at http://indianz.com/News/2005/009449.asp.
47. See, for example, Orit Tamir (1999). 'What Happened to Navajo Relocatees from Hopi Partition Lands in Pinon?' *American Indian Culture and Research Journal.* **23** (4). Pages 71–90.
48. Herbert Gans (1962). *The Urban Villagers.* New York: New Press of Glencoe.
49. Carrington. Op. cit. Page 274.
50. Mervyn Brown (2001). *War in Shangri-La: A Memoir of Civil War in Laos.* London: The Radclifffe Press.

Global threats, global futures

51. Shawn Pogatchnik (30 May 2009). '111 Nations, but not US, Adopt Cluster Bomb Treaty.' Associated Press.
52. Brown (2001). Op. cit. Page 18.
53. Grant Evans (2002). *A Short History of Laos: The land in between.* Crows Nest, Australia: Allen and Unwin. Page 93.
54. According to Brown (2001, op. cit., pages 20–21) who was stationed in the British Embassy in Laos in the early 1960s, 'The principal outside force was by now the USA which . . . exercised a major influence on the government. This influence was to be exercised to prevent the integration of the Pathet Lao on any terms other than virtual Pathet Lao surrender.'
55. See Christopher Robbins (2000). *The Ravens: Pilots of the secret war of Laos.* Bangkok: Asia Books.
56. U.S. Department of State, Bureau of East Asian and Pacific Affairs (March 2008). 'Background Note: Laos.' Page 2.
57. *Ibid.* Page 3.
58. 'Academic Ranking of World Universities' (2007). Available at http://www.arwu.org/rank/2007/ARWU2007_top100.htm.
59. See Rand Corporation (2005b). 'Proven Benefits of Early Childhood Interventions.' Rand Labor and Population Research Brief. Santa Monica, CA: The Rand Corporation.
60. American Society of Civil Engineers (ASCE). Available at http://www.asce.org/150/150years.html.
61. ASCE (2009). 'Report Card for America's Infrastructure: 2009 grades.' Page 4. Available at http://www.asce.org/reportcard/2009/grades.cfm.
62. *Ibid.* Page 1.
63. Lynn A. Karoly, M. Rebecca Kilburn and Jill S. Cannon (2005). '*Early Childhood Interventions: Proven results, future promise.*' Santa Monica, CA: The Rand Corporation.
64. *Ibid.* Summary. Page xv.
65. Rand Corporation (2005). '*Children at Risk: Consequences for school readiness and beyond.*' Rand Labor and Population Research Brief: Santa Monica, CA: The Rand Corporation.
66. Karoly *et al.* Op. cit. Page xv.
67. *Ibid.* Page xvi.
68. *Ibid.* Pages xvii and xix.
69. *Ibid.* Page xix.
70. *Ibid.* Page xxv.
71. *Ibid.* Page xxviii.
72. UNICEF (2007). '*Child Poverty in Perspective: An overview of child well-being in rich countries.*' Innocenti Research Center Report Card 7. Florence, Italy: UNICEF. Page 1.
73. *Ibid.* The top four were three Scandinavian countries and the Netherlands.
74. *Ibid.* Page 13.
75. *Ibid.* Page 23.
76. Public Policy Institute of California (June 2008). 'Predicting Success on the California High School Exam.' Research Brief. San Francisco, CA: PPIC.
77. *Ibid.* Pages 1–2.
78. 'US Expert Panel See Algebra As Key to Improvements in Math.' *Science* (7 December 2007b). **318**. Page 1534.
79. For 2009, American Society of Civil Engineers (ASCE). Op. cit. Page 1. For ASCE (2008), see 'Raising the Grades: Small steps for big improvements in America's failing infrastructure: An action plan for the 110th Congress.' Available at http://www.asce.org/reportcard/2005/actionplan07.cfm.
80. Dan Weikel and Jeff Rabin 10 June 2008. 'More rough roads ahead.' *Los Angeles Times.*

81. William L. Graf (1999). 'Dam Nation: A geographic census of American dams and their large-scale hydrological impacts.' *Water Resources Research.* **35**. Pages 1305–1311.
82. ASCE (2009). Op. cit. Page 2.
83. ASCE (2005a). Report Card for America's Infrastructure: Dams.' Available at http://www.asce.org/reportcard/2005/page.cfm?id=23.
84. Wayne Graham (26 June 2001). 'Human and Economic Consequences of Dam Failure.' Paper Presented at the *FEMA Workshop on Issues, Resolutions, and Research Needs related to Embankment Dam Failure Analysis.* Oklahoma City. 26–28 June.
85. Quoted by T.R. Read (28 June 2006). 'The Superhighway to Everywhere.' *Washington Post.*
86. *Ibid.* Page 2.
87. ASCE (2005b). 'Report Card for America's Infrastructure: Roads.' Available at http://www.asce.org/reportcard/2005/page.cfm?id=30.
88. ASCE (2009). Op. cit. Page 4.
89. Nic Paget-Clarke (29 May 2004). 'Interview with Chalmers Johnson: Part 2: From CIA analyst to best-selling scholar.' Available at http://www.inmotionmagazine.com/global/cj-int/cj-int2.html.
90. Harry Kreisler (29 January 2004). 'Interview with Chalmers Johnson: American Empire.' Page 2.
91. United States Government (17 January 1961). President Dwight D. Eisenhower's Farewell Address.
92. Nic Paget-Clarke (29 May 2004). 'Interview with Chalmers Johnson: Part 1: An empire of more than 725 military bases.' Available at http://www.inmotionmagazine.com/global/cj-int/cj-int1.html.
93. *Ibid.*
94. Harry Kreisler (7 March 2007). 'Interview with Chalmers Johnson: 737 Military Bases and Counting.' Page 2.
95. Harry Kreisler (29 January 2004). Op. cit. Page 2.
96. Chalmers Johnson (2006). *Nemesis: The last days of the American republic.* New York: Metropolitan Books. Page 5.
97. *Kiplinger Letter* (9 February 2007).
98. Harry Kreisler (29 January 2004). Op. cit. Page 2.
99. *Ibid.* Page 3.
100. Johnson (2006). Op. cit. Page 6.
101. Nic Paget-Clarke (29 May 2004). Op. cit. Page 7.
102. Harry Kreisler (29 January 2004). Op. cit. Page 2.
103. David Vine (2009). *Island of Shame: The secret history of the U.S. military base on Diego Garcia.* Princeton, NJ: Princeton University Press. Page 65.
104. *Ibid.* Page 79.
105. *Ibid.* Page 113.
106. Library of Congress. 'For European Recovery: The Fiftieth Anniversary of the Marshall Plan. Truman Signed the Economic Assistance Act.' Home Page. Available at http://www.loc.gov/exhibits/marshall/mars3.html.
107. IPSOS Public Affairs (12–16 June 2008). 'The Associated Press Poll: Political study.' Project #81-5681-88.
108. CNN.com. (5 July 2008). 'CNN Poll: Most say Founding Fathers wouldn't be impressed.' Available at http://www.cnn.com/2008/us/07/04/us.poll/.
109. The Morrill Acts of 1862 and 1890 were passed by Congress to provide each state with government land for a public institution that would offer a broad and practical education, including the agricultural sciences.
110. Bartels. Op. cit. Page 34.
111. *Ibid.* Page 3.

# 5. People's Republic of China

## INTRODUCTION[1]

Deng Xiaoping, while China's paramount leader, made two momentous decisions that underlie China's current political economy. The first decision in the second half of the 1970s produced the household responsibility system (HRS). The second, in 1989, was to use the Red Army to repress in Tiananmen Square the pro-democracy student demonstrations. Together they show both the strengths and weaknesses of a political economy in which a single person, committee or party can influence the future. The result of the first decision was to release the energy and initiative of China's rural majority as private sector entrepreneurs. The second decision led to new leadership which sabotaged the rural private sector capitalism and wellbeing released under the HRS and replaced it during the 1990s with a non-sustainable capital-intensive form of state-controlled industrial development and urbanization. The shift from facilitating household-based rural enterprise development to reliance on foreign-directed investment and State Operated Enterprises (SOE) was glaring – in the first three years of the 1990s the growth rate of SOEs 'tripled over that in the 1980s.'[2]

Deng's decisions were not without opposition. Underlying the household responsibility system was Deng's belief that creating wealth at the household level, and hence differences in wealth between households, was to be encouraged, contrary to previous policies of the Communist Party. Violently repressing student demonstrations in 1989 was contrary to the recommendations of others within the Party, including Zhao Ziyang, the Party's general secretary, who 'advocated using "democracy and the rule of law" to settle the crisis'[3] – a position that resulted in house arrest until his death sixteen years later.

The chapter sections that follow start with an analysis of the importance for China and the world's future of the household responsibility system as documented by the initiative of two responding villages. This emphasis on the ongoing need, indeed requirement, for releasing and fostering local initiative in dealing with local, national and global issues has been a major thrust throughout this book. The first of the two villages, Kaihsiengkung, is adjacent to Lake Tai in the Yangtze delta region and within a three-hour bus drive from Shanghai. Village life and development there has been studied since 1936. The second village, New Sky, is close to Lake Dongting and Wuhan on the Middle Yangtze.

During my 1986–87 visits to rural China I was impressed by the ability of villagers, having adopted the HRS, to move from the subsistence cultivation of food grains to private and collective farm and non-farm commercial activities in less than ten years in spite of pre-independence poverty and the post-independence Great Leap Forward, the Great Famine and the Cultural Revolution in the 1950s, 1960s and first half of the 1970s. The speed and poverty-reduction nature of that transition, which I have yet to observe elsewhere, warrants careful analysis as a model for global emulation not just for reducing impoverishment and improving wellbeing but also for reducing the income and wellbeing gap which is currently widening throughout China because of the policy shifts of the 1990s.

Discussion then shifts to consideration of current national threats associated with China's rapid economic growth and increasing dependence on external natural resources, including fuels, metals and timber. As household consumption rises, so too there is an increasing gap between rich and poor as well as new poverty as people are evicted to make way for new industrial zones and urbanization. Poverty is also exacerbated by factory closures and increasing unemployment due to the world's current economic crisis. A related problem for China's citizens is pollution of water resources, which, like loss of farmland and housing, is associated with an increasing number of complaints and protests.

Emphasis then shifts to other environmental problems associated with declining aquifers on the North China Plain and future problems posed by retreating glaciers in the Himalayas and throughout the Tibetan Plateau. Glacial retreat not only threatens China's major rivers but also the Ganges in India, the Indus in India and Pakistan and rivers in Bangladesh and throughout South East Asia. This phenomenon is only one case where China's problems also occur in other countries. That is especially the case in India, where analogous problems due to rapid industrialization and urbanization occur at the expense of the country's rural and urban poor as illustrated – as in China – by special economic zones, river basin development policies, extractive industries and urban redevelopment. China's global impacts, however, far exceed India's due to increasing industrial demand for imported natural resources, a wide range of exports and a highly competitive foreign aid program.

# THE HOUSEHOLD RESPONSIBILITY SYSTEM (HRS)

## Introduction

The emergence of Deng Xiaoping as China's Paramount Leader follow-ing Mao's death and the arrest of the Gang of Four in 1976 was followed by state approval of the HRS as a national reform in 1981 and a series of supportive economic reforms during the 1980s. They warrant some detail because rural initiative cannot operate in a vacuum. It requires opportuni-ties and supportive government policies. Especially important for releasing household, village and township initiative in China were five documents issued by the Party's Central Committee between 1982 and 1985.[4] They were called Number 1 documents to emphasize their importance and were issued at the beginning of each year.

The first Number 1 document 'was intended to signal that the rural reforms were a top policy priority of the government'[5] while the four that followed addressed issues as they arose. The first was restricted to agricul-tural development and marketing. The second widened market access to urban areas and began to explore expediting agro-industry and non-farm enterprises. The third and fourth dealt with employment of workers, financial and other institutions and industrialization. The fifth Number 1 document dealt with such social consequences as income inequalities arising from the rapid development that had occurred during the first half of the 1980s, and with areas with persistent poverty.

The various economic and financial reforms were also associated with less well-known social changes, including participatory governance at the village level, which may eventually – in spite of Deng's second momentous decision – have an impact on China's political institutions. Intellectuals who had been sidelined during the Cultural Revolution in the 1960s re-emerged, universities increased and expanded, new government institu-tions were created and formerly ostracized disciplines in the behavioral and social sciences re-emerged.

In 1977 I was a member of the Committee on International Health of the U.S. National Academy of Sciences' Institute of Medicine. We were discussing China and I was pushing the importance of the behavioral and social sciences for strengthening China's health programs. A colleague who was president of a major foundation condescendingly reminded me that the Chinese did not favor the social sciences. I remember replying with satisfaction that China didn't have foundations either but that was no reason for assuming their irrelevance for Chinese conditions. Indeed, though I did not know it at the time, the Chinese Academy of Social Sciences was established under the State Council in May 1977. Its basic mission included 'to make Marxism-Leninism, Mao Zedong thought and Deng Xiaoping theory as guiding principles.'[6]

Deng Xiaoping theory emphasized economic development and political stability, with initial emphasis on poverty alleviation and development of China's rural villages and towns. It emerged from a plenary session of the party's Central Committee in 1978, where participants 'shifted the focus of the work of the whole Party onto economic development and carried out reform and opening to the outside world; this ushered in a new era of development in the socialist cause.'[7]

The extension of the household responsibility system throughout China after 1978 was greatly facilitated by Deng Xiaoping and his supporters. The changes were revolutionary for they first shifted responsibility for agricultural and then off-farm production from the brigade or other production teams to a combination of household and collective enterprises. Thereafter, once the government's food grain quota had been met, individual households, larger private sector enterprises and collective enterprises could sell, or otherwise use for their own purposes, any surplus they produced. Villages varied as to how their leaders and committees decided to benefit from the incentives provided. Some allocated quotas to each household. Others specialized by assigning responsibility for meeting the obligatory quotas to the best farm households, who were then provided with additional land, while other households initiated various sideline industries such as aquaculture, ducks or pigs, or any of a wide range of non-farm commercial enterprises, or joined with other households in private and collective village farm and non-farm enterprises.

Opinions vary as to the origin of the responsibility system; more specifically, as to whether it came from below due to village experimentation following decades of poverty and uncertainty or from communist party (CCP) leaders outside the village. In the 1960s, villages and towns in Zhejiang Province pioneered what became known as the Wenzhou Model of village and town development, while in 1978 production teams in another province 'began to contract land, other resources, and output quotas to individual households.'[8] On the other hand, in 1975 the CCP general secretary experimented with the household responsibility system in Sichuan Province. Substantially larger yields caught the attention of the state leadership, which, as in past experiments, initially restricted the reform to poor arable lands. Of course, increased yields also caught the attention of production teams with good farmland, with the result that the HRS began to spread rapidly throughout China. When the authorities under the leadership of Deng Xiaoping formally launched the HRS in 1981, 41 per cent of China's production teams were already using the system; this rose to 94 per cent by the end of 1983.[9]

Opinions also vary among China researchers as to the relative importance of collective village and town industries versus private sector enterprises. MIT political economist Yasheng Huang argues persuasively that private sector enterprises dominated throughout the 1980s except in a few provinces and areas where government control remained strong. His analysis is based on a study of household income data provided during surveys by government departments. His analysis, for example, of 1985 Ministry of Agriculture data on 12 million township and village enterprises indicated that 'more than 10 million were purely private.'[10] That conclusion further buttresses my argument on the global benefits that can be expected when governments place far more emphasis on promoting farm and non-farm household, village and town development. In the Chinese case, not only was growth of rural household income during the 1980s twice that in the 1990s, but it significantly increased demand for consumer goods and services. Social wellbeing also increased.

During the 1990s, state-controlled industrialization and urbanization was pushed at the expense of the rural sector. According to Huang, 'many of the productive reforms in the 1980s were partially or completely reversed in the 1990s. Fiscal decentralization . . . was largely reversed in 1994 . . . The financial innovations to lend to rural households to start non-farm businesses and to allow financial intermediation were discontinued.'[11] The urban industrial sector was also favored by increasing rural taxation. Fees levied on self-employment businesses reduced their number. Illiteracy increased because of rising school fees and deterioration of educational infrastructure. Rural health also deteriorated due to increasing medical expenses at clinics and hospitals, including even for inoculations.

### Kaihsiengkung Village: 1936–1987

#### Introduction

Kaihsiengkung is the site of one of the longest long-term studies in anthropology.[12] Chinese anthropologist Fei Hsiaotung began the study in 1936. Fei (1910–2005) was born nearby in the Yangtze delta and studied anthropology in Beijing, where he met and married another anthropologist. Together they commenced fieldwork among ethnic minorities in southwest China. As Fei later recalled, 108 days after their marriage, his wife drowned while crossing a river to get help for Fei, who had been badly injured after falling into a tiger trap.

While recuperating during 1936, Fei visited his sister in Kaihsiengkung, where she was helping villagers revitalize the domestic silk industry which dated back over a thousand years.[13] His PhD dissertation at the London School of Economics, published in 1939 as *Peasant Life in China*, was based on fieldwork during his two-month convalescence. He revisited Kaihsiengkung in 1957 to follow up on research by former classmate and Australian anthropologist William Geddes. During that visit Fei noted that while grain production had increased significantly since China's independence, people were still poor because, in Fei's opinion, government policy was ignoring the potential of a diversified system of household enterprises (sidelines in the Chinese literature) and rural industries. Emphasizing that point in a series of published articles, he was denounced as a 'rightist,' fired from official positions held and forbidden to teach. His partial rehabilitation during the period of rectification (1962–1966) that followed the Great Famine in 1959–1961 ended during the Cultural Revolution, when he and his family were required to work for six years as farm laborers.

Complete rehabilitation only occurred after the 1978 plenary session of the Communist Party's Central Committee. Fei was first assigned to the Academy of Social Sciences 'to restore and organize the teaching of sociology, which had been suspended more than twenty years earlier in Chinese universities.'[14] One of his activities was to establish in 1981 a field station in Kaihsiengkung for ongoing research by government sociologists so that the village might 'serve as a portal through which the outside world can view the changes, achievements, new developments, and new problems in one part of rural China.'[15] The previous year Fei had also carried out further research in the village, which was published in his 1983 *Chinese Village Closeup*. I visited Fei in Beijing in 1987, at which time he arranged for me to make a two-day visit to Kaihsiengkung.

### Kaihsiengkung: 1936–1981

Kaihsiengkung was a small village at the time of Fei's first visit, with a population of 1458. The large majority were living in poverty. The main occupation of three-fourths of the 360 households was subsistence agriculture. Rice cultivation was combined with small household vegetable gardens, livestock management and common-property use of plentiful aquatic resources surrounding the village. Mulberry trees were also grown to feed silkworms that spun cocoons for the silk factory or for family specialists who spun raw silk on consignment to town silk industries. Arable land was scarce, amounting to only 3065 mu (204 hectares), 90 per cent of which was cultivated in rice. Little use was made of animal traction because most households' small fields were split into separate holdings. Distribution of the inadequate arable land base was also unequal, with three-quarters of the extended families owning no land or less than half a hectare while 18 per cent owned less than one hectare.

Small-scale agriculture was combined with fishing and a range of services, except for a few immigrant households which were landless traders and other service providers. Most households owned a boat for water transport along the maze of canals and waterways that provided the main access to the nearest market town four kilometers distant. Ownership of land was complex. More than half was owned by absentee landlords who leased cultivation rights to village tenants. The village land-owning unit was the extended family of parents and married and unmarried children. Married sons usually lived in the same house as their parents while married daughters joined the household and kin group of their husbands.

Following Fei's initial study, poverty worsened during the thirteen years prior to Chinese independence, with farm production either stagnant or declining.[16] In addition to an inadequate arable land base, inequitable land tenure, taxation and crime, the main reasons were the 1938 Japanese invasion and the Chinese civil war. By the late 1940s Fei wrote that about 75 per cent of the households farmed rented land. Most were indebted: 'Usually, they sold their food grains immediately after each harvest to clear their debts and then again borrowed money to buy food for the rest of the year.'[17]

The first major beneficial change after independence was the land reform of 1952. Thereafter land was owned by the state but leased for use to villages through agricultural cooperatives. Grain production per mu nearly doubled between 1949 and 1956. Communes were formed in 1958. Initially living standards and production increased because adding skill to work performed provided some incentive over the previous coopera- tive system. Village affairs and production suffered, however, during most of the1958–1977 period due to the 1958–1960 Great Leap Forward, the 1958–1961 Great Famine, during which one-third of the villagers became beggars, and the 1966–1976 Cultural Revolution. The major exception was during the 1962–1966 period of rectification, at the beginning of which the state allocated a small plot of land to each household 'for permanent use as private land.'[18]

During the 1980s, the Household Responsibility System initiated the first of two 'quiet revolutions' which combined collective and private household agricultural and non-farm enterprises.[19] Into the mid-1990s, both the state and local government emphasized the primary impor- tance of collective production, as did Fei for both villages and small towns. The primacy of the collective over private household enterprises came to be known among development specialists and academics as the Southern Jiangsu Model, as distinct from the later Wenzhou Model, which emphasized only private enterprise at the village and town level.

Explanations as to which model China's villages followed emphasize the degree of central government control. The Southern Jiangsu Model was named after the southern portion of Jiangsu Province, in which

Kaihsiengkung and Lake Tai were located. That area during the 1980s already had attracted state interest and control as one of China's leading provinces in regard to the development of collective village, town and urban industries. Wenzhou, on the east coast in Zhejiang Province, was both geographically and politically isolated. The province had a large rural area tied to a small urban one. Much of the rural zone was isolated within three mountain ranges. The province also had been economically (in terms of government investment) and politically isolated under Mao because it was Chiang Kai-shek's home province.[20] For such reasons, University of California political scientist Alan Liu argues that rural villages were left relatively free to develop as they wished.

High rates of labor migration to Hong Kong and close ties to the political leadership of Shanghai also characterized Wenzhou villagers, as did their market orientation in regard to commercial crops and crafts. The introduction of the Household Responsibility System legitimized and accelerated previously illegal privatization activities that became the Wenzhou Model for China's development. That second 'quiet revolution' that shifted collective enterprises to privatized ones was delayed in Kaihsiengkung and throughout Jiangsu Province until the second half of the 1990s because tighter central government control continued to favor collective enterprises.

In Kaihsiengkung during the early years of the household responsibility system, per capita income more than doubled between 1979 and 1981. Both collective and household enterprises were involved. Livestock sidelines had become a popular source of household income, especially rabbits.[21] Collective enterprises, however, provided the major source of income. They included grain cultivation, various agricultural sidelines (especially cultivation of mulberry trees for silkworm production) and four village industries established in 1979.

Collective grain production had increased by 39 per cent during the last two years of the 1970s. The village silk industry, destroyed following the Japanese invasion in 1938, had been reintroduced as a collective enterprise in 1966 during the period of rectification. It had two components. One was collective cultivation of mulberry trees on reclaimed land for feeding silkworms, whose cocoons were then sold to the state, which then resold the silk back to village collectives for processing. Kaihsiengkung had two collective silk processing industries – a silk reeling filature and a silk weaving workshop. Hardly an efficient set-up granted the state's involvement as an intermediary, but sufficient to further increase household per capita income along with collective production of tofu in two soybean mills. Overall in 1980, collective agriculture provided 41 per cent of per capita income, collective industry 40 per cent, and household sidelines 19

per cent.[22] Construction of new houses and purchase of household furnishings was the major use of increasing incomes, with 50 new houses built in
one section of the village during 1980. Bicycles and sewing machines were
now owned by most households.

**Kaihsiengkung: 1987**

I visited Kaihsiengkung for two days in September 1987. The village, population 2377, was the largest of 21 neighboring villages that constituted an
official township which collectively owned a number of rural industries.
One, a silk factory, was in Kaihsiengkung. The communal system had
ended in 1983. It was replaced by 19 village groups, each of which had a
two-wheeled tractor used primarily for collective grain cultivation. Each
household with access to land also grew rice for subsistence purposes. Due
to village expansion, arable land had been reduced to 3024 mu (201 ha),
of which 740 mu (49 ha) were planted with collectively farmed mulberry
trees. Silkworm cocoons were still required to be sold to the state and
then repurchased for processing. A 20th group collectively exploited 80
hectares of water that fell within the village area.

Breakdown of village output was 60.5 per cent from village collective
industry, 26.5 per cent from household sidelines and 13 per cent from collective agriculture. Income per capita had more than doubled since 1981.
Of the village labor force of 1429 people, 693 were primarily employed in
village industries, 355 in agriculture, 278 in sidelines and 103 in various
services. There were still four major collective industries in the village: the
two silk factories as in 1981 and the two soybean mills. Minor collective
enterprises included a small cinema, a shop and a clinic.

Major improvements in village infrastructure and institutions were the
road and a new junior middle school. For a village previously connected
to the outside world primarily by the use of hand-powered small boats that
took two and a half hours to reach the closest town, it is hard to overempha-
size the importance of the road's construction in 1983. It must have been
a major undertaking, for three bridges over waterways were required. Its
timing, including provision of a bus station, I suspect was due in large part to
Fei's influence in establishing the village as a sociological research station.

As in 1981, most marriages continued to be within the village, while
young married couples, as before, lived with the husband's parents.
Increasing income continued to be used to build and furnish new houses
and enlarge old ones, with at least 125 now having two stories. Though all
houses were electrified, none had running water or a courtyard water pipe.
Furnishings for the 608 families[23] included 7 color and 180 black and white
televisions, 10 washing machines and 6 refrigerators. Seven individuals
had motor cycles.

In reply to my query as to why some households were better off than others, I was told that key factors were the size of a household's labor force, the nature of their involvement in village industries and the side-lines they chose. There certainly were a large number of sidelines to choose from, including raising pigs and ducks, growing vegetables, raising silkworms and running a private business such as one of the two small restaurants in the village.

At the end of my visit, I asked the village leadership about their plans for the future and for their recommendations for developing the new villages to which Three Gorges' resettlers would be moved. Plans continued to emphasize the primacy of collective enterprises. As for Three Gorges resettlement planning, they recommended collective village industry for the youth but, as in their case, agriculture during the summer when the silk factories closed. In effect, as Fei himself had once emphasized, 'leave the fields but not the village.'[24]

**New Sky: 1986–1987[25]**

Throughout our feasibility study of the Three Gorges Project (TGP), the 100-person Canadian team, which I served as an adviser, worked closely with Chinese colleagues. In December 1986 several of us dealing with resettlement asked to visit an existing village that illustrated the Southern Jiangsu Model that the government wished to implement in resettled TGP villages. New Sky (Xin Nong) on the Middle Yangtze flood plain and located 11 kilometers from the large city of Wuhan was selected for two visits: one in December 1987 and the other in April 1988.

When I visited Kaihsiengkung six months later I was struck by similarities between the two villages in addition to both representing the Southern Jiangsu Model. Population size and agricultural conditions (including a restricted agricultural base) were broadly similar. The main difference, however, was New Sky's proximity to a major city, which influenced the speed with which the village leadership was able to increase the number and variety of its village industries. Another difference was what I call being a 'World Bank Village,' which means the type of model village that government officials ask donors to visit to convince them that the development plans they are financing are, in fact, being implemented as planned.[26] But in this case, the selection was appropriate in that it did give us an idea of the potential of the Southern Jiangsu Model.

Like Kaihsiengkung, New Sky's responsibility before the implementation of the household responsibility system was to produce food grains for the state. According to the village leadership, 93 per cent of the labor force was employed in agriculture before 1978. The first village collective industries, a pig bristle brush factory and a casting factory, had already been implemented. Ten other village industries followed during the 1980s, dealing with, among other activities, concrete fabrication, manufacturing plastics and park benches, and cap making, sewing and embroidery. Altogether we found 15 collective industries that employed 868 workers. Four were owned collectively with 22 surrounding township villages; the others were owned by New Sky. Because of unreliable electricity – a continuing problem in China today – in this case from the grid serving Wuhan, the village had built its own coal-fired power plant. That plus the 15 industries and a busy tarred road passing through the village, gave the impression of a small town.

We were especially interested in how the village leadership financed the various enterprises and how they decided who would be employed in which industry as well as in collective agricultural activities and sidelines. Financing was done in two major ways. One was to arrange to become a future supplier for a Wuhan industry, get a loan from that industry to construct the agreed-upon factory and then to repay the loan in previously agreed-upon supplies. As for other new industries, they were capitalized with profits from the most successful collective industries.

How the village moved a population of farmers to collective village industry was especially interesting. The first step was to ask the leaders of the village's 11 groups to describe the education and skills of its labor force – women aged 16 to 50 and men aged 16 to 60. The first priority was to select the best farm families, for the leadership had decided that they wanted specialists to provide the village's food grain quota to the state. Twenty-four families were selected and provided with holdings for growing two crops of rice a year. The decision was a wise one for those families grew substantially more than the required quota to the extent that their incomes were in the village's upper range.

Equally ingenious was the leadership decision to give all the other families with former land rights (over 700 of the 737 families) enough arable land to meet their subsistence needs in rice. Even then, it took three years before the majority agreed that the new system would not only meet their own food grain requirements but also allow living standards to increase, with more than a fivefold increase in per capita income since 1980. During a Sunday visit, we saw the importance of those smallholdings as security against unexpected events, including destructive changes in government policies as in the past, when we found a young couple, who were employed in village industries during the week, plowing on weekends with a buffalo in the family garden.

As with the 24 farm family specialists, the same system was used to recruit labor not just for the various collective factories but also for exploiting the village's aquatic resources (26 families) and citrus holdings (no families but 14 laborers). In contrast to Kaihsiengkung's 49 per cent, 87 per cent (1118 workers) of the labor force was employed in collective village enterprises. The private sector employed 168 laborers drawn from 97 of the village's 737 households, which owned rice mills, worked in crafts or used privately owned two-wheel tractors as taxis and other modes of transport. There were also 64 community workers, including teachers and 15 employed in village government. At the time of our visits, available opportunities in the village were able to absorb over 90 per cent of those joining the labor force – an accomplishment made easier by enforcement of the government's one child policy. As for future plans, they included agro-industries based on processing and canning fish, poultry and pigs.

Preferred marriage, especially for daughters, continued to be in the village. As elsewhere, rising incomes were invested in new houses and household furnishings. Of the 737 houses, 278 were two-storied in 1987. Over 90 per cent of families also owned television sets, 285 had washing machines, 15 had refrigerators, four had motor bikes and four had trucks.

**Kaihsiengkung: 1996–2007**

Sociologist Xiangqun Chang picked Kaihsiengkung as the setting for her PhD dissertation[27] because it was the site of Fei's long-term research. Her research on social support networks and reciprocity among villagers and between villagers and the state was completed over a three-month period in 1996. Since 1997 she has communicated with the village by email and telephone, with short visits between 2004 and the present.

At the commencement of her research in the first half of 1996, Xiangqun found that living standards of the large majority of households had continued to improve under the household responsibility system but that incomes were stagnating. New houses numbered 510, up from none in the late 1970s. Every family now had tap water and three-fourths used bottled gas for cooking. On the other hand, continued overdependence on inefficient, indebted and bankruptcy-prone collective enterprises had left the village 'in a depressed situation.'[28]

Between 1996 and the present, 'the second quiet revolution' occurred, whereby the villagers pioneered the change from collective enterprises to private capitalism or, in other words, from the Southern Jiangsu to the Wenzhou System. By the mid-1990s, villagers had increasingly come to believe that dependence on collective industries was holding them back. In 1996, when a village entrepreneur (Zhou Yonglin) was expanding the only privately owned industry in the village, CCP leaders sent thugs to tear the additions down 'to limit private business development size.'[29] That same year, in a doomed effort to redirect village interest back to collective industries and state-approved activities, and away from other belief systems, 3000 temples were also destroyed in surrounding villages.

Xiangqun's 1996 research was underway at that time. Though concerned about the risk of conflict occurring between villagers and local government, she reported that the transition from collective to private enterprise subsequently occurred peacefully over a two-month period as a result of an interactive process in which villagers played a major role. As a result they currently believe that 'their current living conditions of free market economy and loosened political control by the state are in part their own creation. In other words, they believe that they and the state can change and shape each other in a reciprocal way over a long period.'[30] The prefecture bought into the transition later in 1996 by establishing a 'new policy of privatization of collective enterprises system.'[31]

During the process whereby villagers took increasing responsibility for their own affairs, they arranged for Zhou, though not a Party member and therefore ineligible to take over the number one leadership position of general secretary, to be appointed to another position in which he 'was in charge of everything.'[32] Zhou remained in that position for six years until he was replaced by a CCP member in 2003. Under his leadership all collective enterprises were privatized and the number of village leaders requiring government approval was reduced to five (which the villagers interpreted as illustrating a loosening of political control). Debt was dealt with by leasing various collective enterprises to village entrepreneurs, who raised capital from external sources and signed a village contract agreeing to hire half of the enterprise's skilled workers.

By 2002 there were 12 privately owned enterprises. Eighty per cent of village income came from private industry, 7 per cent from fishing and other aquatic resources and 13 per cent from agriculture and sidelines. Fourteen households, however, remained very poor and some others were vulnerable because of insufficient labor resources.[33] By 2004 the village was connected to a circular road around Lake Tai and the villagers had built a 6 kilometer circular macadamized road around the village. Due to improved communications, an increasing number of families were bussing their children to a better staffed town school even though the village's educational system continued to improve.

Village assets included 21 cars, 650 motorcycles, 730 new houses, 850 installed air conditioners, 1230 mobile phones and 720 telephones, while 'nearly one quarter of the village households had broadband internet access.'[34] Two years later villagers owned 28 private cars and 850 motorcycles.[35]

In spite of being one of China's richer villages, Xiangqun continued to consider Kaihsiengkung a normal village since Fei first described it in 1936. This conclusion was based in large part on the village's self-sufficiency and enterprise and especially on an ever-present informal and dynamic networking system that included all villager categories as well as the ancestors and 'the local gods and goddesses . . . This informal system can be viewed as the real power that holds the local society together . . . and which mediates changes in the relationships between the state and the villagers.'[36] As with the large majority of China's rural villages, state social security coverage was small in Kaihsiengkung. Even before 1996, village collective institutions played 'a very small role in the support of villagers' major events.'[37]

# CHINA'S POLITICAL ECONOMY TODAY AND ASSOCIATED THREATS

## Introduction

Global living standards will become much worse by the end of this century unless China and the United States agree to make and actually implement transformational changes in their political economies. Currently the governments of these two dominant nations are expansionist in ways that exceed the regenerative capacity of the atmosphere and of terrestrial, freshwater and marine ecosystems. China's global impact is relatively recent and is fueled by a demand for global subsurface and surface resources to drive a state-dominated, capital-intensive export-oriented economy which has grown at an average rate of 10 per cent per annum during 1992–2006[38] in contrast to the United States' long-term growth rate of 2 to 5 per cent.

China's contribution to global warming is an example of the magnitude of its adverse environmental impact. As a signatory of the Kyoto Convention, in 2004 China released greenhouse gas figures for 1990 and 1994. Though low per capita in comparison with the United States, it was estimated that China's total greenhouse gas emissions could exceed those of the United States by about 2020. In fact, China's production of greenhouse gases had passed that of the United States by 2007.[39]

### China's Economy Today

During the present century China has become a 'planetary power.'[40] Regardless of which of two methods one uses for calculating a country's Gross Domestic Product,[41] China's growing economy could equal in size that of the United States by 2040 according to one estimate.[42] China's consumption of such basic commodities as grain, meat, coal and steel had already exceeded that of the United States by the end of 2004.[43] The figures are impressive. China's consumption of grain exceeded that of the United States by 104 million tons, meat by 26 million tons, coal by 226 million tons and steel by 154 million tons.

Through the mid-1990s the growth of the Chinese economy largely reflected two activities. As in Kaihsiengkung and New Sky, one activity was the continued privatization by tens of millions of resident households of collective village and township industries along with the formation of new household, village and township enterprises. The other, mandated by the central government, involved the privatization of bankrupt and inefficient state industries so that by early 2008 only a third of the economy 'was directly state-controlled.'[44]

A major change, however, began in the late 1990s as the government shifted emphasis from light industrial development to heavy industry, a change that continues today in spite of government efforts to hold it back by restricting credit and by other state policies. Production of steel for domestic use as China industrialized and urbanized, and then for export, is an important example. Starting in the late 1990s, China bought, dismantled with Chinese labor and shipped to China dozens of Germany's antiquated steel mills as well as secondhand industrial plants in other European countries.[45] More recently, after China's National Development and Reform Commission set higher standards, emphasis shifted to construction in China of state-of-the-art facilities. By the end of 2007 China's steel mills had 'increased their output fivefold over the decade, to about 38 per cent of the World's total.'[46]

Over 50 per cent of China's steel production is by state-owned facilities, with some level of government holding 'a majority interest in nine of the top ten Chinese producers.'[47] These producers are both expansionist and increasingly international. Sinosteel Corporation, for example, has 76 subsidiaries, of which 23 are outside China, with the corporation having established 'iron ore and chrome resource bases in Australia and South Africa.'[48] State-owned Shougang Corporation, one of China's oldest, most famous and largest steel companies, illustrates how Chinese industry is diversifying and reinventing itself through upgrading.

Until recently Shougang's headquarters and major steel factory were located inside Beijing. In 2005 Shougang announced that the factory would be transferred to Hebei Province and replaced by a major recreational area, non-polluting enterprises such as real-estate projects, high-tech companies, service industries and perhaps an industrial museum. While the timing of the decision no doubt was influenced by China's hosting the

2008 Olympics, how Shougang planned to reinvent itself is instructive. The new site selected was Caofeidian – initially an insignificant offshore sand spit in the Bohai Gulf's Economic Circle some 220 kilometers east of Beijing. Currently under development as a major port and industrial site, the much-enlarged man-made site is expected to cover several hundred square kilometers, be connected to the mainland and adjacent to one of the few deep water areas along China's northern coastline.

There, along with over 40 other industries, Shougang in partnership with another state-owned iron and steel group started construction in 2007 of a new steel plant on a 21 square kilometer plot. By 2010 the completed plant is expected to be China's largest, with 'a designed production capacity of 9.98 million tons of iron, 9.7 million tons of steel and 9.13 million tons of rolled steel a year.'[49] The plant's design has been carefully vetted by the State Environmental Protection Administration (SEPA), with the new site approved by the State Council. According to SEPA's evaluation, the plant's new technologies 'will ensure 99.5 per cent of the solid waste and 97.5 per cent of waste water are recycled.'[50]

In addition to coal and iron ore, China's demand for aluminum and copper also exceeds that of the United States. Any state-of-the-art efforts to reduce pollution associated with steel production, however, are overwhelmed by China's increasing use of coal. Dependency on coal, currently generating 80 per cent of the country's energy,[51] is longstanding and overwhelming. During my visits to New Sky in the late 1980s, I observed household users making briquettes for cooking from coal dust while the village had its own coal-burning thermal plant to provide energy to its own industries because of unreliable supplies from the local grid. Countrywide demand for energy jumped with the shift from light to heavy industry, with steel production alone using '16 per cent of China's power, compared with 10 per cent for all the country's households combined.'[52]

In recent years the importance of domestic consumption in the Chinese economy has been closing in on, and perhaps overtaking, the importance of exports.[53] In China's villages and townships, increased consumption followed the spread of the household responsibility system in the 1980s, as shown by construction of new houses and purchase of household furnishings in Kaihsiengkung and New Sky. Household consumption surged following the privatization of collective enterprises in the later half of the 1990s. During that time span Chinese mobile phones increased from under 10 million to 269 million versus 159 million in the United States.[54] By 2008 China was also expected to exceed the United States in number of internet users.[55] By 2000, China had 374 million TV sets as opposed to 243 million in the United States, while China produced more refrigerators than the U.S. that same year.[56]

To feed its population, by 2004 China was using double the tonnage of fertilizers used in the United States and had become a major importer of grain (for both people and livestock), soybeans and other food stuffs.[57] Granted the country's dependence on such bulk products as metals, coal, fertilizers and grains, a major effort is currently underway to develop Chinese infrastructure. To meet the challenge, 'China has embarked upon the world's biggest program of railway construction since the nineteenth century.'[58]

## China's Increasing Global Impact

### Introduction
In a world with limited natural resources, China's increasing demand for imports, fuels and metal especially, understandably has caused concern among international financial institutions and OECD and G8 countries as well as environmental and human rights NGOs. That was especially the case several years ago, when increasing media attention was paid to China's growing influence in Africa following China's October 2006 summit in Beijing for over 40 African countries. The World Bank and the International Monetary Fund (IMF) stated concerns that Chinese loans would exacerbate African indebtedness, a point emphasized by the Bank's then president. The IMF also complained that a Chinese loan of $2 billion with 'minimal rates of interest, a generous payback period and none of *IMF's "conditionalities"*'[59] caused the Government of Angola to break off prior loan negotiations with the Fund in 2004. Other critics noted that the Chinese loan 'effectively lowered transparency standards, making it more difficult for western companies and governments to push for anti-corruption schemes like the Extractive Industries Transparency Initiative,' and that the loan condition allowing the Chinese to bid on 70 per cent of construction contracts would slow the development of Angolan skilled labor and enterprises.[60]

In November 2006 the President of the European Investment Bank stated that the 'competition of the Chinese banks is clear . . . They don't bother about social or human rights conditions.'[61] The World Wildlife Fund, focusing on China, noted how the 'current unsustainable consumption patterns in developed countries are spreading to other parts of the world, thereby triggering a global hunt for natural resources and causing the environmental ecosystem to collapse.'[62]

Aside from environmental concerns, such complaints exaggerated China's impact. Citing UNCTAD figures, Firoze Manji, editor of Pambazuka News and former chief executive of the Aga Khan Foundation, wrote that China's foreign direct investment (FDI), aid and trade in Africa were not only 'dwarfed' by similar activities of the United States and European countries but were 'often smaller than those of other Asian countries.'[63] As examples he noted that China's FDI to Africa during 2002–2004 was an annual average of $1.2 billion versus $30 billion, $19 billion and $11.5 billion from the United Kingdom, the United States and France respectively in 2003.

More recently, in response to criticism, China has begun to cooperate with international agencies in joint economic and political activities. According to *The Economist,* in December 2007 'The World Bank and China agreed to develop aid projects in Africa together,' while UNDP's resident representative in the Congo noted that Chinese officials had begun attending donor round table meetings in Kinshasa.'[64] Early in 2008, China also participated in round table meetings addressing the financial and development needs of Liberia and Mauritania. Political activities include providing troops for UN peace-keeping missions in Liberia and the Congo, and agreeing to an African Union/United Nations peace force in Darfur. On the other hand, progress has been inadequate in dealing with illegal exports of timber from Angola, Mozambique and Tanzania,[65] among other countries, and in dealing with social and human rights issues, as shown by China's intention to deliver arms to Zimbabwe as recently as April 2008.

### China's economic activities in Africa

Expanding rapidly, to date China's demand for natural resources has focused on Africa. China's current[66] programs seek out countries rich in natural resources, especially oil and minerals essential for China's ongoing development. They are initiated on a government-to-government basis that requires African partners to accept China's one-country policy in regard to Taiwan. Thereafter a wide range of development assistance is available, with rights to minerals and oil complemented by physical, social and cultural infrastructure, agriculture, training in China and exchange of students. The major source of government-to-government funds is provided by China's Export-Import (ExIm) Bank, which had 259 mainly infrastructural projects in 36 African countries by September 2006.[67]

The largest ExIm Bank loan through 2007, $5 billion, was to the Democratic Republic of Congo. In return for export rights to cobalt, copper, timber and eventually to other minerals, as well as cash repayments from use of infrastructure, China will fund, among other projects, a 3400 km road linking the northeastern portion of the country to Zambia, a 3200 km railroad to the coast, hospitals and health centers and two universities.[68] In the Sudan, where China funds oil exploration and is the largest recipient of Sudanese oil, the ExIm Bank funded construction of the controversial Merowe Dam[69] and in Guinea, the ExIm Bank will fund construction of the $1 billion Souapiti Dam. Due to ExIm Bank policies which require that 'at least 50 per cent of the materials must be sourced from China,'[70] such dams tend to be designed and built by Chinese state and private companies which bring Chinese managers, technicians and laborers with them. In oil-rich Nigeria, the state company that built China's Gezouba and Three Gorges dams on the Yangtze River is expected to build the 2600 MW Mabilla Plateau hydropower installation.[71]

China is also pursuing other ways to finance African development. In June 2007 the government formed the China–Africa Development Fund with capital of $1 billion as a Chinese version of a private equity fund for helping African private industry. The Fund will be managed by the government's China Development Bank (CDB), 'which forecasts a 50-year lifespan for what's being called the world's largest single fund aimed at African development.'[72] More recently CDB entered a partnership with Nigeria's United Bank of Africa, which, though not involving equity, will 'expand the Chinese bank's ability to finance infrastructure projects in Africa.'[73] At about the same time the government's Commercial Bank of China was in the process of acquiring a $5.56 billion stake in South Africa's Standard Bank.[74]

In 2008, the head of China's ExIm Bank encouraged unemployed and under-employed Chinese rural workers to move to Africa to farm in countries that have 'plenty of land, but food output is not up to expectations.'[75] In a 2007 speech in Chongqing, where urban development projects are expected to uproot millions of rural residents, he said, 'The bank will give full support to the farmers in terms of capital investment, project development and product-selling channels.'[76] Some 300–400 Chinese farmers already have leased about 4050 hectares in Uganda, on which they employ hundreds of laborers. Negotiations are currently underway to lease arable land outside Nairobi in Kenya, where the Chair of the China–Africa Baoding Business Council explains that Chinese farmers will bring improved seed varieties, methods and equipment such as two-wheel tractors.[77]

The most significant criticism of Chinese aid in comparison to that of other donors relates to adverse economic, socio-cultural and human rights impacts on local communities, as illustrated by the Sudan case. Oilfield development there also illustrates China's strength in competing with the West for Africa's natural resources. By the late 1970s, Chevron had found significant oil deposits in the Bentiu area. Though the oilfields straddled the border between Northern and Southern Sudan, the main residents were non-Islamic Nilotic peoples who identified with the southern region, which had its own legislature and chief executive following the

1972 Addis Ababa Agreement that brought to an end the first phase of the North–South civil war. I was working in the Southern Sudan at the time as a UNDP consultant dealing with the social impacts of the Jonglei Canal and development of the Nilotic artisanal fishery in the Sudd Region of the Nile that was adjacent to the Bentiu area.

In my 1990 book review of *The Jonglei Canal: Impact and Opportunity*,[78] I accused the editors of ignoring the role of the canal in renewing the civil war (1983–2005). Another contributing factor of even greater importance to civil war renewal was the effort of the government of the Sudan to incorporate, by redrawing boundaries, the oilfields within Northern Sudan. Both factors led to attacks by southern forces on construction activities along the canal and on Bentiu oilfield installations. Chevron withdrew in 1984 after three expatriate workers were killed by southern fighters.

The renewal of the civil war, Chevron's withdrawal and the Sudan government's increasing isolation from the West, especially after the military coup by Islamic militants in 1989, left the door open for the Chinese and other Asian countries, after an initial government attempt to rely on other Muslim oil-producing states was unable to link financial assistance to oil extraction and transport.[79] In the mid-1990s, state-owned China National Petroleum Corporation (CNPC) contracted to build in Khartoum Sudan's first oil refinery. At the same time CNPC acquired the largest interest (40 per cent) in the Greater Nile Petroleum Operating Company, which commenced building a 1600 kilometer pipeline from the Bentiu oilfields to Port Sudan via Khartoum. Both facilities were operational by 1999.

More recently CNPC has acquired a major interest (41 per cent) in the PetroDar Operating Company to exploit the oil reserves in the Melut Basin in adjacent Upper Nile Province, with exports through Port Sudan by another pipeline that was completed in 2006. Together the two pipelines are reported to carry 500 000 barrels a day, with 60 per cent exported to China, which currently is estimated to get 10 per cent of its oil from the Sudan.[80]

According to Christian Aid, compliance of Chinese interests with the government's 'scorched earth' policy against southern ethnic groups[81] has come at a major cost to local communities in the oilfields and along pipeline routes. Christian Aid starts a 2001 report by stating that '[i]n the oil fields of the Sudan, civilians are being killed and raped, their villages burnt to the ground.' During Christian Aid's visit eyewitnesses reported that 'government forces are ruthlessly clearing the way for oil over an ever larger area. In one area of Eastern Upper Nile where a new consortium began prospecting in March 2001, 48 villages have been burned and 55 000 people displaced in the past 12 months.'[82]

Though Christian Aid criticized all Western and Asian companies involved in Sudanese oil production, China is the major beneficiary. Moreover China 'is the key player in the Sudan's arms effort and has sold arms to successive Sudanese governments since the early 1980s, becoming a major supplier in the 1990s.' Deliveries since 1995 'include ammunition, tanks, helicopters and fighter aircraft.'[83] Chinese firms have also built 'arms factories in Sudan, which have proved particularly handy since the UN imposed an arms embargo in 2004.'[84] Some of these arms are distributed to various government-supported militias.

### New Poverty in China and a Rising Gap Between Rich and Poor

There is no question that China, like India, has an impressive poverty reduction record in recent years. Still that record should not obscure the fact that well over 100 million citizens are still impoverished, with the number rising during the current (2009) global recession, in which millions of workers are losing their jobs as factories close down or reduce operations as demand drops for Chinese exports. Furthermore, emphasis on poverty alleviation in academic, international financial institutions and media writing largely ignores the new poverty that is arising as a direct result of China's urbanization, infrastructure (dam construction, in particular) and capital-intensive industrialization policies.

While accurate information on the numbers involved is not available, piecing together what information does exist indicates that the number falling into new poverty in China exceeds 50 million. Estimates of those relocated in connection with dam construction range from 10 million over a 40-year period to 10 million involuntarily resettled from one river alone, the Yangtze. In both cases, available evidence suggests that the large majority were further impoverished.[85] Then there are the countless millions of downstream residents whose agriculture and fisheries are adversely affected when dams alter natural river flows. More recently, urbanization has caused far more involuntary resettlement and new poverty. In 2007 anthropologist Matthew Erie referred to a report from China's Ministry of Labor and Social Security that 'stated that 40 million farmers lost their land over the past decade due to urbanization and another 15 million will suffer the same fate in the next five years.'[86] When the head of China's ExIm Bank stated that over 12 million Chinese would have to leave land surrounding Chongqing by 2020, presumably he was referring to further expansion of a city of over 30 million people.[87]

There are also countless millions of rural residents who are displaced by extractive industries, coal in particular, and more recently by local governments which expropriate collective land leased to farmers for sale to real-estate developers and industry. Then there are demobilized soldiers, with many – who are in that majority coming from rural areas – finding no employment on their return home. According to *The Economist*, in recent years the Red Army's downsizing has released hundreds of thousands of soldiers in addition to regular turnover, while an estimated seven million enlisted men were demobilized in a ten-year period before 2004. Though their unemployment is not an example of new poverty as such, it results in a form of relative poverty of danger to the state since demobilized soldiers 'could act as a "bond" to bring together isolated disaffected groups.'[88] In 2007, 2000 demobilized soldiers 'rioted in two cities 770 miles apart.'[89]

Rural farmers have good cause to be disaffected. With an inadequate safety net when landless, their control over land cultivated on 30-year leases from the state through local collectives was further weakened by a March 2004 constitutional amendment passed by the People's Congress that 'stipulated that the state can legally appropriate land and take back the land-use rights from peasants.'[90] That provision puts rural farmers in direct opposition to corrupt township and county leaders who, as representatives of the state, can sell use rights to that land at a large profit to developers while inadequately compensating the current users. In one case in Fujian Province, local officials offered farmers only $2800 per mu (one-fifteenth of a hectare) after selling the land, 'reportedly earmarked to build luxury villas, to a developer for $92,800 per mu.'[91]

Numbers of protests and organizational capacity have increased significantly in the past ten years even though protesting farmers are apt to be silenced by an overwhelming local police force, or sentenced to prison by local courts. Local protests have increased from 8709 in 1993 to over 32000 by 1999 and to over 87000 in 2005.[92] Moreover, 'after 1998, Chinese peasants' resistance became far more organized . . . Their speakers or representatives are often demobilized soldiers, retired government officials . . . and former government cadres.'[93] Such 'peasant-soldiers are the government's biggest headache,' according to the Beijing Institute of Technology's Hu Xingdou. 'Taught idealism in the army . . . they go back to no work and a countryside rife with corruption.'[94]

The central government is well aware of the threat of rural discontent over loss of land use as illustrated by the recent emphasis on slowing growth 'to redress the growing inequality between the prosperous coastal provinces and the poorer interior ones, and between cities and the countryside.'[95] New policies emphasize the need for a harmonious society and social stability. But such untested policies and slogans as well as new laws are a questionable response to the Communist Party's weak control over provincial, county, township and village governments. Control over provincial governments is weakened by the equal status of provincial governors and central ministers and by the desire of provincial and sub-provincial governments to accelerate the economic growth of their own cities, infrastructure and industries. Furthermore, in a country of over 1 billion people, there are just too many local governments. That fact is one reason why more control was given to village cadres and village households under the responsibility system, an action which amounted in effect to institutionalizing village democracy. But, aside from some experimentation at the township level, democracy stops at the village level so that villagers have no institutional capacity to challenge their exploitation by corrupt officials at township, county and provincial levels. Until the central government deals with that problem, local protests, and the risks they present, can be expected to increase.

## Environmental Degradation, Water Scarcity and Pollution

### Introduction

China has been following in the footsteps of the former USSR by industrializing at the expense of its environment. Along with the rising gap between rich and poor, increasing environmental degradation and pollution have become major concerns of the central leadership. Recent strengthening of the State Environmental Protection Administration (SEPA) is only a small step in the right direction since it remains in the interest of industry to ignore or pay fines rather than control polluting and environmentally degrading activities. Moreover, for a population four times that of the United States, SEPA has only 10 per cent of the staff of America's Environmental Protection Agency.[96]

More effective are reductions in energy consumption subsidies, higher fuel-economy standards for cars (but lower for more polluting diesel-powered trucks) and energy-efficient standards for appliances.[97] On the other hand, 'Overall environmental efforts have lacked effectiveness and efficiency, largely as a result of an implementation gap,' while 'a lack of strong monitoring, inspection and enforcement capabilities and associated penalties are limiting the effectiveness of otherwise sound policies, laws and regulations.'[98] As for China's recent success in controlling logging and implementing reforestation to reduce degradation on sloping land and on the loess plateau and to reduce desertification of arid and semi-arid areas, that has caused China to seek timber elsewhere, including large-scale legal and illegal importation of round logs from Africa, Indonesia and Russia.

Especially constraining are the environmental implications of China's increasing demand for electricity and natural resources to sustain its dependence on heavy industry. According to a World Bank/SEPA report, between 2000 and 2005, total energy consumption increased by 70 per cent.[99] Surging demand, with accompanying brownouts, has been associated with more use of diesel generators, hence increasing China's dependence on oil imports, and with construction of more coal-fired thermal stations, which in 2007 required China for the first time to complement its large national coal resources with coal imports.[100] Construction of hydrodams, currently supplying about 17 per cent of China's electricity, is also increasing since only about 15 per cent of China's hydropower potential has been tapped.[101] Adverse hydropower environmental impacts are many. They include reservoir pollution, reduced river flows (many years the Yellow River no longer reaches the South China Sea), saline encroachment, as in the lower reaches of the Yangtze River, and production of greenhouse gases.

Together air and water pollution have major health, economic and political costs for China. In 2008 *The Economist* referred to an OECD article that estimated that air pollution 'reduces the country's output by between 3 per cent and 7 per cent a year, mainly because of respiratory ailments that keep workers at home,' while a World Bank report estimated that air and water pollution together cost '$100 billion a year, or about 5.8 per cent of GDP.'[102] Pollution has also become a major source of citizen complaints, with Pan Yue, SEPA's dynamic deputy minister, telling *The Economist* that pollution and environmental complaints were second in number only to complaints over land, with 50 000 such protests recorded by the authorities in 2005, 30 per cent increase over 2004.[103]

That such protests are becoming a major threat to the state gains support from recent mortality valuation surveys in Shanghai and Chongqing; these 'suggest that people in China value improvements in health beyond productivity gains'.[104] They also appear to be well informed on the detrimental impacts of pollution on their health. Anthropologist Bryan Tilt's six-months study in 2003 of citizen perceptions of industry-related environmental risks in an urban setting in Sichuan Province illustrates not only the breadth and depth of concern but also an understanding of the risks involved. Tilt's informants 'in all occupational groups reflect a wide spread concern about pollution from township and village industries.' Moreover, 'Their nuanced understanding of the effects of pollution was sometimes startling . . . Many informants discussed in great detail how emission levels had changed through time, how pollution affected the livelihoods and health of their families.'[105] It is no wonder that pollution is also an increasing cause not just of citizen complaints but also of protest, which, as in the case of land protests, continues to be countered in a negative fashion by overwhelming local government force.

Lake Tai is one of the three largest in China. At the time of China's independence, it provided villagers, including those from Kaihsiengkung, with ample aquatic resources including fish and shrimp. Now, highly polluted, it suffers periodic algae blooms due to inflow of chemical wastes, sewage from people and livestock and from agricultural run-off. In 2007, for example, 'at least two million people who live amid the canals, rice paddies and chemical plants around the lake had to stop drinking, or cooking with, their main source of water.'[106] Wu Lihong, a local resident who had been protesting against the lake's pollution for over ten years, had acquired national fame as a 'crusading peasant' who had been declared an 'Environmental Warrior' in 2005 by the People's Congress. That did not protect him, however, from the ire of local officials pushing industrial development agendas. Both he and his wife lost their jobs, while he was 'summoned, detained and interrogated' by local police. Arrested in 2007, he was sentenced that August to three years by a local court.[107]

## Water scarcity and pollution

China's water scarcity and pollution problem is a major threat to the country's wellbeing which will worsen in the years ahead. In 2004, China's Ministry of Water Resources estimated an annual agricultural water shortage for the country of about 30 billion cubic meters and an 'annual shortage of urban and industrial water is about 6 billion m³', with water shortages in 400 of China's 660 cities adversely affecting 160 million people.[108]

Per capita availability of water is only one-fourth of the world's average, while distribution of surface water varies significantly within and between years. Both surface and ground water are also poorly distributed in relationship to demand. Relatively plentiful in Southern China, water resources are inadequate in the four northern river basins. Those basins contain '46 per cent of the national population, 45 per cent of the national GDP, 65 per cent of the national farm land, 59 per cent of the national irrigated farm land, but less than 20 per cent of the national water resources.'[109]

The situation is especially severe in the North China Plain, which includes the lower reaches of the Yellow, Huaihe and Haihe rivers, as well as such major cities as Beijing and Tianjin. Those plain areas 'account for 1/3 of the national GDP and industrial output, but only 7.7 per cent of national water resources.'[110] Demand already exceeds supply in spite of improved irrigation efficiency and a shift in priorities from agriculture to urban residential and industrial use between the early 1970s and the present.

Availability of water is decreasing. In 2002, groundwater supplied 51 per cent of North China's water supply versus only 14 per cent in the rest of China.[111] Not only are supplies being deleted due to falling groundwater tables, but quality is suffering from industrial pollution and chemical run-off as well as from salinity.[112] In a joint 2001 report sponsored by China's Ministry of Water Resources, the World Bank and Australian AID, the authors state that 'the acute water shortage and pollution problems in north China will soon become unmanageable – with catastrophic consequences for future generations – unless much more significant, comprehensive and sustained commitments are made.'[113]

The government's main plan for dealing with water deficits in North China, aside from conservation and water pricing reform, is to divert water from the Yangtze River basin. I suspect actual diversion plans date back at least to the late 1950s, when the State Council approved the construction of the Danjiankou Dam on a major northern tributary of the Yangtze, which is by far China's largest river. In 1987 during the Canadian-funded feasibility study for the Three Gorges Dam, I visited Danjiankou to assess what could be learned from the largest previous dam resettlement in the Yangtze River Basin.[114] While there I noticed on the northern edge of the dam what was a much larger diversion canal than would be needed for downstream irrigation or flood management. At the time my Chinese colleagues did not support my speculation that its major future use would be as part of China's South–North Water Diversion Project.

The government's intention to complete the South–North Water Diversion Project was officially announced in 1995, with the general development program approved by the State Council in 2002.[115] The project is mind-boggling in scale. It involves three South–North routes intended to deliver annually 44.8 billion cubic meters of water, which would be approximately 10 times the current capacity of California's vast North–South project[116] and 'equal to water quantity of the Yellow River.'[117] The cost over a 50-year period is estimated at over $60 billion.[118]

Though planning for the western route has yet to begin (and may never begin because of technical, financial and environmental problems), construction on the eastern and central routes is under way. The first stage of the central route is intended to deliver 9.5 billion cubic meters to Beijing and surroundings. It starts from the Danjiankou Reservoir, the capacity of which has recently been increased by two-thirds by heightening the dam 15 meters – and required involuntary resettlement of over 300 000 people, some for the second time. Should reservoir water decline, flows could be augmented from the Three Gorges reservoir. As for the eastern route, it too will be over 1000 km long. Part will include the ancient Grand Canal. Each year, 14.8 billion cubic meters will be delivered to Tianjin and surrounding areas.

Water scarcity varies in different parts of China; water pollution is a problem everywhere. Though the greatest pollution occurs in the North China Plain's river basins, 'in the period between 2001 and 2005, on average about 54 per cent of the seven main rivers in China contained water deemed unsafe for human consumption. This represents a nearly 12 per cent increase since the early 1990s.'[119] Run-off from polluted rivers into the ocean is reported to have contaminated 160 000 square kilometers.[120] Depending on which analytical approach is used, the total cost of China's air and water pollution in 2003 ranges from 2.68 per cent of GDP to 5.78 per cent,[121] bringing the cost of 'water scarcity associated with water pollution to . . . about 1 per cent of GDP.'[122]

## SUMMARY

What is most impressive for global replication about China's development over the past thirty years is the entrepreneurial activities and capacity of China's rural majority in creating and responding to the household responsibility system (HRS). Even before the state formalized the HRS under the leadership of Deng Xiaoping in 1981, 41 per cent of China's production teams were already using the system; this rose to 94 per cent by the end of 1983. Literally hundreds of millions of people were implementing in less than ten years a dramatic transformation from the subsistence cultivation of food grains to private and collective farm and non-farm commercial activities.

Premier Deng also deserves credit for a shift that significantly raised household income and improved living standards. Under his leadership China's central banks supported private sector enterprise in rural villages and towns with favorable lending policies. The resulting combination of local rural initiative with supportive central government policies has global applicability not just in late-developing countries but also in the United States and elsewhere.

On the other hand, Deng's use of the Red Army in 1989 to repress the pro-democracy student demonstrations reasserted state control. The Tiananmen Square massacre, at least indirectly, also led to a shift from a rural development partnership between local people and the government to large-scale state-controlled industrial development and urbanization. MIT political economist Yasheng Huang argues persuasively that such a transition was due in large part to a shift from central government leaders who supported rural development to those favoring urban development and capital-intensive industrialization at the expense of China's rural majority.[123] Not only was rural finance no longer available, but rural areas were now expected to subsidize the urban industrial sector through increased taxation and higher-cost social services.

China's emphasis on rapid growth of large-scale capital-intensive industry since the early 1990s is largely responsible for the wide range of current threats. Contributing to the rising gap between rich and poor is a much slower increase in the income of rural households during the 1990s than during the 1980s. Increases in new poverty follow from the ease with which township, county and provincial leaders can acquire village leasehold lands for dam construction or for industrial and urban development. The central government is well aware of the threat of rural discontent but corrective policies are hampered by weak control over often corrupt leaders at the township and higher levels. Control over provincial governments, for example, is weakened by the equal status of provincial governors and central ministers and by the desire of provincial and sub-provincial governments to accelerate their own economic growth.

Increasing demand for such natural resources as minerals, fuels and timber is having adverse global impacts. Within China, industrial pollution of water and air is adversely affecting health and becoming a major source of increasing citizen complaints. As of 2007, China has become the major contributor of greenhouse gases, a trend which can be expected to continue so long as a new coal-fired thermal plant starts operating each week. Groundwater resources are being depleted in China's larger urban and industrial areas while expensive infrastructure projects to transfer water from the Yangtze River to the cities and rivers of the more densely populated North China Plain are threatened by glacial retreat, caused by global warming, on the Tibetan Plateau.

China's leadership since 2004 is well aware of the threats posed by social discontent and environmental degradation. The need for greater security of rural household and village leasehold is at least under discussion as are more friendly economic and social policies for rural areas. More clout is being given to the State Environmental and Protection Agency (SEPA), though its strength is still weak in comparison to that of large state and provincial industries and urban authorities. Meanwhile China continues its unsustainable policy of capital-intensive industrial and urban growth.

# NOTES

1. Since the 1970s I have visited mainland China on six occasions. The first visit was as a tourist on a brief one-day bus tour through villages adjacent to Macao. In 1986 and 1987 I visited China on three occasions while an adviser to a Canadian consortium involved in a detailed feasibility study of the Three Gorges Project in collaboration with senior engineers of China's Ministry of Water Resources and Electric Power. During that period, while traveling extensively in the Yangtze River Basin, I was able to visit villages and towns not accessible to outsiders. Of particular importance to this book were visits which enabled me to evaluate the effectiveness of Premier Deng Xiaoping's Household Responsibility System (HRS).

I returned to China in May–June 1994 as a member of the newly formed International Environment Protection and Resettlement Panel of Experts for the Longtan Hydroelectric Project in Southwest China's Guangxi Zhuang Autonomous Region. Longtan had been designed as a high dam on the upper reaches of the Pearl River to export 5000 MW to rapidly growing Guangdong Province and to funnel water downstream via a cascade of dams. Subsequent visits of our five-person panel, which included three government engineers, were canceled after the government decided to proceed without World Bank assistance. My last visit to China was in March 2005 as a team member of The Nature Conservancy's China Dams Strategy Assessment, during which we traveled extensively in Yunnan, including visits to the upper reaches of the Mekong, Yangtze and Nu/Salween Rivers.

2.   Yasheng Huang (2008). *Capitalism with Chinese Characteristics*. Cambridge: Cambridge University Press.
3.   Perry Link (3 April 2008). 'He Would Have Changed China.' *The New York Review of Books*.
4.   Yasheng Huang. Op. cit. Pages 89–91.
5.   *Ibid*. Page 89.
6.   Chinese Academy of Social Sciences, http://bic.cass.cn/English – Chinese Government's Official Web Portal.
7.   Communist Party of China (23 June 2006). 'Ideological Foundation.' Available at http://english.cpc.people.com.cn/66739/4521326.html.
8.   Justin Yifu Lin (May 1987). 'The Household Responsibility System Reform in China: A peasant's institutional choice.' *American Journal of Agricultural Economics*. **69** (2). Page 410.
9.   *Ibid*.
10.  Yasheng Huang. Op. cit. Page 33.
11.  *Ibid*. Page 172.
12.  Several cautions are needed in analyzing Kaihsiengkung data. On most occasions research was completed during short visits of several months or less, although in Fei's case he spoke the local dialect before his first visit. Quantitative data such as production and per capita income were usually acquired from the village leadership rather than being gathered by the researcher, while its analysis is difficult because of non-existent information on rates of inflation during different periods. Data on population and number of households was influenced by periodic incorporation and removal of outlying hamlets. Nonetheless, based on villager comments and on changes in housing and family consumption, the trends noted are clear.
13.  Fei Hsiaotung (1983). *Chinese Village Closeup*. Beijing: New World Press. Page 94.
14.  *Ibid*. Page 11.
15.  *Ibid*. Page 12.
16.  Fei Hsiaotung (1981). 'The New Outlook of Rural China: Kaihsiengkung revisited after half a century.' Huxley Memorial Lecture for 1981. 18 November.
17.  *Ibid*.
18.  Xiangqun Chang (2004). 'Lishang-Wanglai: Social support networks, reciprocity and creativity in a Chinese village' PhD dissertation. London School of Economics.
19.  The second was a shift in the second half of the 1990s to privatization of former collective enterprise 'within two months time without any social chaos.' See Xiangqun Chang (2005). 'Changing Relationships between Villagers and the State in a Chinese Village over 70 years: An analysis with a Chinese model of reciprocity *(lishang-wanglai)*.' Paper presented at the *Fourth International Convention of Asian Scholars (ICAS4)*. Shanghai. August 2005. Page 15.
20.  Alan P.L. Liu. 'The "Wenzhou Model" of Development and China's Modernization.' *Asian Survey*. **32** (8). August 1992. Pages 696–711.
21.  Fei (1981). Op. cit. Page 1.
22.  Fei (1983). Op. cit. Page 209.

23. Some confusion exists as to whether reference is to households or to families, two or more of which could belong to a household.
24. Fei Hsiaotung (16 September 1987). Verbal communication to the author in Beijing.
25. The New Sky section is based on my December 1987 and April 1988 field notes and on CIPM Yangtze Joint Venture (1988). 'The New Sky Experience.' Appendix B of Volume 9 '*Resettlement. Three Gorges Water Control Project: People's Republic of China.*'
26. As opposed to New Sky's employment of 87 per cent of its labor force in village industry, surrounding villages employed about 50 per cent. Reasons given for the difference included being closer to Wuhan, historic relations with relatives and others living in Wuhan, exceptional village leadership and educated youth.
27. Xiangqun Chang (2004). Op. cit. Page 1.
28. Ibid. Page 10.
29. Xiangqun Chang (2005). Op. cit.
30. *Ibid.* Page 1.
31. Xiangqun Chang (2004). Op. cit. Page 11.
32. Xiangqun Chang (2005). Op. cit. Page 17.
33. Xiangqun Chang (2004). Op. cit. Page 13.
34. *Ibid.* Page 3.
35. Xiangqun Chang (2007). '*Lishang-wanglai*: A Chinese model of social relations and relatedness.' Paper presented at the *International Colloquium on New Discourses in Contemporary China*. Management School. Lancaster University. 20–21 September. Page 13.
36. Xiangqun Chang (2005). Op. cit. Pages 13–14.
37. *Ibid.* Page 13.
38. OECD (2007). 'Environmental Performance Reviews: China.' OECD.
39. Bloomberg News (20 June 2007). 'China overtakes U.S. in Greenhouse Gas Emissions.' *International Herald Tribune.*
40. See Christopher Flavin and Gary Gardner (2006). 'China, India and the New World Order.' In *State of the World 2006*. New York: W.W. Norton and Company for Worldwatch Institute. Page 3.
41. One method converts a country's GDP into dollars at market exchange rates. The other converts GDP into dollars based on the purchasing power for a country's lower-income majority of a carefully designed cross-cultural and international basket of goods and services.
42. *The Economist* (16 September 2006). 'The New Titans. A Survey of the World Economy.' Page 5.
43. Lester Brown (16 February 2005). 'China Replacing the United States as World's Leading Consumer.' Washington DC: Earth Policy Institute.
44. 'China's economy.' Economist.com (18 March 2008). Page 1.
45. Joseph Kahn and Mark Landler (21 December 2007). 'China Grabs West's Smoke-Spewing Factories.' *The New York Times.*
46. *Ibid.*
47. Alan H. Price, D.S. Nance and Christopher B. Weld (Fall 2006). 'China's Failure to Comply with its WTO Commitments: Subsidies to the Chinese steel industry.' *Global TradeMarkets*. Available at http://www.wrf.com/docs/newsletter_issues/458.pdf.
48. 'About Sinosteel.' Available at http://en.sinosteel.com/zggk/jtjj/.
49. Beijing 2008 (2007). 'Shougang Begins Construction of New Plant outside Capital.' Available at http://en.Beijing2008.cn/07/47/article214024707.shtml.
50. *Ibid.*
51. *The Economist* (15 March 2008a). 'A Ravenous Dragon: A special report on China's quest for resources.' Page 18.
52. *The Economist* (15 March 2008b). Leader, 'The New Colonialists: China's hunger for natural resources is causing more problems at home than abroad.' Page 13.
53. World Bank Office, Beijing (February 2008). *Quarterly Update*. See References for

web address. 'The slowdown in the global economy should affect China's exports and investment in the tradable sector, but the momentum of domestic demand should remain robust and a limited global slowdown could contribute to rebalancing of the economy.' See also *The Economist* (16 February 2008). 'Economics Focus: From Mao to the Mall: Amid all the global doom, the good news is that China is turning into a nation of spenders, as well as sellers.' Page 86.

54. Lester Brown. Op. cit. Page 2.
55. *The Economist* (9 February 2008). 'Briefing: Technology in emerging economies: Of internet cafés and power cuts.' Page 75.
56. Lester Brown. Op. cit. Page 2.
57. *Ibid.*
58. World Bank Office, Beijing (February 2008). Op. cit. Page 25.
59. Ben Schiller (20 December 2005). 'The China Model.' Available at http://www. opendemocracy.net/democracy-china/china_development_3136.jsp. Page 1 (original emphasis).
60. *Ibid.* Page 2.
61. Quoted by Peter Bosshard (June 2007). 'China and the West in Africa: Shared interests?' *China Monitor.* Available at http://www.ccs.org.za/downloads/monitors/ ccsChina Monitor June 2007.pdf.
62. D. Pamlin and Long Baijin (April 2007). 'Re-think China's Outward Investment Flows.' See References for web address.
63. Firoze Manji (27 March 2008). 'China Still a Small Player in Africa.' *Pambazuka News.* Available at http://www.pambazuka.org/en/category/features/46990.
64. *The Economist* (15 March 2008a). Op. cit. Page 13.
65. Lesley Wroughton (2008). 'World Bank sees change in China's African role.' Johannesburg. 5 February (Reuters).
66. China did not totally neglect Africa in the past. Its involvement, however, was more related to political than economic reasons. An example was China's funding and building the Tan-Zam railroad in the 1970s to give Zambia port access in Tanzania after railway connection through Angola and to South African ports was severed.
67. Peter Bosshard (May 2007). 'China's Role in Financing African Infrastructure.' Berkeley, CA: International Rivers Network.
68. Available at http://www.news.bbc.co.uk/2hi/Africa/7000925.stm (18 September 2007). 'China opens coffers for minerals.' Page 1.
69. Bosshard (May 2007). Op. cit.
70. *Ibid.* Page 4.
71. International Rivers (no date). 'Mambilla Dam, Nigeria.' Available at http://www. internationalrivers org/en/africa/mambilla-dam-nigeria.
72. Zhang Yuzhe (26 July 2007). 'China's Unique Cash Pool for Building Africa.' *Caijing Magazine.*
73. Matthew Green and Jamil Anderlini (30 October 2007). 'China's CDB Seals Nigerian Deal.' *Financial Times.*
74. *Ibid.*
75. Richard Spencer (12 February 2008). '750 000 Poor Chinese Head to Africa to Exploit Resources.' *The Daily Telegraph.*
76. Dominique Patton (6 April 2008). 'China Eyes Idle Farmland in Country.' *Business Daily* (Nairobi).
77. *Ibid.*
78. Thayer Scudder (1990). 'Review of *The Jonglei Canal: Impact and Opportunity.* Paul Howell, Michael Lock and Stephen Cobb (eds).' Pages 1073–4.
79. Ali Askouri (14 December 2006). 'China's Investment in Sudan: Destroying communities.' *Pambazuka News.* **282.**
80. *The Economist.* (15 March 2008a). Op. cit. Page 14.
81. Christian Aid (March 2001). 'The Scorched Earth.' See References for web address.

I previously found Christian Aid's reporting on India's Sardar Sarovar Dam Project and Lesotho and South Africa's Highlands Water Project to be accurate.

82. *Ibid.* Executive Summary. Page 1.
83. *Ibid.* Page 19.
84. *The Economist.* (15 March 2008a). Page 16.
85. See Scudder (2005).
86. Matthew Erie (May 2007). 'Land Grade Here and Real Estate Market There: Property law reform in the People's Republic of China.' *Anthropology News.* Page 36.
87. Dominique Patton. Op. cit. Page 2.
88. *The Economist* (20 November 2007). 'Beware of Demob: A reserve of unemployed ex-servicemen worries China's leaders.' Pages 49–50. The quote refers to comments from the article that follows by the Chinese Academy of Social Sciences' Yu Jianrong.
89. Yasheng Huang. Op. cit. (note 2). Page 259.
90. Yu Jianrong (Spring 2007). 'Social Conflict in Rural China.' *China Security.* **3** (2). Page 6.
91. Mark Magnier (27 May 2006). 'Organizer of Land Seizure Protest in China is Sentenced.' *Los Angeles Times.* Page A21.
92. Yu Jianrong. Op. cit. Page 5.
93. *Ibid.* Page 6.
94. *The Economist.* (20 November 2007). Page 50.
95. *The Economist* (15 March 2008a). Op. cit. Page 17. Some of the analysis in this introduction draws heavily on this excellent 14-page report which concludes 'that the impression remains that the government is fighting a losing battle' (page 21).
96. *Ibid.* Page 21.
97. *Ibid.* Page 20.
98. OECD. Op. cit. (note 37) Pages 2 and 4.
99. World Bank / State Environmental Protection Administration (SEPA) (February 2007). *Cost of Pollution in China: Economic estimates of physical damage.* Washington DC: World Bank.
100. *The Economist.* (15 March 2008a). Page 17.
101. Power Technology (no date). 'Xiaolangdi China Hydro Electric Power Plant.' Available at http://www.power-technology.com/projects/xiaolangdi/
102. *The Economist.* (15 March 2008a). Page 18.
103. *Ibid.*
104. World Bank / SEPA (February 2007). Op. cit. Page xv.
105. Bryan Tilt (2006). 'Perceptions of Risk from Industrial Pollution in China: A comparison of occupational groups. *Human Organization.* **65** (2). Page 124.
106. Joseph Kahn (14 October 2007). 'In China, a Lake's Champion Imperils Himself.' *New York Times.*
107. *Ibid.*
108. 'Water Resources in China.' Home Page of the Ministry of Water Resources, People's Republic of China (2 August 2004). Available at http://www.mwr.gov.cn/english/20040802/38161.asp. Page 7.
109. *Ibid.* Pages 4–5.
110. *Ibid.* Page 5.
111. CCAP-UC Davis China Water Resource Team (no date). 'Groundwater in China: Development and Responses.' Power Point Presentation. Available at http://www.iwmi.cgiar.org/Assessment/files/Synthesis/China%20CCAP_Davis%20Team.ppt
112. *Ibid.*
113. World Bank. (2 April 2001b). *China: Agenda for water sector strategy for North China. Volume 1: Summary report.* Report No. 22040-CIIA.Washington DC: World Bank. Page vii.
114. 383 000 people were resettled.

115. Ruxiang Zhu (no date). 'China's South-North Water Transfer Project and its Impacts of Social and Economic Development.' See References for web address.
116. Richard Stone and Hawk Jia (25 August 2006). 'Hydroengineering: Going against the flow.' *Science.* **313**. Pages 1034–1037.
117. Ruxiang Zhu. Op. cit.
118. 'South-to-North Water Diversion Project, China' (no date). *Water Technology.* Available at http://water-technology.net/projects/south_north/.
119. World Bank/SEPA. Op. cit.
120. *The Economist.* (15 March 2008a). Op. cit. Page 18.
121. World Bank/SEPA. Op. cit. Page xvii.
122. World Bank/SEPA. Op. cit. Page xvi.
123. Yasheng Huang (2008). Op. cit. (note 2).

# 6. Zambia

## INTRODUCTION

In April 2007, 16 donors wrote in the country analysis of their Joint Assistance Strategy for Zambia (JASZ) 2007–2010 that 'from being a middle income country at independence in 1964, . . . the country is at present among the poorest in the world.'[1] Zambian business consultant Silane Mwenechanya states that in 2005, 78 per cent of Zambia's employed population worked, 'without any legal protection,' in the informal sector of the economy. The earnings of most were insufficient to afford a 'Basic Needs Basket' of essential foods, shelter, energy, water and other essentials.[2]

This chapter explains the reasons for this decline and the constraints that must be overcome before Zambia, as in its Vision 2030 and Fifth National Development Plan (2006–2010), can once again achieve middle-income status. Some of the issues examined can be generalized to other African countries.[3] Dealing with constraints to development will be very difficult. Zambia is a complex and highly diverse country. Donors and government officials, while emphasizing the importance of capacity building, continue to underestimate and neglect the development potential and characteristics of Zambia's citizens. Those citizens have shown the ability to innovate and improve their livelihood, as in China and the United States, when opportunities are available. They have also shown patience under difficult political conditions; Zambia which became independent in 1964, is one of the few African countries which have avoided ethnic violence and civil war prior to and since independence. Avoiding such conflicts is a major accomplishment in a country with over 70 ethnic groups that speak more than 40 languages. It reflects well on Zambia's citizens as does the increasing amount of inter-ethnic marriage among villagers and among the educated elite.

Zambia is a landlocked country of 750 000 km² with 11.5 million people in 2007[4] and a population density of 15 per square kilometer. Sixty per cent of the population is rural, with 81 per cent – as opposed to 34 per cent for urban residents – falling below the national poverty line in 2006.[5] Per capita income was only $490 in 2005.[6] Such overviews, however, are not very informative unless complemented with details on the country's geography, and on how Zambians make a living and have been impacted by, and responded to, unfavorable national and World Bank development policies.

More informative in a global context is Zambia's poor standing among other nations. Zambia is ranked 165 of 177 nations, for example, in the United Nations Development Programme's 2007/2008 Human Development Index, 117 of 128 countries in the 2007 Global Competitive Index and 116 of 178 countries in the 2008 'Doing Business' ranking.[7] Even among countries in Sub-Saharan Africa, Zambia's ranking is in the lower half. Governance challenges include being among the 'poorer performers in the control of corruption.'[8] Especially worrisome is Zambia's weak system of education. In primary schools, the mean reading and math scores of fifth grade children were second from the bottom of 15 Sub-Saharan countries while secondary school enrollment rates 'are lower than the average for Sub-Saharan Africa.'[9]

Zambia is exceptionally well endowed with forest, land, mineral and water resources, which, along with the enterprise of its citizens, were a major reason for the country being middle income at the time of independence. English is the official language, while four of seven regional languages are spoken by over half a million people. One of the four, Tonga, includes the Gwembe Tonga, whom my colleague Elizabeth Colson and I have been studying since 1956. Small-scale agriculture employs two-thirds of Zambians, including most Gwembe Tonga. Increases in their purchasing power for locally grown foods, locally manufactured goods and locally provided services are as essential for Zambia's development as they are in other African countries in the earlier stages of industrial development.

Increasing agricultural productivity will not be easy for local, national and international reasons. At the local level a starting point needs to be greater awareness of the differing potential of Zambia's 36 agro-ecological zones.[10] Current national problems include irregular rainfall, increasingly adverse impacts expected from global warming and a history of government neglect of agriculture. International problems include adverse international terms of trade, including especially destructive agricultural subsidies for farmers in the European Community and the United States, and donor neglect of small-scale commercial agriculture. These are just some of the constraints that will be assessed in this chapter.

## MY ZAMBIAN EXPERIENCE

I first traveled to Zambia in September 1956 to initiate with Elizabeth Colson what has become the most systematic long-term study of an African society and quite possibly of any society outside the United States,

Europe and Japan. At that time Zambia was still Northern Rhodesia, a Protectorate under the British Colonial Service, while I had just completed my second year as a graduate student in anthropology at Harvard. Colson, now retired in Zambia and California, had been asked to lead the study under the auspices of the British-financed Rhodes-Livingstone Institute located on the outskirts of the capital city of Lusaka. One of the world's most prominent social anthropologists and a member of the U.S. National Academy of Sciences, Colson was the logical person to direct the study because she was a former director of the Institute and had already carried out detailed research in an ethnically similar area.

Aside from a year in Bermuda as a child during the 1930s' depression I had never been overseas, let alone lived in an isolated, disease ridden, semi-arid rift valley in which the first full primary school had just been opened for a total population of about 80 000 people. My luck in having Colson as my mentor during my first fieldwork became obvious immediately after our arrival. When inviting Colson to lead the study, the Institute's Director, Henry Fosbrooke, had requested that she bring with her someone to study the human geography of the future Kariba reservoir basin. Since I was only a graduate student and the director was a geographer, as well as a strong-willed former British colonial official, he assumed that he would be responsible for overseeing my work. That was not Colson's intention. 'Look,' she said, 'Scudder is my colleague and we will work together as colleagues. Your views on research topics will, of course, be welcome, but how we work together and how we share research topics will be Scudder's and my responsibility alone.' That was that. Subsequently Fosbrooke became a close friend, who in later years taught me to water ski when my wife Eliza and I visited him at his retirement home close to Masailand (where he had been a district commissioner) and overlooking a volcanic lake within a short distance of Tanzania's Mount Kilimanjaro.

Colson and I arrived in the Middle Zambezi Valley during the hottest time of the year, with daily temperatures exceeding 100 degrees Fahrenheit. Colson could already speak Tonga; I knew only a few words of greeting. For the first few weeks we had only one vehicle and pitched our tents side by side on the edge of one of the larger villages. During the first few days I was overwhelmed, and on one occasion, after returning to our camp, I told Colson that I was uncertain as to whether I could stick it out. Her reply was only, 'Well, that will have to be your own decision.' That night, as on previous nights, I put so much copper sulfate into my canvas bath to kill the parasites that carried schistosomiasis that the water turned blue. Then after we drank our nightly gin and tonic and prepared for bed, I barricaded myself within my tent with no thought to what I would do if a poisonous snake or other wildlife was already resident inside.

A few weeks later, I received my own Land Rover – a short wheel base four-wheel drive vehicle which I could turn into a convertible and crank down the windshield to a horizontal position. Next it made sense for me to move into 'my own village' to broaden our research and to keep from getting on each other's nerves. To keep in touch we agreed to exchange copies of our typed research notes (in those days we used portable type-writers) and to meet at least once a fortnight to share experiences and insights.

I picked Mazulu – a small village of 126 people and 20 households that were strung out along an ancient, elevated terrace overlooking the Zambezi. A very large Indian tamarind tree, under which I pitched my tent, divided the village into two sections. Finally on my own, the next ten months were among the most intensive and intellectually profitable of my career. Since then I have returned to Zambia and Mazulu on eighteen occasions, varying in length from several weeks to a year.

I also expanded my research and consulting between 1956 and 2002 to four other countries in the vicinity. Some of what I have learned in Zambia, Zimbabwe, Botswana, Lesotho and Mozambique about a local people's strengths and weaknesses, about culture change and continuity, about the strengths and weaknesses of colonial, national and international development policies, and about how local people have responded to those policies informs this chapter.

## LOCAL INITIATIVE: THE GWEMBE TONGA CASE

### Introduction

There have been very few long-term studies of the same individuals, house-holds, communities and ethnic groups in a late-industrializing country. I can think of only five that have continued for over fifty years,[11] one of which is our study of the Gwembe Tonga. It is also the most detailed long-term study of the impacts of a major development intervention (the Kariba Dam) and of national independence on a society's members. It is the gathering of comparable time-series data on a people's environment, demography, society and culture that make long-term studies so valuable. Few such studies had been initiated at the start of our research in the 1950s. Even today, the number is far too few for improving our under-standing of the dynamics of change and continuity and, more specifically, on how members of low-income societies are impacted by, and respond to their incorporation within a wider national and international political economy.

In the 1950s, most detailed anthropological studies of specific communities or wider social and political units were 'one-shot studies' averaging about a year, that occasionally were followed by short revisits ten or more years later. The initial detailed study was often completed by a graduate student and written up as a PhD dissertation. The best dissertations were often those of scholars who sought employment in colleges and universities at that time; their findings were then revised and published in book form to meet tenure requirements. The time spent doing research in the 'field' among real people was just too short for formulating a science of society and, in particular, of social change and continuity.

In the 1950s, lack of time-series data based on long-term studies influenced most anthropologists and other social scientists to view small-scale societies as relatively closed and conservative 'traditional' systems. China's Kaihsiengkung Village, described in the previous chapter, is one of the five community studies on which we have detailed time-series data for over 50 years. When Fei began his research in 1936, the large majority of households were impoverished subsistence farmers living in a relatively closed community dominated by absentee landlords. By 2004, however, the 790 households had 730 new houses and their members owned 650 motor cycles and 1230 mobile phones. The ancestors of the large majority were the impoverished villagers Fei studied in 1936. The rapidity of change in that village has seldom been achieved in other countries. The nature of that change from a relatively closed society to an open one, however, is relatively common.

University of California anthropologist George Foster also documented increasing social change in the Mexican community of Tzintzuntzan between the 1940s and the 1990s. While analyzing data from the 1940s he concluded that the village's conservatism was due to its inhabitants' 'culture of poverty', which caused them to perceive their social, economic and political environment as a zero-sum game in which any household's gain was at a neighbor's expense. What in fact restricted people's wellbeing was access to limited opportunities in what was then an unfavorable political economy at local, provincial and national levels. When economic conditions improved, Foster found the people of Tzintzuntzan actively improving their livelihood not just in Mexico but also as labor and permanent migrants to the United States.

Among my colleagues in the social sciences there has also been a tendency to view human societies as equilibrium systems, a viewpoint influenced by models taken from the natural sciences. While evidence from long-term studies as well as from history rejects that interpretation, social anthropologists have yet to come to an agreement on just what kind of system a social system is or if it is a system at all. During the 36 years I taught social anthropology at Caltech, I noted that practically all the students majoring in astronomy took my courses – a situation different from other Caltech disciplines. I concluded that their interest was because they too were intrigued by what I called 'messy complex systems' that we do not fully understand.

Yes, the members of a society can behave as if their society is an equilibrium system, especially when it is stressed, as with the Gwembe Tonga, by such extreme events as involuntary relocation in connection with dam construction. Colson and I noted that during the first few years after removal, the majority tried to recreate the familiar. They not only rebuilt similar houses but 'circled the wagons' by increasing the number of kin living in close proximity, including kin who had previously lived apart due to various conflicts and misunderstandings. But, as elsewhere, such responses proved to be temporary. Subsequently the Gwembe Tonga, like members of other forcibly resettled communities, once again began to behave as members of a dynamic, open-ended coping system. Such systems are characterized by varying degrees of change and continuity. But their members also have the capacity to rapidly change values and institutions, including even the very nature of society and culture, as well as to protect important institutions and values that they do not wish to change.

Also influencing the perception of anthropologists that low-income communities were relatively conservative, in that their cultures were slow to change, was the common observation during fieldwork that little experimentation occurred. That was also my perception of the Gwembe Tonga following my initial period of fieldwork in 1956–57. But we learned during subsequent fieldwork that different individuals and households were experimenting with new economic or other activities during each revisit.

Many of the economic experiments failed due to environmental constraints or, of increasing importance as people began to experiment with cash crops, the government's unfavorable agricultural and other development policies. Throughout our fieldwork, the colonial government and different Zambian governments have favored the urban industrial sector. Rural feeder roads for marketing produce have been neglected, as have marketing institutions and favorable pricing policies for rural produce. Yet in spite of such constraints, during each generation we have documented a majority of households accepting a range of innovations with the potential for improving their livelihood.

### The Gwembe Tonga in the 1950s

In the 1950s, the Gwembe Tonga were one of the most isolated ethnic groups in Zambia. Approximately 80 000 people lived in the Middle

Zambezi rift valley in villages grouped around the more fertile alluvial soils along the banks of the Zambezi and its major tributaries. The valley, located well below the surrounding plateaus, was hot and disease-ridden, but the fertility of its riverine alluvia supported one of the highest rural population densities in central Africa.

The villagers coped with irregular rainfall and periodic droughts during the November–March rainy season by evolving and altering an ingenious economic system that combined crop production with livestock management, gathering of wild food plants, fishing, hunting, barter and labor migration to the farms of Northern Rhodesia and the mines and cities of Southern Africa. Central to the cropping system was the twice-yearly cultivation of the more fertile alluvial soils. The main planting of three cereals (maize, sorghum and bulrush millet), legumes and cucurbits was at the beginning of the rains, with the harvest expected just before the Zambezi flooded at the end of the rains in March–April. Then a second, smaller area was planted behind the retreating flood in tributary deltas and along the Zambezi's banks, with those crops harvested before the river began to rise again following the commencement of the rains.

Major problems required adaptive management. Drought was periodic. Some years the Zambezi flooded early and high so that most crops were destroyed. In other years flooding was deficient so that less land could be sown during both cropping seasons. Population increase since the end of the First World War was another problem. Villagers coped by emigrating to the adjacent Northern Rhodesian plateau. They also opened up an entirely new system of agriculture on forested bush soils well back from the river. Using aerial photographs and farmer interviews I dated the system's commencement to the late 1940s. Its initiation was aided by the gradual replacement of hoe cultivation by use of ox-drawn plows and by less risk of crop loss due to reduction of elephants and other large herbivores. The initiators were local entrepreneurs with less access to alluvial soils. By 1956 most of the new land was under cultivation.

Other components of the valley production system also had constraints. Animal trypanosomiasis (sleeping sickness) slowed the introduction of cattle, while sheep, goats and fowl were susceptible to epidemic outbreaks of other diseases. While gathering (including lengthy processing of poisonous seeds and tubers in hunger years), fishing and hunting could provide alternate foods for short periods when crops failed, their main use was to complement, and not replace, grain crops. Crop replacement either required moving in with, or begging from, kin in villages (including those of other Tonga speakers on the Northern Rhodesian Plateau) or men spending longer periods as labor migrants outside the valley.

The first Gwembe Tonga became labor migrants to South Africa and the two Rhodesias in the last few decades of the 19th century. By 1956–57, approximately 42 per cent of adult males left their village to work elsewhere. Most returned in time to help with farming during the next rainy season although at times a minority would be absent for several years. Earning money for buying food was a major reason for labor migration, especially when crops failed. The major reason for those with adequate harvests was to earn money to pay the colonial government's hut tax, to buy consumer goods such as clothes and to help with marriage payments.

**Ability to Experiment and Innovate**

**Introduction**
The policies of the British colonial government in Northern Rhodesia already had had a major impact on the Gwembe Tonga before Colson and I began our research in the mid-1950s. Taxation forced men to earn wages as poorly paid farm, mining and urban workers. Restricting favorable agricultural policies to European farmers reduced the opportunity for Africans to develop local economies based on cash crops. Halting of inter- and intra-tribal raiding, elimination of smallpox and provision of famine relief during periods of drought favored rapid population increase throughout the twentieth century and especially after the end of the Second World War. Establishing clinics and schools became a church responsibility, with the government favoring a different denomination for each of the seven British-established Gwembe Tonga chieftaincies.

Labor migration widened the horizon of Gwembe men but involved few women. Population increase had a major impact on village agriculture. Initially farmers tried to increase the output of older, less frequently flooded alluvial soils by reducing the length of necessary periods of fallow. That was a negative response because by the 1950s many such soils were no longer farmed due to hard-to-control wild grasses which grew over a meter high from a dense network of roots. More positive was the previously mentioned pioneering of non-alluvial soils at a distance of one or more kilometers from riverine villages.

But the major innovation under way in 1956–57 consisted of efforts by risk-taking individuals to shift from hoe cultivation to plowing alluvial and non-alluvial soils with oxen. Ox traction not only allowed larger areas to be cultivated but also increased yields through early planting and a turning under of initial weed growth. The major risk in some areas was that cattle would die of sleeping sickness, which was transmitted from wild game to domestic stock by tsetse flies.

Efforts to build up herds in the valley were not assisted by the colonial government; indeed the Middle Zambezi was designated a quarantined area in order to protect the herds of European and African farmers on the plateau. As a result cattle could be brought into the valley but not exported. Between 1914 and 1956, however, the number of cattle mentioned in official reports increased from under 1000 to 21 000 in 1956, while ox plows increased from 81 in 1936 to 1691 in 1956. Government assistance only began in 1948, when Department of Agriculture veterinary assistants were issued a prophylactic drug to inoculate against sleeping sickness.

Construction of the Kariba Dam in the second half of the 1950s was the major event incorporating the Gwembe Valley and the Gwembe Tonga into the political economy of Northern Rhodesia. Dam site preparation included an improved road that traversed two of the district's seven chieftaincies and part of a third before joining the paved road linking the two Rhodesias. Because the large majority of the Gwembe Tonga wished to resettle close to the reservoir, feeder roads to resettlement sites opened up other areas. Bush clearance in a portion of the future reservoir, though temporary, provided the first major employment opportunity within the valley. Insistence of the Gwembe Tonga on tsetse control through their district council opened up most of the valley for cattle. Gwembe Tonga initiative in responding to new opportunities was most obvious in the development of an artisanal fishery in the new reservoir, initiating cash cropping of grain crops and cotton and a gradually increasing demand for primary, secondary and tertiary education.

**Development and multiplier effects of the Kariba reservoir inshore fishery**
The development of the inshore (artisanal) fishery in the Northern Rhodesian portion of the Kariba reservoir was a major success that became a model for reservoir fisheries elsewhere because it was well planned by members of the colonial government's political administration for the benefit of the Gwembe Tonga. Planning was not without opposition. Officials in the overarching Central African Federation, which included Northern Rhodesia from 1953 to 1963, wanted a large-scale commercial fishery controlled by a white settler corporation as well as a sport fishery for settlers and tourists. Officials in the fishery section of the Northern Rhodesian government doubted that the Gwembe Tonga had the interest and capacity to exploit the fishery's potential.

The Gwembe District Commissioner distributed gill nets to selected individuals, including Gwembe Tonga, primary school teachers and myself, while the dam was being constructed. He also arranged for instruction by Department of Fishery personnel. I was called on to teach a group of young men from Mazulu Village, who soon mastered how to set, harvest and mend the net. The dam was sealed in December 1958. Eight months later, 407 Gwembe Tonga were fishing the reservoir using 748 gill nets. When Colson and I returned in 1962, over 2000 Gwembe Tonga resettlers and hosts were using over 5000 gill nets. That year recorded fish landings exceeded 3000 short tons (over 2.7m kg), with over 4000 short tons recorded during 1963.

The spread effect of income earned during those two years, complemented by cash compensation received during the resettlement process, improved living standards throughout the district. Individual fishers usually were dependent on older non-fishing relatives to finance their nets and improved boats. They operated out of government-organized fish camps with feeder road access, market structures and local government and fish department personnel who recorded output. They also had the opportunity to take short courses at a newly built fishery training center. Credit was available for purchase of nets and boats with an excellent repayment rate. The existence of fish camps also drew Gwembe women into a market economy when they came from surrounding villages to sell foodstuffs and brew beer.

In the mid-1960s, income from the fishery became the major means to buy cattle, ox plows and ox-drawn carts, which revolutionized Gwembe agriculture, to build and stock village shops, tea rooms and beer taverns and to pay primary and secondary school fees and other expenses. Between 1959 and 1969 the number of cattle more than doubled from 17 930 to 40 813. Tsetse control operations associated with the resettlement program enabled ownership of cattle to spread to villages throughout the district. During the 1960s, village agriculture was revolutionized, as most households shifted from hoe cultivation to the use of ox plows for the cultivation of both food and cash crops such as maize, sorghum and cotton. Farmers with larger herds also began to sell surplus stock as a cash crop. Village diets, housing and furnishing were transformed. Daily consumption of animal protein increased. Square huts built from sun-dried bricks and furnished with spring beds and mattresses began to replace unfurnished wattle and daub round huts. New clothing fashions spread widely as did bicycles and radios.

There were three main reasons for the initial development of the fishery. The first was the ability of district officials to plan and implement a state-of-the-art fishery program. The second, of equal importance, was the speed with which Gwembe Tonga resettlers and hosts responded to a new and major development opportunity. The third reason was timing the development of the fishery to coincide with the known explosion of biological productivity that occurs in tropical reservoirs in the years immediately after dam closure. At that time the release of nutrients from flooded soil and vegetation increases phytoplankton on which herbivorous fish feed. At the same time predators are dispersed as the reservoir fills so that species of fish that can adapt to reservoir conditions multiply, allowing the Gwembe Tonga to harvest the temporary increase. Production increased annually until the reservoir's full storage level was reached in July 1963 – four years after the dam was sealed. Fish yields continued to increase through 1964 but then began to decline, diminishing in 1967 to only 1000 short tons. But by then the fishery had provided the capital needed for increasing agricultural productivity and financing non-farm enterprise and education.

**Increasing demand for education**
There was little demand for western schooling prior to Zambian independence in 1964. In the early 1950s, Gwembe District was one of three in which only 25 per cent or less of children were enrolled in primary schools. A major reason for lack of interest in formal education was a realistic perception on the part of children's guardians of inadequate employment opportunities in the colonial political economy. Another reason was inadequate school infrastructure. There was only one full primary school for over 50 000 villagers when we arrived in October 1956 and that had only opened earlier in the year.

It was the transition to independence in 1964 that caused a dramatic change in demand as jobs opened up to replace departing colonial officials and to staff the new African government. Gwembe primary school infrastructure had improved by then, with full primary schools being built in the larger resettlement villages. Also in 1964 the first secondary school opened in the district, with the first graduates assured of starting jobs with good promotion opportunities in the police and the Zambian army. Primary school students were now aware of new employment opportunities and realized the importance of achieving a high pass in their final examinations in order to be admitted to one of the few secondary schools.

Between 1956 and 1972, the number of Gwembe students enrolled in the final year of primary schools within the district increased from 30 to 1267, of which an estimated 253 were accepted for secondary schooling. Competition during the final years of primary school was strong; it was common for those not accepted to repeat a full year to improve their chance of acceptance.

In the mid-1960s we began to collect the names of students attending secondary school in Gwembe and adjacent districts with the intention of surveying at a later date the impact of education on their careers and on Gwembe Tonga society. By the 1970s we had a list of the first 500 Gwembe Tonga secondary school leavers. School leavers we defined as students who had completed at least one full year of the five-year secondary school curriculum before a December 1972 cut-off date.[12] The actual list included 518 Gwembe Tonga, which we estimated were more than 90 per cent of the district's initial secondary school leavers. Over a four-year period (1973–1976) we interviewed 176 (34 per cent of the 518) and in 1976 we also obtained occupational data on 417 (80 per cent).

These school leavers were just starting their careers, since the age of the large majority was under thirty. Some 77 per cent were employed in a wide variety of government institutions as opposed to only 6 per cent in the private sector. Eight per cent were pursuing further education, while only 3 per cent were unemployed. The remaining 6 per cent were mainly self-employed in the informal sector of the economy. The major employer was the Ministry of Education (27 per cent), followed by the security forces (11 per cent), and the Ministry of Health (8 per cent).

Currently we are updating our information on the careers of the 176 people interviewed in the 1970s. Although we have yet to analyze the data, it is clear that education has been responsible for the stratification of what was formerly an egalitarian society, with the most successful graduates joining the Zambian middle class and playing an important role in Zambia's political economy. It is also clear that due to weak government policy toward private sector manufacturing, formal employment continues to be primarily in government services.

The proportion of Gwembe students who are accepted in secondary schools remains lower than in urban areas and in less isolated rural areas because teachers view the hot, dry and isolated Zambezi Valley as an African version of Siberia. Teacher turnover is high, leading to poor teaching quality. Of the first 500 school leavers on our list, only 12 per cent were girls due to a persistent bias of their guardians against education for women. As for girls who reached secondary school, they tended to be younger than boys. They also had a higher graduation rate in spite of hostility from boys toward high-achieving girls and risk of expulsion should they become pregnant.

Poverty also continues to be a constraint to educating children beyond primary school in both Mazulu village and elsewhere in the district. In the 1980s, my wife Eliza and I decided to experiment with educational outcomes by agreeing to help with the expenses of any Mazulu student accepted in secondary school provided thereafter they received good grades and sought supplemental funds. Soon we realized we had made a mistake by concentrating on secondary school education because the number accepted had increased faster than our finances and because unemployment rates among secondary school graduates had risen due to a downturn in the Zambian economy. So we shifted our attention to graduates accepted into the University of Zambia and other tertiary educational institutions.

To date four Mazulu students have graduated from the university and two others are in attendance. Of the graduates, one is currently on a full scholarship while pursuing an MSc degree in electrical engineering at the University of Leeds in the United Kingdom. Another, with a BA degree in education, is teaching in an urban secondary school. The third graduated with a degree in law and then received his practicing certificate from the Zambian Institute of Advanced Legal Education. He was admitted to the Bar in February 2008 and currently is an associate at the law firm that had also sponsored him. The fourth graduated in 2007 and currently is a clinical care expert in the Ministry of Health. In June 2008 he married. Eliza and I contributed a cow to his marriage payments.

In addition to those six University of Zambia students, we have also assisted nine other students to complete different two-year courses following secondary school graduation. They include agriculture, natural resources and business management, telecommunications engineering and water supply operation. All are courses relevant to building the type of national capacity that Zambia's various governments have failed to provide.

Our 'experiment' in funding tertiary education illustrates the potential of every African village to contribute to capacity building at the national level. It also points up the tragic and unacceptable wastage of human resources due to the inadequate political commitment of Zambian and other countries' governing institutions to financing education at the village level. More than finance is needed, however. Also important are examples and mentoring provided by well-trained, adequately paid and dedicated teachers and village workers who will instill a desire in young children for education starting at the primary school level.

Mazulu's record on achieving tertiary education for its children is very relevant to addressing global threats because one of my major conclusions is that global action requires a much better educated and activist global citizenry. Tertiary education is essential. It is essential to help the graduate find a job since a secondary school degree even in countries like Zambia is no longer sufficient. Tertiary education is also essential to build capacity and citizen activism in all countries, but especially in middle-income countries like China, India and Brazil, with large numbers still living in poverty, and in low-income countries like Zambia.

# BANKRUPTING ZAMBIA'S POLITICAL ECONOMY

**Introduction**

What were the causes for Zambia's decline in a single generation from a middle-income country at independence in 1964 to becoming one of the poorest countries in the world? To what extent are the causes also applicable to other countries in Sub-Saharan Africa? Harvard political scientist Robert Bates theorizes[13] that African governments are the main culprits. I agree based on my own research and consulting in 20 African countries. In the Zambian case, which also figures prominently in Bates's book, I would emphasize government corruption from the national to the local level. Also warranting special emphasis are the Zambian government's development policies, which continue to favor the urban industrial sector, mining especially, at the expense of the small-scale rural farming community.

The nature of Zambia's governing institutions at the center, corruption and adverse rural–urban terms of trade have been the major causes of downturn throughout Zambia's history. There are also a number of important contributory causes at particular times. Zambia suffered as a frontline state throughout the war for Zimbabwe's independence. Another cause, apparent since the 1980s, is the impact of HIV/AIDS. Crop failure due to drought and livestock diseases, especially East Coast Fever, has periodically ravaged southern Zambia.

Climate change and environmental degradation can be expected to play an increasing role in Zambia's future. Such extreme climatic events as drought and floods appear to be increasing as a result of global warming. Southern Zambia, and the Middle Zambezi Valley in particular, are more susceptible to drought since the 1980s, with villagers more dependent on food aid. Scientists James Hurrell and Martin Hoerling attribute such droughts to warming of the Indian Ocean: 'In our models, the Indian Ocean shows very clear and dramatic warming into the future, which means more and more drought for Southern Africa . . . It is consistent with what we would expect from an increase in greenhouse gases.'[14] Zambia adds its own contribution to greenhouse gas emissions due to the combined effect of the mining industry and land use change.[15]

Since the turn of the century, increased Zambezi River flooding has required the flood gates of the Kariba and Cahora Bassa dams to be opened at short notice on several occasions with downstream loss of life and extensive flooding of communities and cropland. In February 2008 President Mwanawasa declared a national emergency after extensive flooding on the Zambian plateau.

Most of Zambia's '19 national parks and 34 game management areas are degraded.'[16] Poaching continues to be a serious problem with 'bush meat' having a ready market in town and urban centers. Deforestation is causing serious environmental degradation. Though over 50 per cent of Zambia is forested, 'between 1990 and 2005 Zambia lost 13.6 per cent of its forest cover' with the rate of deforestation increasing 1 per cent per annum between 2000 and 2005.[17] That is one of the highest rates of global deforestation. The use of charcoal as the principal fuel of 90 per cent of Zambia's rapidly urbanizing population is a major cause.[18]

## The Government Role

### Introduction
Two political parties vied for control at the time of independence. The winning party, the National Independence Party (UNIP) under President Kenneth Kaunda, won again in 1968, and then entrenched its position by becoming a one-party state in 1972 with a new reinforcing constitution and supporting national elections in 1973. Increasing opposition resulted in the renewal of multi-party elections in 1991, when the Movement for Multi-Party Democracy (MMD) won the presidency from Kaunda with 81 per cent of the vote and won over 80 per cent of elected seats in Parliament. Fredrick Chiluba served as president during the two five-year terms allowed under yet another new constitution. In the 2001 and 2006 elections, MMD won again with Levy Mwanawasa elected president on both occasions. Following Mwanawasa's death in 2008, MMD's Rupiah Banda was elected as his replacement for the remaining three years.

Bates's argument for Zambia, as for other African nations, is that 'independence represented the capture of the state by local political elites who then used power to accumulate wealth.'[19] Within the party in power, senior politicians also competed for and dominated the major government positions. Trying to distribute benefits among party members and their supporters, as well as to co-opt opponents, required Kaunda to spread the wealth at hand and to continually seek new wealth as competition increased.

Before Zambia became a one-party state, Kaunda sought new wealth by launching several economic reforms. In the first the government took over a number of foreign-owned firms, the management and assets of which Kaunda used to compensate those supporters 'who lost out in the competition for power.'[20] When one disenchanted province joined the opposition after the 1968 general election, Kaunda nationalized the copper industry to gain additional assets. That was followed by nationalizing the banking and insurance industries when a former vice-president threatened, with his supporters in two other provinces, to form a new party. Hence on each occasion 'the president extended the scope of the government's control over the economy.'[21] He also appointed senior party members to the boards of nationalized firms and as bureaucrats of government agencies overseeing those firms.

Once Zambia became a one-party state in 1972, membership in UNIP 'became a form of citizenship.'[22] Card-carrying party members were given preference for jobs, credit, housing and other benefits. By 1972, however, the good years were coming to an end. Thereafter the Kaunda government began to borrow heavily to acquire new funds for patronage and to subsidize food for urban residents and inefficient government industries. Zambia's external debt rose to $3.26 billion in 1980 and to $7.336 billion by 1991.[23]

**Economic downturn**
From 1964 to the time of writing, the mining of copper and cobalt has provided 70 to 80 per cent of Zambia's foreign exchange. Since independence, policies on expenditure have favored the urban industrial sector at the expense of agriculture and the rural majority. Towns and cities proliferated along the railway line that split Zambia into eastern and western sections. The largest collection of towns was around the copper mines close to the border with the Congo. Lusaka in the central region was the largest city and the capital, while Livingstone dominated the area across the border from Zimbabwe. Roads fanned out from these urban areas into the rural areas, which, however, were not well interconnected.

During the Kaunda era, industrial policy favored the copper industry, and, as an import substitution policy, the assembly of such luxury items as refrigerators, air conditioners, TVs and automobiles for the small Zambian elite.[24] When Fabian Maimbo and James Fry documented[25] for Zambia's Rural Development Studies Bureau in 1975 the implications of adverse rural–urban terms of trade for the 1960–1973 period, Kaunda was praised for emphasizing the paper's importance and the critical need for change. I certainly believed him at the time, but no major policy changes occurred then or later. Lack of capital, according to economist Ann Seidman, was not really a problem. Rather 'the necessary institutional changes have not been made to ensure that these surpluses are directed to the appropriate expansion of productive sectors, in order to reduce dependence on copper exports and increase employment throughout the whole economy.'[26]

In 1974 copper prices dropped at the same time that mining efficiency decreased in the now nationalized industry. The simultaneous jump in the price of petroleum imports and petroleum-based products such as fertilizer worsened the situation. So also did intensification of the war for Zimbabwe's independence, with closure in 1973 of the border with Zambia. No longer were existing export routes through Mozambique and South Africa available so that an alternate and more expensive rail and road routing through Tanzania was required.

Comprehensive international documentation of Zambia's increasing rural and urban poverty started with the International Labour

Organization's 1975 and 1979 surveys of the Zambian economy.[27] By then:

> [T]he fact of rural decline is well known. Senior Zambians, describing the villages where they were brought up, have frequently said to members of the Mission that they now find these villages in decline with poorer quality of life, a lack of goods and resources and deepening poverty . . . The Mission cannot state too strongly that the weight of evidence . . . confirms that very large numbers of rural households are severely deprived, suffer acute seasonal shortages and stress, and are much worse off than they were.[28]

> In addition, the effectiveness of government field staff has been sharply reduced in the last few years through transport difficulties and lack of petrol . . . Our own analysis of the budget allocations for petrol and vehicle maintenance of the Ministry of Agriculture shows a reduction by 1980 to one-fifth the level in 1973, in spite of an increase of both vehicles and staff. We have found officers confined to base for months on end through lack of transport. [As for other services] many rural clinics are having to operate without even minimal supplies of medicines and equipment, including soap, dressings, anti-malarial drugs, etc. . . . Schools too are suffering, especially primary schools, through extreme lack of books and other most basic equipment, [while] many government programmes to assist rural communities to meet basic needs . . . have had to be cut back often to levels so small as to be negligible.[29]

French agronomist René Dumont, who visited Zambia on two occasions at the invitation of President Kaunda, made similar comments in 1979 in referring to 'an almost total collapse of government services at the village level.' Where provision of agricultural services does occur, 'everything' is late: 'finance, supplies, marketing, payment for crops.' As for Zambia's 500 000 'forgotten farmers,' they are provided with 'no incentives whatsoever, except speeches.'[30]

Three subsequent donor reports provide further documentation on Zambia's downturn through April 2008. The first was the World Bank's five-volume *Zambia Poverty Assessment* in late 1994,[31] the second the Cooperating Parties' *Joint Assistance Strategy for Zambia (JASZ) 2007–2010* and the third the World Bank's 2008 *Country Assistance Strategy for the Republic of Zambia.*

According to the Bank's *Zambia Poverty Assessment*, 69 per cent of Zambians were living in poverty in 1991, with the prevalence of rural poverty 76 per cent. While the second and third reports note positive macroeconomic growth since 1999–2000, the Cooperating Partners still list Zambia 'at present among the poorest in the world.'[32] The 2008 Bank report states that despite 5–6 per cent increases in Gross Domestic Product since 2000, '64 per cent of the Zambian population . . . live below the national poverty line' according to 2006 government estimates. The rural poverty estimate is now 81 per cent versus 34 per cent urban poverty because 'the rural economy has stalled.'[33]

**Inadequate capacity building and human development**
The intention of the April 2007 Joint Assistance Strategy for Zambia 2007–2010 (JASZ), produced by the 17 cooperating donors, is to help the government achieve the goals of its Fifth National Development Plan and Vision 2030. The JASZ donors assessed nine country risks. The first related to institutional capacity constraints.[34] To date, 'in terms of improving human development outcomes, results are lacking.' Moreover, results during the first nine years of independence (1964–72) were better than those during the more recent 1999–2005 period.[35]

The donors mention education as the first topic in their commentary on the government's social sectoral plans. They place too much emphasis, however, on universal primary education as if it existed in a vacuum. The same is true for the UN's Millennium Development Goal for Zambia and elsewhere. Such a goal should not be treated as an end in itself. It must be related to Zambian and African needs and, more specifically, to improved and increased secondary and tertiary education. Yet, according to the World Bank's 2008 Country Assistance Strategy, both secondary and tertiary education are being neglected by the Zambian government.[36] Secondary school enrollment rates at '24 per cent, are lower than the average for Sub-Saharan Africa and much lower than the average for low-income countries.'[37] Educational infrastructure is aging. No new government secondary schools have been built since 1970. As for the whole educational system, it is 'characterized by high drop-out rates between primary, secondary and tertiary levels of schooling.' That is hardly surprising since '[f]or more than 30 years, little has been invested in secondary and tertiary education.'[38]

**Corruption**
The Corruption Profile in Transparency International's 2006/7 Country Study Report starts by stating that '[c]orruption in Zambia has been described as endemic. It can be traced back to the First Republic although it became more rampant following political change and liberalization of the economy in the early 1990s.'[39] After Kaunda declared Zambia a one-party state in 1972, dissent of any kind became dangerous until after the restoration of multi-party democracy in 1991. My own experience provides an example. During the 1980s, Kaunda attempted to establish large commercial farms in each district. In Gwembe District, 2100 hectares of the more productive land were selected for irrigated double cropping in cotton and wheat. The agri-business was dominated by Lummus, an

American builder of cotton gins, with 70 per cent of the shares. Hoescht (Zambia), a subsidiary of the German chemical company of the same name, the government's Lint Corporation of Zambia and a cooperative dominated by local elite each had 10 per cent of shares.

Nine Gwembe Tonga villages with a combined population of over 2000 had customary rights to use the land in question for cultivation and for grazing nearly 3000 cattle and 3000 goats. The state leased that land to the company with no involvement of the local villagers. Three of the nine villages were forced to resettle with minimal compensation, three others lost all their rainy season farmland and the remaining three lost part of their fields and grazing. Six of those villages had already been involuntarily resettled in the late 1950s because of the Kariba Dam project, while a seventh had been forced to move twice – once because of Kariba and once to make way for Zambia's first coal mine.

Though compensation land was inadequate and cash compensation for lost production was minimal, no formal development plan was implemented for the villagers' benefit and no research has since been carried out on how those involved have fared. Anecdotal evidence is that an unknown number had no recourse but to leave the valley to settle in the hilly country of the adjacent escarpment, 'where their cultivation on slopes contributes to deforestation and erosion.'[40]

While the joint venture was under implementation, I made a brief survey of the situation with a Zambian colleague. I was so appalled that I wrote a critical report,[41] which I arranged to be delivered to a prominent member of UNIP's governing Central Committee. I was later told that my report was not appreciated by the President and that I should consider not coming back to Zambia for a while.

The stultifying impact on dissent of the later years of the Kaunda regime made it 'only natural that the seed of corruption would flourish with the coming into power of the MMD Government in 1991 because Zambians had already been indoctrinated into a culture of silence . . . During the first ten years of the MMD rule, corruption became rampant to a point of being institutionalized.'[42] The Attorney General's Report for 1999 showed that:

> President Chiluba himself openly created an illegal fund – the infamous slush fund – that he used to appropriate public funds and 'dole' them out to favoured or politically useful persons or groups without accounting for them. Surprisingly, Parliament allowed criminal funds to be operated throughout President Chiluba's tenure of office . . . On 4th May 2007, Chiluba [and nineteen others] were found liable of defrauding the Zambian Government of more than US $41 million, by the London High Court. The London judgment has since been registered in the Lusaka High Court.[43]

In the last year of Chiluba's presidency 86 per cent of the 91 countries in Transparency International's 2001 Corruption Perceptions Index had less corruption than Zambia.[44]

### Misuse of public funds[45]

Government funds for improving low-income urban suburbs and constructing low-income housing were not available during the Second National Development Plan (1972–76). Yet, according to the 1981 ILO report, 'expenditure on medium- and high-cost housing exceeded the planned provision.' Moreover, subsidies 'on houses provided for government and parastatal employees continued to be given most generously . . . while no loans or grants were available to villages.'[46]

During 1975–80, public sector salaries and allowances were increased. The most advantageous allowances went mostly to highly paid officials 'who are eligible for . . . commuter car allowances, entertainment allowances, payment of electricity and water bills, the provision of one or two servants and a security guard, as well as for generous subsistence allowances when traveling abroad.'[47]

International travel on occasion actually was at the expense of the rural majority. A potential cash crop in the Gwembe Valley was an early maturing malting sorghum which villagers were beginning to grow and which was in increasing demand for an opaque beer manufactured by a government parastatal.[48] Rather than government assisting its production in Zambia, that opportunity was lost when more expensive overseas imports were arranged following government travel to Australia.[49]

Reaching the same conclusion as Seidman, who reported that the funds were there for rural development in the early 1970s, the ILO report stated for the 1975–1979 period:

> [A]lthough funds and manpower were available, they were not used according to the pronounced objectives of meeting the needs of the poorer sections of the population. . . . the total annual additional cost of the salary awards . . . exceeds the sum we estimate to be required to meet basic needs in water, health, education and housing over the next five years.[50]

### The World Bank Role

#### National impacts

The World Bank has made two closely linked, fundamental mistakes in dealing with the Zambian people. The first was its 'one fits all' approach whereby the same growth strategy was applied to all African borrowers in spite of differences between them. The second mistake was the weakness of the strategy applied. The Bank paid little attention to what would likely happen if Zambia followed its policies, nor did it stipulate how they should be implemented. The Bank's strategy called for major reductions in government funding that were bound to produce cuts in social services, including education and health services. It over-emphasized the importance of improving exports, especially copper and cash crops, at the expense of manufacturing and other industries. And it called for public companies to be privatized and for trade liberalization, that is, tariff reduction. Only in the Bank's April 2008 Country Assistance Strategy (CAS) for Zambia for fiscal years 2008–11 has the Bank attempted to correct these weaknesses.

The World Bank's own reports critique its Zambia program. The Bank's Operations Evaluation Department (now the Independent Evaluation Group that reports to the Bank's Board) concluded that 'the Bank's assistance strategy and its performance had been unsatisfactory' during 1996–2001.[51] At the end of fiscal year 2005, half of the Bank's twelve projects were 'deemed to be at risk.'[52] Reasons given for such an unenviable record included too much emphasis on 'far reaching reforms, derived from first-best principles.' Those principles were based on a systematic attempt to apply the Washington Consensus (Chapter 1) without sufficient monitoring to ascertain adverse impacts on poverty alleviation, including employment and social services. As the Bank-assisted 2008 *Growth Report* emphasized, no generic development formula 'exists. Each country has specific characteristics and historical experiences that must be reflected in its growth strategy.'[53]

Other weaknesses included inadequate understanding of the regional implications of rapid tariff reduction, especially in relation to South Africa; delayed acknowledgement of the seriousness of HIV/AIDS; emphasis on special project units (rather than building capacity in existing government agencies and civic society); over-reliance on highly paid international consultants and project infrastructure (housing, vehicles and so on); and inadequate supervision.

Too rapid elimination of national tariffs as opposed to the type of phased reduction preferred by China led to the bankruptcy of a wide range of Zambian private and government-owned business enterprises that were just getting started. In the early 1970s I was impressed when shopping in Lusaka by the gradual appearance of Zambian dairy products and canned beef and fruits. By the 1990s they had been replaced by South African produce and sold by South African supermarkets. I suspect that, as in the demise of a local aquaculture industry in Zimbabwe based on *Tilapia* fish farming, predatory pricing by South African firms was involved. On the government side, corruption was involved in the privatization of some government companies with new politically connected owners making an immediate profit by selling off inventory and equipment.

By the mid-1970s, Zambia's per capita income had begun a gradual decline before leveling off in 1996 and starting a gradual but slight increase in the present century.[54] Throughout, growth in village agriculture has stagnated. Rural poverty today is still about 80 per cent and 64 per cent of the total population live below the national poverty line. The large majority of workers are underemployed in the informal sector, with only 10 per cent employed in the formal sector.[55]

**Impacts on the Gwembe Tonga**
As throughout Zambia, international aid increased in the Gwembe Valley as government services deteriorated. Assistance from bilateral donors and the World Bank has been disappointing in comparison to assistance provided by the local NGO Harvest Help/Zambia. Staffed entirely by Zambians, Harvest Help/Zambia has brought social services and economic development to the Gwembe's most isolated chieftaincy. Their approach has been to require village participation in all planning and implementation tasks. If villages want a primary school they must form the necessary committee, select the site and provide local materials, while Harvest Help provides technical assistance and helps finance construction.

The two largest Gwembe donors have been Germany's government-owned technical cooperation agency (GTZ) and the World Bank. GTZ launched an ambitious project in the early 1990s to develop a lake transport system on the reservoir and an ambitious agricultural and forestry program in two chieftaincies. The lake transport system failed and today there is scant evidence of any major agricultural or other improvements.

I was responsible for initiating the World Bank's first involvement in the Gwembe Valley since completion of Stage 1 of the Kariba Dam Project in 1960 and Stage 2 in 1976/77. In 1995 I was continuing my Zambian research when I heard that a World Bank team had arrived to prepare a country-wide power rehabilitation project with the Zambian Electricity Supply Corporation (ZESCO). The Bank's task manager was Donal O'Leary, with whom I had worked in Lesotho. I invited the Bank team to visit a major resettlement area to see at first hand the adverse impacts of the Bank-financed Kariba Project on resettled villages and on the environment. My hope was that their visit might lead to a bi-national reparations project for the benefit of 150 000 resettlers and their descendents. That would directly benefit the Gwembe Tonga in both Zambia and Zimbabwe and a small number of Kore Kore in Zimbabwe. It would also enable the Bank to pioneer the first donor-financed project to correct new poverty caused by donor-financed development and to show that the Bank really did care about those adversely affected by Bank-financed projects.

Members of the team made two visits. The first visit to the Lusitu (Chapter 3 in this book) included only the team's social and environmental experts who reported to O'Leary the appalling poverty and habitat destruction that they had observed (the Bank's ecologist estimated that it would take the habitat 40 years to recover – if no people lived there!) Some days later, when my fellow researchers and I were resident in another resettlement area, O'Leary and ZESCO's general manager arrived to see the situation first hand. That visit led to a Gwembe Tonga development project being inserted within the $200 million Power Rehabilitation Project at the time of its September 1997 appraisal.

The ambitiously named Gwembe Tonga Rehabilitation and Development Project was inaugurated in December 1998 with a budget of $12.4 million under encouraging conditions. All seven chiefs were present as well as the area's three Members of Parliament. Professor Mwindaace Siamwiza, a resettled Gwembe Tonga and Zambia's leading scientist, gave the introductory speech. Seven years later, including a two-year extension, the Gwembe Tonga project came to an end on 31 December 2005 without completing, indeed scarcely starting, the project's key component. That was rehabilitation of a defunct 750 km road system, referred to as the Bottom Road, which linked all seven chieftaincies to the outside world and was essential for marketing purposes.

Reasons for failure were several, including delayed donor funding on the part of a World Bank partner agency, an unanticipated and expensive program of road demining and weak ZESCO involvement. But I place the major blame on the World Bank, which neglected to become involved in an evolving bi-national project, did not take direct responsibility for financing design, construction and supervision of the Bottom Road, and opted not to become directly involved in financing a planned stage 2 to complete the Bottom Road progress on which the Bank itself considered 'highly unsatisfactory.'[56]

On 27 July 2007 the seven Gwembe chiefs sent a letter to the World Bank's Washington DC office outlining 'the wrongs the Bank has done – background on current suffering of the displaced people following relocation.'[57] The first wrong listed was:

> The Bottom Road Priority for the Gwembe Tonga People. The economic benefits of the Bottom Road can not be over-emphasized as it will open up the valley and as such:

> ● Improve trade along the lake shore,
> ● Ease movement of people

- Improve food security
- Ease marketing of produce and other merchandise in the valley and beyond
- Exploit the tourism potential and abundant mineral resources.
- Improve fishery and setting up aquaculture industries.

# HIV/AIDS

Zambia has one of the worst HIV/AIDS epidemics in the world. By 2007, 1.1 million adults and children, 9.2 per cent of the national population, were estimated to be living with HIV.[58] That year the estimated proportion of adults (aged 15–49) living with HIV was 15 per cent. Women were especially at risk.

Economic impacts are devastating. Avert refers to a 2004 *Times of Zambia* article that quoted the Zambia Business Coalition as linking 82 per cent of identified causes of employee deaths to HIV and 17 per cent of staff recruited are replacements for employees whose death or departure was HIV-related.

Agriculture is especially affected, with Avert noting that 'AIDS is believed to have made a major contribution to the food shortages that hit Zambia in 2002, which were declared a national emergency.'[59] Education is also adversely affected, with John Nyamu reporting in a 2003 news release that 'some 2,000 teachers have died annually during the past two years.'[60] Such deaths not only reduce the number of teachers, but they also help explain the higher prevalence of HIV/AIDS among younger women through teacher–pupil intercourse.

A major reason why HIV/AIDS got out of control in Zambia was that only in 2002 (almost twenty years after the first case of HIV/AIDS was diagnosed) did the government, under President Mwanawasa, take the epidemic seriously. That year a National HIV/AIDS/STD/TB Council began operations as a legally established institution that could receive funding. In 2004 the President 'declared HIV/AIDS a national emergency.'[61]

# DOWNTURN AND THE GWEMBE TONGA

Until the mid-1970s, it was a pleasure to return to the Gwembe Valley for it was obvious to Colson and me, and to the Gwembe Tonga, that living standards had improved significantly. As elsewhere in rural Zambia, those living standards were adversely affected by Zambia's downturn[62] – a decline in wellbeing that still exists. Kariba resettlement has been a contributing factor, as was the war for Zimbabwe's independence. In most resettlement areas there was insufficient land to support the second generation when they married and started their own families. Because national unemployment was increasing at the same time due to Zambia's downturn, young men became more dependent on their elders for land, use of oxen and assistance with school fees and marriage payments – a situation that increased social tensions within the family, kinship networks and villages.

During the war for Zimbabwe's independence, Rhodesian forces drove Zambian boats and fishers off the Kariba reservoir. During land incursions, they terrorized villagers, laid landmines and destroyed bridges. Residents in several of our sample villages were killed, while government services, deteriorating throughout the country, worsened. Some programs, like control of the tsetse fly, stopped entirely, so that sleeping sickness (bovine trypanosomiasis) in cattle increased. The combination of more cattle deaths and inability to purchase new stock because of increasing poverty adversely affected crop yields, forcing more and more households to revert from ox traction to hoe cultivation.

Critical infrastructure, including roads and clinics, deteriorated. Some schools no longer had roofs, tables and chairs. As elsewhere in the country, all services – agricultural, health and educational – deteriorated. Teachers, for example, became increasingly responsible for traveling to district headquarters to get their salaries because of lack of government vehicles and gasoline.

One only had to walk through a village to see how living standards had declined. Ox-pulled carts stood idle with broken axles and no tires. Discarded bicycle frames leaned against houses or hung from trees. Plow parts, broken spring beds and other equipment and furnishings littered the ground.

Less obvious to an observer was the deterioration in social conditions. Intra-village theft of food from fields and granaries had increased as had theft of money and other valuables from houses. Theft also increased within families, with sons stealing the chickens, goats and cattle from parents and other kin to sell on the neighboring plateau to satisfy their own needs. Alcohol abuse increased among both men and women, as did violence-induced injuries including death. There was more abuse of women and children and more suicide.

Misfortunes of any kind increasingly were attributed to witchcraft, which had replaced ancestor worship as the dominant feature in the Gwembe Tonga belief system. Malice toward those who were better off, or who were attempting to improve their wellbeing, increased. Malcontents in the village I know best poured boiling water on the dogs of those they envied, maimed their cattle and poisoned their chickens and other domestic animals. In one case a young man planned to take 30 chickens to sell in Lusaka. After he had accumulated 29, all were poisoned the night before he planned to travel. Categories of people suspected to be witches expanded to include fellow workers and close kin including fathers[63] and, more recently, mothers.[64]

Those are among the negative impacts of the downturn. More positive are ways in which the Gwembe Tonga tried to cope with downturn by further diversifying their household economies and village and religious institutions. A significant number of households left resettlement villages to seek arable land along the shores of the Kariba reservoir or close to the Zambezi below the dam. A still larger number of households emigrated from the valley to farm underdeveloped areas on the plateau.

Women in particular have become more active participants in the informal sector of the Zambian economy, which nationwide employs the largest number of people. In the valley they market produce to local towns. Others have moved to the busy international border town of Chirundu, which is expanding along the main road between Lusaka and Harare. Some are trans-border traders while others have started small businesses, including prostitution, within Chirundu. Other Gwembe Tonga have become active traders in the markets of Lusaka and various towns along the railroad line.

In response to the increased number of NGOs and churches in the valley, the Gwembe Tonga have modified previous political institutions and donor policies to form committees for addressing issues of economic development and religion. Most secondary and tertiary school leavers and graduates consider themselves Christians. Within villages, membership in a widening range of fundamentalist churches is increasing. Church membership is seen by some as a way to reduce the risk of witchcraft. However, German anthropologist Ulrich Luig interprets Christian beliefs 'as manifestation of the desire for change.'[65]

# SUMMARY: CAN THE NATIONAL DOWNTURN BE REVERSED?

**Introduction**

I have not been back to Zambia since President Mwanawasa's election in 2001. During that period the World Bank states that gross domestic product has been growing at 5–6 per cent annually. My colleagues Elizabeth Colson and Lisa Cliggett have also informed me of the noticeable growth of towns and cities along the railroad line. Two obvious changes according to Colson are:

> rapid growth of small towns such as Monze and the emergence of a Zambian middle class. Everywhere building is going on – houses large and small, businesses, private schools, private clinics. More and more private cars. Shops stocked with goods. Shopping malls. Restaurants. These are catering to Zambians as well as expatriates.[66]

Cliggett also refers to the growing middle class and the number of Zambians with cars (the traffic in Lusaka is 'truly unbelievable'), cell phones and shopping at malls.[67]

My research assistant Jairos Mazambani also refers to development because of changes in the city of Lusaka and provincial towns, new expatriate investors, white farmers from Zimbabwe, new shops including 'show rooms for new vehicles on sale, filling stations built [and] goods in abundance for sale.'[68]

Certainly a growing middle class is essential for development, although I would like to know its size. Nonetheless in 2006, '64 per cent of the Zambian population, or approximately 7.5 million people, live below the national poverty line.'[69] In rural areas, where 'the economy has stalled,'[70] poverty affects 81 per cent of the population. To help them, the World Bank estimated in early 2008 that the then current expansion of GDP at 6 per cent annually needed to grow still more.

In regard to constraints as seen from below, Mazambani's perception is that:

> Zambia has no factories to manufacture goods and has got more shops for selling already finished commodities which makes it a dumping place . . . There are less jobs in Zambia because it is just a selling country instead of being a manufacturing point . . . Zambia will remain the same or undeveloped if the issues of unemployment, corruption and political interference are not checked.

**The Vision 2030**

In 2005 the government held meetings in all of Zambia's 72 districts to prepare the Vision 2030, which was considered necessary, in President Mwanawasa's words, 'because the various national development plans were not prepared within the context of a long term perspective.'[71] The purpose of the Vision was to 'serve as the guide for all development efforts.'[72] Five-year development plans, starting with the Fifth National Plan (2006–2010), and annual budgets will be the means for operationalizing the Vision, whose main goal will be for Zambia to become

'**A Prosperous Middle Income Country by 2030**' (bold as written in the Vision).[73]

The Vision's definition of a prosperous middle-income country is one in which opportunities would be available for everyone's wellbeing in a country committed to socio-economic justice. Deserving special emphasis would be: '(i) gender responsive sustainable development; (ii) democracy; (iii) respect for human rights; (iv) good traditional and family values; (v) positive attitude towards work; (vi) peaceful co-existence; and private–public partnerships.'[74] The overall goal for Zambia's political economy would be 'devolved political systems and structures' and a 'diversified and balanced and strong industrial sector, a modern agricultural sector and an efficient and productive services sector.' Requirements would be to gradually improve annual real economic growth rates from 6 and 10 per cent; 'to attain and maintain a moderate inflation rate of 5 per cent; to reduce national poverty head count to less than 20 per cent of the population.'[75]

**Will the Necessary Political Will and Capacity Exist?**

Ethnic groups such as the Gwembe Tonga cannot develop on their own. They need good governance, employment opportunities and government planning capabilities and services at district, provincial and central levels. Will the Vision be implemented or just become a modern version of the 'speeches' which Rene Dumont mentioned in 1979 as the only government response to Zambia's forgotten farmers? The question is a legitimate one granted the emphasis of previous governing elites on enriching themselves and their principle supporters and the extent to which each government has ignored the country's rural and urban poor, who time and again have been referred to derogatively as 'the masses.' Do Zambia's leaders at central, provincial and district levels have the interest to change their values and priorities, and if they do, will they have the capacity to implement the Vision? A similar question is applicable to African leaders throughout the continent.

**Other Threats and Constraints to Success**

Unfortunately during Zambia's recent period of growth, the government did not take the opportunity to build up financial reserves and diversify an economy overly dependent on copper mining. By the first half of 2009, copper prices had dropped from nearly $9000 a ton in mid-2008 to about $5000 a ton, inflation had increased and the Zambian currency had depreciated. The International Monetary Fund had been approached in 2009 for a loan on $200 million in addition to a loan of $79 million received the previous June.[76] Doubts had also arisen about the government's ongoing commitment to address corruption.[77]

Zambia's pervasive poverty, current rate of population increase (2.9 per cent) and lack of employment opportunities remain major threats to development as elsewhere in Africa. Major environmental constraints are global warming and ongoing deforestation (one of the highest rates in the world). Capacity building and human resource development are slowed due to inadequate attention paid to secondary and tertiary education for the country's low-income majority. Disease, especially HIV/AIDS, cholera, tuberculosis, malaria and waterborne diseases result in Zambia having one of the highest death rates in the world.

Donor-supplied finance has enabled the government to provide free antiretroviral drugs to an increasing proportion of those with AIDS, thus improving their health and extending their life expectancy. Recommended improvements in diet and transportation to clinics can, however, be major problems for the sick. One of my research assistants, who bicycles regularly to the hospital in Chirundu, is a beneficiary of this program, which might have helped three of my other research assistants, who died with AIDS before its initiation. But Zambia's government has scarcely begun to address the problem in 2007 of an estimated 600 000 AIDS orphans, of whom it is estimated that 340 000 have lost both parents.

Zambia also has one of the world's lowest life expectancies at birth, a major reason for Zambia being 165th of 177 countries in UNDP's 2007/2008 Human Development Index. Malnutrition is another reason: 47 per cent of Zambia's children are stunted, 28 per cent underweight and 5 per cent wasted.[78] Poor infrastructure results in transport costs being 'five times higher than those in industrial country markets, and even within the region, the cost of exporting a container from Zambia is 45 per cent higher than from Malawi, another land locked country.'[79]

Increases in the prevalence of witchcraft beliefs since independence are another constraint not just among the Gwembe Tonga but elsewhere in Zambia and Africa. Such beliefs are one response to a situation where the majority have little control over the context in which they live, where often corrupt government officials do not provide necessary services and where life, to a considerable extent, is viewed as a zero sum game. This is not a novel conclusion of mine. South African anthropologist Isak Niehaus has associated witchcraft with 'misery, marginalisation, illness, poverty and insecurity' in the South African lowveld at the end of the twentieth century.[80] Other social scientists warn against marginalizing Africa by considering witchcraft there as an identifying characteristic. Drawing on Mary Douglas's research on risk and culture, anthropologist Pat Caplan explores whether or not fear of terrorism in the United States exemplifies what she refers to as 'similar "occult" economies outside of Africa.'[81]

In sum it remains to be seen whether poverty continues among the majority of Zambians, whether the country becomes a failed state like neighboring Zimbabwe or whether through improved governance the country is able to capitalize on its industrious population and favorable natural resources. Absolutely essential is increased priority given to commercialization of small-scale agriculture, which continues to employ a majority of Zambian households, whose increased purchasing power is required at this stage of Zambia's national development.

## NOTES

1.  Joint Assistance Strategy for Zambia (JASZ) 2007–2010 (April 2007). Page 5.
2.  Silene K. Mwenechanya (August 2007). 'Legal Empowerment of the Poor: Labour rights in Zambia.' An issue paper prepared for UNDP – Commission on Legal Empowerment of the Poor. See References for the web address. Mwenechanya's figures are taken from the 2005 Labour Force Survey of the government's Central Statistical Office (CSO). The contents of a basic needs basket were calculated by Zambia's Jesuit Centre for Theological Reflection (see JCTR's 'Basic Needs Basket: A comprehensive overview.' 2006 Edition. Lusaka: JCTR). The cost for such a basket in Lusaka for a family of six would be approximately US$390 while Mwenechanya states that the average monthly earnings in the informal sector are only US$28 according to CSO figures.
3.  On governance at the national level see Robert H. Bates (2008). *When Things Fell Apart: State failure in late-century Africa*. New York: Cambridge University Press.
4.  Population Reference Bureau. Available at http://www.prb.org/Countries/zambia.aspx.
5.  World Bank International Development Association (8 April, 2008). 'Country Assistance Strategy for the Republic of Zambia.' Report No: 43352-ZM. Washington DC: World Bank.
6.  JASZ. Op. cit. Page 5.
7.  World Economic Forum, World Bank and African Development Bank (2007). 'Africa Competitiveness Report.' See References for web address.
8.  World Bank. Op. cit. Pages iv and 7.
9.  *Ibid.* Pages 15 and 18.
10. J. Weitze, Kevin Veldkamp, W. Jeanes and Francis K.M. Shalwindi (1990). 'Agro-Ecological Perspectives in Planning.' In Adrian P. Wood, Stuart A. Kean, John T. Milimo and Dennis Michael Warren (eds). *The Dynamics of Agricultural Policy and Reform in Zambia*. Aimes, IA: University of Iowa Press. Page 76.
11. The other four studies are: a study of the Mexican village Tzintzuntzan by George Foster and his colleagues; the Indian village of Karipur studied by William and Charlotte Wiser and Susan Wadley; Evon Z. Vogt and colleagues' Chiapas project in Mexico; and Fei Hsiaotung's study of Kaihsiengkung Village in China.
12. Reasons for leaving school included poor grades, inability to pay school fees, sickness, marriage and pregnancy.
13. Bates (2008). Op. cit.
14. In the University Corporation for Atmospheric Research (24 May 2005). 'A Continent Split by Climate Change: New study projects stronger drought in Southern Africa, more rain in Sahel.' Available at http://www.ucar.edu/news/releases/2005/hurrell.shtml.
15. World Bank. Op. cit. Page 11. Zambia is eleventh globally in 2000 in regard to greenhouse gas emissions per capita.

16. *Ibid.* Page 8.
17. Mongabay.com. 'Zambia Deforestation Rates and Related Forestry Figures.' Available at http://rainforests.mongabay.com/deforestation/2000/Zambia.htm.
18. Anne Chileshe (July 2001). 'Forestry Outlook Studies in Africa (FOSA): Zambia.' Lusaka and Rome: Forestry Department, Ministry of Environment and Natural Resources and Food and Agriculture Organization of the United Nations.
19. Bates. Op. cit. Page 37. To support his case Bates draws both on other sources and on his own statistical analysis.
20. *Ibid.* Page 68.
21. *Ibid.*
22. *Ibid.* Page 50.
23. Transparency International. 'Country Study Report: Zambia 2006/7.' Page 4. See References for web address. As a heavily indebted nation, most of Zambia's debt was written off in 2005.
24. See Ann Seidman (1974). 'The Distorted Growth of Import-Substitution Industry: The Zambian case.' *Journal of Modern African Studies.* **12**(4). Pages 601–631.
25. Fabian Maimbo and James Fry (1971). 'An Investigation into the Change in Terms of Trade between the Rural and Urban Sectors of Zambia.
26. Seidman. Op. cit. Page 611.
27. ILO (1981). *Basic Needs in an Economy Under Pressure.* Addis Ababa: International Labour Organization.
28. *Ibid.* Page 27.
29. *Ibid.* Pages xxvi–xxvii.
30. René Dumont (1979). Sections on the ILO report and on René Dumont are from my unpublished August 1985 mimeographed manuscript: 'A History of Development in the Twentieth Century: The Zambian portion of the Middle Zambezi Valley and the Lake Kariba Basin.' Binghamton, NY: Institute for Development Anthropology.
31. World Bank (November 1994). 'Zambia Poverty Assessment.'
32. JASZ. Op. cit. (note 1). Page 5.
33. World Bank. Op. cit. (note 5). Pages 6 and i.
34. The second risk related to governance. Under governance slow progress was noted first in dealing with corruption. Next, 'limited civil society involvement and oversight over the development process by Parliament and other democratically elected bodies could weaken ownership.' JASZ. Op. cit. Page 29. Dealing with such risks requires institutional reform and human development.
35. JASZ. Op. cit. (note 1) Pages 7–8.
36. One response to government neglect of education has been a major increase in private schools from preschool through skill training at the tertiary level.
37. World Bank. Op. cit. (note 5). Page 15.
38. *Ibid.* Page 18.
39. Transparency International. Op. cit. Page 5.
40. Thayer Scudder (2007). 'Development and Downturn in Zambia's Gwembe Valley.' In C. Lancaster and K.P. Vickery (eds). *The Tonga-Speaking Peoples of Zambia and Zimbabwe.* Page 334.
41. Thayer Scudder (1986a). 'The Gwembe Valley Development Company in Relationship to the Development of the Southern Portion of Gwembe District.' Mimeo.
42. Transparency International. Op. cit. Page 5.
43. *Ibid.* Pages 5–6.
44. Following his election in 2001, President Mwanawasa spoke out strongly against corruption. In 2002 a Task Force on Corruption was established. However, during its first five years of operation 'it has secured only three convictions,' two of which have been appealed (Transparency International. Op. cit. Page 9).
45. Examples in this section are taken from my 1985 manuscript 'A History of Development in the Twentieth Century: The Zambian portion of the Middle Zambezi Valley and the Lake Kariba Basin.' Binghampton, NY: Institute for Development Anthropology. Mimeo.

46. ILO. Op. cit. Page xl.
47. *Ibid.* Page 130.
48. The major exception to the manufacture of luxury goods for the elite (from imported parts) was the mass production of beer and cigarettes that 'had reached 40 per cent of the manufacturing value added in Zambia' by 1972. See Ann Seidman (1979). Op. cit. (note 24). Page 42.
49. Thayer Scudder field notes.
50. ILO. Op. cit. Page 115.
51. Quoted in World Bank. Op. cit. Page 20.
52. *Ibid.* Page 23.
53. Commission on Growth and Development (2008). 'The Growth Report: Strategies for Sustained Growth and Inclusive Development'. Commission on Growth and Development. Washington DC: World Bank. Page 2.
54. *Ibid.* Page 116.
55. JASZ. Op. cit. (note 1). Page 9.
56. World Bank (30 October 2006). 'Implementation Completion Report.' Page 7.
57. 27 July 2007 letter from The Royal Highnesses Chiefs in the Gwembe Valley along Lake Kariba. 'The Wrongs the Bank has done – Background and Current Suffering of the Displaced People Following Relocation.'
58. WHO/UNAIDS/UNICEF (July 2008). 'Epidemiological Fact Sheet on HIV and AIDS: Zambia.' Page 5.
59. Avert. 'HIV and AIDS in Zambia.' Available at http://www.avert.org/aids-zambia. htm. See also Mweeta, S. (2004). 'Lets Fight HIV/AIDS Stigma.' *Times of Zambia*: 29 December. See References for web address.
60. John Nyamu (February 2003). 'Famine and AIDS Batter Southern Africa: Action needed to avert collapse, Stephen Lewis warns.' *Africa Recovery*. News Releases.
61. Avert. Op. cit. Page 2.
62. ILO (1981) and René Dumont (1979). Op. cit. (notes 1 and 29).
63. Elizabeth Colson (2000). 'The Father as Witch.' *Africa*. **70** (3). Pages 333–358.
64. Thayer Scudder fieldnotes.
65. Ulrich Luig (1996). *Conversion as a Social Process: A history of missionary Christianity among the Valley Tonga, Zambia*. New Brunswick, NJ: Transaction Publishers.
66. Elizabeth Colson (14 July 2008). Email to Thayer Scudder.
67. Lisa Cliggett (4 August 2008). Email to Thayer Scudder.
68. Jairos Mazambani (13 August 2008). Email to Thayer Scudder.
69. World Bank. Op. cit. (note 5). Page 6.
70. *Ibid.* Page i.
71. Levy Patrick Mwanawasa (December 2006). 'Foreword'. In *Vision 2030: A prosperous middle income country by 2030*. Lusaka: Government of Zambia.
72. *Ibid.*
73. Vision 2030 (December 2006). Executive Summary. Lusaka: Government of Zambia.
74. *Ibid.*
75. *Ibid.*
76. Sarah Childress (26 March 2009). 'Zambia's Economy Falls With Price of Copper.' *The Wall Street Journal.* Available at http://online.wsj.com/articles/SB123803357232044061. html.
77. See Celia W. Dugger (10 June 2009). 'Battle to Halt Graft Scourge in Africa Ebbs.' *The New York Times.*
78. World Bank. Op. cit. (note 5). Page 14, based on Republic of Zambia. *Zambia Demographic and Health Survey 2001–2002.*
79. World Bank. Op. cit. Page 13.
80. Isak Niehaus (2001) *Witchcraft, Power And Politics: Exploring the occult in the South African lowveld.* London: Pluto Press.
81. Pat Caplan (2006). 'Terror, Witchcraft and Risk.' *The Anthroglobe Journal.* http:// www.anthroglobe.ca/info/caplanp_witchcraft_060119.htm.

# 7. Transforming global societies

## INTRODUCTION

Current global threats will surely lower living standards during the 21st century since national governments and international institutions have neither the will nor the knowledge to address them. A major contributing cause to a majority of these threats is the single-minded pursuit of growth as measured by global and per capita gross domestic product (GDP).

The 2008 Growth Report of the World Bank-assisted Commission on Growth and Development illustrates this bias. Ten of its 20 members were, or had been, ministers of finance or in charge of equivalent ministries and three were heads of major banks. The Chair was a Nobel prize-winning economist and the Vice Chair a World Bank vice president. The Commission's focus was on how to sustain high inclusive annual growth of 7 per cent or higher over several decades. Conclusions were drawn from collaborating academic experts and the experience of 13 countries, including Brazil, China, Indonesia, Korea and Japan, that had achieved such growth for at least 25 years since the end of the Second World War.

I have emphasized in previous chapters global threats about which I am most knowledgeable – poverty, fundamentalism and environmental degradation. I have also referred in the text to other global threats associated with nuclear energy, civil strife, militarization, war, too high levels of consumption and population increase (especially in the more impoverished nations), urbanization, global climate change and the present (2009) financial and economic crisis. Other unnamed global threats exist and then there are future threats that will be unexpected.

All identified threats must be addressed. Some, however, will require more immediate attention at different times. Requiring immediate attention now are the spread of nuclear weapons, global warming and unsustainable consumption of natural resources. Other global threats, however, must not be ignored, for threats tend to be synergistically interrelated. Poverty, especially the relative poverty associated with the rising gap between rich and poor, can influence conflict (nuclear included), as can fundamentalism.

### Spread of Nuclear Weapons

I have been concerned about risks from global threats since early in my professional career. My first professional article after coming to Caltech was in a 1965 issue of the *Bulletin of the Atomic Scientists*. In 1947 the cover of the first issue of the *Bulletin* featured the Doomsday Clock with the hands set at 5 minutes before midnight to show how close the world was to catastrophe. Since 1947 the clock has been reset 19 times.[1] On two occasions during the Cold War the clock was set at a minute before midnight, but after the Cold War's end the minute hand was set back in 1991 to 17 minutes before midnight – the lowest setting to date. Since then the minute hand has advanced steadily, with the last setting in 2007 again 5 minutes from midnight. The advance is due to an increasing number of states with, or seeking, a nuclear capacity and to the international trade in nuclear materials.

The clock is set by the Board of Directors of the *Bulletin* after consultation with a Board of Supervisors that includes 18 Nobel Prize winners. In a 17 January 2007 announcement, the Board stated:

> We stand at the brink of a second nuclear age . . . North Korea's recent test of a nuclear weapon, Iran's nuclear ambitions, a U.S. renewed emphasis on the military utility of nuclear weapons, the failure to adequately secure nuclear materials, and the continued presence of some 26,000 nuclear weapons in the United States and Russia are symptomatic of a larger failure to solve the problems posed by the most destructive technology on Earth.[2]

The situation is actually even more serious than during the Cold War since the Board has added climate change, a threat that poses dangers 'nearly as dire as those posed by nuclear weapons,'[3] to threats influencing the setting of the Doomsday Clock. Members of the scientific community, such as Stephen Hawking, professor of mathematics at the University of Cambridge, and Martin Rees, a recent president of the United Kingdom's Royal Society,[4] take these threats very seriously. Since the last clock setting in 2007, the associated risks have worsened.

### Global Climatic Change

Systematic international investigation of the risks and uncertainty imposed by global climate change accelerated in 1988 with the establishment of the Intergovernmental Panel on Climate Change (IPCC), which received the Nobel Peace Prize in 2007. IPCC reports do not make recommendations. That is the responsibility of political leaders, for whom each report is accompanied by a separate 'Summary for Policy Makers.' Four comprehensive assessments have been produced, the latest (at the time of writing) being in 2007.

Throughout, emphasis has been on achieving a consensus among authors chosen from different countries and representing different viewpoints and disciplines. That approach was considered essential granted the seriousness of the issues, the major implications for people, national political economies and the world and the inevitability of criticism regardless of what was written. The 2007 report, for example, has been criticized by scientists for paying insufficient attention to positive feedback loops whereby global warming would cause changes in marine and terrestrial ecosystems that amplify warming trends. Examples mentioned include accelerated melting of glaciers and snowpacks, which reflect more heat back into the atmosphere than the underlying surface; a weakening between 1981 and 2004 of the Southern Ocean sink to absorb carbon dioxide;[5] increased release of $CO_2$ and methane from thawing permafrost in the circumpolar zone; release of $CO_2$ from more fire-prone boreal forests; and various synergisms that can be expected to cause sea levels to rise faster than IPCC reports forecast.[6]

Changes in global climate since the turn of the century were such that the authors of the February 2007 IPCC assessment wrote, with very high confidence, 'that the globally averaged net effect of human activities since 1750 has been one of warming.'[7] More specifically, the April 2007 report to policy makers stated that 'coasts are projected to be exposed to extreme risks, including coastal erosion, due to climate change and sea-level rise,'[8] while, with high confidence, 'in the course of the [present] century, water supplies stored in glaciers and snow cover are projected to decline, reducing water availability in regions supplied by melt water from major mountain ranges, where more than one-sixth of the world population lives.' Moreover, 'The resilience of many ecosystems is likely to be exceeded by an unprecedented combination of climate change, associated disturbances . . ., and other global change drivers,'[9] which include 'unsustainable development policies.'[10]

Leading experts emphatically emphasize the risks involved. According to the Scientific Expert Group of 18 authors, 'The human race . . . has never faced a greater challenge, and there is no time for further delay.'[11] Jim Hansen, Director of the American Goddard Institute for Space Studies, made the same point: 'we have at most ten years – not ten years to decide upon action but ten years to alter fundamentally the trajectory of global greenhouse emission.'[12]

Especially relevant to my own critique of the current unsustainable emphasis on global growth is the 2006 Stern Report. Sir Nicholas Stern is an economist who was Chief Economist and Senior Vice-President of the World Bank for a number of years before becoming a permanent secretary in the UK Treasury and head of the government economic service. In the first sentence of the Executive Summary of his 700-page report, Stern stated, 'The scientific evidence is now overwhelming: climate change presents very serious global risks, and it demands an urgent global response' now, there being 'a high price for delay.'[13]

Throwing down the gauntlet to his colleagues in economics, Stern went on to state that '[c]limate change presents a unique challenge for economics: it is the greatest and widest-ranging market failure ever seen.' A wide range of analytical techniques will be required to analyze and deal with 'the possibility of major, non-marginal change.' Those techniques must place 'at centre stage' the economics of risk and uncertainty. In other words, as long as an economic calculus based largely on cost-benefit analysis continues to dominate policy discussions, there will be little shift away from business as usual.

### Consumption as a Threat

Consumption is a necessary component of every nation's political economy. In the United States, for example, personal and household consumption has been responsible for up to 70 per cent of GDP. It far exceeds government spending, investment and net exports.[14] I personally was overwhelmed when I first came across that 70 per cent figure for it indicated not just the magnitude of consumption in the United States, but the difficulty of changing its nature and content because of its macroeconomic significance and especially its importance for employment generation. The same is also true in India, where personal and household consumption was reported to be 56 per cent of GDP[15] before the recent financial and economic crisis.

Global private and public consumption has been expanding rapidly since the end of World War II. In 1998, expenditures were $24 trillion, which was six times the level in 1950.[16] Private expenditures for goods and services far exceed public ones. Household expenditures, for example, increased from $4.8 trillion in 1960 to over $20 trillion in 2000. Since then private expenditures have been increasing even more rapidly throughout the world, and especially in Asia. In China, India and Vietnam the main consuming age group is under 40, which suggests even more rapid increases in the future as their more conservative elders die off.

Current levels of consumption pose a global threat because they exceed the capacity of the world's natural resources to provide for them and to process associated liquid and solid waste products. According to 'preliminary and exploratory assessment' based on the ecological footprint concept,[17] humanity's demand for natural resources overshoots the regenerative capacity of the globe by 20 per cent. More specifically, 'humanity's load corresponded to 70 per cent of the capacity of the global biosphere in 1961, and grew to 120 per cent in 1999.'[18] In other words, not only have we already passed the 'tipping point' by exceeding the world's carrying capacity of people's current consumption, but consumption and its adverse impacts continue to increase annually.

**Can People and Nations Cope with Global Threats?**

Coping with global threats will require transformational changes in human values and behavior and in societies and nations. Such changes have been made in the past. Examples are many. For reasons such as drought, human-induced environmental change and population increase, gathering and hunting societies independently invented agriculture in at least five different parts of the world. Since then there have been many examples of how people, societies and cultures have adapted to changes in technology in agricultural, industrial and now post-industrial societies.

Recent research on human behavior is also encouraging since it suggests that altruism, cooperation, fairness, sharing and trust are basic human characteristics that extend beyond ties of blood and kinship. Whether these characteristics are primarily due to the co-evolution of human genetics and culture or are primarily the result of random mutations and natural selection associated with biological evolution is irrelevant from our point of view. What is important is the strong evidence that they exist. Hence the potential exists that they can be expanded to encompass a global approach to threats.

People's active involvement must be the starting point if the necessary transformations are to occur.[19] Global Boomer Julian Simon was right when he emphasized that 'the ultimate resource is people – skilled, spirited and hopeful people.' His emphasis was primarily on individuals exerting 'their wills and imaginations for their own benefit'[20] whereas I place equal importance on their active and decisive involvement in civic society's efforts to foster transformational change. Unfortunately in the United States, active participation in such civil institutions as labor unions, parent–teacher organizations and such fraternal organizations as the Rotary Club has been declining in recent decades. In China, strong and influential non-governmental organizations continue to be opposed by the central government.

# TRANSFORMATIONAL CHANGE

I emphasize transformational changes that could reduce the rate and magnitude of decline in living standards without necessarily reducing other quality of life indicators. In the sections that follow, the first two deal with transforming values and the empowerment of women. Sections on transforming economic, social and cultural systems follow. Emphasis is on localizing and enriching the variety of economic, social and cultural opportunities and activities in interconnected rural areas while linking them to cities, ports and global markets. Special attention is paid to poverty alleviation, agricultural development and employment generation in late industrializing nations. The World Bank and the World Environment Organization examples in the section on transforming international governance illustrate the need for global institutions which have the authority and the power to overrule national policies and activities. The last two sections relate transformation of educational systems to dealing with future threats and uncertainty, and, more specifically, to religious fundamentalism.

The text draws on what my own experience suggests is needed to slow the rate and magnitude of decline and to put people back in charge of their lives. The relevance of my suggestions will vary from society to society and within any one society at different times. Where attempted, such strategies must be carefully monitored and adapted, for example, to new technology. As the 2008 Commission on Growth and Diversity realized, the best one can do is try to identify the necessary 'basic ingredients.'[21]

I am not optimistic about the future of the world in which *Homo sapiens* is the dominant species. The various incremental changes that are under way at present, dealing, for example, with global warming, are non-transformational and totally inadequate. As for the type of transformational changes needed now, I doubt that they will occur during my lifetime or that of my children and hence they will be too late to avoid downturn not just in living standards but also in quality of life.

I am especially worried about the continuing emphasis in government and international financial institute policies on growth and specifically on people's increasing consumption of material possessions. On the one hand, growth and consumption are essential to eliminate poverty. On the other hand, throughout my career, I have studied case after case where people, having exited poverty, join the rest of us whose continued consumption is destroying the natural resource base on which our survival depends. That conclusion applies to Gwembe Tonga who have managed to join Zambia's small but growing middle class. It applies to the residents of formerly impoverished Kaihsiengkung village in China, where a population of about 3000 in 2004 had 650 motor cycles and 730 new houses furnished with 850 air conditioners. Two years later residents owned 850 motor-cycles. Cars had increased from 21 to 28, with International Monetary Fund economists estimating that by 2050 China alone will have nearly 600 million cars, which was the global total in 2005.[22] This year, during my latest visit to Laos, I noticed that the same trend had begun in the reservoir basin behind the new Nam Theun 2 dam among ethnic minorities who ten years ago were among the poorest of the poor in one of the poorest countries in the world.

## TRANSFORMING VALUES

Transforming people's values will be the key to whether humankind will be able to shift from a primary focus on increasing per capita income and improving living standards to a less-materialistic emphasis on other quality of life characteristics. Change will be easiest in response to cata-strophic events such as the current global financial and economic crisis or more frequent and severe droughts, floods and hurricanes related to global warming. But then it may be too late. Being too late is especially a problem with more gradual changes that occur over decades and which are not evident in everyday life. Environmental degradation and loss of biodiversity are examples. California has already lost 90 per cent of its wetlands, yet pressure continues to degrade those that remain. Biologists have tried for years, with no success, to get the international community to set up an institutional response to loss of biological diversity similar to the Intergovernmental Panel on Climate Change.

Values vary widely within and between cultures and within belief systems, such as the great world religions, that overlay cultures. In all cases they are passed on to children by parents and within informal and formal systems of education. In all cases they are susceptible to change. Crisis events and charismatic leaders can and do change people's values in a short time span. Even though initially opposed by a majority, govern-ing institutions can legislate and motivate changes that gradually lead to value change. Examples are affirmative action for the benefit of oppressed minorities, and quotas for the participation of women in governing insti-tutions and national service, all of which I believe should play a role in addressing current and future threats.

Cultures and belief systems also vary in their resistance to value change. Such will especially be the case with some of the value changes that I believe will be necessary. Granted the importance I ascribe to empowerment of women and to science, current societies in which Islam is the major religion may be initially at a disadvantage. Unlike the situation a thousand years ago, when Muslim societies pioneered and valued mathematics and science, basic scientific research no longer plays a major role in the education and research of most Islamic countries. That is a major weakness.

A more hopeful sign is that some necessary global changes in values are occurring slowly, including the need to address climate change and to empower women. I deal next with women's empowerment because it is so important to a range of transformational changes.

## EMPOWERING WOMEN

### Introduction

It is common knowledge in development agencies and among social scientists that gender equality and the empowerment of women benefit both sexes as well as society as a whole. The World Bank stated in its 2001 report, *Engendering Development*, that 'gender equality is a core development issue – a development objective in its own right.'[23] According to the Bank '[t]he evidence presented shows that societies that discriminate by gender tend to experience less rapid economic growth and poverty reduction.'[24] Klaus Schwab, the World Economic Forum Founder and Executive Chair, states: 'we recognize that the advancement of women is an important economic, business and societal issue with a significant impact on the growth of nations.'[25] The background introduction to the UN's 44 pages of 'Guidelines on Women's Empowerment' refers to the increasing recognition during the 1990s 'of the centrality of women's empowerment to the success of development programmes.'[26]

Economist and Nobel Laureate Amartya Sen emphasizes that empowerment requires the free agency of women as well as their wellbeing:

> No longer the passive recipients of welfare enhancing help, women are increasingly seen, by men as well as women, as active agents of change: the dynamic promoters of social transformations that can alter the lives of *both* women and men. [Indeed,] the limited role of women's active agency seriously afflicts the lives of *all* people – men as well as women, children as well as adults.[27]

Benefits of women's empowerment are many. Control of women's own fertility through family planning and use of contraceptives reduces unwanted pregnancies, which the London School of Hygiene and Tropical Medicine estimates at 41 per cent of global pregnancies. Roughly one-fifth of those pregnancies are terminated by induced abortion, with unsafe abortions being a major cause of maternal mortality.[28]

Women's desire for fewer and better spaced children slows population growth and reduces child mortality and malnutrition, while equal educational opportunities for future mothers further decreases child mortality rates and increases educational opportunities for children, and especially for girls. Overall benefits of fewer and better spaced children also include 'greater subsequent productivity, gendered empowerment of girls, and enhanced opportunities for women to participate in economic and political life.'[29]

My own comparative and cross-cultural research on government-implemented large-scale land settlement projects documents how women's status and decision-making authority within the family improve when women's unpaid housework is complemented by earned income from their own farming and business activities. A woman's status as a wage earner directly benefits the nutrition, clothing and education of children. This is true among the Gwembe Tonga as well as with women elsewhere using income from sale of crops and livestock and from business activities.

Women are more concerned about local-level environmental issues than men and are more well-disposed toward environmental activists.[30] A cross-cultural study involving older men and women in four high-income countries showed women as more concerned about environmental problems and risks. They also placed more emphasis than men on environmental quality and the protection of nature and the environment.[31]

*The Economist* argues that women have become in recent years 'the most powerful engine of global growth.' That argument is based on the observation that the increased employment of women in the market economy 'has accounted for a big chunk of global growth in recent decades,' with women since 1970 filling 'two new jobs for every one taken by a man.' Furthermore, *The Economist* refers to research that indicates that women are better investors than men because they 'earn higher returns.' That also applies to American companies with more women in top positions, perhaps because teams composed of both sexes are better at problem solving and risk assessment or because women may be better 'at building teams and communicating.' Another survey noted by *The Economist* emphasizes the growing ability of women to influence global futures because they 'make perhaps 80 per cent of consumers' buying decisions – from health care and homes to furniture and food.'[32]

Unfortunately, if the behavior of women and of their better educated children emphasizes growth and material consumption, their increased participation in the global economy will speed up the magnitude and rate of living standard decline. That is a definite risk. Why then do I put so much emphasis on women's empowerment? I do so because I believe that there is evidence that once alerted to the nature and implications of global threats, empowered women will be more effective as individuals, spouses, mothers, teachers and business and political leaders in addressing threats without the need for major changes in their values.

Take poverty. Poverty rates are higher among women and their children because of 'political, legal, economic, and educational inequalities that perpetuate women's lack of access to resources, control over decision-making, and participation in public life.'[33] It is reasonable to assume that reduction of those inequalities will reduce the number and proportion of the impoverished.

Empowerment of women will definitely reduce the rate of population increase in those countries where 90 per cent of future global increase is expected to occur and where educational and employment opportunities are less apt to be available for incorporating existing youth bulges within a viable society. One of my long-held assumptions has been that married women with children have greater concern than men about the issue of environmental quality. That assumption is based on my own observations that environmental degradation increases the amount of time that rural women in late-industrializing countries must spend getting fuel and water while water pollution and pollution from use of charcoal adversely affect the health of urban women and children. I also assume that married women with children in the United States and other industrial counties would be more concerned than men and unmarried women about the effects of pollution.

**The Empowerment Record to Date**

Incremental global empowerment of women is occurring, but the rate of change is too slow and uneven. Of the Millennium Development Goals affecting women, most disappointing is the fact that global maternal mortality decreased less than 1 per cent per year between 1990 and 2005. In 2005 the difference in mortality rates between the industrialized and late-industrializing countries remained unacceptably high, being 9 per 100 000 in the former and 450 in the latter. Sub-Saharan Africa continued to have the highest maternal mortality (900 deaths per 100 000 births), followed by South Asia (490).[34]

The most detailed international surveys dealing with the empowerment issue are the 2006 and 2007 editions of 'The Global Gender Gap Report' by Hausmann *et al.* for the World Economic Forum. Equality was measured by economic participation and opportunity, educational attainment, health and survival and political empowerment. Each category was subdivided into two to five variables. The three under political empowerment, for example, were ratios of women to men with seats in parliament and at ministerial level, and number of years of a female head of state.

There were 128 countries, with over 90 per cent of the global population, involved in the 2007 report. Sweden had the best result, with 81 per cent of its gender gap closed.[35] Four other Scandinavian countries were in the top ten along with New Zealand, the Philippines, Germany, Ireland and Spain. The United States was number 31, having closed 70 per cent of its gender gap, China was number 73 (gender gap 66 per cent closed) and Zambia number 101 (63 per cent).

Islamic countries as a category fared worst. Indonesia was number 81, Malaysia 92, Iran 118, Egypt 120, Saudi Arabia 124 and Pakistan 126. On the other hand, Uzbekistan, with over 85 per cent of its population Muslim, was in the upper third of countries. Moreover, significant changes are occurring among the lower third as well. In Iran in recent years, over 60 per cent of those accepted at universities have been women, with graduates competing with men in the professions. The rapidity of their rise may not be sustainable, however, because the fundamentalist government is concerned about the impact of educated women on family and society.[36] In Iraq the government continues to emphasize female well-being as opposed to their free agency. As soon as the government took over from American forces, a program was stopped in which over 1000 women had been trained since 2003 to serve in the security forces, and those who had been trained were reassigned to safer positions than they had been trained for.[37]

By 2007, all 128 countries had closed nearly 92 per cent of the educational attainment gap and 96 per cent of the health and survival gap. On the other hand, only 58 per cent of the economic empowerment gap and 14 per cent of the political empowerment gap had been closed. China (59 per cent) and the United States (69 per cent) were in the middle on political empowerment. In the United States the proportion of women in the US Congress was only 17 per cent in 2009 in both the Senate and the House of Representatives.[38] Worldwide, the proportion of women in national legislating bodies in 2002 was about 14 per cent.[39] That statistic illustrates a major problem if I am correct about the political role women must play in dealing with declining living standards.

Looking to the future, educational systems and governments must play a stronger role in empowering women. Gender neutral, non-sexist education, for example, must apply to all activities and disciplines from the preschool level through national service, while governing institutions should apply minimum quotas for women in economic and political institutions. Again, gradual changes are under way. Non-sexist education is generally accepted in public schools in the United States, while 77 countries had 'constitutional, electoral or political party quotas for women'[40] by the end of 2003.

# TRANSFORMING ECONOMIC AND SOCIAL SYSTEMS

## Introduction

Many experts have attempted to establish procedural guidelines for a more sustainable future. One useful starting point is environmental economist Herman Daly's 65-page Index of Sustainable Economic Welfare.[41] More attention must also be paid to cultural, social and political self-sufficiency at the community, locality and regional levels. A greater degree of economic self-sufficiency, however, should not be at the expense of major advantages associated with global trade. Even at the national level it makes little sense for arid and semi-arid countries to seek food self-sufficiency when necessary staples or opportunities are more reliably available at cheaper prices from food crop exporters or from countries with unexploited arable lands. It makes sense, as examples, for African countries such as Botswana and Senegal to purchase rice from Thailand and for food deficit countries to invest in agricultural projects or lease land in Africa, as Chinese, Japanese and Middle Eastern Arab countries already are doing.

My strategic vision for a more sustainable society at local, national and global levels situates the concepts of previous 'Wake-Up Call' authors in a 21st century global context. Essential as a starting point is a re-emphasis on social and economic relations at the local or community level and a transition from rampant individualism to more participatory societies or, as Daly and Cobb state, 'From cosmopolitanism to communities of communities.'[42]

Such a trend has commenced in most high-income democratic societies, especially in Europe, New Zealand and Australia. In Europe, there are over 30 politically active green parties, some of which have elected members in national governments while the Greens in Germany have participated as a party in coalition governments. The European Federation of Green Parties, formed in 1993, has a small number of seats in the European Parliament. The word 'green' symbolizes the importance of environmental sustainability, but other Federation goals are 'equity and social justice as well as self-reliance of local and regional economies, encouraging a true sense of community.'[43] New Zealanders claim to have started the first national green party in 1972. Their guiding principles are 'ecological wisdom, social responsibility, appropriate decision-making and non-violence.'

In the United States emphasis has been more on community activities and national service, with both gaining prominence during periods of national crisis. Community examples include the community garden movement. In Los Angeles County the University of California's Extension Program began to assist low-income families with community gardens in the late 1970s. By the end of 2005 there were 60 such gardens open to the public with over 4000 gardeners. In 1933, during the depression years, the Civilian Conservation Corp was established during President Roosevelt's first 100 days in office. During 2008 bipartisan support increased in Congress for a Serve America Act. The act was supported by both presidential candidates and was passed by Congress and signed by President Obama in 2009.

Linkages between local economies and societies must extend laterally as well as up to the global level. Rural areas should be linked with adjacent rural areas rather than just to the nearest city, and linked through cities and ports to global markets. Old concepts, such as regional development and integrated river basin development, must be dusted off, redefined and linked down to sub-regions and up to global markets.

My discussion will start with development strategies based on commercializing employment-generating, small-scale agriculture linked to agribusiness, followed by rural non-farm enterprises and manufacturing linked to urbanization and industrialization. Such a model, especially necessary for modernization of low-income countries with large rural populations, is also applicable to middle- and high-income countries. Small-scale commercial agriculture, for example, supports permanent farmers' markets in Californian cities and rotating markets in smaller towns.

The ongoing transition from rural to urban and from crafts to post-industrial employment will continue for most of the world's citizens. It will take generations, however, for this to be realized in those lower- and middle-income countries where 90 per cent of future population increase will occur. There, as in high-income countries, commercialized rural farm and non-farm enterprises within communities and small towns are essential for poverty reduction and employment generation. For such reasons, future government-sponsored and private research, extension and agricultural development projects must correct the current imbalance between small-scale commercial agriculture and agribusiness.

**Rural Development**

Prior to the 1970s, economists were inclined to downplay the importance of rural area linkages between agriculture and non-farm employment and enterprise development. More recent research shows the opposite – as their incomes increase, farm households purchase more locally provided goods and services as well as diversifying into non-farm enterprises and occupations. I was fascinated to observe during my evaluations of land settlement projects for USAID in the late 1970s the frequency with which settler households around the world made similar production and consumption decisions as their incomes increased. Early investments included agricultural equipment, sewing machines, improved housing with additional rooms added for family members, for rental and for an in-house business, purchasing livestock and educating children.

Improved housing was furnished with spring beds and mattresses, a kitchen table and chairs, a stuffed sofa and chairs suite and a glassed-in cabinet for a tea or coffee set and prized items collected during pilgrimages and other travels. All such items were made in-country so that their purchase stimulated the non-farm employment and enterprise development so important during the early stages of industrialization. Previously impoverished resettlers in Laos's Nam Theun 2 project have begun to acquire similar furnishings. Ten years earlier they lived in non-furnished houses.

Michigan State University agricultural economists Enyinna Chuta and Carl Liedholm concluded from a study of 18 late-developing countries that in the majority, 'one fifth or more of the rural labor force is primarily engaged in nonfarm activities.'[44] In India, 20 per cent were so engaged, and 28 per cent in the Philippines. A World Bank publication generalized further that rural non-farm activities provided approximately one-third of employment opportunities if rural towns were included, with the proportion growing to 40 per cent when rural town populations reached 20000 to 30000 people.[45]

In Indonesia Lubell noted that '[t]he bulk of manufacturing employment and production is in small scale enterprises, most of which are in rural areas . . . In Sri Lanka, 72 per cent of total employment in manufacturing in 1971 was rural.'[46] Clearly manufacturing must be carefully integrated into any process of rural development in order to provide employment for primary and secondary school graduates, to provide locally available goods for purchase and to orient people's ingenuity more directly toward current threats.

### Chinese, Sri Lankan, Brazilian and American examples

In lower- and middle-income countries, government support of agricultural and non-farm employment and enterprise development can be as effective as increases in GDP and individual income associated with industrial and urban development. The response of China's rural majority to the government's household responsibility system in the 1980s clearly illustrates this fact. China's annual economic growth rate of approximately 10 per cent over the last thirty years is based on two very different development policies, as analyzed in Chapter 5.

During the 1980s the government emphasized releasing the potential of the rural majority through the household responsibility system. Related economic reforms, called Number 1 Documents to emphasize their importance, dealt with agricultural production and marketing, village and township agro-industry and manufacturing, and supportive financial and other institutions. After the Tiananmen Square massacre in 1989, new leadership switched emphasis to state-controlled industrial and urban development. Both strategies have achieved similar growth rates. But personal income grew faster than GDP in the 1980s and slower than GDP in the 1990s.[47] There was also greater improvement in the majority's wellbeing in the 1980s as well as less environmental degradation.

A Sri Lankan case involves Minneriya – a medium-sized irrigation project in which cash cropping stimulated non-farm employment generation and enterprise development and the emergence of a dynamic rural town.[48] Non-farm employment in the 1980s was estimated to be 50 per cent more than on-farm employment. The success of the project is attributed to two major factors. One was good plan implementation that provided small-scale commercial farmers with reliable water supplies and service facilities and farm and household allotments large enough to absorb the second generation. The other was the diversified production system of farming households that included rice cultivation, several high-value crops and non-farm enterprises. Farm family consumption of farming equipment, household furnishings and other consumption goods, including children's toys, stimulated the emergence of what was probably the most dynamic rural town in Sri Lanka's dry zone. This is not a unique case – analogous results were achieved by government-sponsored land settlement projects in Indonesia and Malaysia.

In Brazil a private sector land development company, after extensive surveys, gave title to small-scale farmers to grow coffee in a frontier area. Agricultural development was coordinated with building a railroad, along which towns were built. Within 50 years population had risen from less than 100 000 to over 1 500 000. Though figures are not available on the ratio of farm to non-farm jobs, 'it would appear that at least one non-farm job had been created for every farm job.'[49]

The recent growth of America's clean energy economy is an example of the kind of individual initiative on the part of scientists and engineers, universities, business and venture capitalists that is essential if global warming and other threats are to be reduced. It has also been an important source of new employment, having generated job growth twice as fast as total job growth during 1998–2007. California again leads as America's most innovative state by having twice the number of clean energy businesses and jobs than the next highest state and approximately half of the nation's clean energy venture capital.[50]

**Transforming Global Agriculture**

The upside of the current (2009) crisis in global financial markets is that finally the world's leaders realize that markets, essential as they are, require regulation; not 'too much' but, equally important, not 'too little.'[51] National leaders have yet to realize that global agriculture requires transformation. Far too little attention by policy makers and economists has been paid to the role in the commercializing of agriculture. Providing and distributing sufficient food to an increasing population is of obvious importance. Less obvious is the critical historical role that commercializing agriculture has played in enabling rural societies to industrialize and urbanize. Equally important is the contemporary role that agriculture must play if late-industrializing countries are to make the necessary transition to a post-industrial society. That role applies to any society with a rural majority, whether it is found in Africa, China or India.

Transformation could start today, for we have the necessary knowledge and technology. The problem is lack of political will in the United States, the European Union and elsewhere. In industrialized countries, politically-driven agricultural subsidies are restricting the transition, especially in Africa, Latin America and South Asia, from consumption-oriented small-scale agriculture to commercial agriculture. The situation is especially serious in regard to subsidies for cotton, food grains and soybeans. African countries have, for example, complained that American cotton subsidies have driven millions of farmers further into poverty. The United States paid out over $4.2 billion in subsidies to 25 000 American cotton farmers in 2005. Removing them would have raised 'the price of cotton on the international markets by an average of 12.9 per cent' according to one credible source.[52]

Unfair subsidies, according to World Trade Organization policies, also characterize agriculture in a number of European countries. But the key problem is a policy of the European Union that prohibits the importation of genetically modified crops from African and other countries.[53] As with any new technology there are costs as well as benefits. Risks of contaminating wild cultigens are major and need to be dealt with. How crops are genetically altered also requires caution. In the 1990s the opposition of poor African (the Gwembe Tonga included) and Indian farmers to

Monsanto's high-yielding genetically modified food grains, which could not reproduce themselves, was understandable because farmers could not afford to purchase new seed each year.

The present and future benefits of GM crops far outweigh their costs. Already genetically modified food grains can increase yields and reduce storage losses. Looking to the future, drought- and salt-resistant crops could play a major role in both dry land and irrigated agriculture. Such a role is especially important in southern, central and east Africa, where global warming is expected to increase aridity, and in Asia, where land salinity is a major threat to irrigated agriculture.

## A Better Balance between Small-Scale Commercial Agriculture and Agribusiness

### Introduction

Both small-scale commercial agriculture and agribusiness have their advantages. What is important is correcting the current imbalance between the two so as to benefit from the strengths and avoid the weaknesses of each. Not only is small-scale agriculture still the number one source of global employment, but increases in productivity and income are important for late-developing countries to proceed through the initial stages of industrialization.

Small-scale agriculture can have greater ecological, employment and social benefits. It also can have a comparative advantage over agribusiness for certain high-value crops best tended on smaller holdings. On the other hand, the large majority of small-scale farmers are less efficient and less productive than agribusiness. That major development problem is primarily a result of weak government policies and capacities and inadequate legal tenure, credit availability, infrastructure (roads especially) and marketing – all weaknesses that can be corrected. In recent years, for example, increased use of cell phones for identifying markets and prices has made small-scale farmers more competitive in countries, especially in Africa, with inadequate rural electrification. Increased availability of micro-credit is having a similar effect, while advances in finance already allow international labor migrants to wire home wages to diversify and commercialize production systems there.[54]

### Ecological benefits

By far the largest number of small-scale farmers are in the tropics and subtropics. Most practice diversified agricultural systems, based on a variety of crops cultivated at any one time, and livestock management. When income increases with commercialization, more attention is paid to improved housing, diets, education of children and higher income-generating non-farm enterprises. Such small-scale diversified production systems are less susceptible to plant diseases and fungal and rust infections, which are an ongoing threat to agribusiness mono cropping. New production techniques such as organic farming, drip irrigation, minimum tillage, mulching and integrated pest control are best implemented on relatively small holdings, require less water and make less use of petroleum-based fertilizers and pesticides. The United Nations Food and Agricultural Organization has strongly promoted organic farming as a global rural development strategy that provides healthier produce and more jobs per hectare than other farming systems, has lower environmental costs and 'in some areas, it can reverse problems of natural degradation.'[55]

**Social and economic benefits**

Unfortunately there are few studies that compare and contrast the benefits of small-scale agriculture and agribusiness. Most relevant for my purposes is a study by anthropologist Walter Goldschmidt, in which he compared living standards in two communities in California's Central Valley during the 1940s. One, Dinuba, was dominated by family farms and the other, Arvin, by more specialized agribusinesses cultivating larger holdings. Both were in desert areas that required irrigation and practiced intensive, specialized agriculture, the dollar value of which was similar. In addition both were dependent on intensive use of immigrant and local seasonal labor. The fact that much of the local labor was provided by the families of former immigrants emphasizes the importance for agriculture of national policies that favor ongoing immigration and integration.

Dinuba's population was 7404 and Arvin's 6236, with approximately half in both communities living in town and half in the surrounding countryside. The major agricultural difference was in farm size, number of farming units and proportion of residents who were farm laborers. In family farm Dinuba there were 624 field crop and orchard farms under 32 ha versus only 53 such farms in agribusiness Arvin. At the other end of farm size, Arvin had 7 farms over 518 ha and 15 between 259 ha and 518 ha that covered 67 per cent of the farmed area. In Dinuba there was one farm larger than 518 ha and four between 259 ha and 518 ha, and these totaled less than 10 per cent of the farmed area. Resident families providing farm labor, other than foremen and managers, constituted 24 per cent of Dinuba's families and 58 per cent of Arvin's.

Summing up differences as they related to economic and social viability Goldschmidt noted the following:

- Dinuba supported 62 separate business establishments versus 35 in Arvin.
- Based on analysis over a one-year period, Dinuba's volume of retail trade was $4 383 000 versus $2 535 000 in Arvin.
- Dinuba families had a 'better average standard of living'.
- More than half of Dinuba's employed personnel were 'independently employed businessmen, persons in white-collar employment, or farmers.' In Arvin the proportion was less than a fifth. Conversely less than a third of Dinuba's employed personnel were either landless or low-income agricultural laborers versus two-thirds of those employed in Arvin.
- Dinuba had over twice as many 'organizations for civic improvement and social recreation' than Arvin as well as much better 'physical facilities for community living.' Dinuba's facilities included four elementary schools and one secondary school versus a single elementary school offering fewer services in Arvin, three recreational parks versus one, two newspapers versus one and twice as many churches.

Summarizing his data, Goldschmidt concludes:

> [R]eported differences in the communities may properly be assigned confidently and overwhelmingly to the scale-of-farming factor. The reasons seem clear. The small-farm community is a population of middle-class people with a high degree of stability in income and tenure, and a strong economic and social interest in their community. Differences in wealth among them are not great and the people generally associate together in those organizations which serve the community.

Especially important in Goldschmidt's summary was the larger number of non-farm, private sector businesses, civil improvement organizations and recreational opportunities in Dinuba. This outcome needs to be expanded in small towns everywhere in low-, middle- and high-income countries. Take farmers' markets as one example. Economist Norman Reynolds proposed combining them in Botswana with delivery of a wide range of government services.[56]

Reynold's concept is equally applicable to the United States, where farmers' markets could be expanded to provide social, recreational and other services in addition to government ones. In smaller towns citizens could be provided with financial services, including credit, from mobile banks on a fortnightly or monthly basis. Government officials would be available to provide advice on starting a business or on such issues as taxation, workers' compensation, unemployment insurance, social security, health and retirement. Legal and social service providers would be available to provide adjudication and counseling services as an alternative to time-consuming and expensive lawsuits. Evening recreation could be organized by the host community in the form of sporting events, music, dance and other entertainment.

**Requirements for commercializing small-scale agriculture**
A wide range of requirements warrant more attention. They include assessing the strengths as well as the weaknesses of existing farming systems; better marketing infrastructure and opportunities; more agricultural research and extension, contract farming, security of ownership, credit facilities and land reform; elimination of agricultural subsidies in industrial nations; and legalization of drug crops. Critical are favorable government policies (and finance for implementing them) that include both agricultural production and marketing. Marketing produce requires a reliable road network, which all too often does not exist in late-industrializing countries. Maintenance and improvement of existing rural road systems tend to be defective, as was the case with the Bottom Road in the Middle Zambezi Valley (Chapter 6).

Agricultural research is essential and cost-effective. It is crucial at the international level, for example, to increase funding for expanding collections and cooperative sharing of seed banks so that plant breeders have access to the best available resources for developing new crop varieties when fungal and other diseases threaten famine, as is currently the case with stem rust on wheat.[57] Research also needs to be targeted more directly at better understanding, as well as improving, small-scale farming in high-, middle- and low-income countries.

In April 2008 the UN's Food and Agriculture Organization established a Contract Farming Resource Centre with its own website, to coordinate the growing interest in contract farming between small-scale commercial farmers and agribusiness as a major way to adapt vulnerable small farmers to increasing competition. The least risky model for both partners is where a centralized private or government agribusiness with a nuclear estate and processing facilities buys a single crop from a large number of small farmers.

Annual crops including vegetables, sweetcorn, cut flowers, condiments, tobacco and cotton all have been effectively grown, processed and marketed in many countries in Africa, Asia and Latin America. Nuclear estates, where present, can provide a means for agribusiness to pass on to farmers the result of research as well as to increase output. More risky for the farm family is where the agribusiness is primarily a distributor of fresh produce that is either air-freighted to international next-day markets, or sold in neighboring countries. Contract farmers have also successfully grown more risky tree crops, including coffee, rubber and palm oil, raised poultry, swine and fish and provided dairy products.

Contract farming is not a panacea. It has risks for both the small farmer and agribusiness. Small farmers, for example, risk over-reliance on a contract crop by neglecting other income sources and food crops. Nonetheless contract farming is an effective way for small farmers to acquire a more reliable source of inputs (including credit, improved seed and technical assistance) and income and to outsource marketing.

In Africa agribusinesses combine nuclear estates and processing facilities with a network of small-scale farms growing cotton, rubber, sugar cane or tobacco. Or they may concentrate on collecting tropical crops from contract farmers and marketing them to countries in which such crops are not available during the winter season. Green beans in Kenya were an early example. They were flown from Nairobi airport to Europe for next-day delivery. Cut flowers are another African example. In Zambia, all cotton, including that grown by Gwembe Tonga villagers, is grown by contract farmers.

In Sri Lanka, I have worked in villages where farmers have benefited from the contract farming of tobacco and sale of dairy products. In Malaysia, I researched the government's Federal Land Development Agency's land settlement schemes, where recruited small-scale settler households benefit from growing oil palm. In Laos, contract farming is more risky where contracts are with expatriate traders who export to Thailand and Vietnam, than it is when growing tobacco for a local processor. On the other hand, large-scale government projects like Laos's Nam Theun 2 provide an opportunity to introduce contract farming to thousands of rural households.

Unpopular with national and international financial institutions, land reform remains controversial but is of importance in countries like Brazil and the Philippines. The least controversial way of carrying it out is through large-scale government land settlement and river basin development projects where government-acquired or -owned lands are used. One example is Sri Lanka's Mahaweli project, where 75000 households received 1 hectare farms. In such cases, it is critical for farm households to receive large enough holdings and certificates of ownership or other documents which will encourage them to make permanent improvements and enable them to receive credit.

There are other problems that place small-scale farmers at a major disadvantage which require international attention. Agricultural subsidies in the United States, France and other European countries and Japan, which should be considered illegal under a reformed World Trade Organization, are a major constraint for small-scale cotton producers throughout Africa, wheat farmers in India and maize producers in Mexico. Another problem, the solution of which requires legalizing cultivation of drug crops for medical and other purposes, is how to allow small-scale farmers to grow high-value coca, marijuana and opium crops in areas where they have a major comparative advantage over other crops.

# TRANSFORMING INTERNATIONAL GOVERNANCE

## Introduction

My involvement with international institutions has been primarily with UN specialized agencies and with the World Bank Group. Criticisms of the United Nations system disproportionately refer to the UN Security Council. That is unfortunate, for the various specialized agencies have played a major role in dealing with a wide range of important international issues. Included are agriculture, climate change, the protection of working people, development, education and science, environment, food relief, health, international peace keeping, nuclear energy, refugees and urbanization. I see no substitutes for such organizations. Among them, the United Nations Development Programme has played an important ambassadorial and funding role, helping to coordinate relations between the UN family, the international community of donors and late-developing countries.

Toward the end of the Second World War a series of meetings in the mid-1940s produced the United Nations, the World Bank and the International Monetary Fund. All three need to be reinvented to relate them to changed and changing power relations among UN members with new regulatory institutions created where necessary. Several months ago I doubted that the United States and China, for example, would allow such institutions to infringe upon their short-term national interests. But perhaps the global impacts of the current financial and economic crisis will cause them to rethink the need for more powerful international institutions.

In what follows I restrict my comments to the World Bank and to the need for a World Environment Organization with close ties to a reformed World Bank Group, World Trade Organization and World Court.

## The World Bank

I have had a close relationship with the World Bank as an adviser, consultant and independent panel member for Bank-assisted large dams since 1964. That year, on a part-time basis, I joined three economists and an agronomist on a three-year study that published what may still be the most definitive study of African small-scale agriculture.[58] Since then I have worked closely with World Bank colleagues in Washington and overseas.

A World Bank is essential for poverty alleviation and development in late-developing countries, but the present Bank needs to be radically restructured to address those goals. External oversight by a board or committee of internationally respected development experts is essential to complement the current Executive Board of politically-appointed directors from member countries. Also essential is making the Bank's Inspection Panel into an independent body with greater clout. The current panel reports to, and can be ignored by, the Board, which in turn is influenced by Bank management.

External professional oversight is needed for two major reasons. The first is because the Bank has few staff members who have actually studied poverty while living in rural and urban communities. This fact diminishes the Bank's proclamation that a world without poverty is its main priority. Too many major Bank policies have actually worsened poverty, including a too rapid implementation of 'one fits all' structural adjustment policies and downplaying the importance of agriculture and employment. The Bank's role in worsening poverty was recently emphasized in the September 2008 report of the Independent People's Tribunal on the World Bank in India.[59] Testimony was collected over a two-year period and heard by a thirteen-member jury that included three retired Supreme Court and High Court justices, former secretaries of finance and water resources for the government of India, four professors and four social activists. All were Indian citizens except for two of the social activists.

In a one-page summary the jury members unanimously:

> drew attention to the fact that the World Bank tends to legitimize its action through its self-proclaimed mandate of poverty reduction and development. While in reality, its actions exclude the poor in the best of cases, and hurt and worsen their situation in most other cases . . . To exclude and hurt the majority of Indian citizens in the name of development and poverty alleviation is not merely callous, it verges on a social crime.

The summary was followed by 28 Charges. Charge 1 is that '[t]he World Bank has not reduced poverty in India'; Charge 3 is that 'World Bank policies have increased hunger in India'; Charge 4 is that '[t]he World Bank contributes to India's agricultural depression and farmers' suicides;' and Charge 5 is that 'World Bank led development has not improved employment levels in India.' One jury member added a qualification which placed even more blame on the policies of the central and state governments.

The second reason why independent oversight is important is the overriding policy influence of the Bank's senior management, themselves unduly influenced by member country finance ministers, the US Treasury and national leaders in countries like Brazil, India and China, which are major recipients of Bank assistance. One result is that management emphasizes funding such prestigious large-scale projects as dams. Project task managers are rewarded for moving large amounts of funds as fast as possible. This makes them reluctant to use Bank staff or consultants who might slow progress by insisting on a more careful assessment of environmental and socio-economic costs as well as a wider range of development benefits. In the process, less expensive and more complex, longer-term projects that directly target poverty alleviation at the district and community level are neglected.

It is Bank management that resists strengthening environmental and social safety net provisions associated with urban development, infrastructure and mineral extraction projects and special economic zones. The Bank's stance has been reactive rather than proactive, when civic society, for example, complains about inadequate attention paid to issues relating to the environment, resettlement and indigenous people. One way to placate critics was to agree to world commissions on dams and extractive industries. These commissions produced state of the art reports whose major recommendations were then ignored by the Bank. In the 2008 report of the Indian people's tribunal, the central government's retired secretary for water resources stated that there is 'reason to believe that in 2000–01 the World Bank worked actively to sabotage the Report of the World Commission on Dams.'[60] I was in Laos when the Bank's two-person team arrived to assess the government's reaction to the commission's report. The team's one-sided approach dealt primarily with the ministry most responsible for dam construction.

Dam-related Bank management decisions both at headquarters and in the field also have undercut the recommendations of the Bank's own experts. In a 2001 publication on dam-induced resettlement, the three authors stated: 'Above all, displacees must be beneficiaries of the project.' Bank management rejected that recommendation in favor of the Bank's existing policy that allowed only restoration of living standards – a policy that the Bank's own research, as well as independent research, showed would create new poverty among the majority.

The Inspection Panel was formed at the Board's request in 1993 to 'provide an independent forum to private citizens who believe that they or their interests have been or could be directly harmed by a project financed by the World Bank.'[61] Complaints are first directed to Bank management for comments. Should the Panel believe a fact-finding non-judicial investigation is warranted after reviewing such comments, the Board must give its approval. Should a complaint then be investigated, it is the Board that decides what action, if any, is to be taken. Such a procedure not only results in the Bank evaluating itself, but also leads to Bank management not taking Panel reports seriously – a conclusion warranted by report after report in which the Inspection Panel criticized staff for ignoring the Bank's safety net guidelines.

Let's take a look at a recent Inspection Panel report. It deals with the four-country West African Gas Pipeline Project, which the Bank's Board discussed in August 2008. The Board confirmed the Panel's discovery of 'significant flaws and shortcoming in the application of the Bank's Policy on Involuntary Resettlement' – a finding identical to those in previous Panel reports on Uganda's Bujagali Dam and Argentina's and Paraguay's Yacyretá. The Panel's findings also replicate conclusions in the 1992 report of the Bank-financed Independent Review of India's Sardar Sarovar Projects.

The World Bank's environmental record is as poor as its implementation of its social safety net guidelines. Robert Goodland, former Chief Environmental Adviser to the World Bank Group, writes in a co-authored 2008 publication:

> [the] World Bank is contributing significantly to climate change by financing fossil fuels, deforestation and livestock production . . . The WBG [World Bank Group] is aware that it handles generic environmental issues poorly. Nearly one-third of all Bank-financed 'environment' projects . . . are judged as unsatisfactory or worse, making it the worst-performing sector by a large margin.'[62]

On the other hand, Goodland, like me, is a member of the Bank's loyal opposition. The title of his paper is 'How the World Bank Could Lead the World in Alleviating Climate Change.'

Solving the management problem will require major reorganization for the Bank to adequately deal with environmental, poverty and social issues. Social scientist Robert Wade recommends matrix management as especially appropriate in reducing conflicts between country and sector department staff.[63] Currently country directors make the key decisions and control budgets while sector technical experts not only have 'little budget of their own' but must negotiate from a position of weakness with country directors how they will approach the Bank's safety net and other operational directives.

**A World Environment Organization**

Ten years ago on 23 April 1999, a panel session was held at the Harvard Law School on the topic 'Do We Need a World Environmental Organization?' The chair was MIT political scientist Eugene Skolnikoff. The other four panellists were senior experts from two other universities, the Woods Hole Research Center and the US Department of Defense. At the end of a ninety minute debate, Professor Skolnikoff 'repeated that the panel's judgment was that a new **world environmental organization** should not be created. Instead, we would be better advised to build upon existing organizations.'[64]

Since then the deterioration of the global environment has accelerated. In 2005 the *Millennium Ecosystem Assessment* reported that 60 per cent of 24 global ecosystems assessed 'are being degraded or used unsustainably.'[65] Moreover, substantial losses of ecosystem services and degradation are growing. As with global warming, 'there is *established but incomplete* evidence that changes being made in ecosystems are increasing the likelihood of nonlinear changes in ecosystems (including accelerating, abrupt, and potentially irreversible changes) that have important consequences for human-wellbeing.'[66]

Loss of biodiversity is another environmental crisis. According to a 2006 report of the UN Convention of Biological Diversity, 'we are currently responsible for the sixth major extinction event in the history of the earth, and the greatest since the dinosaurs disappeared 65 million years ago.'[67] Also that year *Nature* reported the conclusions of 19 influential scientists that 'there is clear scientific evidence that we are on the verge of a major biodiversity crisis.'[68] In October 2008 the World Conservation Union (IUCN) released results of a new study on the world's mammals confirming an extinction crisis 'with almost one in four at risk of disappearing forever.'[69]

Clearly, merely building on existing organizations has failed to deal with our environmental crisis. Reasons are many. There are too many competing organizations, none of which has the World Trade Organization's authority to make and enforce international regulations. That reason alone is why a World Environment Organization is needed. Another reason is that the world's global powers have intentionally kept existing organizations weak. The Intergovernmental Panel on Climate Change is one of many examples. It has no binding decision-making capacity but can only report a scientific consensus on global warming causes, risks and possible responses. If governments have no political will to act on IPCC conclusions, necessary actions will not be taken. The situation is even worse with biodiversity, where necessary action involves millions of species as opposed to a small number of greenhouse gases, since a similar organization does not even exist which might at least try to get the attention of governments.

A World Environment Organization, to be effective, should be modeled on a reformed World Trade Organization. Responsibilities should include negotiating, implementing and enforcing agreements and regulations relating to such global commons as the climate and the oceans as well as to critical trans-boundary resources such as river basins, groundwater and glaciers. That is the type of transformational change that I believe is necessary. Close cooperation with the World Trade Organization would be essential, while enforcement would require cooperation with, and a new environmental capacity within the World Court.

Support for a World Environment Organization has been growing since the release of the IPCC's 2007 reports on climate change. Following the February release of the first working group's report, *Climate Change 2007: The Physical Science Basis*, France's President Chirac, backed by leaders of 46 other countries, called for such an organization. Support has also come from two recent World Trade Organization directors. Lack of political will on the part of China, Russia and the United States will be the main obstacle to setting up a World Environment Organization within the United Nations system, since any one of the three could veto its establishment as a threat to its national sovereignty. An alternative would be for the new global organization to be established outside the UN system, as is the case with the World Trade Organization and the World Court. That would facilitate linkage with those two organizations but would require rethinking the future of UNEP.

# TRANSFORMING EDUCATIONAL SYSTEMS

## Introduction

Global threats imply that society can no longer rely on families alone to educate their children before they enter primary school. Such a statement may seem a heresy for a social anthropologist, granted the emphasis in our profession on the family as a cultural universal and as society's basic building block. Experiments to design family substitutes, such as the Israeli kibbutz, have not survived the test of time simply because they have been unable to improve or replicate in one institution such family functions as reproduction, sex, socialization of children, companionship and family maintenance through economic activities. Combining such functions in the family remains crucial, as does the existence of the family itself. But the family, wider kin networks and closed communities can no longer be the only institutions for socializing and educating the world's children.

Coping with the future requires an ability to deal not just with risks but also with increased uncertainty. Because of their rigidity, special efforts need to be made to alter fundamentalist belief systems. Necessary are efforts to offset automatic transfer of values to children and students by giving them the type of education that will enable them to choose their own values rather than automatically replicating those of parents and community.

Universal formal education should start at the preschool level and it should include primary, secondary and tertiary levels as well as national service. The goal is to assist in preparing children, adolescents and young adults to cope better with future risks and uncertainties, to find satisfying employment and livelihood and to contribute to a more sustainable global society. The challenge is to design a program that starts at birth but does not end up superimposing a uniform value system and approach to life. The emphasis in the paragraphs that follow is on preschool education and national service since those are topics yet to be integrated into national systems of education.

**Preschool Education**

Rand Corporation studies discussed in Chapter 4 emphasized four benefits of preschool education for three to five year olds. One was the development of skills that would better prepare children for further education. Included were cognitive learning skills as well as character-building skills, which help children relate to themselves and to others. A second benefit was to help children cope with such constraints as poverty, single-parent households and parents unfamiliar with a national language. Third were benefits to parents when they were specifically targeted in disadvantaged areas. The first three benefits not only helped children acquire skills but also improved children's health, future employment success and avoidance of delinquency and crime. The fourth benefit was economic: not just for the children involved but also for government and society.

Though I am unaware of any countries that promote a national program of preschool education for all children, there are innumerable individual programs. The Rand Corporation included in its study of early childhood interventions, 20 programs in the United States. Eleven involved early childhood education combined with home visiting or parent education, eight programs dealt only with home visiting or parent education and one program considered only early childhood education.

In terms of educational goals I am impressed with Italy's Reggio Emilia system. Reggio Emilia is a city of about 142 000 people, which is the capital of the Province of the same name. During the twentieth century its citizens resisted and were oppressed by Mussolini's fascist government and were devastated by the Second World War. Following liberation in 1943, women in a nearby village wanted to build a preschool 'to provide a new form of education that would ensure that they would never bring up a generation of children that would tolerate injustice and inequality.' A primary school teacher, Loris Malaguzzi, provided inspiration and ideas and the first pre-school was opened in 1945. Finance was provided by 'the sale of a tank, a few horses and a truck abandoned by the retreating Nazis.'[70] Others followed, including the Diana preschool, which *Newsweek* in 1991 called the 'most avant-garde early childhood institution in the world.'[71] Until his death in 1994, Malaguzzi and colleagues continued to develop the Reggio Emilia system, which not only places the child at the center of learning but provides the child with some control over the learning process. The roles of teachers and parents were to create the best possible learning environment, in which children could each explore themselves, others and the surrounding world.

The non-profit Children's Center at Caltech (the Center) is a current variant of this system which has been greatly influenced by association with one of the world's great research and teaching universities. I use the Center as an example of the type of preschool education that is necessary for future generations if they are to cope successfully with existing and future threats. The Center serves children aged six months through their fifth year with a well-trained staff. Students number about 100, with a student/teacher ratio of three to one for infants and toddlers and six to one for preschool students. Parents are expected to be actively involved in the school's programs, with resources available to support both parenting and staff development. Enrollment is open to the community, although children with a formal association with Caltech have priority.

The Center's philosophy views each child as an independent and individual learner. The educational program draws on research that 'children learn best through their senses, needing many opportunities to initiate learning on their own, and needing periods of choice that alternate with periods of guidance.'[72] Active hands-on learning is emphasized, which includes pre-math, pre-reading and science activities at the appropriate time.

Over the years director Susan Wood has emphasized integrating math and science into the curriculum without neglecting the arts and humanities, and has developed a staff capable of encouraging each child's learning in such subjects.[73] A major step forward was the opening of an Outdoor Science Laboratory in 2007. All children aged 3–5 are encouraged to participate in experiments dealing, for example, with what is life and the nature of machines.[74] Observations and hypotheses are noted in journals, in which the children draw and in which an adult writes down their exact statements. At the end of each experiment, group discussions are held in which each child is encouraged to speak. Results are written out on posters and displayed so that children can see their work.

Such an approach to learning, including the curriculum and activities pursued, is, in many respects, experimental. Careful monitoring is essential to track students after they leave the Center to learn how they perform during later schooling and their careers and to feed back that knowledge into the Center's program.

### Primary, Secondary and Tertiary Education

Education, at primary, secondary and tertiary levels, is stressed by all nations. The need for ongoing improvement in financing, management and curricula is widely acknowledged. Further research is needed on how best to continue the Caltech Center's emphasis on mathematics and science in primary and secondary school curricula without diminishing the importance of the arts and humanities, which are so important for improving one's quality of life. Perhaps not sufficiently acknowledged in the Center's preschool curriculum is the danger of developing individual awareness and competence at the expense of the social networking skills that a viable society requires. At all ages children need to learn that they are above all social beings whose identity is formed through relationships with other individuals, social groupings and social situations. Especially in upper primary and secondary school, students need instruction in culturally appropriate sexual relationships as well as such universal social institutions as marriage and parenthood. In other words, schooling must deal with all aspects of children and adolescents being culture-bearing social animals.

### Government-Initiated National Service

Calls for national service increase in the United States and elsewhere in times of economic, political and social crisis. During the first 100 days following his 1933 inauguration, President Roosevelt signed the Emergency Conservation Act, which established the Civilian Conservation Corp (CCC). During his first hundred days, President Obama signed into law the Serve America Act for expanding community and national service.

The CCC was one of Roosevelt's pet projects. Its purpose was to provide employment for hundreds of thousands of young men who were jobless because of the Great Depression. The speed with which it was up and running shows that dynamic political leadership can achieve major goals during a short time span even in a complex democracy. Within three months of its establishment, 250 000 young men were involved 'in the greatest peacetime mobilization of American youth.'[75] By the end of 1935, approximately 500 000 men were at work at 2600 camps located in every state as well as in various overseas territories. Success depended on different government departments working together. The Department of Labor was responsible for recruitment. The War Department mobilized the necessary transportation to deliver enrollees to the various camps, where the Departments of Agriculture and Interior were responsible for developing a work program which would directly benefit the nation without competing with the ongoing work of other agencies. Work was also integrated with an education program which varied from one camp to another. Over 40 000 illiterate youth learned how to read and write.[76]

Aside from the employment and education received, perhaps the greatest achievement of the CCC was increasing the nation's environmental awareness. Over a ten-year period the CCC coordinated and developed America's state park system in 41 states. Elsewhere, drainage systems were built on over 32.4 million ha of arable land. Planting over three billion trees played an important role in the rehabilitation of the dust bowl, where agriculture-related land degradation and wind erosion had left bare soil in several mid-western states. Other tasks were disaster-related. The CCC emphasized fire fighting, which included construction of nearly 100 000 miles of fire roads and thousands of fire watch towers. Flood, disease and insect control also were emphasized.

In 1940, Congress, responding to the possibility of U.S. involvement in the Second World War, passed the Selective Training and Service Act, which required all men between the ages of 21 and 35 to register for possible military service. More recently, concerns about international poverty were instrumental in establishing the Peace Corps in 1961 as an independent federal agency. In 1964 a sister agency, Volunteers in Service to America (VISTA), was established under the Economic Opportunity Act to recruit citizens for working in low-income American communities. The 1993 National and Community Trust Act created the Corporation for National and Community Service and the Office of the Inspector General for implementing and overseeing four social service programs, including VISTA.

Since the 11 September 2001 terrorist attacks on New York and Washington DC, efforts have intensified to promote national civic service through a Universal National Service Act. The 10 September 2007 cover of *Time Magazine* showed a poster of an attractive working woman to illustrate the case for national service. A prominent and wide-ranging group of citizens formed a Service Nation Campaign, which led to the Serve America Act, which the Congress passed and the president signed in 2009.

I see a major need for such programs in every country. Other than to address pressing national problems (poverty, high secondary school dropout rates and unemployment were emphasized in explaining the need for the Serve America Act), national service should combine self-respect and personal development with social networking and environmental awareness. Perhaps an appropriate UN agency, such as UNESCO, could promote the concept of national service and provide various forms of assistance to be financed through a revitalized World Bank Group, the business community and appropriate NGOs.

How the concept is planned and implemented presumably would vary from country to country. Key issues to be considered would include whether national service would be compulsory or voluntary. Compulsory service might be especially relevant in late-industrializing countries with small populations. In countries with large populations, problems of finance and logistics might require moving from voluntary to compulsory service over a longer period. Other critical issues include how best to incorporate both men and women as well as ethnic minorities, how best to involve civic society and the private sector, the relationship between work and educa-tion, the selection of work and educational priorities as they relate to local, national and global problems, the timing and length of national service, and the absorption of graduates into the national political economy.

Zambia could be a useful case for the review and restructuring of an existing but failing national service program, which has been in existence since independence in 1964. Since its beginning, the program has been implemented under the government's national security services. Initially secondary school leavers were enrolled and emphasis was on agriculture. In the mid-1970s three months of military training became compulsory for senior secondary school and university graduates, as well as government employees, until the military aspect was discontinued in 1980. Thereafter emphasis has been shifting back to agriculture, with skills training camps established by the government in 2004. In 2006 a program was initiated for street children. None of the agricultural development programs have proved successful because of policy, planning and implementation inade-quacies. The same has been the case with street children. Two major prob-lems were lack of planning for what would happen to street children after their two-year stint and no involvement of civic society, including local secular and religious NGOs with the most knowledge of the street children problem.

# ADDRESSING RELIGION AND RELIGIOUS FUNDAMENTALISM

**Introduction**

It is appropriate to return to belief systems and values as the last major topic before a brief summary. When I was a one-year special student at the Yale Divinity School studying comparative religion, I would occasionally sit in the Yale Chapel trying to understand the difference between me and fellow students sitting nearby. I had no faith-based belief system. That made me different. I had no reason for the difference and still do not.

Neuroscience provides evidence that religious belief systems have evolutionary value in creating humanity's genetic heritage. So too are religious belief systems part of our cultural heritage. Not only are they a cultural universal, but efforts by political fundamentalists in China, Russia and elsewhere to stamp out religion have failed. As many writers have explained, there are also numerous reasons for individuals to want to believe in a system which provides moral guidance and rewards a 'good life' with a better hereafter – a heavenly paradise, nirvana, reincarnation, union with the ancestors or some other reward. I include union with the ancestors for I see no real difference between the worldwide religions and the belief systems of such groups as the Gwembe Tonga in the 1950s and the Navajo today.

All religious belief systems draw on myths and I do not understand how intelligent people can find meaning, inspiration and solace in such myths. Yet much to my surprise, the tendency today is for the world to become more, not less religious and for religion and global politics to become increasingly interrelated.[77] At the June 2008 interfaith conference at Yale University, which brought together 140 religious leaders, participants noted that the world 'is growing more religious, not less, and more dangerous.'[78] In the United States, more educated and wealthier people are joining evangelical and Pentecostal churches than before, while such churches now contain a majority of all Protestant Christians.

I personally would prefer a future without religion. Reasons why I have placed so much emphasis on preschool education is to provide future generations with a greater ability to better understand the nature of the world in which they live and to question any belief system that their parents, communities and schools impose upon them. Rejecting religious beliefs later in life can be a very traumatic experience, as paleontologist Stephen Godfrey found out when he rejected Christian creationism. There is the hurt and deep unhappiness among parents who 'worried whether their son could endorse an old Earth and remain a Christian' and the question of what stance to take with a devout wife and one's children. On the other hand, there was the 'bitterness, anger and disappointment about having been deceived for so many years.'[79] If we are to cope with current and future threats, more science will be required in children's schooling. Do we want to subject them to similar conflicts? Then there is the unacceptable tendency of Christian evangelicals and Pentecostals, innumerable Hindus and Muslims and Orthodox Jews to reject the empowerment of women by subjecting their roles to the whims of their menfolk.

But a future without religion may not be possible, so we must also address how to live with 'the best' that each religion has to offer while avoiding 'the worst.' Militant fundamentalism is certainly 'the worst.' It exists in all of the great world religions and is responsible for a growing list of atrocities. But the problem of religion is not restricted just to fundamentalism. Catholicism's official stance on the use of condoms and legalized abortion is an example of 'the worst' in that religion. When Mozambique's archbishop of the capital city of Maputo riled against condoms as intentionally infected with HIV/AIDS to kill Africans, commentators were puzzled by the lack of correction from the Vatican. They shouldn't have been. Alfonso López Trujillo was the Vatican enforcer at that time. Following his death the following year, *The Economist* wrote 'Condoms were the first enemy . . . To the Cardinal nothing was safe about them.'[80] I find the Roman Catholic Church's stand against legalized abortion equally appalling granted the Church's knowledge of the unacceptably high death rate among women worldwide who, in desperation, seek illegal abortions.

As for 'the best' in religion, the world would be a less desirable place without the art, architecture, music and poetry that religion has inspired. Not that secular masters are unable to produce equally inspirational works, for they have done so. Especially worrisome would be the loss of the good works and ethical behavior that are attributed to religious beliefs that I mentioned in the Introduction.

The Barna Group, a Christian faith-based firm, released results of a survey in 2007 that compared Christians with 1055 adults self-identified as atheists, agnostics and people with no faith.[81] As a sample, the people with no faith were younger, better educated, wealthier and 'more likely to be male and unmarried' than the faith community to which they were compared. While further surveys that correct for those biases are necessary to further explore differences between the faith and non-faith communities, the results of the Barna group survey are disturbing in that the non-faith sample showed a greater degree of 'cultural disengagement and sense of independence . . . in many areas of life.' They were less apt to participate in community activities, to volunteer in non-profit organizations and to donate to charity. Such differences may be primarily due to sampling errors. Nonetheless I suspect those who willingly place themselves at risk to do good works, as is the case with Doctors without Borders (they won the Nobel Peace Prize in 1999), are more apt to be devout members of the faith community. Is the same the case with Ashoka's more than 2000 social entrepreneurs working in over 60 countries? If the answer is yes, humanity has a problem that anti-religious commentators such as Richard Dawkins and Sam Harris need to address.

**Self-Policing and the Role of Governments**

To date the world religions have not been effective in controlling the worst fundamentalist sects in their midst. A basic question is the extent to which global society should be more supportive in helping them 'clean up their act.' Another alternative would be for governments, for example, to follow the wisdom of America's founding fathers in separating church and state, or to prohibit missionary activities in such 'hot spots' as Northern Nigeria, or to close down fundamentalist schools.

Commentators on the religious scene such as Gustav Niebuhr refer to an unprecedented trend toward interfaith contacts. Since the 11 September 2001 Al Qaeda attack on the United States, such contacts increasingly have been linked to global economic and political issues. In 2004 the World Economic Forum was responsible for setting up the Council of West and Islam Dialogue (C-100), which is composed of 100 business, media and opinion, political and religious leaders. In 2005 the United Nations sanctioned the Alliance of Civilizations following the initiative of the governments of Spain and Turkey. The Alliance's aim 'is to help counter the forces that fuel polarization and extremism' by improving 'understanding and cooperative relations among nations and peoples across cultures and religions.'[82]

In 2007, 138 Muslim religious leaders requested a dialogue between Muslims and Christians. One response was the one-week long 2008 Yale conference, which was to be followed by similar events in England, Jordan, the United States and the Vatican. The hope is to initiate the type of interfaith dialogue which has previously involved Christians and Jews. The task will not be easy, granted misunderstandings between religions, the belief of some that they are the only 'true' religion and competitive missionary activities between Christianity and Islam. As Niebuhr has emphasized, for any interfaith dialogue to be effective in influencing religious behavior, it must go 'beyond tolerance.'[83]

# SUMMARY

Addressing global threats will require major transformations, including a radical improvement in the ability of nations to work together to address global threats and to achieve global goals. The international response to the 2007–2009 global financial and economic crisis, certainly the worst since the depression, shows that global action may be possible in addressing immediate and future threats. But addressing the current crisis will probably not involve major changes in values such as will be necessary if humankind is to shift from a primary focus on increasing per capita income and living standards to a less-materialistic emphasis on other quality of life characteristics. The current pursuit of higher growth rates by national and international financial institutions is a major contributing cause, for example, to absolute and relative poverty (and associated conflict and civil war), unsustainable consumption and degradation of the global environment.

New threats can be expected to arise during a more uncertain future just as priorities in addressing old threats can be expected to change. The magnitude of the threats posed by global warming and nuclear weapons require immediate action by national and international leaders. New policies for reducing greenhouse gases are essential. Their implementation also requires additional funding for basic and applied research to improve old technologies and invent new ones and to launch comprehensive programs of energy conservation. Equally essential is a re-emphasis on social networking and social relationships at the community level and a transition away from rampant individualism.

Addressing current and future threats will require major changes in gender relations so that women achieve full equality in family, community, national and international governance. Also essential are much improved formal systems of education that, starting at the preschool level, enable children better to choose between alternatives (including different belief systems), deal with uncertainty and acquire the background in mathematics, science and the humanities to gain meaningful employment under changing global conditions.

Emphasis must be on both change and continuity. Globalization as currently being implemented pays insufficient attention to quality of life issues and to employment generation, including through village and town enterprises that have existed for thousands of years. Indeed, throughout this book I have emphasized that a wide range of more sustainable employment generation options have been neglected by development planners.

The global transition from rural to urban and post-industrial employment can be expected to continue. Achieving this transition will take generations, however, in those lower- and middle-income countries where 90 per cent of future population increase will occur. There as elsewhere rural farm and non-farm enterprises and small town development, as in China during the late 1970s and the 1980s, are essential not just for poverty reduction and employment generation but also to foster a higher quality of social and cultural life. In lower- and middle-income countries where a majority of households still farm, much more attention needs to be paid to commercializing small-scale agriculture and to its linkage to agribusiness so as to speed up the transition to industrial and post-industrial society.

On the other hand, the economies of scale and comparative advantages associated with globalization must also receive more emphasis as an essential means for achieving food security in those many nations where food self-sufficiency is an unrealistic option. And in every country, more attention needs to be paid to the integrated development of national heart-lands such as river basins and to potential multiplier effects associated with all types of national programs (including research) and development projects.

Regarding international governance, reforming the World Bank is central to improving the world's inadequate and unacceptable record in dealing with global poverty. External oversight is essential to ensure that the Bank actually gives poverty the priority which management falsely claims has been the case. A second essential change is to make the Bank's Inspection Panel independent of Bank control so that its conclusions are not neglected, as has all too frequently been the case in the past. To better deal with environmental issues, an institutional first step is to set up a World Environment Organization which is closely linked with a strengthened World Trade Organization and World Court.

The growing worldwide importance of religion and religious fundamentalism and their engagement in politics are major concerns. In my research and travels I have observed an incompatibility between many religious beliefs and the type of thinking necessary to cope with the major threats and uncertainty that will continue to challenge humanity. Looking to the future, history indicates that people can learn from mistakes and misconceptions and can implement changes when they feel threatened and see a better way forward. What is uncertain is whether we will have the answers to what is needed and whether those powerful individuals and institutions that have the most to lose initially will be willing to adapt. I doubt that the transformational changes required will occur during my life span but the potential is there for them to begin.

# NOTES

1. See Doomsday Clock Timeline. Available at http://thebulletin.org/content/doomsday-clock/timeline.
2. *Bulletin of the Atomic Scientists* (17 January 2007). Page 66. See References for web address.
3. *Ibid.* Page 66.

4. Geoff Brumfiel (17 January 2007). 'Doomsday Draws Two Minutes Closer. Atomic Scientists Add Climate Change to the Threats to Humanity.

5. C. Le Quéré *et al.* (22 June 2007). 'Saturation of the Southern Ocean $CO_2$ Sink Due to Recent Climate Change.' *Science.* **316**. Pages 1735–1738.

6. See Richard A. Kerr (9 February 2007). 'US Policy: A permanent sea change?' *Science.* **315**. Page 757.

7. IPPC (2007a). 'Summary for Policymakers.' In Susan Solomon, Dahe Qin, Martin Manning *et al.* (eds) *Climate Change 2007: The physical science basis.* Cambridge: Cambridge University Press. Page 5. Very high confidence means a 9 out of 10 chance of being correct.

8. IPCC (2007b). '2007: Summary for Policymakers.' In M.L. Parry, O.F. Canziani, J.P. Palutikof, P.J. van der Linden and C.E. Hansen (eds) *Climate Change 2007: Mitigation of climate change.* Contribution of Working Group III to the Fourth Assessment Report of the Intergovernmental Panel on Climate Change. Cambridge: Cambridge University Press. Pages 7–22 (page 12 in April 2007 release).

9. *Ibid.* Page 11.

10. IPCC (2007c). '2007: Summary for policymakers.' In B. Metz, R. Davidson, P.R. Bosch, R. Dave and L.A. Meyer (eds) *Climate Change 2007: Impacts, adaptation and vulnerability.* Contribution of Working Group II to the Fourth Assessment report of the Intergovernmental Panel on Climate Change. Cambridge: Cambridge University Press. Page 4 in May 2007 release.

11. Rosina M. Bierbaum and Peter H. Raven (6 April 2007). 'A Two-Pronged Climate Strategy.' *Science.* **316**. Page 17. The Scientific Expert Group on Climate Change and Sustainable Development had been organized by the scientific research society Sigma Xi and the UN Foundation. The Group's report, *Confronting Climatic Change: Avoiding the unmanageable and managing the unavoidable*, was presented to the UN Secretary-General. It was produced by a team of 18 experts from 11 nations over a two-year period at the request of the UN Department of Economic and Social Affairs.

12. Jim Hansen (13 July 2006). 'The Threat to the Planet.' *New York Review of Books.* **53** (12). Page 10.

13. The quotes that follow are taken from the 27-page Executive Summary of the Stern Report (2007).

14. Stanford University's Hoover Institution (19 December 2006). Available at www. hoover.org/research/factsonpolicy/facts/4931661.html.

15. Erika Kinetz (31 August 2009). 'India's Economic Growth Accelerates to 6.1 per cent.'

16. United Nations Development Programme (1998). *Human Development Report 1998.* New York: Oxford University Press. Page 1.

17. The ecological footprint concept was presented in the early 1990s by University of British Columbia ecologist William Rees, expanded in the doctoral dissertation of his student Mathis Wachernagel and published in a jointly authored book in 1996. Its purpose is to assess impacts of current rates of consumption on the capacity of a given area of ecologically productive land and water to regenerate the resources used and to absorb the waste products produced. Although the concept has been criticized, criticism relates more to efforts to apply the footprint to specific areas, cities for example, than to the world as a whole.

18. Mathis Wackernagel *et al.* (9 July 2002). 'Tracking the Ecological Overshoot of the Human Economy.' *Proceedings of the National Academy of Science.* **99** (14). Pages 9266–9271.

19. The current situation in the United States and China is not too hopeful, having deteriorated further in the U.S. under the previous Bush administration and continuing to deteriorate currently in China. Possibilities have expanded under the present Obama administration but it remains to be seen whether the emphasis will be on preparing for the future or trying to recreate the unsustainable economic growth of the past.

20. See www.juliansimon.com/writings/Ultimate_Resource/TCONCLUS.txt. Page 10.

21. World Bank (2008). 'The Growth Report: Strategies for sustained growth and inclusive development.' Washington DC: World Bank on behalf of the Commission on Growth and Development.
22. IMF figures reproduced in *The Economist* (13 November 2008). 'The Art of the Possible: Cars in emerging markets.' Available at http://economist.com/specialreports/displaystory.cfm?story_id=12544947.
23. World Bank (2001a). 'Engendering Development: Through gender equality in rights, resources and voice.' Summary. Washington DC and Oxford: World Bank and Oxford University Press.
24. The World Bank (2001a). Op. cit.
25. Klaus Schwab (2007). 'Preface'. In Ricardo Hausmann, Laura D. Tyson, and Saadia Zahidi. *The Global Gender Gap Report*. Cologne/Geneva: World Economic Forum.
26. United Nations Population Information Network (no date). 'Guidelines on Women's Empowerment.' Available at http://www.un.org/popin/unfpa/taskforce/guide/iatfwemp.gdl.html.
27. Amartya Sen (1999b). *Development as Freedom*. New York: Anchor Books. Author's italics. Pages 189–191.
28. See All Party Parliamentary Group on Population, Development and Reproductive Growth (January 2007). 'Return of the Population Growth Factor.' London: APPG. Pages 40–41.
29. *Ibid*. Page 34.
30. *Ibid*. Pages 9 and 1.
31. Anna D. Eisler, Hannes Eisler and Mitsuo Yoshida (March 2003). 'Perception of Human Ecology: Cross-cultural and gender comparisons.' *Journal of Environmental Psychology*. **23** (1). Pages 89–101.
32. *The Economist* (12 April 2006). 'Finance and Economics: A guide to womenomics: The future of the world economy lies increasingly in female hands.' Pages 73–74.
33. World Bank (2000). *World Development Report 2000/2001: Attacking poverty*. Washington DC: The World Bank. Page 118.
34. World Health Organization, UNICEF, UNFPA and The World Bank (2007). 'Maternal Mortality in 2005. Estimates Developed by WHO, UNICEF, UNFPA and The World Bank.'
35. Klaus Schwab (2007). Op. cit.
36. Golnaz Esfandiari. 'Iran: Number of female university students rising dramatically.' Available at http://parstimes.com/women/women_universities.html.
37. Molly Hennessy-Fiske (18 September 2007). 'Female Police and Soldiers Battle Sexism.' The World. *Los Angeles Times*.
38. Center for American Women and Politics (2009). 'Fact Sheets. Women in Elective Office 2009. Available at http://www.cawp.rutgers.edu/fast-facts/index.php.
39. C.R. Bello (November 2003). 'Women and Political Participation.'
40. *Ibid*. Page 2.
41. Herman E. Daly and John B. Cobb, Jr. (1994). *For the Common Good: Redirecting the economy toward community, the environment, and a sustainable future*. Appendix. 'The Index of Sustainable Economic Welfare.' Boston, MA: Beacon Press.
42. *Ibid*. Pages 176–189.
43. European Green Party. 'History.' Available at http://www.europeangreens.org/cms/default/rubrik/9/9114.history.htm.
44. Enyinna Chuta and Carl Liedholm (1979). 'Rural Nonfarm Employment: A review of the state of the art.' Michigan State University Rural Development Papers. Number 4. East Lansing, MI: Michigan State University, Department of Agricultural Economics.
45. See World Bank (1978). *Rural Enterprise and Nonfarm Employment*. World Bank Paper. Washington DC: The World Bank.
46. Harold Lubell (1980). *Small Scale Enterprises, Employment and Foreign Aid*. Washington DC: USAID and New Delhi: Tata McGraw-Hill Publishing Company. Page 92.

47. Yasheng Huang (2008). *Capitalism with Chinese Characteristics*. Cambridge: Cambridge University Press. Page 253.
48. See Kapila P. Wimaladharma (1982). 'Nonfarm employment in the major settlements of Sri Lanka.' In Kapila P. Wimaladharma (ed.). *Land Settlement Experiences in Sri Lanka*. Colombo: Karunaratne and Sons; also Thayer Scudder (2005). *The Future of Large Dams*. London: Earthscan. Page 102.
49. Thayer Scudder (1986b). 'Increasing the Employment Potential of New Land Settlements in the Tropics and Subtropics.' In *Transforming Rural Livelihoods: A Search for Asian Alternatives*. Colombo: Marga Institute. On the Brazilian scheme see Martin T. Katzman (1977). *Cities and Frontiers in Brazil: Regional dimensions of economic development*. Cambridge, MA: Harvard University Press, and Michael Nelson (1973). *The Development of Tropical Lands: Policy issues in Latin America*. Baltimore, MD: Johns Hopkins University Press for Resources for the Future.
50. See The Pew Charitable Trusts (2009). 'The Clean Energy Economy: Repowering jobs, businesses and investments across America.' Washington DC and Philadelphia, PA: Pew.
51. Arthur Lewis (1955). *The Theory of Economic Growth*. London: George Allen and Unwin.
52. Oxfam (2006). 'A Recipe for Disaster: Will the Doha Round fail to deliver for development?' Oxfam Briefing Paper 87. Page 7.
53. See Paul Collier (November–December 2008). 'The Politics of Hunger: How illusion and greed fan the food crisis.' *Foreign Affairs*. **87**(6). Pages 67–79.
54. Wages from labor migration exceed international and national foreign aid.
55. FAO (2007). 'Organic Agriculture and Food Security.' Report prepared for the 3–5 May *International Conference on Organic Agriculture and Food Security*. Rome: FAO. Page 16.
56. Norman Reynolds (1992). 'Community Development and Resource Management.' Paper written for the IUCN Southern Okavango Integrated Water Development Project Review Team. Pasadena, CA: Scudder archives.
57. See Elizabeth Finkel (12 June 2009). 'Plant Breeding: Scientists seek easier access to seed banks.' *Science*. **324.**
58. John C. de Wilde with the assistance of Peter F.M. McLoughlin, Andre Guinard, Thayer Scudder and Robert Mabouché (1967). *Experiences with Agricultural Development in Tropical Africa*. Two volumes. Baltimore, MD: Johns Hopkins Press for the World Bank. De Wilde, a Bank economist and former Acting Director of the Bank Economic Staff, was principal author and study director.
59. Independent People's Tribunal on the World Bank in India (11 September 2008). 'Findings of the Jury.' Verdict from the Independent People's Tribunal held at Jawaharlal Nehru University, New Delhi. 21–25 September 2007. See References for web address.
60. *Ibid*. Ramaswamy R. Iyer. 'A Note of Qualification.' Pages 24–25.
61. The Inspection Panel. 'About Us.' Panel Process. Available at http://tinyurl.com/n76kjg.
62. Robert Goodland and Simon Counsell (2008). 'How the World Bank Could Lead the World in Alleviating Climate Change.' In Laura Westra and Klaus Bosselmann (eds). *Reconciling Human Existence with Ecological Integrity*. London: Earthscan. Pages 240–242.
63. Robert H. Wade (2001). 'The US Role in the Malaise at the World Bank: Get up, Gulliver.' Paper presented at the 28–30 August *Annual Meeting of the American Political Science Association*. San Francisco.
64. Google cache of http://law.harvard.edu/academics/graduate/cwe/chayes/enviro.html (emphasis in original).
65. Millennium Ecosystem Assessment (2005). *Ecosystems and Human Wellbeing: Synthesis: Summary for decision-makers*. Washington DC: World Resources Institute. Page 1.
66. *Ibid*. Page 2.

67. Secretariat of the UN Convention on Biological Diversity (March 2006). 'Global Biodiversity Outlook 2.' (Emphasis in original.) See References for web address.
68. Loreau et al. (20 July 2006). 'Diversity without Representation.' *Nature*. **442**. Page 245.
69. IUCN (6 October 2008). 'Red List Reveals World's Mammals in Crisis.' Available at http://www.iucn.org/about/work/programmes/species/red_list/?1695/3.
70. 'Loris Malaguzzi and the Reggio Approach to Early Childhood Education.' Available at http://baliadvertiser.biz/articles/teach_children/2007/loris.html.
71. *Ibid.*
72. The Children's Center at Caltech. 'The Children's Center at Caltech.' Available at http://www.ccc.caltech.edu.
73. Dan. D. Gutierrez (Science Café Field Reporter). 'Field Report #6: Children's Center at Caltech.' Available at http://www.meetup.com/SoCal-Science-Cafe/messages/boards/thread/5327083.
74. See 'Random Walk: Serious fun at the outdoor science lab' (2007). *Engineering and Science*. **LXX** (3). Available at http://eands.caltech.edu/articles/LXX3/seriousfun.html.
75. John C. Page (1985). *The Civilian Conservation Corps and the National Park Service 1933–1942: An administrative history*. Chapter 5: 'Overall Accomplishments 1993–1942'. Washington DC: National Park Service.
76. Civilian Conservation Corps. Alumni (no date). 'Roosevelt's Tree Army: A brief history of the Civilian Conservation Corps.' Available at http://www.geocities.com/ccchistory/treearmy.html.
77. See *The Economist* (3 November 2007). 'In God's Name: A special report on religion and public life.' Pages 3–22.
78. Neela Banergee (September–October 2008). 'Ayatollahs, Evangelicals, Shaykhs, and Rabbis meet at Yale to Ask: Can we all just get along.' *Yale Alumni Magazine*. **LXXII** (1). Pages 51–55.
79. 'Evolution: Crossing the Divide' (22 February 2008). *Science*. **319**. Pages 1034 and 1036.
80. *The Economist* (3 May 2008). 'Alfonso López Trujillo.' Page 93.
81. The Barna Group. 'Atheists and Agnostics Take Aim at Christians.' See References for web address.
82. Mission Statement. Available at http://www.unaoc.org/content/view/39/187/lang,english/.
83. Gustav Niebuhr (2008). *Beyond Tolerance: Searching for interfaith understanding in America*. New York: Viking Penguin.

# References

Adema, Guy W., R.D. Karpilo, Jr. and B.F. Molnia (no date). 'Melting Denali: Effects of climate change on the glaciers of Denali National Park and Preserve.' Available at http://www.nps.gov/akso/AKParkScience/ClimateChange/adema.pdf. Accessed 2 September 2009.

Adeniyi, E.O. (1973). 'Downstream Impact of the Kainji Dam.' In A.L. Mabogunje (ed.). *Kainji: A Nigerian man-made lake, socio-economic conditions.* Kainji Lake Studies. 2. Ibadan: University of Nigeria Press for Nigerian Institute of Social and Economic Research. Pages 169–177.

All Party Parliamentary Group on Population, Development and Reproductive Growth (January 2007). 'Return of the Population Growth Factor'. London: APPG.

Al-Wahaid, Adnan (no date). 'Border Closures and Nutrition in Gaza.' Available at http://www.fex.ennonline.net/20/border.aspx.

American Bird Conservancy and Defenders of Wildlife (August 2006). 'Pesticide Ban Follows Millions of Bird Deaths.' Press Release. Available at http://www.abcbirds.org/newsandreports/releases/060803.html. Accessed 2 September 2009.

American Museum of Natural History and Lewis Harris and Associates (20 April 1998). 'Biodiversity in the Next Millennium.' New York: American Museum of Natural History.

American Society of Civil Engineers (ASCE) ([2002?]). '150 years of Civil Engineering.' Available at http://www.asce.org/150/150years.html. Accessed 2 September 2009.

American Society of Civil Engineers (ASCE) (2005a). 'Report Card For America's Infrastructure: Dams.' Available at http://www.asce.org/reportcard/2005/page.cfm?id=23. Accessed 2 September 2009.

American Society of Civil Engineers (ASCE) (2005b). 'Report Card For America's Infrastructure: Roads.' Available at http://www.asce.org/reportcard/2005/page.cfm?id=30. Accessed 2 September 2009.

American Society of Civil Engineers (ASCE) (2008). 'Raising the Grades: Small steps for big improvements in America's failing infrastructure: An action plan for the 110th Congress.' Available at http://www.asce.org/reportcard/2005/actionplan07.cfm. Accessed 2 September 2009.

American Society of Civil Engineers (ASCE) (2009). 'Report Card for America's Infrastructure: Report card 2009 grades.' Available at http://

www.asce.org/reportcard/2009/grades.cfm. Accessed 2 September 2009.

Asian Development Bank (1999). 'Fighting Poverty in Asia and the Pacific: The poverty reduction strategy.' Manila: Asian Development Bank.

Asian Development Bank (2007). 'Special Chapter – Highlights.' In 'Inequality in Asia: Key indicators 2007.' Manila: Asian Development Bank.

Asiatics Agro-Dev, International (Pvt) Ltd (2000). 'Tarbela Dam and related aspects of the Indus River Basin Pakistan: Final report.' Available at http://www.dams.org/docs/kbase/studies/cspkmain.pdf. Accessed 2 September 2009.

Askouri, Ali (14 December 2006). 'China's Investment in Sudan: Destroying communities.' *Pambazuka News*. **282**.

Audubon Society ([2007?]) 'White-Throated Swift.' Available at http://www.audubon2.org/watchlist/viewSpecies.jsp?id=216. Accessed 2 September 2009.

Avert (no date). 'HIV and AIDS in Zambia.' Available at http://www.avert.org/aids-zambia.htm. Accessed 2 September 2009.

*Bali Advertiser* (2007). 'Loris Malaguzzi and the Reggio Approach to Early Childhood Education.' Available at http://baliadvertiser.biz/articles/teach_children/2007/loris.html. Accessed 2 September 2009.

Ballis, Robert, M. Ezzati and D.M. Kammen (1 April 2005). 'Mortality and Green House Gas Impacts of Biomass and Petroleum Energy Futures in Africa.' *Science*. **308**. Pages 98–103.

Banergee, Neela (September–October 2008). 'Ayatollahs, Evangelicals, Shaykhs, and Rabbis meet at Yale to Ask: Can we all just get along.' *Yale Alumni Magazine*. **LXXII** (1). Pages 51–55.

Barna Group (no date). 'Atheists and Agnostics Take Aim at Christians.' Available at http://www.barna.org/barna-update/article/12-faithspirituality/102-atheists-and-agnostics-take-aim-at-christians. Accessed 2 September 2009.

Bartels, Larry M. (2008). *Unequal Democracy: The political economy of the new gilded age*. New York: Russell Sage Foundation.

Bates, Robert H. (2008). *When Things Fell Apart: State failure in late-century Africa*. New York: Cambridge University Press.

Beehner, Lionel (27 April 2007). 'The Effects of "Youth Bulge" on Civil Conflicts.' Backgrounder. New York: Council on Foreign Relations.

Beijing 2008 (2007). 'Shougang Begins Construction of New Plant Outside Capital.' Available at http://en.Beijing2008.cn/07/47/article214024707.shtml. Accessed 2 September 2009.

Bello, C.R. (November 2003). 'Women and Political Participation'. Available at http://www.onlinewomeninpolitics.org/beijing12/03_1201_wip.htm.

Bhatia, Ramesh, R. Cestti, M. Scatasta and R.P.S. Malik (eds) (2008). *Indirect Economic Impacts of Dams: Case studies from India, Egypt and Brazil*. New Delhi: Academic Foundation for the World Bank.

Bierbaum, Rosina M. and Peter H. Raven (6 April 2007). 'A Two-Pronged Climate Strategy.' Editorial. *Science*. **316**. Page 17.

Birdlife International (2005). 'A Biodiversity Indicator For Europe: Wild bird indicator update 2005. Available at http://www.birdlife.org/action/science/indicators/pdfs/2005_pecbm_indicator_update.pdf. Accessed 2 September 2009.

Birdlife International (2008). 'State: What birds tell us about condition and change.' Available at http://www.birdlife.org/action/science/sowb/state/index.html. Accessed 2 September 2009.

Birdlife International (2008). 'Declines Can Be Quick and Catastrophic.' Available at http://www.birdlife.org/action/science/sowb/state/10.html. Accessed 2 September 2009.

Birdlife International (2008). 'Species Are Becoming More Threatened.' Available at http://www.birdlife.org/action/science/sowb/state/16.html. Accessed 2 September 2009.

Bloomberg News (20 June 2007). 'China Overtakes U.S. in Greenhouse Gas Emissions.' *International Herald Tribune*.

Bosshard, Peter (May 2007). 'China's Role in Financing African Infrastructure.' Berkeley, CA: International Rivers Network.

Bosshard, P. (June 2007). 'China and the West in Africa: Shared interests?' *China Monitor*. Available at http://www.ccs.org.za/downloads/monitors, CCS China Monitor June 2007.pdf. Accessed 2 September 2009.

Boushey, Heather and Jeffrey Wenger (30 October 2001). 'Coming Up Short: Current unemployment insurance benefits fail to meet basic family needs.' Brief. Washington DC: Economic Policy Institute.

British Broadcasting Company News (18 September 2007). 'China Opens Coffers for Minerals.' Available at http://www.news.bbc.co.uk/2hi/Africa/7000925.stm.

Brown, Lester (28 January 2004). 'Update 33.' Washington DC: Earth Policy Institute.

Brown, Lester (16 February 2005). 'China Replacing the United States as World's Leading Consumer.' Washington DC: Earth Policy Institute.

Brown, Mervyn (2001). *War in Shangri-La: A memoir of civil war in Laos*. London: The Radcliffe Press.

Brumfiel, Geoff (17 January 2007). 'Doomsday Draws Two Minutes Closer. Atomic scientists add Climate Change to the Threats to Humanity.' *Nature News*. Available at http://www.nature.com/news/2007/070117/full/news070115-8.html.

B'Tselem (no date). 'About B'Tselem.' Available at http://www.btselem. org/english/About_BTselem/Index.asp. Accessed 2 September 2009.

*Bulletin of the Atomic Scientists* (no date). 'Doomsday Clock: Timeline.' Available at http://thebulletin.org/content/doomsday-clock/timeline. Accessed 2 September 2009.

*Bulletin of the Atomic Scientists* (17 January 2007). 'It is 5 Minutes to Midnight.' **63** (1). Pages 66–71.

Caplan, Pat (2006). 'Terror, Witchcraft and Risk.' *The Anthroglobe Journal.* http://www.anthroglobe.ca/info/caplanp_witchcraft_060119. htm. Accessed 2 September 2009.

CARE International (5 August 2002). CARE releases preliminary findings from two health and nutrition surveys which find high rates of malnutrition and anemia in the West Bank and Gaza. Reports with the technical assistance of Johns Hopkins University and funded by the United States Agency for International Development.

Carey, Roane and Jonathan Shainen (eds) (2002). *'The Other Israel: Voices of refusal and dissent.'* New York: New Press.

Carrington, Paul D. (2005). *Spreading America's Word: Stories of its lawyer-missionaries.* New York: Twelve Tables Press.

CBC News (10 June 2009). 'Rae "dumbfounded" after Sri Lanka denied him entry.' Available at http://www.cbc.ca/world/story/2009/06/10/rae-detain-sri-lanka-tamil-tigers285.html.

CCAP-UC Davis China Water Resource Team (no date). 'Groundwater in China: Development and Responses.' Power Point Presentation. Available at http://iwmi.cgiar.org/Assessment/files/Synthesis/China%20 CCAP_Davis%20Team.ppt. Accessed 2 September 2009.

Center for American Women and Politics (2009). 'Fact Sheets. Women in Elective Office 2009.' Available at http://www.cawp.rutgers.edu/ fast_facts/levels_of_office/documents/elective/pdf.

Cernea, Michael M. (1999a). 'Why Economic Analysis is Essential.' In Cernea, Michael M. (ed.). *The Economics of Involuntary Resettlement: Questions and Challenges.* Washington DC: World Bank. Pages 5–49.

Cernea, Michael M. (ed.) (1999b). *The Economics of Involuntary Resettlement: Questions and Challenges.* Washington DC: The World Bank.

Cernea, Michael M. (2000). 'Risks, Safeguards, and Reconstruction: A model for population displacement and resettlement.' In Michael M. Cernea and Christopher McDowell (eds). *Risks and Reconstruction: Experiences of resettlers and refugees.* Washington DC: The World Bank. Pages 11–55.

Chidumayo, Emmanuel N. (no date). 'Inventory of Wood Used in Charcoal Production in Zambia.' Available at http://www.worldwildlife.

org/bsp/publications/africa/inventory-wood/inventory.html. Accessed 2 September 2009.

Children's Center at Caltech ([2009]). 'The Children's Center at Caltech.' Available at http://www.ccc.caltech.edu. Accessed 2 September 2009.

Childress, Sarah (26 March 2009). 'Zambia's Economy Falls with Price of Copper.' *The Wall Street Journal*. Available at http://online.wsj.com/articles/SB123803357232044061.html. Accessed 2 September 2009.

Chileshe, Anne (July 2001). 'Forestry Outlook Studies in Africa (FOSA): Zambia.' Lusaka and Rome: Forestry Department, Ministry of Environment and Natural Resources and Food and Agriculture Organization of the United Nations.

Chinese Academy of Social Sciences, http://bic.cass.cn/English.

Christian Aid (March 2001). 'The Scorched Earth.' London: Christian Aid. Available at http://www.reliefweb.int/library/documents/2001/chr_aid-sud14mar1.pdf. Accessed 2 September 2009.

Christison, Kathleen (2 May 2002). 'Before There was Terrorism.' *Counterpunch*.

Chuta, Enyinna and Carl Liedholm (1979). 'Rural Nonfarm Employment: A review of the state of the art.' Michigan State University Rural Development Papers. Number 4. East Lansing, MI: Michigan State University, Department of Agricultural Economics.

Cincotta, Richard (1 March 2005). 'Youth Bulge, Underemployment Raise Risks of Conflict.' State of the World 2005 Global Security Brief #2 Washington DC: Worldwatch Institute. Available at http://www.worldwatch.org/node/76. Accessed 2 September 2009.

CIPM Yangtze Joint Venture (1988). 'The New Sky Experience.' Appendix B of Volume 9. *Resettlement: Three Gorges Water Control Project: People's Republic of China*. Toronto: Sponsored by Canadian International Development Agency.

Civilian Conservation Corps Alumni (no date). 'Roosevelt's Tree Army; a brief history of the Civilian Conservation Corps. Available at http://www.geocities.com/ccchistory/treearmy.html.

Clower, R.W., G. Dalton, M. Harwitz and A.A. Walters (1966). *Growth without Development: An economic survey of Liberia*. Evanston, IL: Northwestern University Press.

CNN.com (5 December 2000). 'Israeli Ban Tripled Palestinian Unemployment, Says U.N. Report.' Available at http://edition.cnn.com/2000/WORLD/meast/12/05/mideast.02/index.html. Accessed 2 September 2009.

CNN.com (5 July 2008). 'CNN Poll: Most say Founding Fathers wouldn't be impressed.' Available at http://www.cnn.com/2008/US/07/04/us.poll/. Accessed 2 September 2009.

Cohen, Roger (12 February 2009). 'Eyeless in Gaza.' *The New York Review of Books.* **56** (2).

Collier, Paul (1999). 'On the Economic Consequences of Civil War.' *Oxford Economic Papers.* **51**. Page 175.

Collier, Paul (November–December 2008). 'The Politics of Hunger: How illusion and greed fan the food crisis.' *Foreign Affairs.* **87** (6). Pages 67–79.

Colson, Elizabeth (2000). 'The Father as Witch.' *Africa.* **70** (3). Pages 333–358.

Commission on Growth and Development (2008). *The Growth Report: Strategies for sustained growth and inclusive development.* Washington DC: The World Bank.

Communist Party of China (23 June 2006). 'Ideological Foundation'. Available at http://english.cpc.people.com.cn/66739/4521326.html. Accessed 2 September 2009.

Dahl, Robert A. (1961). *Who Governs? Democracy and Power in an American City.* New Haven: Yale University Press.

Daly, Herman E. (September 2008). 'Growth and Development: Critique of a credo.' Notes and Commentary. *Population and Development Review.* **34** (3). Pages 511–518.

Daly, Herman E. and J.B. Cobb, Jr. (1994). *For the Common Good: Redirecting the economy toward community, the environment, and a sustainable future.* Boston, MA: Beacon Press.

Day, Kathleen (17 September 2006). 'Retirement, Squeezed: As traditional plans decline, workers face a less certain future.' *Washington Post.*

de Wilde, John C. with the assistance of P.F.M. McLoughlin, A. Guinard, T. Scudder and R. Mabouché (1967). *Experiences with Agricultural Development in Tropical Africa.* Two volumes. Baltimore, MD: Johns Hopkins Press for the International Bank for Reconstruction and Development (World Bank).

Diamond, Jared (2005). *Collapse: How societies choose to fail or succeed.* New York: Viking.

Dickson, I.W., R. Goodland, P.H. Leblond, F.L. Leistriz, C. Limoges and T. Scudder (1994). 'Hydro-Quebec's Grande Baleine Environmental Impact Study: An assessment report prepared for Hydro-Quebec.'

Dissanaake, Gamini (April 1981): 'Inaugural Speech at the April 1981 Conference on Land Settlement Experiences in Sri Lanka.' Published in May 1982 under the same title in Kapila P. Wimaladharma (ed.). *Land Settlement Experiences in Sri Lanka.* Colombo: Karunaratne and Sons. Pages 1–5.

Douglas, Mary (1986). 'The Social Preconditions of Radical Skepticism.'

In J. Law (ed.). *Power, Action and Belief: A new sociology of knowledge.* London: Routledge and Kegan Paul. Pages 261–277.

Douma, Pyt (December 1999). 'Poverty, Conflict and Development Interventions in Sub Saharan Africa.' Paper presented at the *First Global Development Conference.* Bonn, Germany. 6–8 December.

Dugger, Celia W. (10 June 2009). 'Battle to Halt Graft Scourge in Africa Ebbs.' *The New York Times.*

Dumont, René (1979). 'Towards Another Development in Rural Zambia.' Mimeographed manuscript.

Easterlin, Richard A. (1995). 'Will Raising the Incomes of All Increase the Happiness of All?' *Journal of Economic Behavior and Organization.* **27** (1). Pages 35–47.

*Economist* (29 March 2003a). Book Review. 'The Other Israel: Voices of refusal and dissent.'

*Economist* (29 March 2003b). 'Walling them in. Israel's security barrier.'

*Economist* (12 April 2006). 'Finance and Economics: A guide to women-omics: The future of the world economy lies increasingly in female hands.' Pages 73–74.

*Economist* (16 September 2006). 'The New Titans. A survey of the world economy.' Page 5.

*Economist* (11 August 2007). 'Income Inequality in Emerging Asia is Heading Toward Latin American Levels.' Page 36.

*Economist* (13 October 2007). 'China Beware.' Leaders. Page 15.

*Economist* (3 November 2007). 'In God's Name: A special report on religion and public life.' Page 3–22.

*Economist* (20 November 2007). 'Beware of Demob: A reserve of unemployed ex-servicemen worries China's leaders.'

*Economist* (9 February 2008). 'Briefing: Technology in emerging economies: Of internet cafés and power cuts.' Page 75.

*Economist* (16 February 2008). 'Economics Focus: From Mao to the Mall: Amid all the global doom, the good news is that China is turning into a nation of spenders, as well as sellers.' Page 86.

*Economist* (15 March 2008a). 'A Ravenous Dragon: A special report on China's quest for resources.'

*Economist* (15 March 2008b). 'The New Colonialists: China's hunger for natural resources is causing more problems at home than abroad.' Page 13.

*Economist* (3 May 2008). 'Alfonso López Trujillo.' Page 93.

*Economist* (26 July 2008). ' Unhappy America.' Leaders. Page 15.

*Economist* (13 November 2008). 'The Art of the Possible: Cars in emerging markets.' Available at http://www.economist.com/specialreports/displaystory.cfm?story_id=12544947. Accessed 2 September 2009.

Economist.com (18 March 2008). 'China's economy.' Available at http://www.economist.com/research/backgrounders/displayBackgrounder.cfm?bg=747710.

Eisler, Anna D., H. Eisler and M. Yoshida (March 2003). 'Perception of Human Ecology: Cross-cultural and gender comparisons.' *Journal of Environmental Psychology*. **23** (1). Pages 89–101.

*Engineering and Science* (2007). 'Random Walk: Serious fun at the outdoor science lab.' LXX (3). Available at http://eands.caltech.edu/articles/LXX3/seriousfun.html. Accessed 2 September 2009.

Erie, Matthew (May 2007). 'Land Grab Here and Real Estate Market There: Property law reform in the People's Republic of China.' *Anthropology News*.

Esfandiari, Golnaz ([2003]). 'Iran: Number of female university students rising dramatically.' Available at http://parstimes.com/women/women_universities.html. Accessed 2 September 2009.

European Green Party (no date). 'History.' Available at http://www.europeangreens.org/cms/default/rubrik/9/9114.history.htm. Accessed 2 September 2009.

Evans, Grant (2002). *A Short History of Laos: The land in between*. Crows Nest, Australia: Allen and Unwin.

Fei Hsiaotung(1939). *Peasant Life in China: A field study of country life in the Yangtze Valley*. London: G. Routledge and New York: Dutton.

Fei Hsiaotung (1981). 'The New Outlook of Rural China: Kaihsiengkung revisited after half a century.' Huxley Memorial Lecture for 1981. 18 November.

Fei Hsiaotung (1983). *Chinese Village Closeup*. Beijing: New World Press.

Feit, H.A. (1995). 'Hunting and the Quest for Power: The James Bay Cree and white men in the 20th century.' In R.B. Morrison and C.R. Wilson (eds). *Native Peoples: The Canadian experience*. Toronto: McClelland and Stewart. Pages 171–207.

Finkel, Elizabeth (12 June 2009). 'Plant Breeding: Scientists seek easier access to seed banks.' *Science*. **324**.

Fithen, Caspar and Paul Richards (2005). 'Making War, Crafting Peace: Militia solidarities and demobilization in Sierra Leone.' In Paul Richards (ed.). *No Peace, No War: An anthropology of contemporary armed conflicts*. Athens, OH and Oxford: Ohio University Press and James Curry. Pages 117–136.

Flavin, Christopher and Gary Gardner (2006). 'China, India and the New World Order.' In *State of the World 2006*. New York: W.W. Norton and Company for Worldwatch Institute. Pages 3–23.

Food and Agriculture Organization (2007). 'Organic Agriculture and Food

Security.' Report prepared for the 3–5 May *International Conference on Organic Agriculture and Food Security*. Rome: FAO.

Foster, George, T. Scudder, E. Colson and Robert Van Kemper (eds) (1979). *Long Term Field Research in Social Anthropology*. London: Academic Press.

Frederiksen, Harald (2003). 'Water: Israeli strategy, implications for peace and the viability of Palestine.' *Middle East Policy*. **X** (4). Pages 69–86.

Frederiksen, Harald (June 2007a). 'Water in the Israeli/Palestinian Conflict: A history that leaves few options.' Presentation at the *Fifth International Water History Association Conference*. Tampere, Finland.

Frederiksen, Harald (2007b). 'A Federation of Palestine and Jordan: A chance for peace?' *Middle East Policy*. **XIV** (2). Pages 30–43.

Frederiksen, Harald (2009). 'The World Water Crisis and International Security.' *Middle East Policy*. **XVI** (4). Pages 76–89.

Frederiksen, Harald (no date). 'Return of water: One component for attaining an Israel-Palestine peace and a more secure Middle East.' Presentation at the *Third Annual Conference of the Center for Macro Projects and Diplomacy*. Roger William University, Bristol, RI.

Friedman, Thomas L. (2005). *The World Is Flat: A brief history of the twenty-first century*. New York: Farrar, Straus and Giroux.

Gans, Herbert (1962). *The Urban Villagers*. New York: New Press of Glencoe.

Gardner, Gary T. (2006). *Inspiring Progress: Religion's contribution to sustainable development*. New York: W.W. Norton and Company.

Gardner, Gary, E. Assadourian and R. Sarin (2004). 'The State of Consumption Today.' In *State of the World 2004*. New York: W.W. Norton and Company for the Worldwatch Institute. Pages 3–21.

Gay, John (2005). 'An Analysis of "*The End of Poverty*" and the Millennium Development Goals.' *Higher Education in Europe*. **XXX** (3–4). Pages 249–265.

Gertner, Jon (21 October 2007). 'The Future is Drying Up.' *New York Times Magazine*.

Girion, Lisa (8 July 2008). 'WellPoint Settles with California Hospitals over Rescissions.' *Los Angeles Times*.

Gisha (January 2008). 'Israel Still Preventing at least 625 students from Leaving Gaza.' Available at http://www.gisha.org/index.php?intLanguage=2&intItemId=930&intSiteSN=113&OldMenu=113. Accessed 2 September 2009.

Global Development Research Center (1998). News Release (6 January 1998). 'Troubled Waters: A call for action.' Available at http://www.gdrc.org/oceans/troubled.html.

Global Witness (January 2001). 'The Role of Liberia's Logging Industry: Briefing to the UN Security Council on National and Regional Insecurity.' Available at http://globalpolicy.org/component/content/article/194/39174.html. Accessed 2 September 2009.

Goodland, Robert and S. Counsell (2008). 'How the World Bank Could Lead the World in Alleviating Climate Change.' In Laura Westra and K. Bosselmann (eds). *Reconciling Human Existence with Ecological Integrity.* London: Earthscan. Pages 240–242.

Google cache of http://law.harvard.edu/academics/graduate/cwe/chayes/enviro.html. 'Do we need an environmental organization?' Found at http://209.85.173.104/search?q=cache:1M8wdhtp6BHJ::www.law.harvard.edu/academics/graduate/cwe/chayes/enviro.html.

Gosselin, Peter (2008). *High Wire: The precarious financial lives of American families.* New York: Basic Books.

Graf, William L. (1999). 'Dam Nation: A geographic census of American dams and their large-scale hydrological impacts.' *Water Resources Research.* **35.** Pages 1305–1311.

Graham, Wayne (26 June 2001). 'Human and Economic Consequences of Dam Failure.' Paper presented at the *FEMA Workshop on Issues, Resolutions, and Research Needs Related to Embankment Dam Failure Analysis.'* Oklahoma, City, 26–28 June.

Green, Matthew and J. Anderlini (30 October 2007). 'China's CDB Seals Nigerian Deal.' *Financial Times.*

Gunaratna, Malinda H. (1988). *For a Sovereign State.* Ratmalana: Sarvodaya Book Publishing Services.

Gutierrez, Dan D. (no date). 'Field Report #6: Children's Center at Caltech.' Available at http://www.meetup.com/SoCal-Science-Cafe/messages/boards/thread/5327083. Accessed 2 September 2009.

Gwembe Tonga Rural Authority (27 July 2007). 'Letter from the Royal Highnesses Chiefs in the Gwembe Valley along the Lake Kariba: The wrongs the Bank has done – background and current suffering of the displaced people following relocation.' Muyumbwe: Gwembe Tonga Rural Council.

*Ha'aretz* Service and Reuters (26 February 2009). 'Israel's Next Government Will Be "More Jewish and More Zionist".' Available at http://tinyurl.com/nsj4nq. Accessed 2 September 2009.

Haberli, W. and M. Hoelzle (2001). 'The World Glacier Monitoring Service.' Available at http://nerc-bas.ac.uk/public/icd/icsi/WGMS.html.

Hamburger, Tom and P. Nicholas (18 June 2008). 'Partying Hard on Soft Money.' *Los Angeles Times.* Pages A1 and A13.

Hamlet, A.F., P.W. Mote, M.O. Clark and D.P. Lettenmaier (2005). 'Effects of Temperature and Precipitation Variability on Snowpack

Trends in the Western United States.' *Journal of Climate.* **18**. Pages 4545–4561.

Hansen, Jim (13 July 2006). 'The Threat to the Planet.' *New York Review of Books.* **53** (12).

Hausmann, Ricardo, L.D. Tyson and S. Zahidi (2006). 'The Global Gender Gap Report.' Cologne/Geneva: World Economic Forum.

Hausmann, Ricardo, L.D. Tyson and S. Zahidi (2007). 'The Global Gender Gap Report.' Cologne/Geneva: World Economic Forum.

Hennessy-Fiske, Molly (18 September 2007). 'Female Police and Soldiers Battle Sexism.' The World. *Los Angeles Times.*

Hoover Institution (19 December 2006). 'Fact on Policy: Consumer Spending.' Available at www.hoover.org/research/factsonpolicy/facts/4931661.html. Stanford, CA: Hoover Institute, Stanford University.

Human Rights Watch (13 January 2009). 'Israel: End Gaza's humanitarian crisis at once.' Available at http://www.hrw.org/en/news/2009/01/12/israel-end-gaza-s-humanitarian-crisis-once. Accessed 2 September 2009.

Independent People's Tribunal on the World Bank in India (11 September 2008). 'Findings of the Jury.' Verdict from the Independent People's Tribunal held at Jawaharlal Nehru University, New Delhi. 21–25 September 2007. Available at http://worldbanktribunal.org/WB_Tribunal_Findings.pdf. Accessed 2 September 2009.

Indianz.com (22 July 2005). 'McCain Prods Tribes, Government on Tribal Land Dispute'. Available at http://indianz.com/News/2005/009449.asp. Accessed 2 September 2009.

Inspection Panel. 'About Us.' Available at http://tinyurl.com/n76kjg. Accessed 2 September 2009.

*International Herald Tribune* (11 October 2008). 'Nobel Peace Prize Winner Wants Jobs for the Young.'

International Labour Organization (1981). *Basic Needs in an Economy Under Pressure.* Addis Ababa: International Labour Organization.

International Labour Organization (24 January 2006). 'ILO Annual Jobs Report Says Global Unemployment Continues to Grow, Youth Now Make Up Half Those Out of Work.' Press Release. Available at http://www.ilo.org/global/About_the_ILO/Media_and_public_information/Press_Releases/lang--en/WCMS_O65176/index.htm. Accessed 2 September 2009.

International Rivers (no date). 'Mambilla Dam, Nigeria.' Available at http://www.internationalrivers.org/en/africa/mambilla-dam-nigeria.

IPCC (2007a). 'Summary for Policymakers.' In Susan Solomon, Dahe Qin, Martin Manning *et al.* (eds) *Climate Change 2007: The physical science basis.* Cambridge: Cambridge University Press.

IPCC (2007b). '2007: Summary for Policymakers.' In M.L. Parry, O.F. Canziani, J.P. Palutikof, P.J. van der Linden and C.E. Hansen (eds). *Climate Change 2007: Mitigation of climate change.* Contribution of Working Group III to the Fourth Assessment Report of the Intergovernmental Panel on Climate Change. Cambridge: Cambridge University Press.

IPCC (2007c). '2007: Summary for Policymakers.' In B. Metz, R. Davidson, P.R. Bosch, R. Dave and L.A. Meyer (eds). *Climate Change 2007: Impacts, adaptation and vulnerability.* Contribution of Working Group II to the Fourth Assessment report of the Intergovernmental Panel on Climate Change. Cambridge: Cambridge University Press.

IPSOS Public Affairs (12–16 June 2008). 'The Associated Press Poll: Political study.' Project #81-5681-88.

Israel (28 January 2003). 'Elections for the 16th Knesset: National Unity (Halchud HaLeumi): Platform. Available at http://www.knesset.gov.il/elections16/eng/lists/plat_27-e.htm. Accessed 2 September 2009.

IUCN (12 September 2007). 'Extinction Crisis Escalates: Red List shows apes, corals, vultures, dolphins in danger.' News release. Available at http://www.iucn.org/media/materials/releases/?81/Extinction-crisis-escalates-Red-List-shows-apes-corals-vultures-dolphins-all-in-danger. Accessed 2 September 2009.

IUCN (6 October 2008). 'Red List Reveals World's Mammals in Crisis.' Available at http://www.iucn.org/about/work/programmes/species/red_list/?1695/3. Accessed 2 September 2009.

Iyer Ramaswamy R. (11 September 2008). 'A Note of Qualification.' In Independent People's Tribunal on the World Bank in India. 'Findings of the Jury.' Verdict from the Independent People's Tribunal held at Jawaharlal Nehru University, New Delhi. 21–25 September 2007. Pages 24–25. Available at http://worldbanktribunal.org/WB_Tribunal_Findings.pdf. Accessed 2 September 2009.

Jesuit Centre for Theological Reflection (2006). 'Basic Needs Basket: A comprehensive overview.' Lusaka: JCTR.

Johnson, Chalmers (2000). *Blowback: The cost and consequences of American empire.* New York: Henry Holt and Company.

Johnson, Chalmers (2004). *The Sorrows of Empire: Militarism, secrecy, and the end of the republic.* New York: Henry Holt and Company.

Johnson, Chalmers (2006). *Nemesis: The last days of the American republic.* New York: Metropolitan Books.

Johnston, Bruce F. and Peter Kilby (1975). *Agriculture and Structural Transformation: Economic strategies in late developing countries.* New York: Oxford University Press.

'Joint Assistance Strategy for Zambia (JASZ) 2007–2010' (April 2007).

Joint Meeting of the American Association for the Advancement of Science and the American Philosophical Society with members of the National Academies of Science (27–29 April 2007) with sponsorship by The Annenberg Foundation Trust at Sunnylands. Available at http://www.sunnylandstrust.org/programs/programs_show.htm ?doc_id=450010.

Josupeit, Helga (January 2006). 'Aquaculture Production and Markets.' Rome: FAO Globefish. Available at http://www.globefish.org/dynamisk.php4?id=2713.

Kahn, Joseph (14 October 2007). 'In China, a Lake's Champion Imperils Himself.' *New York Times*.

Kahn, Joseph and M. Landler (21 December 2007). 'China Grabs West's Smoke-Spewing Factories.' *The New York Times*.

Kammen, Daniel M. and D.J. Lew (1 March 2005). 'Review of Technologies for the Production and Use of Charcoal.' Renewable and Appropriate Energy Laboratory Report. Berkeley, CA: University of California, Berkeley.

Kanbur, Ravi (January 2004). 'Growth, Equity and Poverty: Some Hard Questions.' Commentary Prepared for *State of World Conference*, Princeton University, February 13–14.

Kanbur, Ravi (July 2005). 'The Development of Development Thinking.' Text of a public lecture given at the Institute for Social and Economic Change, Bangalore, India, 10 June 2004.

Kanbur, Ravi (March 2006). 'Three Observations on the Challenges of Growth and Poverty Reduction in Asia.' Available at www.arts.cornell. edu/poverty/kanbur/AsiaGrowthThreeObservations.pdf. Accessed 2 September 2009.

Karoly, Lynn A., M.R. Kilburn and J.S. Cannon (2005). *Early Childhood Interventions: Proven results, future promise*. Santa Monica, CA: The Rand Corporation.

Katzman, Martin T. (1977). *Cities and Frontiers in Brazil: Regional dimensions of economic development*. Cambridge, MA: Harvard University Press.

Kerr, Richard A. (9 February 2007). 'US Policy: A permanent sea change?' *Science*. **315**. Page 757.

Kiljunen, Kimmo (ed.) (1984). *Kampuchea: Decade of the genocide: Report of a Finnish Inquiry Commission*. London: Zed Books Ltd.

Kinetz, Erika (31 August 2009). 'India's economic growth accelerates to 6.1 per cent.' Available at htpp://www.newsvine.com/ _news/2009/08/31/3210132-indias-economic-growth-accelerate.

Kiplinger, Knight (1998). *World Boom Ahead: Why business and consumers will prosper*. Washington DC: Kiplinger Books.

*Kiplinger Letter* (9 February 2007). 4 pages. Available at www.kiplingerbiz. com.

Kirchmeier, Felix (July 2006). 'The Right to Development: Where do we stand?' State of the Debate on the Right to Development. Dialogue on Globalization. Occasional Papers No. 23. Geneva: Friedrich Ebert.

Kreisler, Harry (29 January 2004). 'Interview with Chalmers Johnson: American empire.' Institute of International Studies, UC Berkeley's 'Conversations with History' series.

Kreisler, Harry (7 March 2007). 'Interview with Chalmers Johnson. 737 Military bases and counting.' Institute of International Studies, UC Berkeley's 'Conversations with History' series.

Landsberg, Mitchell (28 December 2006). 'Jobs Scarce for China's Graduates.' *Los Angeles Times*.

Lawson, M.L. (1994). *The Dammed Indians: The Pick-Sloan Plan and the Missouri River Sioux, 1944–1980.* Norman, OK: University of Oklahoma Press.

Leakey, Richard and Roger Lewin (1995). *The Sixth Extinction: Patterns of life and the future of humankind.* New York: Anchor Books.

Le Quéré, C., E.T. Rodenbeck, T.J. Buitenhuis, *et al.* (22 June 2007). 'Saturation of the Southern Ocean $CO_2$ Sink Due to Recent Climate Change.' *Science*. **316**. Pages 1735–1738.

Levy, Dawn (25 October 2006). 'Forum Examines Technologies Aimed at Reducing Greenhouse Gasses.' Stanford Report. Stanford News Service.

Lewis, Arthur (1955). *The Theory of Economic Growth.* London: George Allen and Unwin.

Library of Congress (no date). 'For European Recovery: The fiftieth anniversary of the Marshall Plan: Truman signed the Economic Assistance Act.' Home Page. Available at http://www.loc.gov/exhibits/marshall/mars3.html. Accessed 2 September 2009.

Lin, Justin Yifu (May 1987). 'The Household Responsibility System Reform in China: A peasant's institutional choice.' *American Journal of Agricultural Economics*. **69** (2). Pages 410–415.

Link, Perry (3 April 2008). 'He Would Have Changed China.' *The New York Review of Books*. Pages 40–43.

Liu, Alan P.L. (August 1992). 'The "Wenzhou Model" of Development and China's Modernization.' *Asian Survey*. **32** (8). Pages 696–711.

Loreau, M., A. Oteny-Yeboah, M.T.K. Arroyo *et al.* (20 July 2006). 'Diversity without Representation.' *Nature*. **442**. Pages 245–246.

*Los Angeles Times* (30 August 2002).

Lubell, Harold (1980). *Small Scale Enterprises, Employment and Foreign Aid.* Washington DC: USAID and New Delhi: Tata McGraw-Hill Publishing Company.

Luig, Ulrich (1996). *Conversion as a Social Process: A history of missionary Christianity among the Valley Tonga, Zambia.* New Brunswick, NJ: Transaction Publishers.

Maclean, Ilya (no date). 'Effects of Edge Habitat Type on the Density of Papyrus Endemic Bird Species.' Available at http://www.britishecologicalsociety.org/articles/grants/reports/SEPG1925. Accessed 2 September 2009.

Magnier, Mark (27 May 2006). 'Organizer of Land Seizure Protest in China is Sentenced.' *Los Angeles Times.* Page A21.

Maimbo, Fabian and James Fry (1971). 'An Investigation into the Change in Terms of Trade between the Rural and Urban Sectors of Zambia.' *African Social Research.* **12.** Manchester: Manchester University Press for Institute of African Studies, University of Zambia.

Manji, Firoze (27 March 2008). 'China Still a Small Player in Africa.' *Pambazuka News.* Available at http://www.pambazuka.org/en/category/features/46990. Accessed 2 September 2009.

McDonald, M. and J. Muldowny (1982). *TVA and the Dispossessed: The resettlement of population in the Norris Dam area.* Knoxville, TN: University of Tennessee Press.

Mead, Walter Russell (2006) 'God's Country?' *Foreign Affairs.* **85** (5). Pages 24–43.

Meadows, Donella, J. Randers and D. Meadows (2004). *Limits of Growth: The 30-year update.* White River Junction, VT: Chelsea Green Publishing Company.

Millennium Ecosystem Assessment (2005). *Ecosystems and Human Well-Being: Synthesis: Summary for decision-makers.* Washington DC: World Resources Institute.

Millennium Ecosystem Assessment (2006). *Marine and Coastal Ecosystems and Human Well-being: A synthesis report based on the findings of the Millennium Ecosystem Assessment.* Nairobi: UNEP.

Ministry of Water Resources, Peoples Republic of China (2 August 2004). 'Water Resources in China.' Home Page. Available at http://www.mwr.gov.cn/english1/20040802/38161.asp. Accessed 2 September 2009.

Mongabay.com ([2006?]). 'Zambia Deforestation Rates and Related Forestry Figures.' Available at http://rainforests.mongabay.com/deforestation/2000/Zambia.htm. Accessed 2 September 2009.

Mwanawasa, Levy Patrick (December 2006). 'Foreword'. In *Vision 2030: A prosperous middle income country by 2030.* Lusaka: Government of Zambia.

Mweeta, S. (29 December 2004). 'Let's Fight HIV/AIDS Stigma.' *Times of Zambia.* Available at http://www.times.co.zn/news/viewnews.cgi?category=8&id=1104355761. Accessed 2 September 2009.

Mwenechanya, Silene K. (August 2007). 'Legal Empowerment of the Poor: Labour rights in Zambia.' An issue paper prepared for UNDP – Commission on Legal Empowerment of the Poor. Available at http://www.undp.org/LegalEmpowerment/reports/NationalConsultation Reports/Country Files/26_Zambia/27_5_Labor_Rights.pdf. Accessed 2 September 2009.

Narayan, Deepa (ed.) (2000). *Voices of the Poor: Can anyone hear us?* New York: Oxford University Press for World Bank.

National Coalition on Health Care (2008). 'Facts on Health Insurance Coverage.' Available at http://www.nchc.org/facts/coverage.shtml. Accessed 2 September 2009.

Nelson, Michael (1973). *The Development of Tropical Lands: Policy issues in Latin America.* Baltimore, MD: Johns Hopkins University Press for Resources for the Future.

New Israel Fund (no date). 'Religious Pluralism and Tolerance: Why is religion Israel's touchiest issue?' Available at http://www.nif.org/issue-areas/religious-pluralism. Accessed 2 September 2009.

New York Academy of Medicine. Newsroom (28 May 1982). 'Baltimore Criticizes Bush Administration's Restrictions on Scientific Research at Annual Spring Stated Meeting.' Available at http://www.nyam.org/news.1982.html.

Niebuhr, Gustav (2008). *Beyond Tolerance: Searching for interfaith understanding in America.* New York: Viking Penguin.

Niehaus, Isak (2001). *Witchcraft, Power and Politics: Exploring the occult in the South African lowveld.* London: Pluto Press.

Nixon, Will (1996). 'Rainforest Shrimp'. *Mother Jones.* March/April. Available at http://www.motherjones.com/politics/1996/03/rainforest-shrimp. Accessed 2 September 2009.

Nyamu, John (February 2003). 'Famine and AIDS Batter Southern Africa: Action needed to avert collapse, Stephen Lewis warns.' *Africa Recovery.* News Releases.

Obeysekera, Gananath (1984). 'Political Violence and the Future of Democracy in Sri Lanka.' In *Sri Lanka: The ethnic conflict: Myths, realities and perspectives.* New Delhi: Navrang. Pages 70–94.

OECD (2007) 'Executive Summary'. In *OECD Environmental Performance Reviews: China.* (2007). Paris: OECD. Pages 1–7.

*OECD in Washington* (August/September 2003). 'Subsidies to Agriculture: Why?' **46**. Page 1.

Ortolano, L and K. Cushing (2000). 'Grand Coulee Dam and the Columbia Basin Project USA.' Case study report prepared as an input to the World Commission on Dams, Cape Town. Available at www.dams.org/docs/kbase/studies/csusmain.pdf. Accessed 2 September 2009.

Oxfam (2006). 'A Recipe for Disaster: Will the Doha Round fail to deliver for development?' Oxfam Briefing Paper 87.

Páez-Osuna, Federico (2001). 'The Environmental Impact of Shrimp Aquaculture: Causes, effects and mitigating alternatives.' *Environmental Management.* **28** (1). Pages 131–140.

Page, John C. (1985). *The Civilian Conservation Corps and the National Park Service 1933–1942: An administrative history.* Washington DC: National Park Service.

Paget-Clarke, Nic (29 May 2004). 'Interview with Chalmers Johnson: Part 1: An empire of more than 725 military bases.' Available at http://www.inmotionmagazine.com/global/cj_int/cj_int1.html. Accessed 2 September 2009. Part 2: From CIA analyst to best-selling scholar. Available at http://www.inmotionmagazine.com/global/cj_int/cj_int2.html. Accessed 2 September 2009.

Pamlin, D. and Long Baijin (April 2007). 'Re-think China's Outward Investment Flows.' Available at http://assets.wwf.no/downloads/wwf_re_think_chinese_outward_investment.pdf. Accessed 2 September 2009.

Patton, Dominique (6 April 2008). 'China Eyes Idle Farmland in Country.' *Business Daily* (Nairobi).

Petit, C., T. Scudder and E. Lambin (2001). 'Quantifying Processes of Land-Cover Change by Remote Sensing: Resettlement and rapid land-cover changes in south-eastern Zambia,' *International Journal of Remote Sensing.* **22** (17). Pages 3435–3456.

Pew Charitable Trusts (2009). 'The Clean Energy Economy: Repowering jobs, businesses and investments across America.' Washington DC and Philadelphia, PA: Pew.

Pew Research Center (23 June 2008). 'Religion in America: Non-dogmatic, diverse and politically relevant.' Religious Beliefs and Practices/Social and Political Views: Report 2.

Pew Research Center for the People and The Press/The Pew Forum on Research and Public Life (24 August 2006). 'Many Americans Uneasy With Mix of Religion and Politics.'

Pfeffer, Anshel (15 February 2009). 'A New Jewish State.' *Ha'aretz.* http://www.haaretz.co.il/hasen/spages/1063791.html. Accessed 2 September 2009.

Pogatchnik, Shawn (30 May 2009). '111 Nations, but not US, Adopt Cluster Bomb Treaty.' Associated Press. Available at http://www.thefreelibrary.com/111+nations%2c+but+not+US%2c+adopt+cluster+bomb+treaty-a01611556358.

Population Reference Bureau (no date). 'Zambia.' Available at http://www.prb.org/Countries/zambia.aspx. Accessed 2 September 2009.

Population Resource Center (February 2003). *Executive Summary: Israel and the Palestinian Territories.* Available at http://www.prcdc.org/Files/ Israel.pdf. Accessed 2 September 2009.

Poteba, James, S. Venti and D.A. Wise (2006). 'The Decline of Defined Benefit Retirement Plans and Asset Flows.' Paper prepared for the *Eighth Annual Joint Conference of the Retirement Research Consortium.* Washington DC. 10–11 August.

Power Technology (no date). 'Xiaolangdi China Hydro Electric Power Plant.' Available at http://www.power-technology.com/projects/ xiaolangdi/. Accessed 2 September 2009.

Price, Alan H., D. Scott Nance and C.B. Weld (Fall 2006). 'China's Failure to Comply with its WTO Commitments: Subsidies to the Chinese steel industry.' *Global Trade Markets.* Available at http://www.wrf.com/ docs/newsletter_issues/458.pdf. Accessed 2 September 2009.

Public Policy Institute of California (June 2008). 'Predicting Success on the California High School Exam.' Research Brief. San Francisco: PPIC.

Rand Corporation (2005a). *Children at Risk: Consequences for school readiness and beyond.* Rand Labor and Population Research Brief. Santa Monica, CA: The Rand Corporation.

Rand Corporation (2005b). *Proven Benefits of Early Childhood Interventions.* Rand Labor and Population Research Brief. Santa Monica, CA: The Rand Corporation.

Read, T.R. (28 June 2006). 'The Superhighway to Everywhere.' *Washington Post.*

Rees, W.B. and Mathis Wackernagel (1994). 'Ecological Footprints and Appropriate Carrying Capacity: Measuring the natural capital requirements of the human economy.' In Ann Mari Jansson *et al.* (eds.) *Investing in Natural Capital: The ecological economics approach to sustainability.* Washington DC: Island Press.

Reynolds, N. (1992). 'Community Development and Resource Management.' Paper written for the IUCN Southern Okavango Integrated Water Development Project Review Team. Pasadena, CA: Scudder archives.

Richards, Paul (1996). *Fighting for the Rain Forest: War, youth and resources in Sierra Leone.* Oxford and Portsmouth, NH: The International African Institute in association with James Currey and Heinemann.

Richards, Paul (2005a). 'New War.' In Richards, Paul (ed.). *No Peace, No War: An anthropology of contemporary armed conflicts.* Athens, OH and Oxford: Ohio University Press and James Currey. Pages 1–21.

Richards, Paul (2005b). 'Green Book Millenarians? The Sierra Leone war within the perspective of an anthropology of religion.' In Niels Kastfelt (ed.). *Religion and African Civil Wars.* New York: Palgrave Macmillan. Pages 119–146.

Richter, Brian D., S. Postel, C. Revenga *et al.* (forthcoming). 'Lost in Development's Shadow: The downstream human consequences of dams.' Manuscript.

Robbins, Christopher (2000). *The Ravens: Pilots of the secret war of Laos.* Bangkok: Asia Books.

Rogers, Peter P., Kazi Jalal and John Boyd (2006). *An Introduction to Sustainable Development.* The Continuing Education Division. Harvard University and Glen Educational Foundation. Cambridge, MA: Distributed by Harvard University Press.

Running, Steven W. (18 August 2006). 'Is Global Warming Causing More, Larger Wildfires?' *Science.* **313**.

Ruxiang Zhu (no date). 'China's South-North Water Transfer Project and its Impacts of Social and Economic Development.' Available at http://www.mwr.gov.cn.

Sabbagh, Suha (March 1991). 'Behind Closed Doors: Palestinan families under curfew.' *Washington Report on Middle East Affairs.* Available at http://www.wrmea.com/backissues/0391/9103015.htm. Accessed 2 September 2009.

Sachs, Jeffrey D. (2005). *The End of Poverty: Economic possibilities for our time.* New York: Penguin Press.

Salisbury, R.F. (1986). *A Homeland for the Cree: Regional development in James Bay 1971–1981.* Quebec: McGill-Queens University Press.

Schiller, Ben (20 December 2005). 'The China Model.' Available at http://www.opendemocracy.net/democracy-china/china_development_3136.jsp. Accessed 2 September 2009.

Schmidt-Soltau, Kai and D. Brockington (2006). 'Do Conservation and Development Programs Differ when they Displace People?' Manuscript.

Schwab, Klaus (2007). 'Preface'. In Ricardo Hausmann, L.D. Tyson and S. Zahidi. *The Global Gender Gap Report.* Cologne/Geneva: World Economic Forum.

*Science* (23 February 2007). 'AAAS Annual Meeting. Wedging Sustainability Into Public Consciousness.' **315**. Page 1068.

*Science* (26 October 2007) 'AAAS News and Notes: AAAS strikes landmark agreements to build long-term China engagement.' **318**. Page 586.

*Science* (7 December 2007a). 'Chinese Science on the Move'. Editorial. **318**. Page 1523.

*Science* (7 December 2007b). 'US Expert Panel See Algebra As Key to Improvements in Math.' **318**. Page 1534.

*Science* (22 February 2008). 'Evolution: Crossing the divide.' **319**. Pages 1034 and 1036.

*Science Daily* (17 May 2007). 'West Nile Virus Threatens Backyard Birds.' Available at http://www.sciencedaily.com/releases /2007/05/ 070516161 231.htm.

*Science Daily* (22 October 2007). 'Coral Reef on Brink of Disaster.' Available at http://www.sciencedaily.com/releases/2007/10/071021225256.htm.

Scientific Expert Group on Climate Change and Sustainable Development (2007). 'Confronting Climatic Change: Avoiding the unmanageable and managing the unavoidable.' Research Triangle Park, NC: Sigma Xi and the UN Foundation at the request of the UN Department of Economic and Social Affairs.

Scudder, Thayer (1981). *The Development Potential of New Lands Settlement in the Tropics and Subtropics: A global state-of-the-art evaluation with specific emphasis on policy implication*.' Binghamton, NY: Institute for Development Anthropology for U.S. Agency for International Development.

Scudder, Thayer (August 1985a). *A History of Development in the Twentieth Century: The Zambian portion of the Middle Zambezi Valley and the Lake Kariba Basin*.' Binghamton, NY: Institute for Development Anthropology.

Scudder, Thayer (1985b). 'Memo on Mahaweli Report Number 6 to USAID Colombo Office.' December.

Scudder, Thayer (1986a). 'The Gwembe Valley Development Company in Relationship to the Development of the Southern Portion of Gwembe District.' Mimeo.

Scudder, Thayer (1986b). 'Increasing the Employment Potential of New Land Settlements in the Tropics and Subtropics.' In *Transforming Rural Livelihoods: A search for Asian alternatives*. Colombo: Marga Institute. Pages 64–98.

Scudder, Thayer (1990). 'Review of *The Jonglei Canal: Impact and Opportunity*. Paul Howell, Michael Lock and Stephen Cobb (eds).' *American Anthropologist*. **92**. (4). Pages 1073–1074.

Scudder, Thayer (1999). 'The Emerging Global Crisis and Development Anthropology: Can we have an impact?' 1999 Malinowski Award Lecture. *Human Organization*. **58** (4). Pages 351–364.

Scudder, Thayer (2005). *The Future of Large Dams: Dealing with social, environmental, institutional and political costs*. London: Earthscan.

Scudder, Thayer (2007). 'Development and Downturn in Zambia's Gwembe Valley.' In C. Lancaster and K.P. Vickery (eds). *The Tonga-Speaking Peoples of Zambia and Zimbabwe*. Lanham, MD: University Press of America. Pages 307 343.

Scudder, Thayer with the assistance of D. Aberle, K. Begishe, E. Colson, C. Etsitty, J. Joe, J. Kammer, M.E.D. Scudder, J. Serena, B.B.G. Tippenconnie, R. Walters and J. Williamson (1982). *No Place to Go: The impacts of forced relocation on Navajos.* Philadelphia, PN: ISHI.

Scudder, T. and G. Ablasser (1984). 'The Experience of the World Bank with Government-Sponsored Land Settlement.' Report No. 5625. Washington DC: World Bank, Operations Evaluation Department.

Scudder, Thayer and Elizabeth Colson (2002). 'Long Term Research in Gwembe Valley, Zambia.' In Robert V. Kemper and Anya Peterson Royce (eds). *Chronicling Cultures: Long term field research in anthropology.* Walnut Creek, CA: Altamira Press. Pages 197–238.

Scudder, Thayer and Maher Habbob (forthcoming). 'Aswan High Dam Resettlement.' In A.K. Biswas and C. Tortajada (eds). *Conference Proceedings of the February 2007 Cairo Workshop on the Aswan High Dam.* Berlin: Springer.

Secretariat of the UN Convention on Biological Diversity (March 2006). *Global Biodiversity Outlook 2.* Available at http://www.cbd.int/doc/gbo/gbo2/cbd-gbo2-en.pdf. Accessed 2 September 2009.

Seidman, Ann (1979). 'The Distorted Growth of Import-Substitution Industry: The Zambian case.' *Journal of Modern African Studies.* **12** (4). Pages 601–631.

Sen, Amartya (1999a). 'Democracy and Social Justice.' Talk given at the *International Conference on Democracy, the Market Economy and Development.* 26–27 February. Seoul, Korea.

Sen, Amartya (1999b). *Development as Freedom.* New York: Anchor Books.

Shanghai Jiao Tong University, Institute of Higher Education (2007). 'Academic Ranking of World Universities.' Available at http://www.arwu.org/rank/2007/ARWU2007_top100.htm. Accessed 2 September 2009.

Shaohua Chen and Martin Ravallion (2004). *How Have the World's Poorest Fared Since the Early 1980s?* Washington DC: World Bank, Development Research Group.

Simon, Julian. 'Ultimate Resource.' Available at www.juliansimon.com/writings/Ultimate_Resource/TCONCLUS.txt. Accessed 2 September 2009.

Sinosteel (no date). 'About Sinosteel.' Available at http://en.sinosteel.com/zggk/jtjj/. Accessed 2 September 2009.

Spencer, Richard (12 February 2008). '750 000 Poor Chinese Head to Africa to Exploit Resources.' *The Daily Telegraph.*

Speth, James Gustave (2004). *Red Sky At Morning: America and the crisis of the global environment.* New Haven, CT: Yale University Press.

Speth, James Gustave (2008). *The Bridge at the Edge of the World:*

*Capitalism, the environment, and crossing from crisis to sustainability*. New Haven, CT: Yale University Press.

Sri Lanka Government (1951). 'Sri Lankan Census of Population.'

Stern, Nicholas (2007). *The Economics of Climate Change: The Stern report*. Cambridge: Cambridge University Press.

Stern, Nicholas (2009). *The Global Deal: Climate change and the creation of a new era of progress and prosperity*. New York: Public Affairs.

Stokes, Erik (1959). *The English Utilitarians and India*. Oxford: Oxford University Press.

Stone, R. and Hawk Jia (25 August 2006). 'Hydroengineering: Going against the flow.' *Science*. **313**. Pages 1034–1037.

Stonich, Susan C. (2002). 'Farming Shrimp, Harvesting Hunger: The costs and benefits of the blue revolution.' *Backgrounder*. **8** (1). Winter. Available at http://www.foodfirst.org/en/node/54. Accessed 2 September 2009.

Tambiah, S.J. (1986). *Sri Lanka: Ethnic fratricide and the dismantling of democracy*. London: I.B. Tauris.

Tamir, Orit (1999). 'What Happened to Navajo Relocatees from Hopi Partition Lands in Pinon?' *American Indian Culture and Research Journal*. **23** (4). Pages 71–90.

Tekiner, Roselle (January 1990). 'Israel's Two-Tiered Citizenship Law Bars Non-Jews from 93 per cent of its Lands.' *Washington Report on Middle East Affairs*. Available at http://www.washington-report. org/component/content/article/123-1990-january/783-israels-two-tiered-citizenship-law-bars-non-jews-from-93-percent-of-its-lands.html. Accessed 2 September 2009.

Tilt, Bryan (2006). 'Perceptions of Risk from Industrial Pollution in China: A comparison of occupational groups.' *Human Organization*. **65** (2). Pages 115–127.

Tinley, K. (1994). 'Description of Gorongosa-Marrameu Natural Resource Management Area: Section 2: Ecological profile of the region (form, content, process).' Harare: IUCN Regional Office for Southern Africa.

Transparency International (2007). 'Country Study Report: Final report: Zambia 2006/7.' National Integrity Systems Country Study. Available at http://www.transparency.org/policy_research/nis/nis_reports_by_country/africa_middle_east. Accessed 2 September 2009.

Udall, Bradley (6 June 2007). 'Written Testimony.' Hearings on Impacts of Climate Change on Water Supply and Availability in the United States. Sub Committee on Water and Power. Washington DC: US Senate.

Udall, Bradley and Gary Bates (January 2007). 'Climatic and Hydrologic Trends in the Western U.S.: A review of recent peer-reviewed research.' *Intermountain West Climate Summary*. Pages 2–8. Available at http://

www.colorado.edu/IWCS/archive/IWCS_2007_Jan.pdf. Accessed 2 September 2009.

UNICEF (2007). *Child Poverty in Perspective: An overview of child well-being in rich countries*. Innocenti Research Center Report Card 7. Florence: UNICEF.

Union of Concerned Scientists (1993). *World Scientists' Warning to Humanity*. Cambridge, MA: Union of Concerned Scientists.

Union of Concerned Scientists (2004). 'Scientific Integrity in Policy Making: An investigation into the Bush administration's misuse of science.' Available at http://www.ucsusa.org/assets/documents/scientific_integrity/rsi_Fullreport_1.pdf. Accessed 2 September 2009.

Union of Concerned Scientists (no date). 'The A to Z Guide to Political Interference in Science.' Available at http://www.ucsusa.org/scientific_integrity/abuses_of_science/a-to-z-guide-to-political.html. Accessed 2 September 2009.

United Nations (1992). *Water Resources of the Occupied Palestinian Territory*. New York: United Nations.

United Nations (no date). 'Affiliated Ecosystems. Mangroves.' Atlas of the Oceans. Available at http://www.oceansatlas.com/servlet/CDSServlet?status=NDOzMTgzNiY2PWVuJjMzPSo.

United Nations (no date). 'Mangroves.' Atlas of the Oceans. Available at http://www.oceansatlas.com/servlet/CDSServlet?status=NDOxMjczMCY2PWVuJjMzP.

United Nations, Alliance of Civilizations (2005). 'Mission Statement.' Available at http://www.unaoc.org/content/view/39/187/lang,english/. Accessed 2 September 2009.

United Nations, Commission on the Status of Women (March 1990). *The Situation of Palestinian Women in the Occupied Territories*. New York: United Nations.

United Nations Development Programme (1990). *Human Development Report 1990*. New York: Oxford University Press.

United Nations Development Programme (1998). *Human Development Report 1998*. New York: Oxford University Press.

United Nations Development Programme (no date). 'The Importance of Biodiversity.' Available at http://www.undp.org/biodiversity/biodiversitycd/bioImport.htm. Accessed 2 September 2009.

United Nations Environment Programme (2007). *Global Outlook for Ice and Snow*. Nairobi: UNEP.

United Nations Human Settlement Programme Report (2007). *State of the World's Cities Report 2006/7: The Millennium Development Goals and urban sustainability: 30 years of shaping the habitat agenda*. London: Earthscan.

United Nations News Service (18 May 2009). 'Over 11 Million People Displaced in Central and East Africa.' Available at http://www.un.org/apps/news/story.asp?NewsID=30826. Accessed 2 September 2009.

United Nations Population Information Network (no date). 'Guidelines on Women's Empowerment.' Available at http://www.un.org/popin/unfpa/taskforce/guide/iatfwemp.gdl.html.

United States (17 September 2002). 'The National Security Strategy of the United States of America.' Washington DC: The White House.

United States Department of State (31 March 2003). 'Israel and the Occupied Territories.' Country Reports of Human Rights Practices. Bureau of Democracy, Human Rights, and Labor. 2002. Available at http://www.state.gov/g/drl/rls/hrrpt/2002/18278.htm.

United States, Department of State, Bureau of East Asian and Pacific Affairs (March 2008). 'Background Note: Laos.' Washington DC.

United States, Federal Election Commission (no date). 'Presidential Campaign Finance.' Available at http://www.fec.gov/DisclosureSearch/mapApp.do. Accessed 2 September 2009.

United States, Federal Election Commission (no date). '2008 House and Senate Campaign Finance.' Available at http://www.fec.gov/DisclosureSearch/mapHSApp.do?election_yr=2008. Accessed 2 September 2009.

United States, Geological Service (March 2005). 'Changes in Stream Flow Timing in the Western United States in Recent Decades.' Fact Sheet 2005-3018.

United States Government (17 January 1961). President Dwight D. Eisenhower's Farewell Address (1961). Available at http://www.ourdocuments.gov/doc.php?doc=90.

University Corporation for Atmospheric Research (24 May 2005). 'A Continent Split by Climate Change: New study projects stronger drought in Southern Africa, more rain in Sahel.' Available at http://www.ucar.edu/news/releases/2005/hurrell.shtml. Accessed 2 September 2009.

University Corporation for Atmospheric Research (5 July 2006). 'Report Warns about Carbon Dioxide Threat to Marine Life.' Press Release. Boulder, CO: UCAR.

Verba, Sidney, N.H. Nie and J. Kim (1995). *Voice and Equality: The view from the top*. Cambridge, MA: Harvard University Press.

Vine, D. (2009). *Island of Shame: The secret history of the U.S. military base on Diego Garcia*. Princeton, NJ: Princeton University Press.

Visvanathan, Susan (2000). 'The Homogeneity of Fundamentalism: Christianity, British colonialism and India in the nineteenth century'. *Studies in History*. 16 (2) (n.s). Pages 221–240.

Wackernagel, Mathis, N.B. Schulz, D. Deumling, *et al.* (2002). 'Tracking the Ecological Overshoot of the Human Economy.' *Proceedings of the National Academy of Science.* **99** (14). Pages 9266–9271.

Wade, Robert H. (2001). 'The US Role in the Malaise at the World Bank: Get up, Gulliver.' Paper presented at the *Annual Meeting of the American Political Science Association.* 28–30 August. San Francisco.

*Water Technology* (no date). 'South-to-North Water Diversion Project, China.' Available at http://water-technology.net/projects/south_north/. Accessed 2 September 2009.

Weikel, Dan and J. Rabin (10 June 2008). 'More rough roads ahead.' *Los Angeles Times.*

Weitze, J, K. Veldkamp, W. Jeanes and F.K.M. Shalwindi (1990). 'Agro-Ecological Perspectives in Planning.' In Adrian P. Wood, S.A. Kean, J.T. Milimo and D.M. Warren (eds) *The Dynamics of Agricultural Policy and Reform in Zambia.* Aimes, IA: University of Iowa Press. Pages 63–85.

WHO/UNAIDS/UNICEF (July 2008). 'Epidemiological Fact Sheet on HIV and AIDS: Zambia.' Geneva: World Health Organization.

Wickrematunge, Lasantha (11 June 2007). '"Ethnic Cleansing" in Sri Lanka?' *Time.*

Wilkinson, C. (2004). 'Executive Summary.' In Wilkinson, C. (ed.). *Status of Coral Reefs of the World: 2004.* 'Executive Summary.' Available at http://www.aims.gov.au/pages/research/coral-bleaching/scr2004/pdf/scr2004v1-00.pdf. Accessed 2 September 2009.

Wilkinson, Tracy (13 December 2002). 'Mideast Violence Moves to the Home Front.' *Los Angeles Times.*

Williamson, John (1990). 'What Washington Means by Policy Reform.' In John Williamson (ed.). *Latin American Adjustment: How much has happened.* Washington DC: Institute for International Economics. Pages 5–20.

Williamson, John (2002). 'Did the Washington Consensus Fail?' Outline of Speech at the Center for Strategic and International Studies. Washington DC. 6 November.

Wills, Garry (16 November 2006). 'A Country Ruled by Faith.' *The New York Review of Books.* Pages 8–11.

Wilson, E.O. (2006). *The Creation: An appeal to save life on earth.* New York: W.W. Norton and Company.

Wimaladharma, Kapila P. (1982). 'Nonfarm employment in the major settlements of Sri Lanka.' In Kapila P. Wimaladharma (ed.). *Land Settlement Experiences in Sri Lanka.* Colombo: Karunaratne and Sons.

World Bank (1978). *Rural Enterprise and Nonfarm Employment.* Washington DC: The World Bank.

World Bank (November 1994). 'Zambia Poverty Assessment." In Five Volumes. Report No. 12985-ZA. Washington DC: The World Bank.

World Bank (June 1998). *Experience with Post-conflict Reconstruction.* Report No. 17769. Washington DC: The World Bank.

World Bank (2000). *World Development Report 2000/2001: Attacking Poverty: Opportunity, empowerment, and security.* Washington DC: The World Bank.

World Bank (2001a). 'Summary'. In *Engendering Development: Through gender equality in rights, resources and voice.* Washington DC: World Bank and Oxford: Oxford University Press.

World Bank (2 April 2001b). *China: Agenda for water sector strategy for North China. Volume 1: Summary report.* Report No. 22040-CHA. Washington DC: The World Bank.

World Bank (30 June 2005). *Toward a Conflict Sensitive Poverty Reduction Strategy: Lessons from a retrospective analysis.* Report No. 32587 SDVand ESSD. Washington DC: The World Bank.

World Bank (30 October 2006). 'Implementation Completion Report (PPFI-P9660 IDA-30420). Report No: 37848. Washington DC: The World Bank.

World Bank (2008). 'Economic Restrictions: Moving Beyond the "Movement and Access" Approach' and 'West Bank and Gaza: The Economic Effects of Restricted Access to Land in the West Bank.' *West Bank and Gaza Update.* Washington DC: The World Bank.

World Bank and State Environmental Protection Administration (February 2007). *Cost of Pollution in China: Economic estimates of physical damage.* Washington DC: The World Bank.

World Bank, Environment Division (1996). *Resettlement and Development: The Bankwide review of projects involving involuntary resettlement 1986–1993.* Washington DC: The World Bank.

World Bank, International Development Association (8 April, 2008). 'Country Assistance Strategy for the Republic of Zambia.' Report No: 43352-ZM. Washington DC: The World Bank.

World Bank Office, Beijing (February 2008). '*Quarterly Update.*' Available at http://siteresourcesworldbank.org/INTCHINA/Resources/318862-1121421293578/cqu_jan_08_en.pdf. Accessed 2 September 2009.

World Bank, Operations Evaluation Department (1984). *The Experience of the World Bank with Government-Sponsored Land Settlement.* Report No. 5625. Washington DC: The World Bank.

World Commission on Dams (2000). *Dams and Development: A new framework for decision-making.* London: Earthscan.

World Economic Forum, Global Governance Initiative (2006). 'Annual Report 2006.'

World Economic Forum, World Bank and African Development Bank (2007). 'Africa Competitiveness Report 2007.' Available at http://www.weforum.org/en/initiatives/gcp/Africa Competitiveness Report/2007/index.htm. Accessed 2 September 2009.

World Health Organization, UNICEF, UNFPA, and the World Bank (2007). 'Maternal Mortality in 2005. Estimates developed by WHO, UNICEF, UNFPA and The World Bank.' Geneva: WHO.

World Resources Institute (2000). *A Guide to World Resources 2000–2001: People and ecosystems: The fraying web of life.'* Washington DC: World Resources Institute.

World Watch Institute (2006). *State of the World: 2006.* New York: W.W. Norton and Company, Inc.

WWF Nepal Program (March 2005). 'An Overview of Glaciers, Glacier Retreat, and Subsequent Impacts in Nepal, India and China.' Available at http://assets.panda.org/downloads/himalayaglaciersreport2005.pdf. Accessed 2 September 2009.

Wroughton, Lesley (5 February 2008). 'World Bank sees Change in China's African role.' Johannesburg: Reuters.

Xiangqun Chang (2004). *'Lishang-Wanglai: Social support networks, reciprocity and creativity in a Chinese Village'.* PhD dissertation. London School of Economics.

Xiangqun Chang (August 2005). 'Changing Relationships between Villagers and the State in a Chinese Village over 70 Years: An analysis with a Chinese model of reciprocity (*lishang-wanglai*).' Paper presented at the *Fourth International Convention of Asian Scholars (ICAS4).* Shanghai.

Xiangqun Chang (September 2007). *'Lishang-wanglai*: A Chinese model of social relations and relatedness.' Paper presented at the *International Colloquium on New Discourses in Contemporary China.* Management School. Lancaster University. 20–21 September.

Yasheng Huang (2008). *Capitalism with Chinese Characteristics.* Cambridge: Cambridge University Press.

Yu Jianrong (Spring 2007). 'Social Conflict in Rural China.' *China Security.* **3** (2).

Youth, Howard (2003). *Winged Messenger: The decline of birds.* Worldwatch Paper #165. Danvers, MA: Worldwatch.

Yusuf, Feysal Ahmed (no date). 'Environmental Degradation in Somalia.' Available at http://www.cru.uea.ac.uk/tiempo/floor0/archive/issue26/t26art1.htm.

Zambia (December 2006). 'Executive Summary.' In *Vision 2030.* Lusaka: Government of Zambia.

Zambia (no date). *Zambia Demographic and Health Survey 2001–2002.* Lusaka: Government Printer.

Zau, Andrew C. and J.R. Betts (2008). *Predicting Success, Preventing Failure: An investigation of the California high school exit exam.*' San Francisco, CA: Public Policy Institute of California.

Zhang Yuzhe (26 July 2007). 'China's Unique Cash Pool for Building Africa.' *Caijing Magazine.*

# Index

trade liberalization 33, 195
transformational change
  capabilities of people and nations
    211, 212–14
  economic and social systems 218–28
    agriculture and agribusiness 222–8
    rural development 219–21
  education 233–8, 239
  educational systems 233–8
  empowering women 213–18
  international governance 228–33
  religion and religious
    fundamentalism 238–41
  values 213–14
transport 191, 196, 203
  *see also* railways; roads
trees 92, 93
truth as revealed 47
tsunamis 86
two state solution, to Arab–Israeli
  conflict 57, 58, 60

Uganda 48, 99, 160, 231
UN 63, 92–3, 136, 137, 158, 159, 162,
  214, 228, 233
UN Convention on Biological
  Diversity 92–3, 94, 232
UN Declaration on the Right to
  Development 14, 25–7
UN Development Programme
  (UNDP) 10, 30, 92, 159, 161, 176,
  203, 228
UN Earth Summit 91–2
UN Food and Agriculture
  Organization (FAO) 10, 224, 226
UN-Habitat's 2006 report 23
UN Millennium Development Goals
  13–14, 31, 36, 192, 216
UN OCHA 23
UN Resolution 181 (1947) 57, 58, 60
uncertainty 49, 50, 208–9, 210
unemployment
  China 18, 163
  Gwembe Tonga, Zambia 199
  Native Americans 122, 123
  and Palestinian poverty in Gaza and
    West Bank 60, 61–2, 65
  and relative poverty 18, 36–7
  and religious, political and cultural
    fundamentalism in Sri Lanka 53

  and religious and political
    fundamentalism in Israel 56
  United States 118, 138
unemployment insurance 118, 121
*Unequal Democracy* (Bartels) 115–16,
  117–18, 119, 137–8
UNICEF 128–9
Union of Concerned Scientists 69
UNIP (National Independence Party)
  (Zambia) 189–90, 192–3
United Kingdom 98, 126, 159, 187,
  208
United States
  agricultural research 137
  agricultural tariffs and subsidies
    37–8, 222, 227
  assessment of human influences
    on ecosystems and ecosystem
    services 82
  bird decline 94–5, 96, 99, 100–101
  childhood disadvantage 127–8
  and China Agreement on
    Cooperation and Technology
    111
  Christian fundamentalism 67–70,
    115
  civil society institutions, decline 211
  clean energy sector 221–2
  community activities 219
  consumption 30, 210
  cultural and political
    fundamentalism 65–7, 122–6
  democracy, decline 112–13, 115–21,
    137–8
  development definition 27
  economic fundamentalism 72, 121–2
  ecosystem service loss 81
  education 112–13, 118, 122, 126–30,
    234, 235–6
  empowering women 217, 218
  and genocide in Cambodia 20
  and global economic and financial
    crisis 121–2
  and government implemented
    political and cultural
    fundamentalism 65–71
  health care, inadequacies of 112
  infrastructure inadequacies 127,
    130–32
  international leadership 136